SON OF MARY

Australian College of Theology Monograph Series

SERIES EDITOR GRAEME R. CHATFIELD

The ACT Monograph Series, generously supported by the Board of Directors of the Australian College of Theology, provides a forum for publishing quality research theses and studies by its graduates and affiliated college staff in the broad fields of Biblical Studies, Christian Thought and History, and Practical Theology with Wipf and Stock Publishers of Eugene, Oregon. The ACT selects the best of its doctoral and research masters theses as well as monographs that offer the academic community, scholars, church leaders and the wider community uniquely Australian and New Zealand perspectives on significant research topics and topics of current debate. The ACT also provides opportunity for contributors beyond its graduates and affiliated college staff to publish monographs which support the mission and values of the ACT.

Rev Dr Graeme Chatfield
Series Editor and Associate Dean

Son of Mary

The Family of Jesus
and the Community of Faith
in the Fourth Gospel

MARGARET WESLEY

WIPF & STOCK · Eugene, Oregon

SON OF MARY
The Family of Jesus and the Community of Faith in the Fourth Gospel

Australian College of Theology Monograph Series

Copyright © 2015 Margaret Wesley. All rights reserved. Except for brief quotations in critical publications or reviews, no part of this book may be reproduced in any manner without prior written permission from the publisher. Write: Permissions, Wipf and Stock Publishers, 199 W. 8th Ave., Suite 3, Eugene, OR 97401.

Wipf & Stock
An Imprint of Wipf and Stock Publishers
199 W. 8th Ave., Suite 3
Eugene, OR 97401
www.wipfandstock.com

ISBN 13: 978-1-4982-1985-3

Manufactured in the USA.

Dedicated to my family who have shown me so much grace in my own struggle to be faithful as a disciple of Christ and also as a wife, mother, daughter and sister.

Table of Contents

Abbreviations | xi

1. Introduction: The Relevance of Social Sciences to Gospel Studies | 1
    Elaboration Of Questions To Be Addressed In The Book
    Some Initial Clarification
    Use Of Socio-Rhetorical Scholarship
    Why Look At Jesus' Family In The Fourth Gospel?
    Is This Book A Search For The Historical Holy Family?
    Genre Of The Fourth Gospel
    Becoming (More Like) Ideal Readers Of The Fourth Gospel
    Social Location Of The Fourth Gospel
    Sources Of Information And Their Uses
    Conclusions

2. Who Is This Family? | 21
    The Holy Family In Christian Scholarship
    Evidence Within The Fourth Gospel Of A Wider Body Of Knowledge
    Paul's Knowledge About The Family Of The Lord
    Jesus' Family In The Synoptic Gospels, With A Particular Focus On Matthew
        The Hieronymian View
        The Epiphanian View
        The Helvidian View
    Son Of Mary
    Mary And Fourth-Century Christian Asceticism
    Was Mary A Widow?
    Nazareth—Jesus' Hometown
    Conclusions

3 Conflict between Discipleship and Kinship in the Synoptic Gospels and Other First-Century Sources | 53
Definition Of Fictive Kinship Groups
Genealogies
The Function Of Genealogies In Luke And Matthew
Leaving Home
Jesus Rejected By His Home Town
No Turning Back
Cause Or Effect?
Who Are My Mother And My Brothers?
Some Implications
Kinship And Loyalty To God In Other Jewish Writings
    Philo
    Josephus
Conclusions

4 Mother and Son | 83
Honor And Shame In The Family
Household Space
    Was Household Space Gendered?
Economic Realities Of Home Life
Women At Social Occasions
Affective Bonds
Literary Indications Of The Bonds Between Mothers And Sons
    Evidence From The New Testament
    Ancient Greek And Roman Ethical Literature
    Greek Epic And Mythology
        The Iliad
        The Odyssey
        The Plays Of Euripides
        Conclusions From Greek Epic And Mythology
    Roman Historical Literature
        Conclusions From Roman Historical Literature
    Ancient Jewish Literature
Conclusions

5 Patristic Perspectives on the Cana Wedding, with a Comment on Symbolism | 119
    Patristic Puzzlement Over John 2:1–11
The Usefulness Of Early Interpretations
The Miracle As Sign
Timely Exegesis
Initial Conclusions Concerning Patristic Interpretations
Allegorical And Symbolic Interpretation
Conclusions

6 Οἶνον οὐκ ἔχουσιν. Exegesis of John 2:1–11 | 140
   Conundrums in John 2:4
Exegesis
    Justice, Mercy, And Kingship In Israel
    A Man Of God Among Sinners
    When Will My Bride Be Faithful?
To What Does This Sign Point?
What Does This Sign Indicate About Jesus' Mother, Their Family, And
   The Nature Of Kinship Among Disciples?
Conclusions

7 Brotherly Love | 197
Being A Man
Brothers In First-Century Societies: Current Anthropological Research
A View From The Ethicist's Study
   A Greek View
   A Roman View
   A Torah-Informed View
Brothers In Greek Mythology
Brothers in Roman Mythology
The Historian's Perspective
Conclusions

8 Glory and . . . Deception? | 212
Unity
   The Water Libation Ceremony
   The Ceremony Of Light
   The Rite Of Facing The Temple

      Initial Comments On 7:1–10 As An Introduction To The Tabernacles Discourse
          Jewish Ethics Of Deception
          Joseph And His Brothers: A Narrative Template
          A Brief Look At Ethics Of Deception In Greek Narrative
      John 7:11–24
      Do The Brothers Have Representative Function?
      Conclusions

9 Family Fractured and Reconfigured at the Cross | 256
    A Brief Note On Historicity
    Introduction To Exegesis of John 19:17–30, 38–39
    Representative Roles For Jesus' Mother And His Beloved Disciple?
    Conclusions

10 Conclusions and Recommendations | 287
      Summary Of Conclusions
      The Fourth Gospel And The Synoptics
      Recommendations For Future Research
      Final Conclusions

Appendix: Τί ἐμοὶ καὶ σοί in the LXX, the NT and Epictetus | 299

Bibliography | 309

Abbreviations

ANF	Ante-Nicene Fathers
Chron	Chronicles
Cor	Corinthians
Hos	Hosea
JSNT	Journal for the Study of the New Testament
Matt	Matthew
NPNF	Nicene and Post-Nicene Fathers
NT	New Testament
OT	Old Testament
TR	Translation

1

Introduction: The Relevance of Social Sciences to Gospel Studies

Kinship is central to human personhood. Humans are social beings, and our initial social and emotional identity is usually found in the context of family. Therefore a full understanding of the humanity of Christ must include an analysis of the way Jesus operated within his family. The church, as a community of humans, was called into being in all four Gospels using family language. Christians are sisters and brothers of one another and daughters and sons of God. Understanding what kinship meant in the culture in which (and for which and about which) the Gospels were written therefore contributes to our understanding of Jesus and of the church.

This book is one contribution toward that understanding. The focus is on the Fourth Gospel, and in particular the three pericopes within the Gospel that include Jesus' interactions with his mother and his brothers.

This introductory chapter will provide further explanation for why this research has been necessary, and will outline the methodology, which involves making use of socio-historical scholarship in order to approach the mind-set of the implied ideal readers. The genre and social location of the Fourth Gospel will also be discussed briefly in this chapter, along with an outline of the sources that will be drawn upon throughout the book.

Questions to be discussed in this chapter include: [BL 1–5]
- How do I understand the usefulness of socio-historical scholarship in the exegetical task being undertaken in this book?

- In what ways will that scholarship be drawn upon?
- What other sources of information will be accessed?
- What is current research suggesting about the genre of the Fourth Gospel?
- Why is the topic of this book important?

Elaboration of questions to be addressed in the book

This book begins by considering what can reasonably be deduced about the composition and occupation of Jesus' biological family (chapter 2). It then examines how the concept of family is presented in the Synoptic Gospels (chapter 3,) and how mother–son (chapter 4) and fraternal (chapter 6) bonds were understood and experienced in first-century Greco-Roman and Jewish culture. All insights gleaned from this analysis will be used, along with traditional exegetical strategies, to discern the message presented by the Gospel of John concerning family in the three passages in which Jesus interacts with his mother or brothers.

Christological concerns about the social humanity of Jesus are addressed in this book; but ecclesiology is more of the focus. What does the Fourth Gospel add to our understanding of the nature of church as family? Every use of ἀδελφός in the Fourth Gospel prior to Jesus' crucifixion refers literally to a male member of the same family. The only use of the word after Jesus' resurrection (20:17) refers to the disciples as Jesus' brothers for whom Jesus' Father has become their Father also. While Christians since that time have referred to one another as brother and sister, the nature of church as family is not always well understood, and the symbolic undertones of first-century kinship vocabulary have often been forgotten as we read our own cultural understanding of siblinghood into the church-family language of the New Testament.

While kinship relationships are treated with subtlety and brevity in the Fourth Gospel, they are given their own kind of prominence by the way Jesus' mother appears in the narrative at the beginning and end of Jesus' public ministry.

The purpose of this first chapter is to provide a rationale for the project and introduce the reader to the task at hand. That is, it will seek to explain why I believe that a socio-historical analysis of first-century Galilean kinship obligations may enlighten students of the Fourth Gospel and equip them to better read and interpret those enigmatic Johannine conversations between Jesus and his family members. This chapter will briefly examine the sources of information that will contribute to our knowledge of Jesus' family obligations, and it will outline a strategy for making the most appropriate use of those sources.

In summary, this book sets out to address the following concerns:

1. Shared tradition: What can we reasonably assume the author and his original readers knew about Jesus' family?

2. First-century kinship: What may have been the original readers' understanding of the forces and bonds that governed family life at this time, particularly those that governed relationships among brothers and between mothers and sons?

3. Kinship and discipleship in the Synoptics: What message does the Synoptic tradition present regarding Jesus' attitude to family, kinship bonds in general, and the conflict between kinship and discipleship? This issue must be resolved for the sake of comparison and to identify whether the New Testament presents a united message concerning kinship and discipleship.

4. Kinship and discipleship in John: What message does the interaction between Jesus and his family members in the Fourth Gospel present regarding Jesus' attitude to family, kinship bonds in general, and the conflict between kinship and discipleship? Does the Fourth Gospel contradict the other Gospels in this respect? Does it nuance their perspective in some way, or does it in fact present the same picture but in a different way?

5. Patristic perspectives: Might insights of the Church Fathers contribute to a better understanding of these issues? They will be consulted in the hope that their closer cultural proximity to the original readers will have enabled them to see more than we generally see in the Gospel accounts of Jesus' family.

6. Johannine ecclesiology: the Synoptic Gospels depict a real possibility of conflict between kinship group and fictive kinship group (the church). Is this conflict also found in John and what implications may be drawn from its presence or absence?

Some initial clarification

As a literary study of the final form of the canonical Gospel of John it will not be necessary to delve into questions of authorship or of sources. Throughout this book the term "the author" will be used interchangeably with the name "John"; and the terms "The Fourth Gospel," "The Gospel of John," and "John" will also be used interchangeably. This should not be interpreted as a claim that John the son of Zebedee was the author,[1] but simply as the use of traditional language and attribution in relation to this Gospel.

My academic specialty is the study of the New Testament and I make no claim to being an archaeologist or a historian. No original archaeological work will be undertaken and original historical investigation will be limited to readily available literature from and about the period. The major contribution this book will make to scholarship will be in its exegesis of John 2:1–12; 7:1–10; and 19:26–27.

My own philosophical and theological perspectives will obviously influence my methodology. My approach to texts might be described as critical modernist. While I acknowledge that authorial intent may not be entirely accessible through the text even with the assistance of social history, I believe that interpretation must at least endeavor to identify such intent. I believe that valid interpretation does not drive a wedge between the author and the text. Communication theory will therefore be drawn upon to analyze how the meaning of the author is transmitted to the reader via the text. Further, as an evangelical Christian I have a high view of the importance of the canonical Gospels and their capacity to communicate truths about God; and as a feminist I have a particular interest in the portrayal of female characters in the New Testament. My task here is not to defend these positions, since space would not permit this, but to work fluidly within them, while humbly seeking wisdom from all perspectives; recognizing that sometimes I have most to learn from authors whose perspectives are very different from my own.

For brevity, when I will use the word "reader" throughout this book I include the listener. This Gospel would originally have been read aloud in community much more often than it was studied privately.

---

1. I also do not deny that this is possible, or even likely.

Use of socio-rhetorical scholarship

Socio-rhetorical analysis has thrown new light in recent years on many biblical texts. Moxnes's influential work on the letter to the Romans[2] has been followed by significant contributions to New Testament scholarship by people such as DeSilva, Neyrey and Malina. The article, "Despising the Shame of the Cross: Honor and Shame in the Johannine Passion Narrative"[3] by Neyrey has become a frequently cited classic that has turned the attention of scholars to the ways in which language of honor and shame has been employed by the author of the Fourth Gospel in articulating his central concerns. Neyrey[4] and Malina and Rohrbaugh[5] have both produced commentaries on the Fourth Gospel from a social science perspective in recent years.

The book will interact closely with these and other scholars in order to:

- Identify findings that relate to mothers and sons, to brothers and to fictive kinship groups.
- Compare their findings with biblical and historical (literary and archaeological) data. This will be done with humility but is necessary as scholars from a social-scientific perspective are sometimes guilty of "up-streaming"—assuming that present-day anthropological observations of the Mediterranean area can be applied backwards onto the first century CE.
- Apply their insights to the exegesis of John 2:1–11; 7:1–10; 19:25–27.

Why look at Jesus' family in the Fourth Gospel?

Although family imagery is strong in the Fourth Gospel,[6] encounters between Jesus and his family members in the Fourth Gospel are rare. There are only three in all, and each one provides a significant puzzle for the modern reader. In John 2, Jesus says to his mother, Τί ἐμοὶ καὶ σοί; and biblical scholars have argued for centuries over whether or not this

---

2. For example, Moxnes, *Theology in Conflict*.
3. Neyrey, "Despising the Shame of the Cross."
4. Neyrey, *Gospel of John*.
5. Malina and Rohrbaugh, *Social-Science Commentary*.
6. van der Watt, *Family of the King*.

amounted to a refusal of her request and perhaps even a rather impolite rebuff. In John 7, Jesus tells his brothers that he is not planning to go to the Festival of Booths, but then he does go secretly. Why would the author wish to give the impression that Jesus, whom he calls the way, the *truth* and the life (14:6), apparently deceived his brothers? Is there something in this passage that modern exegetes have missed? Finally, in John 19 as Jesus hangs dying on the cross, he tells his mother to take his beloved disciple as a son and tells the disciple to take her as a mother. Would this not have been an enormous affront to Jesus' remaining brothers?

So, an initial answer to the question of why we should look more closely at Jesus' family in the Fourth Gospel is that the passages in which they are found remain puzzling, and so hold promise that closer investigation may yield previously unnoticed insight. A deeper understanding of Jesus' family members as characters in the Fourth Gospel may provide one puzzle piece to help "render intelligible the intricate multiplicity of sources, allusions, and levels of meaning which are part and parcel of our evangelist's challenging artistry."[7]

The Fourth Gospel does not contain any blatant call on disciples to leave family behind and make the community of believers their first priority and primary loyalty. Statements from the Synoptic Gospels such as, "Who is my mother, and who are my brothers? . . . For whoever does the will of my Father in heaven is my brother and sister and mother" (Matt 12:28, 50), are foreign to the tone of the Fourth Gospel. Might it be that a similar message is there, hidden in Jesus' enigmatic encounters with family members in John 2, 7, and 19?[8]

There is value in identifying whether the author of the Fourth Gospel presents an entirely different view of family obligations from that presented by the Synoptic authors, or whether the same view is presented in a different manner. The idea that kinship may be in conflict with discipleship is sometimes seen as strictly limited to Q source material, and absent from the rest of the New Testament.[9] Christians struggling to manage their loyalty to family and to Christ, especially those in Northern Africa

---

7. Dillon, "Wisdom Tradition and Sacramental Retrospect," 272.

8. This point is made briefly in Collins, *These Things Have Been Written*, 181, but will be expanded and demonstrated in much greater detail in the remaining chapters of this book.

9. Note, for example, Barton's analysis of the work of Theissen in this area. Barton, *Discipleship and Family Ties*, 12–14.

and across Asia, need to know whether the New Testament speaks to their concerns with one voice or with two.

These questions also need further research because they reflect on the character of Jesus. Did he honor his parents at all times? Did he consistently tell the truth? And what are the implications if he did not?

Several scholars have recently been calling for these questions to be addressed. Halvor Moxnes points out that to date surprisingly little attention has been paid to the kinship context of Jesus' life.[10] That is not to say that Jesus' family has been neglected in recent scholarship. Indeed, several excellent books have been devoted to them recently.[11] However, these have not tended to focus on the obligations that these relationships would have placed on Jesus or how these obligations are kept, nuanced, or broken by the behavior attributed to Jesus in the Gospels.

There has, to my knowledge, been only one other attempt at this to date, and I discovered it well after beginning my research. The book of J.C. Campbell was published under the title of *Kinship Relations in the Gospel of John*[12] in 2007. Campbell believed her work to be ground-breaking, and indeed before her book there had been no comprehensive examination of the relationships between the two core kinship groups depicted in the Fourth Gospel: the biological family of Jesus and his fictive family of disciples. While her contribution to this discussion is very welcome, she argues from assumptions that I consider dubious and therefore reaches conclusions that are very different from mine. Her work will provide some useful points of comparison and contrast throughout my book, and for these I am grateful to her.

Aside from Campbell's work, there has been a general scholarly neglect of Jesus' kinship context, particularly in the Fourth Gospel. This neglect may reflect a bias towards individualism in Western scholarship. Moxnes notes, "In much of the study of the historical Jesus from the nineteenth century onward, it has been Jesus as the individual hero that has been at the center of interest."[13] While this book does not seek to identify Jesus as anything less than a "hero," it does wish to understand him in his social context, as a son and a brother. Christology generally asks: what does God look like in a human body? This book asks: what does God

10. Moxnes, *Putting Jesus in His Place*, 23.

11. Including: Bauckham, *Jude and the Relatives of Jesus*; Brown, *Mary in the New Testament*; Gaventa, *Mary*; Perry, *Mary for Evangelicals*.

12. Campbell, *Kinship Relations*.

13. Moxnes, *Putting Jesus in His Place*, 24.

look like in a human family? What does it mean that the second person of the Trinity took on "social humanity,"[14] in particular that most important social reality of family?

Along with Marianne Thompson I believe that investigation into passages in the Fourth Gospel that discuss Jesus' human origins is necessary and potentially very fruitful: "By examining the various texts about Jesus' origins and the disputes surrounding them, we hope to gain insights into the Gospel's understanding of Jesus' earthly origins and their relationship to his origin from above, and so also of the Fourth Gospel's view of the humanity of Jesus."[15]

Jerome Neyrey has also expressed a belief that more serious attention should be paid to "the basic social institution of antiquity, namely the family." He gives his assessment that "Issues of family and (fictive) kinship remain undeveloped in scholarship."[16]

An assumption lying behind this book is that some concept of family is fundamental to humanity, and basic to human culture. One of the defining features of any culture is the structure of its families. Conceptions of family often "serve as metaphors for the larger community or the society itself, and thus these groups are linked to society not just in practical ways, but as ideological constructions."[17] Historians have long understood how this was demonstrated in the Roman Empire, where the emperor was considered the *pater familias* of the empire.[18]

One of the keys, then, to thinking ourselves out of our own culture and into another is to learn the language of family in that other culture. This is particularly pertinent to the study of first-century Mediterranean culture because, as Malina claims, "What is typical of this region is *kinship as the focal social institution*."[19] In this world "notice of someone's genealogy, ancestors, clan and parents constituted essential pieces of information about him."[20]

Hanson and Oakman similarly note that in the advanced agrarian society of first-century Palestine, while other political, religious, and

---

14. See Moxnes, *Putting Jesus in His Place*, 24.
15. Thompson, *The Humanity of Jesus in the Fourth Gospel*, 16.
16. Neyrey, "Loss of Wealth," 156–7.
17. Moxnes, *Putting Jesus in His Place*, 29.
18. See, for example, Seneca, "De Beneficiis" I.53-5, where the household is called the seed-bed of the state.
19. Malina, *The Social World of Jesus and the Gospels*, 98, italics added.
20. Neyrey, "Loss of Wealth," 143.

economic institutions were gaining prominence it was still very much the case that "virtually no social relationship, institution or value-set was untouched by the family and its concerns."[21]

It would be surprising if a Gospel that redefines and reorients every other major institution and symbol of the Jewish people—Torah, temple, Sabbath, festivals, and land[22]—left such a focal institution as family untouched. Indeed, van der Watt believes that, far from leaving the family untouched, familial language forms the most essential and pervasive imagery in the Fourth Gospel.[23]

A complex network of different metaphors is woven together to form the family imagery in this Gospel. Kinship forms the focal point of argumentation to which most themes in the Gospel are directly related. Metaphorical use of friends, slaves, orphans, forensic elements and so on form part of the extended family imagery, lending centrality to the concept of family within the Gospel.[24]

Families are culturally (as well as biologically) defined. They have changed dramatically over the last two millennia, and differ considerably between cultures in our own time. Even in the last century in Australia we have seen the definition of family move away from "Mum, Dad, and the kids" towards an array of options, involving various forms of relationship and sexual expression. History often bears witness to societal upheavals being reflected in transformations of family life. The industrial revolution in England is just one dramatic instance of this, where the average family home ceased to be the place where most of the nation's production took place and became, rather, the place where family members returned after their day's labor in places of concentrated production.[25]

Since the specific obligations of family members to one another are subject to such significant variation between cultures we cannot expect to read the Fourth Gospel correctly when we approach the treatment of Jesus' family with only our own twenty-first-century understanding of family.

I will argue in chapter 2 that the family of Jesus serves an ironic function (among others) in the Fourth Gospel. This is one hint that the

21. Hanson and Oakman, *Palestine in the Time of Jesus*, 20.
22. Barton, *Life Together*, 100–1.
23. van der Watt, *Family of the King*, 397.
24. van der Watt, *Family of the King*, 398.
25. See discussion of change in family construction and ideology in Moxnes, *Putting Jesus in His Place*, 25–28, and in Oakman, *Palestine in the Time of Jesus*, 21–23.

paucity of information about that family in the Gospel does not relegate them to minor significance in the narrative. Another hint that Jesus' mother is not insignificant, in spite of being unnamed, is the fact that she participates in the first sign narrative and in the climactic passion narrative.

Sign narratives are among the primary devices that the author of the Fourth Gospel uses to move towards the climax of Jesus' death.[26] The presence of Jesus' mother at the first sign alerts the reader to her importance as a character. The fact that she is unnamed seems to indicate that her significance is not to be found within her individual identity but in her relationship to her son.

James Howard has argued that all the "minor" characters in the Fourth Gospel are models of either faith or unbelief[27] in order to draw the reader into firmer and deeper faith. Jesus' brothers are described as unbelievers (7:5). It appears that Jesus' mother demonstrates faith at the beginning of the Gospel, but tension is raised by the unbelief of her other sons. In the end we find her, against all opposition, at the foot of the cross being identified with a disciple and as a disciple.

Is this book a search for the historical holy family?

The past century of searching for the "historical Jesus" has taught us not to be too ambitious in our search for the "historical Holy Family." Gaventa says, in relation to the "historical quest for Mary," that since the

---

26. Grassi has pointed out that these sign narratives form the following chiastic structure:
(1) The Wedding Feast at Cana (2:1–12)
(2) The restoration of the dying son (4:46–54)
(3) The Sabbath healing at Bethesda (5:1–16)
(4) The multiplication of loaves (6:1–71)
(5) The Sabbath healing of the blind man (9:1–41)
(6) The restoration of Lazarus to life (11:1–44)
(7) The great hour of Jesus: his mother, the cross, and the issue of blood and water from Jesus' side (19:25-37)
Grassi, "The Role of Jesus' Mother in John's Gospel: A Reappraisal," 69. Rae endorses this reading in Bauckham and Mosser, *The Gospel of John and Christian Theology*, 304.

27. Howard, "Minor Characters," 77.

INTRODUCTION 11

actual events of Mary's life are only accessible through the Gospels, "the probability of arriving at a reliable portrait of Mary[28] is slender indeed."[29]

Gaventa then proposes a more modest quest: a literary quest rather than a historical one.[30] She advocates focusing on the characters in the context of the Gospel stories, rather than plundering the stories to find the historical people behind the characters. She believes that, "in the rush to read behind narratives for their historical value, scholars have often slighted the story in and of itself."[31] It is within the story, not behind or outside it, that characters are to be found. The historical Mary might be lost to us in many ways, but the Matthean Mary, the Markan Mary, the Lukan Mary, and the Johannine mother of Jesus have always been there.

Certainly, the family members we have access to appear in the Gospels as characters whose roles are determined to a significant extent by the authors. The real people[32] from whom those characters are drawn inhabited a real world in a real but distant century where we cannot see, touch, or hear them. Naïve devotion and academic hubris aside, I must concede to Gaventa's challenge and begin this endeavor by admitting that I cannot give Mary, Joseph, James, Jude, and the others more flesh and blood than they were given by Matthew, Mark, Luke, and John.

Each of the Gospels maintains such a strong focus on their main character, Jesus, that all other characters are in danger of fading into the background. In the Fourth Gospel Jesus' mother and siblings are not even given names. What the author wishes to communicate about them is not their individual identity but their relationship to Jesus as mother and brothers.

We can assume that the author of the Fourth Gospel has given as complete a portrait of Jesus' family as he believed necessary to convey the message he sought to communicate to the audience he envisioned reading his Gospel. The problem we have as twenty-first-century readers

28. Note Kraemer's comment that we know considerably more about Berenice and Babatha than any other individual Jewish woman of the Roman period. (Kraemer, "Typical and Atypical Jewish Family Dynamics," 133) For all the interest shown in Mary over the ensuing centuries we must confess that we know significantly more about these two women than we do about her.

29. Gaventa, *Mary*, 9.

30. See also Barton, *Discipleship and Family Ties*, 57–58.

31. Gaventa, *Mary*, 20.

32. Of course, scholarly opinion is divided on the genuine historical reality of Mary, Joseph, James, and the rest of Jesus' family.

is that we are not the audience John envisioned. The bare details of the relationship are not sufficient for us because we are not familiar, as the original readers were, with exactly what those relationships meant.

Recognizing the limitations our own socio-historical setting places on us as readers, this book employs socio-historical research in an effort to enable us to observe those characters with eyes more closely akin to those of the original readers. In short, I contend that the place of socio-historical investigation in biblical exegesis is not in extracting characters from their plot but in re-applying to the narratives some of the color that has been lost in translation.

The changing nature of historical investigation over the past half-century has influenced biblical scholars to ask the sort of questions this book investigates, and has also provided many of the resources we need. Historians of today are much more interested than their fathers and grandfathers were in common people and their social realities. Susan Dixon, who has been at the forefront of socio-historical research, explains:

> Slaves, women, children, the free lower classes, and the family have largely superseded battles and consulships within the "territory of the historian." Emotions and sexualities are now acceptable, even commonplace topics of publication. Studies of Roman marriage and family relations in the late republic and early empire are based no longer solely on jurists' opinions from edited legal compilations but on sophisticated source readings, which locate texts historically and distinguish between laws and social ideals.[33]

Hard as it is to distinguish "between laws and social ideals" this book will go further where possible and attempt to distinguish between social ideals and actual practice. Just as, at a literary level, "the laws of the literary genre upheld by Horace the critic are definitely annulled by Horace the poet,"[34] at a social level, the laws of Philo the moralist are sometimes broken by Philo the man, and may be completely ignored by Philo's distant cousin.

While this book will take a largely social-scientific approach, I am fully in agreement with Stephen Barton in asserting that the Gospels are

---

33. Dixon, "Sex and the Married Woman in Ancient Rome," 111.
34. Hack, "The Doctrine of Literary Forms," 30–32.

sophisticated documents that require all the tools on hand to do them justice:

> As the products of a process of transmission from the time of Jesus on, they justify a form-critical analysis. As the products of a creative process of editing and composition at the hands of the respective evangelists, they justify redactional analysis. As narrative texts written with skill to exhort, edify and persuade a particular readership, they justify the use of literary criticism. Finally, though by no means exhaustively, as texts that spring from, and are addressed to, historical communities, the Gospels have a necessarily social dimension which justifies sociological criticism.[35]

Sociological considerations will, therefore, be a focus, but by no means the exclusive focus, of the exegesis sections of this book (chapters 5, 6, 8, and 9). Social science observations will be applied only where necessitated by the text.

Genre of the Fourth Gospel

"Genre is at the heart of all attempts to communicate."[36] It is a contract between author and reader[37] that "communicates to the reader a set of conventions that controls the understanding of the whole intention."[38] Genre gives us the rules of the language game the author was playing so that we may enter the game as accurate readers and interpreters of the text.[39] Vanhoozer believes that if we are to read a text ethically we have a responsibility "to determine to what kind of communicative act a text belongs, and to respond to this communicative act in an appropriate manner."[40]

Genre must be understood within its own historic location. Burridge has pointed out[41] that for more than a century expectations about

---

35. Barton, *Discipleship and Family Ties*, 19.
36. Burridge, *What Are the Gospels?*, 48.
37. Burridge, *What Are the Gospels?*, 105.
38. Osborne, "Historical Narrative and Truth in the Bible," 680.
39. See Hirsch, *The Aims of Interpretation*, 89–126.
40. Vanhoozer, *Is There a Meaning in This Text?*, 395.
41. Burridge, *What Are the Gospels?*, 3–24.

modern biographies have clouded attempts to place the Gospels within a defined genre.

The Gospels will be treated in this book as βίοι. They are ancient biographies designed to paint a portrait of Jesus that highlights certain aspects of his character. We might also call them "narrative history" but we must be careful not to impose our own expectations of narrative history onto these ancient writings.

Ancient βίοι tend to be medium-length works, mostly in prose narrative; their structure is a bare chronology of birth/arrival and death, with topical material inserted; the scale is always limited to the subject; they contain a mixture of literary units, including anecdotes, stories, speeches, and sayings, selected from a wide range of oral and written sources; and they display the subject's character indirectly through words and deeds rather than by direct analysis.[42]

While authorial intention directs the form of all biographies, and all history, that intention need not be seen as opposing the truth. Ancient biographers were "no less concerned than their modern counterparts with differentiating historical truth from falsehood."[43] I assume that authorial intention plays a large part in the Gospels but also believe that one of the intentions of the evangelists was to provide an accurate account of Jesus' life. This is certainly how the author of the Fourth Gospel describes his work (19:35; 21:24). I concur with Grant Osborne that:

> It is clear that in the historical narratives of the Scriptures the authors believed they were retelling the historical past of Israel and the early Church so as to solidify the self-conscious identity of the people in their present time. In other words, there was a historical purpose throughout. At the same time, they were evaluating those events to provide both negative and positive models.[44]

My reading of historical material in the Gospels is guided by critical realism, where "initial observation is challenged by critical reflection but can survive the challenge and speak truly of reality."[45] Although texts and

---

42. Burridge, *What Are the Gospels?*, 140.
43. Provan et al., *A Biblical History of Israel*, 50.
44. Osborne, "Historical Narrative and Truth in the Bible," 684.
45. Wright, *The New Testament and the People of God*, 36.

even inscriptions follow customs of propriety I maintain that these pieces of information are attached to retrievable pieces of history.[46]

Becoming (more like) ideal readers of the Fourth Gospel

Van der Watt believes that family language forms the most prominent metaphor in the Gospel, and that, "If John used a description of the family . . . which was not known or was atypical, the communicative power of the metaphor would have been jeopardized."[47]

As such, we can assume that the author included all the information needed for *the audience he envisioned* to understand any message he was seeking to present about Jesus in relation to his family. This is especially so when we consider the extent to which the author was a master of his genre. His subtle employment of literary devices such as irony, multi-layered metaphor, and sustained keywords, all without resorting to complicated Greek vocabulary, points toward him being a consummate storyteller, as does the great affection in which this Gospel has been held by Christians since it was written.

However, even the best of storytellers could not be expected to foresee what assistance might be required for listeners as far removed as we are from him in time and culture to enable us to enter into the narrative to the same extent as those of his own time and place. Many shared assumptions, especially about the most common experiences of family life, would have been written between the lines of the Gospel and subsequently lost in translation to another time and culture.

When listening to the Gospels, our section of the audience is seated at a great distance from center stage, and several pillars (historical, linguistic, cultural, and literary) obstruct our view.[48] The two historical and cultural pillars blocking the part of the stage that interests us at present are our relative ignorance of Jesus' biological family and our greater ignorance of the kinship obligations that governed that family's relationships. John has presented all that is necessary, but our ignorance of shared information creates blind spots that cause us to miss some of his subtleties.

---

46. Cohick, *Women in the World of the Earliest Christians*, 28.
47. van der Watt, *Family of the King*, 165.
48. See Campbell, *Kinship Relations*, 64.

I will deal with the first pillar in chapter 2 and the second in chapters 4 and 7. We are foreigners to the culture in which the Fourth Gospel is set, the culture out of which it was written, and the culture into which it was directed. Translation from Greek to English is just the first step in allowing readers of our time to fully understand the author's intention. Biblical exegesis is cross-cultural work and cultural translation must also be included.[49]

Malina has pointed out:

> to find out what any text means, it is quite apparent that the social system expressed in the text has to be of prime interest since the meanings in the wordings[50] . . . that make up the written Bible derive from a social system. And the social system in question for biblical studies is that of the original author and his audience.[51]

The author of the Fourth Gospel gave linguistic (John 1:38, 42) and social (4:9) translations where he deemed this necessary.[52] He understood that different readers stood in different positions in relation to his narrative, and sought to bring them closer to the stage, where the view is clear (20:31). However, he could not possibly have imagined a vantage point such as ours, or provided sufficient parenthetical asides to bring us close to the stage.

Hanson and Oakman believe that it is particularly in relation to issues of kinship that ancient authors were most likely to assume their readers shared their own understanding: "Kinship arrangements are so deeply embedded in the consciousness of the ancients that they are often left implicit."[53] Van der Watt agrees:

> The family as primary social order is part and parcel of the everyday life of every person in the ancient Mediterranean world. The general conventions regarding family life were well known. By using this basic and well-known social phenomenon to describe the salvific relationship between God, Jesus and

---

49. This is quite similar to the need to understand the genre in which the text was written. See Burridge, *What Are the Gospels?*, 48–49.

50. E. D. Hirsch, *Validity in Interpretation*, 126.

51. Malina, *The Social World of Jesus and the Gospels*, 97; see also Campbell, *Kinship Relations*, 85.

52. I note that it is also possible that his parenthetical comments were intended for emphasis rather than explanation.

53. Oakman, *Palestine in the Time of Jesus*, 60.

the believer, a remarkable amount of potential associations are communicatively made available in order to describe the spiritual reality. Since these associations are dormant in the (first) readers, it is not necessary for the author to formulate and explain every association. Simply calling a person a *child* of God activates a whole set of socio-cultural associations relating to family life, for instance why a person should heed his or her parents, why he or she should be loyal towards the family, etc. It does, however, pose a problem for the modern reader who does not share this set of ancient associations. By recognizing that a particular imagery is used, the modern reader can fill in these associations, which leads to a clearer understanding of what is said in the text.[54]

In order to fill in those associations we must look elsewhere than in the text itself. We must look at first-century literature and historical artifacts, and also at analogies from traditional Mediterranean cultures of more recent times. Some of these traditional cultures, while certainly having changed in two thousand years, can give an indication of the different values, behaviors, and assumptions that may have been held there in former days. Because of the increasing pace of social change in the region over the past century, the work of early anthropologists such as Raphael Patai[55] is in many ways more valuable than recent observations.

However, I maintain a cautious attitude throughout this book toward such data by seeking corroborating evidence from historical sources. I am particularly aware that the enormous influence Islam has exerted on these populations for over a millennium had not been imagined in the first century.

Social location of the Fourth Gospel

In order to ground my inquiry, I will assume the validity of the conventional wisdom that the Fourth Gospel was written in the late first-century and that the author was based in Ephesus.[56]

54. van der Watt, *Family of the King*, 400–1.
55. See, for example, Patai, *Sex and Family in the Bible and the Middle East*.
56. See, for example, Carson, *The Gospel According to John*, 86–87. The most significant evidence for the Gospel having been written in Ephesus is from Irenaeus, "Against Heresies," 3, I, I. Eusebius indicates that both Polycrates (Eusebius, *History of the Church*, 5, 24, 2–3) and Clement (Eusebius, *History of the Church*, 3, 23, 6–9) believed the Gospel to have been written in Ephesus. See also Campbell, *Kinship*

I am seeking to be rather minimalist in my assumptions here. Having earlier mentioned the lack of certainty possible in relation to the historical Mary, it is reasonable to add that there is significantly less certainty about the historical Johannine community. Though creative attempts have been made, inspired by the work of J. Louis Martyn,[57] to imagine this community, I believe these attempts have not produced, and are unlikely to produce, a great deal of clarity.[58] So, while seeking to identify what may have been the understandings of the first readers of this Gospel about Jesus' family, I am not about to paint a detailed picture of the community into which it was written.

Steven Barton argues well for the kind of analysis attempted in this book, as opposed to that often attempted using social-scientific arguments. I take the liberty of quoting him at length:

> Given the problems associated with attempting to draw correlations between a Gospel text and a social location extrinsic to the text, may it not be the case that social-scientific exegesis is more appropriately directed at clarifying the contours of various groups, communities, and societies within the text? This would do more justice to the nature of the Gospel texts as (for want of a better phrase) kerygmatic biography, thus allowing the insights of literary criticism to be taken more seriously. It would also lessen the danger, so strong in positivist historical and functionalist sociology, of distracting attention away from the text toward what the ingenious scholar can show lies behind the text.

Identifying more precisely and more vividly the social location of the beliefs and behaviors of the characters and groups presented in the Gospel narratives allows the text itself and the author implied in the text to be understood with ever-deeper levels of appreciation. The potential then is for interpretation of the Gospels to run with rather than against the grain of the text.[59]

It is the purpose of this book to identify "more precisely and more vividly the social location of the beliefs and behaviors" of Jesus' family members in the Fourth Gospel, and so to attempt a deeper appreciation of the narrative as it relates to them.

Relations, 23–25.

57. Martyn, *History and Theology in the Fourth Gospel*.
58. See Bauckham, "For Whom Were the Gospels Written?" 20.
59. Barton, "Can We Identify the Gospel Audiences?" 178–9.

Sources of information and their uses

The Gospels, Paul's letters, and other early Christian writings will be the basis upon which I make assertions about what can reasonably be deduced about Jesus' family in chapter 2. Recent scholarship will also be consulted.

Scholarship concerning the Synoptic Gospels, especially scholarship from a socio-historical perspective, will be extensively studied in order to draw conclusions about the Synoptic perspective on the tension between kinship and discipleship.

Knowledge of kinship obligations among first-century Palestinian artisans will be obtained from socio-historians and anthropologists and also, as much as possible, directly from published archaeology and literature of the period.

All that has been discovered to that point will then be put into the service of a thorough exegesis of the three passages in John that we are concerned with.

Conclusions

The Fourth Gospel is an ancient biography, presenting us with a portrait of its main character as the Word made flesh. No character other than Jesus is allowed center stage, so studying Jesus' mother and brothers will require me to closely examine the background detail.

Much of the detail that will need to be examined is not in the Gospel at all. It is assumed knowledge shared between the author and the original readers, but not shared with twenty-first-century Caucasian Australians. This book will seek to gather some of that missing information from the work of socio-historical scholars and from a selection of influential pieces of ancient literature.

Kinship relationships are of vital importance in any culture and, among first-century Jews living around the Mediterranean, those relationships were seen as particularly predictive of a person's character, obligations, and prospects. There is no doubt that readers of the Fourth Gospel would have been eager to know more about Jesus' family. Yet the author gives them so very little. Two sentences of Jesus are addressed to his mother. One conversation is included between Jesus and his brothers. The significance of this family to this narrative is easy for us to miss. Yet the first readers would not have missed it. Their ears were tuned to the nuances of family language and family expectation. We need to tune our ears to their frequency so that we too might also catch the subtle message regarding kinship that these "minor" characters bring to the narrative.

The following chapter will pull together available information to form as accurate an understanding as possible of Jesus' family relationships. From there it will be possible to begin to examine those relationships so as to clarify the obligations that Jesus carried as a son and a brother.

2

Who Is This Family?

When Jesus is spoken of in the Fourth Gospel as a member of a family, what might the ideal early readers have understood about that family and about Jesus' place in it? How might they have imagined the emotional and other bonds that were present as Jesus interacted with his mother and his brothers? This chapter will investigate the material found in the New Testament Gospels and letters for clues about what the writers and readers appear to have known about Jesus' family relationships. It will also look beyond the canon of the New Testament for indications of the early church's knowledge of Jesus' family.

The purpose of discovering what can be known or reasonably guessed about Jesus' family here is to use this information in later chapters to identify what obligations Jesus might have been under as a son and brother in such a family, and also to determine what obligations his mother and brothers might have owed to him. It is particularly important, in this chapter, to establish whether it is reasonable to base future chapters on the claim that Jesus was known to be the eldest son of a widow.

The material will be examined in roughly chronological order, starting with Paul's letters, moving on to the Gospels, with a particular focus on Matthew, and then examining some writings from the early church.

Key questions addressed in this chapter:

- How sure can we be about whether or not Jesus' brothers and sisters were Mary's offspring?
- What was the nature of the family business and therefore of the economic background of this family?

- What would have been the influence of the politics of Galilee?
- Most importantly, how much of this information may have been common knowledge among early Christians.

The holy family in Christian scholarship

Since the very early days of the church, discussion of Jesus' family has been clouded by sentimentality and censure. Two thousand years of theological reflection around the person of Mary, including various waves of dissent and division particularly, in our time, between Protestants and Roman Catholics, have complicated rather than clarified our understanding of Jesus' family. For many Catholics, the idea that Mary may have given birth to other children after Jesus is a heretical denial of the doctrine of her perpetual virginity. For many Protestants, any other conclusion amounts to Mariolatry. The heat and emotion around this question have made it difficult for Catholics and Protestants to sit at the same table and benefit from frank discussion.

Quite recently, some Protestants have begun to cross a denominational Rubicon by giving scholarly attention to the place of Jesus' mother within the New Testament and within Christian theology. These include Perry[1] and Gaventa.[2] Of course, it has been Catholic scholars, such as Raymond Brown,[3] who have led the way in the study of Mary. These scholars, and a growing number of others, have sought to understand Mary as the woman who was the mother of Jesus. My book will seek to understand Jesus as the Word of God who was the son of Mary.

Halvor Moxnes points out that to date surprisingly little attention has been paid to the kinship context of Jesus' life.[4] That is not to say that Jesus' family has been neglected in recent scholarship. Indeed several excellent books have been devoted to them recently, as I have mentioned.[5] However, these have not generally focused on the obligations that these relationships would have placed on Jesus or how these obligations are

---

1. Perry, *Mary for Evangelicals*.
2. Gaventa, *Mary*.
3. Brown, *Mary in the New Testament*.
4. Moxnes, *Putting Jesus in His Place*, 23.
5. Including: Bauckham, *Jude and the Relatives of Jesus in the Early Church*; Brown, *Mary in the New Testament*; Gaventa, *Mary*; Perry, *Mary for Evangelicals*.

kept, nuanced, or broken by the behavior attributed to Jesus in the Gospels.

After beginning this research, I discovered one book that has addressed this deficit. I have found myself in disagreement with Joan Campbell,[6] but am grateful to her for breaking the ground and for giving me a companion with whom to argue as I have formed my own convictions.

The book will also draw upon the extensive scholarship from the past century concerning the historical Jesus. Though this book is not a "search for the historical holy family" (as it looks at their role within the written record rather than looking behind the historical record for their flesh and blood reality) it will benefit from the interest that the search for the historical Jesus has stimulated concerning the historical background of the Gospels. That background information often uncovers the social symbols and presuppositions that would have allowed the original readers to decode the subtleties of Johannine literature more successfully that we often do.

Evidence within the Fourth Gospel of a wider body of knowledge

The Fourth Gospel provides its own evidence that John's ideal original readers had greater knowledge of Jesus' family than the scanty details found in his text, and that he expected this knowledge to contribute to their appreciation of the narrative. We begin to realize this when we notice that John is a storyteller who rarely lays all his cards on the table. What John leaves unsaid is sometimes just as present to the astute reader as what he says.

Many scholars, most recently Duke[7] and Neyrey,[8] have highlighted the use of irony among the storytelling techniques of the Fourth Gospel. Skilful use of irony requires a shared understanding between the author and the audience. According to Duke,

> Irony is a kind of fellowship into which author and sound reader or spectator enter in silence. Together they watch, wink, and smile, because together they share the perspective that blinded

---

6. Campbell, *Kinship Relations*.
7. Duke, *Irony in the Fourth Gospel*.
8. Neyrey, "Sociology of Secrecy." 79–109.

characters and perhaps less adept observers do not share. They form a community of superior knowledge.[9]

John's particular employment of irony appears to be designed to paint characters as being "in the know" or "not in the know" as a way of bracketing "insiders" from "outsiders"; inviting readers to take an "inside" position over against Gospel characters who are antagonistic to Jesus and are therefore "outsiders."

One instance of such irony is in 7:40–44.[10] Here, Jesus' opponents are made to look ridiculous because they lack information: they are unaware that Jesus was born in Bethlehem and that he was descended from David. More than that, their statement, which is intended to discount the possibility that Jesus could be the Messiah, actually provides evidence for his messiahship to readers who are aware of the nativity traditions behind Matthew and Luke.[11] It seems highly unlikely that this is anything other than a skilful use of irony on the part of the Gospel writer.[12]

The irony here seems almost certainly to be deliberate, but has the evangelist given us any clues that this was his intention? While skilful irony will always be subtle, it cannot afford to be so subtle that an astute reader misses it.[13] Quintilian noted that irony reveals its presence through "the delivery, the character of the speaker or the nature of the subject."[14]

The key to understanding the irony of this passage appears to be verse 44: "Some of them wanted to arrest him, but no one laid hands on him." The words about Jesus not being born in Bethlehem of Davidic descent come from the mouths of people in the crowd who want to arrest Jesus. Within John's Gospel, any accusation against Jesus is suspect, and any person who opposes Jesus has missed the point about who Jesus is (See John 1:10–11). It would be unlikely for John to place true statements

---

9. Duke, *Irony in the Fourth Gospel*, 29.

10. Moxnes, *Putting Jesus in His Place*, 33.

11. van der Watt, *Family of the King*, 261.

12. It should be noted that Neyrey believes the irony of this passage has a different focus. Readers of the Fourth Gospel know that Jesus is "from above," therefore assigning him any earthly origin, either Bethlehem or Galilee would be inaccurate. (Neyrey, *Gospel of John*, 149.) It is entirely possible that both levels of irony are in play here. Certainly, John characterizes Jesus as being "from above," yet the reference to Bethlehem is too strong a pointer to Synoptic tradition to be discounted.

13. It should be noted that this mistake has been made on occasion by highly astute authors. Consider, for example, Swift, *A Modest Proposal*.

14. Quintilian, *Institutio*.

in the mouth of such people unless such true statements showed up more significant areas of ignorance.

It is likely that a similar irony is operating in John 6:41–42, where Jesus' opponents claim to know his father and mother, but are unaware of his virginal conception. It is also possible that 1:13[15] and 8:41 show some awareness of the virgin birth.[16]

This could give us one clue to why John gives so much less information about Jesus' family than the synoptic evangelists. If Jesus' family serves an ironic function in this Gospel then an economy of information about them is essential because "the power of irony, as is the case with symbolism, imagery, and metaphor, lies in the eloquent implicitness of its silence."[17]

We would do well not to hang too much on such a fine thread. It would be inappropriate to assume, on this evidence alone, that John had access to copies of the earlier Gospels.[18] However, in light of this passage, the minimum we can conclude is, firstly, that the author of the Fourth Gospel was aware of more information about Jesus' biological origin than we find recorded in the three brief passages where Jesus' family is discussed; and secondly, that this author believed that at least some of his readers were "in the know" and so able to make use of this information in interpreting his words as irony.

We note here Tim Perry's conviction that the nativity narratives in Matthew and Luke point to a body of knowledge that pre-existed the writing of those Gospels. He believes that the virgin birth is highly unlikely to have been a myth adopted from Greek or Jewish sources because of Jewish abhorrence for the former and the paucity of the latter.[19] It is also unlikely that the virginal conception would have been a creation of pure fiction because of the doubts it cast on Jesus' legitimacy. Perry concludes that, "With these alternatives lacking, the best explanation for the authority that both traditions [Matthew and Luke] so quickly acquired is that they testify to a widespread and early Christian belief that the virginal

---

15. Campbell, *Kinship Relations*, 50.

16. Lieu, "The Mother of the Son in the Fourth Gospel," 73.

17. Duke, *Irony in the Fourth Gospel*, 30.

18. I would contend, though, that this is highly likely. Bauckham argues persuasively that the author of the Fourth Gospel shows awareness of Mark, at least, in Bauckham, "John for Readers of Mark."

19. See also Meier, *A Marginal Jew*, 220–2.

conception of Jesus happened."[20] A widespread belief in the virginal conception is clearly not proof of its veracity, but the concern of this book is more with the beliefs of the early Christian community than with the accuracy of those beliefs. If a belief in Jesus' virginal conception circulated in the earliest Christian communities then it is highly likely that such a belief reached the author and early readers of the Fourth Gospel. It is also highly likely that more information than this was contained in the early stories that were circulated about Jesus' earthly origins.

It is very likely then that John and his readers had access to a greater body of knowledge about Jesus' family than is presented in the Fourth Gospel, yet the exact contents of that body of knowledge cannot be precisely determined. How much more did John know? How much might John have assumed that his readers knew about Jesus' biological origin? In considering the first question, we should note that if the author of this Gospel is to be identified with "the beloved disciple" as tradition holds, and if John 19:27 is taken as a historically accurate report, then we could assume that John had access to information about Jesus' biological family that would have been both complete[21] and accurate. Unfortunately, we cannot call on scholarly consensus here[22] and must leave the author's close familiarity with Jesus' mother as a tantalizing probability. What we can be reasonably certain about is that the author's familiarity with Mary was at most removed by only one or two degrees. If the author was not the beloved disciple he appears at least to be a person well informed about the experience of that disciple and most likely known personally to him.

If it is difficult to be certain how much the author knew, it is more difficult to discern what the readers knew. Presumably, John wrote the Gospel for a broad audience, some more "in the know" than others. In fact, the Gospel claims to have been written as a means of drawing readers further into the circle of those who know and believe (20:31).[23] The

---

20. Perry, *Mary for Evangelicals*, 45–46.

21. It is not to be assumed that Mary would have related intimate details concerning her marital relationship with Joseph. She would undoubtedly, however, have explained the nature of her relationship with Jesus' brothers and sisters.

22. Particularly because none of the Synoptic Gospels explicitly mentions Mary's presence at the cross.

23. I am aware, of course, that scholars argue over whether John's purpose statement here is to bring non-believers into belief or to draw believers into deeper belief. My reading of that verse in the context of the whole Gospel is that the author intended his Gospel to draw all readers (wherever their starting point) into fuller belief and more complete discipleship.

ideal reader was to grow in knowledge through reading the Gospel and through interaction with other members of the post-resurrection Christian community.

Paul's knowledge about the family of the Lord

Scholarly certainty around the words and actions of Paul is limited due to the lack of consensus around Pauline authorship of the epistles traditionally attributed to him, and around the historical reliability of the canonical book of Acts. The following analysis will not seek certainty but rather likelihood and possibility, and so will take a deliberately generous approach. All traditional Pauline epistles, with the exception of 1 and 2 Timothy and Titus, will be considered as source documents, along with the book of Acts. Conclusions drawn should be given weight that is appropriate to the weight supportable by such generous assumptions.

The Fourth Gospel was probably written in Ephesus. It is reasonably likely that the church there had, earlier, benefited from the ministry of Paul, in person and by letter.[24] There is no mention of Jesus' family in Paul's letter to the Ephesians, but we can imagine that Paul may have passed on, in person, some of what he knew.

Paul's letters contain very little detail about Jesus' biological and geographical origins. What they do contain will be discussed below, but I will consider first the likely content of his oral teaching about Jesus' human origins.

While Paul, in his letters, often appeals to the message he preached in founding his churches, and reminds those churches of their response to that message (e.g., 1 Thess 1:5; 1 Cor 11:2) we nowhere have a full statement of that message. It may be possible to identify the basic elements of his gospel from the sermons recorded in the book of Acts, but these are certainly only summaries, which barely begin to suggest the curriculum through which he would, for example, have taken the Corinthian church in the eighteen months or so that he spent with them. He stated that his message could be summed up in five words: "Jesus Christ, and him crucified" (1 Cor 2:2); but we can certainly assume that he used more than five words to persuade, teach, and sustain newly established churches.

---

24. Many scholars question the likelihood that Paul wrote the canonical book of Ephesians, as they question the historicity of the book of Acts.

Would it be unreasonable to suppose that Paul would have said something to his churches about the biological origins of Jesus? Without doubt, his listeners would have been curious about their Savior's human origins and would have questioned Paul about them. As I have pointed out in the first chapter, the world in which the gospel first spread was one where people were defined in terms of the family into which they were born.[25] If Paul refrained from teaching his converts these facts it could only be because either he did not know anything about Jesus' human origins or he had some theological objection to passing on that information.

The possibility that Paul knew nothing about Jesus' human origins is slight. Assuming that Acts can be taken as a reasonably reliable source,[26] we can observe that Acts 7:58—8:1 places Paul in Jerusalem at the time of Stephen's stoning, and that in Acts 22:3 Paul is said to have been raised in Jerusalem as Gamaliel's disciple. It is likely then that he would also have been in that city (or at least living in that city) at the time of Jesus' crucifixion. At least, he would have been aware of the events leading to Jesus' death and of the case against him. In his own writings, Paul admits to having been a Pharisee and a zealous persecutor of the church (Phil 3:5). A man of his intellect would, without a doubt, have obtained as much information as he could about this movement he was opposing, and about its crucified leader. His fellow Pharisees who had been following Jesus' career would undoubtedly have had plenty of information to share. Such a body of information would certainly not, at this stage, have included the birth of Jesus in Bethlehem to a virgin mother, though it may possibly have included rumors to that effect.

What Paul thought he knew about Jesus' origins would have been seriously challenged when he was confronted by the risen Lord (1 Cor 15:8). To what degree his reorganized understanding about Jesus' origins after this time depended on revelation rather than the teachings of the Damascus Christians cannot be determined.[27]

Paul did teach about Jesus' origins in his letters, but his approach to this subject was theologically nuanced. Firstly, he saw the flaws in any human wisdom that limited or honored people according to their human

---

25. See, for example, Oakman, *Palestine in the Time of Jesus*, 51 and Neyrey, "Loss of Wealth," 143.

26. This, of course, is not an assumption all scholars would make and so a great deal of weight cannot be made to rest upon it.

27. I would assume that Paul's claim to have not learned the gospel from humans (Gal 1:12) does not extend to the details of Jesus' birth and family.

origins (1 Cor 1:18–31; 10:1–5; 2 Cor 21–22; Gal 1:1; 3:28–9; 6:14; Eph 2:13; Phil 3:4–7; Col 3:11). This may be one reason why Paul does not dwell on Jesus' biological origins.[28] Another reason may be that he, like John, taught that Jesus' origin was not primarily to be understood in terms of a biological family or a geographical setting. Jesus was from God and equal with God (Phil 2:6); the Son of God the Father (2 Cor 1:3); the image of God (2 Cor 4:4; Col 1:15); the agent through whom God has acted (2 Cor 5:18; Col 1:20); the creator of all, and therefore one who has existed before all creation (Col 1:16–7).

Another reason why Paul may have chosen not to stress Jesus' biological origins might be found in Paul's typical address of Christians as brothers and sisters (1 Cor 1:1; 2:1; 3:1; 10:1; 12:1; Gal 1:11; 3:15, etc.) Kinship wrought in Christian fellowship appears to eclipse all other kinship ties in Paul's estimation.

In spite of this, Jesus' biological origins were not irrelevant to Paul. He finds it significant that Jesus was descended from David (Rom 1:3); that he was an Israelite (Rom 9:5,) born under the law (Gal 4:4); and that he was the seed of Abraham (Gal 3:16). Though he, like John, does not name Mary, Paul insists that Jesus was born of a woman (Gal 4:4). Ridderbos notices the use of ἐκ γυναικός rather than διὰ γυναικός and comments, "The woman was not only the medium of His coming in the flesh, but from her He took all that belongs to the human."[29] There appears to be no evidence that Paul had virginal conception in mind here;[30] Jesus' biological origin warranted mention by Paul only to the extent that it established Jesus' humanity and placed him in the right bloodline to fulfill God's promises to Abraham and to David.

The humanity which Paul saw as being imparted by Jesus' mother was not merely that of a physical human body but of a network of relationships that tied him to David and to Abraham and ultimately to Adam. Jesus was born into a family: that of David and Abraham.

In addition to this, Paul speaks of the more immediate network of relationships into which Jesus was born in 1 Corinthians 9:5. Paul was aware that Jesus had brothers. This verse gives us valuable information

---

28. This may be part of what he meant by saying that "though we once knew Christ from a human point of view, we know him no longer in that way." (2 Cor 5:16)

29. Ridderbos, *The Epistle of Paul to the Churches of Galatia*, 155. Capitalization retained from source.

30. So Ridderbos, *The Epistle of Paul to the Churches of Galatia*, 155 and Fung, *The Epistle to the Galatians*, 182.

that we do not find in the Gospels or Acts. We learn from the plural here that James was not the only sibling of Jesus to become a believer after the resurrection.[31] We also learn that these brothers were married and carried out an itinerant ministry.[32]

The brothers of the Lord are mentioned as leaders in the church who, along with Cephas, need no further introduction to the congregation in Corinth. Paul's use of rhetorical questions here implies that he is reminding them of information they already know ("Remember that the Lord's brothers take their wives with them on their missionary journeys") rather than introducing new information.

This brief mention reminds us that knowledge of Jesus' family circulated through the early church not only in the form of nativity traditions but also in the form of flesh-and-blood siblings. The least we can be certain of is that Paul knew of the ministry of Jesus' brothers. In addition we can be reasonably sure that church members in Corinth knew of the ministry of these men before they received this letter.

Paul also mentions one of Jesus' brothers in his epistle to the Galatians, where he speaks of James as a leader of the church (Gal 1:19) whom he met when he visited Jerusalem. This is almost certainly the same James that Paul includes in his list of witnesses to Jesus' resurrection in 1 Corinthians 15:5–8[33] and the same James listed as a brother of Jesus in Mark 6:3.[34]

Although, as noted earlier, it was Paul's custom to speak of fellow Christians as brothers, it is most unlikely that he had such a figurative use of the word in mind in 1 Cor 9:5 or Gal 1:19. Paul speaks of fellow Christians as brothers and sisters of each other and of Paul, not of Jesus.[35] Perhaps brotherhood of the Lord could be extrapolated from Paul's description of Jesus as firstborn in a large family (Rom 8:29) and from the way Paul customarily names God as our Father and as the Father of the Lord Jesus Christ. Yet Paul never makes that extrapolation. In addition we should notice that in these verses from 1 Corinthians and Galatians,

---

31. Fee, *The First Epistle to the Corinthians*, 403–4.
32. Witherington, *Conflict and Community in Corinth*, 207.
33. See discussion in Shanks and Witherington, *The Brother of Jesus*, 107.
34. Fung, *The Epistle to the Galatians*, 73.
35. The significance of this must be left for others to investigate. In the Fourth Gospel, Jesus calls his disciples "brothers" after the resurrection (20:17), and the significance of this will be discussed in chapter 9. Why Paul does not use sibling language to identify the Christian's relationship to Jesus is an interesting question.

other Christians are mentioned alongside the brother(s) of the Lord. Paul's grammar implies that James is a brother of the Lord in a way that Cephas is not.

We can conclude from these brief phrases in the Pauline corpus that Paul was aware that Jesus had a human mother and that Jesus had brothers who were leaders in the post-resurrection Christian community. Paul speaks of having met James, the leader of the church in Jerusalem, and clearly understood him to be Jesus' brother in the sense of belonging to the same biological family group.

We have also noted that the casual manner in which Paul wrote of Jesus' brothers implies that he believed his readers (in Galatia and Corinth at least) would know whom he was talking about or may even know them personally. This is not solid evidence, but it does point to a likely body of knowledge about Jesus' family (including personal relationships with his family members) that was held by the general population of the church in the second half of the first century. If such a body of knowledge existed in Galatia and Corinth, it is highly likely that it would be shared with another of Paul's churches in the important port city lying directly between them: Ephesus, where the author of the Fourth Gospel may have been living.

To this we may add the fact that the earliest Christian communities were Jewish, with a gradual assimilation of Gentile converts. Up until 70 CE Jews of the Diaspora, including Christian Jews, regularly made pilgrimage to Jerusalem.[36] In Jerusalem it is highly likely that they all heard news of Jesus' brothers and that many would have met them.

We are, therefore, able to say with some confidence that many Christians in the second half of the first century CE would have had some knowledge of Jesus' family and that the circulation of such knowledge would have been supported by the important place assigned to kinship in Jewish Greco-Roman society.

It is impossible for us now to be certain about what that body of knowledge included. The Pauline corpus implies that Jesus was known to have a Jewish mother and some brothers who became leaders in the church in Jerusalem. This is little more than we would know from reading John alone. But it is something. Some, at least, of the brothers who are not believers in John 7 were known to be church leaders by the time

---

36. See Thompson, "The Holy Internet," 53–54.

Paul wrote his first letter to the Corinthians. This will be an important consideration when we come to exegete John 7 in detail.

The Pauline corpus has helped us to identify what was probably common knowledge among educated Christians in the mid first century CE. We now turn to the Synoptic Gospels to identify more of the details that would have been known by at least some Christians in the second half of the first century.

Jesus' family in the Synoptic Gospels, with a particular focus on Matthew

Matthew's birth narratives show the baby messiah in danger: threatened by the shame of his unusual conception, threatened with abandonment by the man who was to be his human father, and threatened by a king who would not tolerate rivals.[37] In each danger, God (or the God's angel) intervenes: a star brings honor by the hands of foreigners, Joseph obeys an angel and gives the baby legitimacy, and the young family is warned to escape from the king's violence.

Matthew[38] stresses that Jesus is descended from David (1:1,6,20). The fact that this descent is through Joseph, who is not Jesus' biological father, does not appear to perturb Matthew. By marrying Mary, Joseph adopts Jesus as his son, and gives him the gift of his lineage.

Adoption in the Roman Empire was reasonably common and was legally equivalent to biological parenting. "The Romans considered the bonds of family and kinship to be biologically based but not biologically determined."[39] Augustus himself was an adopted son and the father of adopted sons. However, in the Roman world, unlike our own, the tendency was to adopt adult sons rather than children. Roman law differentiated between *adoptio*, where the son was in the power of a father and in which case the consent of the father was required; and *adrogatio*, where the adopted son was *sui iuris* and in which case any people in his power would be transferred to the adopting family.[40]

---

37. Moxnes, *Putting Jesus in His Place*, 36–7.

38. For the sake of clarity Matthew will be referred to throughout as the author of the Gospel of that name.

39. Saller, *Patriarchy, Property and Death in the Roman Family*, 43.

40. Dixon, *The Roman Family*, 112.

There are problems with applying Roman adoption practice to Jesus' relationship with Joseph. Adoption does not appear to have been as common among Jews, and even in Rome was almost completely limited to the ruling class.[41]

It was Jesus' legal status as a descendant of David that interested Matthew, rather than his genetic similarity to Joseph's ancestors. Perry comments that, "by taking Mary into his home, [Joseph] has guaranteed that this child who is not his own will nevertheless be his heir, and if his heir then David's heir, and if David's heir then possibly the Davidic Messiah."[42]

Rohrbaugh tells us that, "In publicly acknowledging a boy to be his son, that is a member of his genealogical tree, a father not only accepted responsibility for him and made him his heir, he determined his status (honour) in the community as well."[43]

We must note Yigal Levin's arguments against adoption having the same legal status among Jews that it did among Romans.[44] Levin finds no code or precedent for adoption in the Old Testament or first-century Jewish law, and claims that, "to a Judean of the first Century CE, the very concept of legal adoption, in which the adopted son inherits the adopter's legal status, would have been totally foreign."[45] He posits that the authors of Matthew and Luke were more familiar with Roman law and were unaware that Jewish practice was different.[46]

I respond to Levin's contribution[47] in several ways. Firstly, even if adoption was not practiced among first-century Jews, it could not have been an unfamiliar concept, given that it was practiced at the highest levels of the society of their overlords, the Romans. Secondly, his argument is from silence. Extant legal records from that time are far from complete, and among the lower classes marriages and divorces were often carried out without legal contracts. We cannot assume that all adoptions

---

41. Dixon, *The Roman Family*, 113.

42. Perry, *Mary for Evangelicals*, 57.

43. Rohrbaugh, "Legitimating Sonship," 188. See also Oakman, *Palestine in the Time of Jesus*, 54.

44. Levin, "Jesus, 'Son of God' and 'Son of David,'" 418–25.

45. Levin, "Jesus, 'Son of God' and 'Son of David,'" 429.

46. Levin, "Jesus, 'Son of God' and 'Son of David,'" 432–4.

47. It is always important to remember that the Jews, though highly Hellenized and Romanized, very much valued their own law and traditions. Levin is correct to remind us of this.

would appear in the legal record. Thirdly, to the extent to which the Jews understood themselves as God's children, their history taught them that they were adopted children: chosen, begotten after their birth (Psalm 2) as it were. Adoption may not have been common practice among them, but it was enshrined in their covenant with their God. Fourthly, Paul can certainly not be accused, as Luke and Matthew have been, of being unfamiliar with Jewish law; and Paul was equally insistent that Jesus was descended from David.

Finally, and most importantly, the language of adoption is used only by way of an analogy, to help us understand what Matthew and Luke are doing in the genealogies they present. Mary and Joseph's situation, as described in Matthew and Luke, is unique.[48] Joseph is not taking on a responsibility that another man had been unable or unwilling to fulfill. There was no other man.

Certainly, Jesus' descent from David was not straightforward; but the history of their nation summarized in these genealogies shows that God's work rarely is straightforward. That must, at least partly, be the point of the genealogies. The God they were dealing with is one whose purposes have been worked out through Tamar, Rahab, Ruth, and Bathsheba. This God can re-establish the Davidic line through a boy with a teenaged mother and no apparent father.

In light of this discussion, Campbell's argument that use of the word ἀδελφός to describe Jesus' brothers is incompatible with Jesus' virginal conception because the man was seen as the sole generative factor in conception in this culture (so that brotherhood was determined by common paternity),[49] can be immediately dismissed. Under the circumstances described in Matthew, Jesus would certainly be called the ἀδελφός of Mary and Joseph's other children. The shame associated with his unusual conception would have prevented the family from advertising the fact that Jesus was anything other than Joseph's son; and it seems likely that the younger siblings might not have even been told of the anomaly.

We read in Matthew 1:25 that Joseph "had no marital relations with [Mary] until she had borne a son." While the natural sense of this phrase suggests that the couple did have marital relations after Jesus' birth, it is important to note that this is not the point Matthew is making. Matthew is emphasizing the impossibility of Jesus being the biological offspring of

---

48. See Bauckham, "The Brothers and Sisters of Jesus," 690.
49. Campbell, *Kinship Relations*, 119.

Joseph,[50] and perhaps witnessing to the fulfillment of Isaiah 7:14.[51] He is not commenting on the nature of Mary and Joseph's relationship after Jesus was born. This verse should not be used as a proof text against the perpetual virginity of Mary. However, we can observe that the author makes no effort to advance or support the view that Mary did remain a virgin.

We meet Jesus' family again in Matthew 12 where we discover that Jesus has brothers. In this passage (12:46–50) Jesus appears to distance himself from his biological family and establish an alternative kinship group consisting of those who do the will of his Father in heaven. We will not dwell on this distancing now but will return to it in chapter 3. For now our interest is captivated by the brothers themselves.

ἀδελφοι Ἰησου: James, Joses, Jude, and Simon in the Gospels

Matthew, in 13:55, introduces the reader to Ἰάκωβος,[52] Ἰωσῆφ,[53] Σιμων,[54] and Ἰούδας.[55] The same names are given in Mark 6:3, with only a slight variation, and are among the names most frequently given to Jewish males at the time.[56] To avoid confusion with other characters with similar names, we will refer to them as James, Joses, Simon, and Jude. It appears to be impossible to discover the names of Jesus' sisters with any certainty, as various suggestions given by early Christian writers are taken from fictional accounts of Jesus' life, such as the *History of Joseph the Carpenter* and the *Proteuangelion of James*. Bauckham believes that the names most likely to be authentic are Mary and Salome[57] and I can make no better suggestions.

---

50. Matthew may also be reinforcing his description of Joseph as a righteous man. For some Jews, Romans, and Greeks of the time it was unseemly for a man to have intercourse with a woman while she was pregnant. See Allison, Jr., "Divorce, Celibacy and Joseph (Matthew 1:18–25 and 19:1–12)," 7–9.

51. Bauckham, *Jude and the Relatives of Jesus in the Early Church*, 25.

52. James.

53. Joseph.

54. Simon.

55. Jude (or Judas).

56. See Bauckham, *Jude and the Relatives of Jesus in the Early Church*, 6–7.

57. Bauckham, *Jude and the Relatives of Jesus in the Early Church*, 8.

The question that has divided Christians and occupied scholarship for centuries is this: Are these brothers and sisters the younger children of Mary?

Scholars have divided in three directions on this question, with each view named after its fourth-century proponent. The Helvidian[58] view takes the brothers to be sons of Mary and Joseph. The Epiphanian[59] view is that the brothers were elder sons of Joseph by a previous marriage; and the Hieronymian[60] view is that the brothers were Jesus' cousins.

The Hieronymian view

The Hieronymian view, first espoused by Jerome, relies on some unlikely identifications between minor characters in the Gospels[61] along with the assumption that ἀδελφός could mean "cousin."

Linguistic defense of this view relies on the lack of a word for cousin in Hebrew. The Hebrew, *ah*, is usually translated into Greek as ἀδελφός, when it may have originally meant cousin.[62] Meier notes Oberlinner's discovery[63] that only one such translation can be found (1 Chron 23:22) and further points out that because of the ambiguity of *ah* the narrator usually clarifies the nature of the relationship, as in 1 Chron 23:22.[64] Clearly, no such clarification is given in the Gospel writers' use of the word ἀδελφός in relation to Jesus' brothers.

It is also hard to see why Jerome's concerns about "translation Greek" would be relevant to the Gospels, which were all, with the possible exception of Matthew, written in Greek. There is certainly no reason to think

---

58. See Mayor, "Brethren of the Lord."
59. See Lightfoot, "The Brethren of the Lord."
60. See McHugh, *The Mother of Jesus in the New Testament*.
61. For example, that Μαρία ἡ Ἰακώβου τοῦ μικροῦ (Mark 15:40) is the sister-in-law of Mary the mother of Jesus and the James in question is the James called the brother of Jesus. Among the arguments against this is Hegesippius' insistence that James, the Lord's brother, had been identified as James the Just "by all from the time of our Saviour to the present day; for there were many that bore the name of James" (Quoted in Eusebius, *History of the Church* II.XXIII.4). It seems most likely that Mark identified the James of 15:40 as τοῦ μικροῦ in order to distinguish him from Jesus' brother and the many other men called James.
62. Meier, "The Brothers and Sisters of Jesus in Ecumenical Perspective," 16.
63. Lorenz Oberlinner, *Historische ÜBerlieferung Und Christologische Aussage*, 29.
64. Meier, "The Brothers and Sisters of Jesus in Ecumenical Perspective," 17.

that Paul is translating from the Hebrew when he uses τὸν ἀδελφὸν τοῦ κυρίου to describe James in Gal 1:19 where τὸν ἀνεψιὸς τοῦ κυρίου would have been more accurate had James been merely a cousin of Jesus.

Meier points out that the possibility of an earlier, less precise but more authoritative, Aramaic expression lying behind James' identification as τὸν ἀδελφὸν τοῦ κυρίου, is highly unlikely because Greek-speaking Jews were present in the early church from the beginning, so the Greek and Aramaic titles would have both come into use simultaneously.[65] Meier also notes that Josephus' reference to James as ὁ ἀδελφός τοῦ Ἰησοῦ,[66] both further undermines the argument for a set Aramaic title (as he is here "the brother of Jesus" rather than "the brother of the Lord") and, more importantly, gives a use of ἀδελφός which is independent of the New Testament witness. That Josephus was capable of pedantry in translation of *ah* into Greek is demonstrated by his translation of Gen 29:12 in Book 1 of Antiquities where he takes pains to point out that Jacob is Laban's nephew, not his "brother" as the LXX implies.[67]

Meier believes that New Testament[68] usage allows two meanings for ἀδελφός: metaphorically to refer to a tie of kinship that is not determined by blood, and literally as a full or half-brother.[69] In most cases ἀδελφός means literally a brother who is a blood relation, either a full or a half-brother. The only clear New Testament example of its use as half-brother is its application to Philip as Herod's ἀδελφός in Mark 6:17, but one example is enough to leave this option open.

The most decisive argument against the Hieronymian view is found in the writings of Hegesippus that are quoted by Eusebius. Hegesippus

---

65. Meier, "The Brothers and Sisters of Jesus in Ecumenical Perspective," 18.

66. Josephus, "Antiquitates Judaicae," 20.9.1.

67. Meier, "The Brothers and Sisters of Jesus in Ecumenical Perspective," 18–19.

68. He does not deny that αδελφος has a broader meaning in texts outside the New Testament, but believes these to be immaterial because the New Testament non-metaphorical use of the word indicates "only full or half-brother, and nothing else." Meier, "The Brothers and Sisters of Jesus in Ecumenical Perspective", 19–20. Bauckham counters that the writers of the New Testament did not live in their own language ghetto but "participated in the common linguistic milieu of their Greek-speaking contemporaries." If, in that "linguistic milieu," αδελφος could be used more broadly, then how can the New Testament writers be excluded from such a use? In short, "Meier's argument contradicts what nearly all translators and exegetes assume: that the range of use from which the meaning of a word in the NT must be chosen is the range of use in the language, not the range of use in the NT." Bauckham, "The Brothers and Sisters of Jesus," 691–2.

69. Meier, "The Brothers and Sisters of Jesus in Ecumenical Perspective," 19–20.

speaks of James as the Lord's brother,[70] Clopas as the Lord's uncle, and Symeon as the Lord's cousin.[71] He clearly distinguishes between brothers and cousins, indicating that James is the former.[72]

The Hieronymian view will, therefore, not be further considered here.

The Epiphanian view

Were the brothers and sisters of Jesus children of Joseph by a previous marriage?

The most vigorous modern proponent of the Epiphanian view is Richard Bauckham, who appears to feel acutely his isolation from the overwhelming majority of scholars. He argues that this view has been dismissed too lightly.[73] Perhaps Protestant scholars have allowed the academic consensus around the Helvidian view to dull our rigor. I will accept Bauckham's challenge here and examine the Epiphanian view closely.

Bauckham admits that, "the only serious evidence for the Epiphanian view is that it is the only view positively attested in Christian tradition before Tertullian, if Tertullian is correctly interpreted as holding the Helvidian view, or before the late fourth Century, if he is not."[74]

The obvious response to that is to point out that the fact that the Epiphanian view was explicitly expounded earlier in extant literature than the Helvidian view is hardly surprising or meaningful. The Helvidian view is derived from the most straightforward reading of the text and so presumably would have been assumed by the Christian community in the absence of any contradictory evidence. It is only after the Epiphanian view had been expounded that anyone would have thought that the Helvidian view might need to be defended or even clearly expressed.

---

70. "James, *the brother of the Lord*, succeeded to the government of the Church in conjunction with the apostles." Quoted in Eusebius, *History of the Church* II.XXIII.4.

71. "And after James the Just had suffered martyrdom, as the Lord had also on the same account, Symeon, the son of the Lord's uncle, Clopas, was appointed the next bishop. All proposed him as second bishop because he was a cousin of the Lord." Quoted in Eusebius, *History of the Church* IV.XXII.4.

72. As is Jude—see Eusebius, *History of the Church* III.XX.1; See Bauckham, *Jude and the Relatives of Jesus in the Early Church*, 24.

73. Bauckham, *Jude and the Relatives of Jesus in the Early Church*, 24.

74. Bauckham, *Jude and the Relatives of Jesus in the Early Church*, 25–26.

The "only serious evidence" for this view is flimsy indeed, but the rest of Bauckham's argument must be addressed.

The Epiphanian view was clearly spelled out for the first time in the second-century work *Protevangelium of James*. While this is not a work that has traditionally been treated as authoritative or accurate, it has value here because it informs us that such an understanding of Jesus' origins was considered in the second century. Bauckham contends that the Epiphanian view did not originate with the *Protevangelium of James* but was a belief, predating that work, that found expression in at least six Syrian works of literature in the second century.[75]

These works reveal three ideas about Jesus' origins that are not found in the New Testament. Each idea points to an exalted status for Mary.[76] The first is the Davidic descent of Mary; the second is the miraculous birth of Jesus, which preserves Mary's physical virginity; and the third is that James and the others were stepbrothers of Jesus. All three ideas come together only in the *Protevangelium of James*, though there may be reason to believe that a complete version of the *Gospel of Peter*, which is not extant, may also allude to all three.[77] Bauckham summarizes the presence of these ideas in the following table:[78]

	Davidic Descent of Mary	Miraculous Birth of Jesus	Stepbrothers
Ignatius	✓	✓	
Ascension of Isaiah	✓	✓	
Odes of Solomon		✓	
Gospel of Peter			✓
Infancy Gospel of Thomas			✓
Protevangelium of James	✓	✓	✓

Table 1

75. Bauckham, *Jude and the Relatives of Jesus in the Early Church*, 26–8.
76. See Campbell, *Kinship Relations*, 48.
77. Bauckham, *Jude and the Relatives of Jesus in the Early Church*, 27.
78. Bauckham, *Jude and the Relatives of Jesus in the Early Church*, 27.

While narratives of the miraculous birth may point toward the doctrine of the perpetual virginity of Mary, it is also likely that they simply emphasize the literal fulfillment of Isaiah 7:14.[79] They cannot, therefore, be assumed to deny that further children were born to Mary. We are, nevertheless, left with three witnesses to Jesus' siblings being children of Joseph but not Mary, namely the *Gospel of Peter*, the *Infancy Gospel of Thomas*, and the *Protevangelium of James*.

We must wonder whether these witnesses point to a prior tradition about Jesus' stepsiblings. I cannot positively rule out that possibility, but I can propose one that is more likely. When we place these three documents alongside another second-century historical fiction, *Acts of Paul and Thecla*, we note two essential points of similarity. They each glorify a woman and they each glorify virginity.

I would argue, then, that the polemical context of these three Syrian works (or perhaps all six) is not the development of an accurate family tree for Jesus, but rather the second-century debates over the place of women in the church and the (not unrelated) place of asceticism in Christian living.

J.P. Meier says of the Epiphanian view that "It may well be that we are dealing with a solution thought up after the fact to support the emerging idea of Mary's perpetual virginity, which did not become common teaching until the latter half of the fourth Century."[80]

There may also be something to Malina's argument that developments in Mariology in the fourth century, and their precursors, "derive from a Mediterranean male application of the principle of fittingness or propriety."[81] Since Jesus was the second person of the Trinity, equal and co-substantial with God the Father, it was only fitting that his mother should exhibit certain characteristics that set her apart from common women; and it was only fitting that theologians should look for appropriate language to speak of such a woman outside the common linguistic sphere. The logic of this thinking, according to Malina, runs as follows, "if it is proper or fitting it must have been, and therefore it was."[82]

---

79. If a virgin is to give birth (and remain a physically intact virgin) without a caesarean section the birth must be miraculous. It is interesting to note, then, that the notion of the post-partum virginity of Mary may predate the notion of her perpetual virginity.

80. Meier, "The Brothers and Sisters of Jesus in Ecumenical Perspective," 16.

81. Malina, *The Social World of Jesus and the Gospels*, 101.

82. Malina, *The Social World of Jesus and the Gospels*, 101.

I am convinced by Bauckham that "the Epiphanian view has a better claim to serious consideration than is often nowadays allowed."[83] It may well be that scholars of the Helvidian persuasion have become overconfident.[84] However, in the end his arguments in favor of the Epiphanian view are not convincing.

The Helvidian View

The Helvidian view, that Jesus' brothers and sisters were offspring of Joseph and Mary, is the view that a theologically unencumbered reader would arrive at based on a plain reading of the text.[85] It therefore requires less positive evidence than the two alternatives.

Eisenman notes that when Jesus' family is mentioned in the New Testament, "no embarrassment is evinced about the fact of these brothers. Nor is there any indication that they may be half-brothers, brothers by a different mother, or any other such designation aimed at reducing their importance and minimizing their relationship to Jesus."[86]

J.P. Meier argues that,

> when Mark, in 1:29–30, introduces us to James, his brother (*adelphon*) John and their father Zebedee, it never crosses the mind of any exegete or theologian to claim that James and John are really cousins and Zebedee is really their stepfather or uncle. Why an exegete, operating purely on philological and historical grounds, should judge differently in Mark 6:3, where we hear that Jesus is the son of Mary and the Brother (*adelphos*) of James, Jude, and Simeon, is not clear.[87]

Not only is it natural for the reader of the New Testament to assume that Jesus' "brothers" are really brothers, it is also natural to assume that

---

83. Bauckham, *Jude and the Relatives of Jesus in the Early Church*, 31.

84. In Bauckham, "The Brothers and Sisters of Jesus," some glaring holes in Meier's arguments are identified. I will not repeat these here, but refer them to the reader's attention.

85. Meier, "The Brothers and Sisters of Jesus in Ecumenical Perspective," 13–14. It is in the name of ecumenism that the Catholic scholar, Meier, makes his case that the New Testament most probably points in the direction of the brothers and sisters being literal blood kin who are the children of Joseph and Mary; L. Morris, *The Gospel According to John*, 187–8.

86. Eisenman, *James the Brother of Jesus*, 74.

87. Meier, *A Marginal Jew*, 327.

the marriage of Mary and Joseph was really a marriage. According to I.M. Resnick, "if Joseph and Mary remained perpetually virgins . . . they clearly were engaged in a strange and unusual kind of relationship. This chaste union either implied that they were not truly married or implied a definition of marriage that separated it from the carnal act itself."[88]

While there may have been a form of asceticism involving abstinence within Second Temple Judaism, there is no evidence for permanent abstinence within marriage.

There is, of course, evidence in 1 Corinthians 7 that some Christians in that multicultural city were practicing just such sexual asceticism within marriage less than sixty years after Jesus' birth. It is likely, though, that such behavior had its origin in Greek philosophy and cannot be traced to Palestine. It is also significant that Paul disapproves unequivocally of long-term sexual abstinence within marriage. It is natural to wonder whether he would have stated his case so boldly if he had been aware of a tradition implicating Jesus' parents in such a union.

Meier summarizes the evidence for the Helvidian view in this way:

> if—prescinding from faith and later church teaching—the historian or exegete is asked to render a judgment on the New Testament and patristic texts we have examined, viewed simply as historical sources, the most probable opinion is that the brothers and sisters of Jesus were true siblings . . . [Yet] . . . One cannot say that they provide absolute proof that the traditional Catholic interpretation is simply impossible.[89]

Absolute proof is certainly not available, but the balance of probability is heavily weighted in the direction of Jesus' brothers and sisters being the offspring of both Mary and Joseph. I am sufficiently satisfied to allow this to form an assumption for the remainder of this book.

Son of Mary

Another point of controversy has been the designation of Jesus as "Son of Mary" by the people of Nazareth in Mark 6:3. This description differs from Matthew and Luke, and tends to be accepted as therefore more original.[90] Was it a slur on Jesus' legitimacy to call him the son of Mary rather

---

88. Resnick, "Marriage in Medieval Culture," 355.
89. Meier, "The Brothers and Sisters of Jesus in Ecumenical Perspective," 26–7.
90. See Brown, *Mary in the New Testament*, 100–102; 165–6; 196–9.

than of Joseph? Is it evidence that Mark, who does not record details of Jesus' birth, was nevertheless aware of Jesus' virginal conception? Or does it simply imply that Joseph was dead?

Tal Ilan points out that Josephus (in Ant. 16.11; 17.22,230, etc.) refers to Berenice and Antipater as daughter and son of Salome, not as any slur but because Salome held a higher position at court than her husband's.[91] Ilan mentions several other men from the first three centuries CE who bear their mothers' names because of the social (royal, priestly, or later sagely) or moral superiority of their female parent.[92] Certainly, there is no suggestion in the literature that a metronyme was used to cast aspersions on a man's birth.[93]

We cannot, based on Ilan's work, deduce that Mary necessarily held superior lineage. We simply do not possess sufficient information. We can, however, say that it was no insult to call Jesus the son of Mary. Given that it is a fellow resident of Nazareth who speaks of Jesus in this way, it may be that Mary was a more prominent member of her local community than Joseph—or it may simply be that Mary was present during the discussion and Joseph was not (possibly, though not conclusively, because he had died).

Given that these words are placed in the mouths of the townsfolk of Nazareth, who are unlikely to have been aware of,[94] and less likely to have believed, Jesus' virginal conception, this verse tells us nothing about Mark's knowledge of that tradition.

Mary and fourth-century Christian asceticism

For many early church fathers, Mary was significant principally because she guaranteed Jesus' true humanity;[95] and much that we find in their writings is penned in defense of this orthodox belief against Arians, and

---

91. Ilan, "Man Born of Woman...," 29–30.
92. Ilan, "Man Born of Woman...," 30–37.
93. Ilan, "Man Born of Woman...," 45.
94. See Bauckham, "The Brothers and Sisters of Jesus," 689.
95. See, for example, Pauline Allen, "A Case-Study of Augustine's Letters," 216. Consider also that Tertullian, in his anti-Marcionite writing, stated that the mother and brothers were really mother and brothers, to assert the full humanity of Jesus. Tertullian, "The Five Books against Marcion" Book IV, §xix.

earlier against Gnostics. It also seems that the virginity of Mary was believed, by some at least, to guarantee the sinlessness of Jesus.[96]

However, it is also very likely that for some, post-partum virginity was attributed to Mary because of a belief in the honor and sanctity of the virginal state. A full discussion of the connection between fourth-century Christian asceticism and belief in the post-partum virginity of Mary would be worthwhile but is not possible here. However, it is worth briefly noting the contribution of Jovinian, a monk who is known to us through refutations written by Jerome, Ambrose, and Augustine.

Jovinian stood out from the churchmen of his day by denying that virginity was more meritorious than marriage[97] *and* by insisting that Mary lost her (physical) virginity in the process of giving birth.[98] This one example of dissent on both these points does not constitute a proof of a causal connection between them, but it does suggest the possibility.

David Hunter notes that, of all those who objected to the glorification of virginity in the fourth century, Jovinian was the only one to do so on theological grounds. Hunter believes this was because Jovinian saw Manichean tendencies in the asceticism of his time.[99] Manicheans not only rejected marriage but also taught that the human birth of Jesus was not real.[100] Jovinian compared the Christians of his time with Mani and was alarmed by the similarity.

Jovinian was probably quite astute in seeing a connection between Manichaeism and fourth-century Christian asceticism. His mistake (sadly familiar in the history of the church) seems to have been to seek to address the problems he identified through name-calling.[101] His opponents could easily dismiss the charge that they were Manichean without ever addressing the real theological concerns that Jovinian raised. Though Augustine's years as a Manichean are well documented, his rejection of

---

96. Allen, "A Case-Study of Augustine's Letters," 225.

97. See Jerome, "Against Jovinianus" Book I §3; Augustine, "Anti-Pelagian Writings" Ch 13 §vii.

98. Augustine, "Anti-Pelagian Writings" Ch 15. See Ambrose Ep. 42 *Rescriptum ad Siricium*.

99. Hunter, "Resistance to the Virginal Ideal in Late-Fourth-Century Rome," 46.

100. See Augustine, "The Writings against the Manichaeans and against the Donatists" Reply to Faustus the Manichæan XXVI.

101. Since accusing people of heresy could lead to their execution in this newly Christian empire, name-calling was no light matter. See Hunter, "Resistance to the Virginal Ideal in Late-Fourth-Century Rome," 63.

that sect is also well documented. Jerome and Ambrose are unlikely to have been influenced by the teaching of Mani.

Much more likely than Christian asceticism being derived from Manichaeism is the possibility that both were derived from broader influences in the empire. In *Retractions 1.7* Augustine notes that Manichees were campaigning and attracting converts in Rome on the basis of the superiority of their asceticism. If such a strategy was successful then asceticism must have held some attraction for the Roman population.

We can guess the reasons why asceticism had become so attractive. As confidence in the things of this world became decreasingly well founded, as Rome lost its hold on the Mediterranean world—and even on the city of Rome—room was left for otherworldly fascination. Cultures that don't believe they have a future in this world tend to renounce marriage. Cultures that are fighting to push back the forces of chaos tend to venerate self-control.

Was Mary a widow?

That Joseph had died before the start of Jesus' public ministry is widely assumed. He disappears from the Gospel narratives after Jesus' childhood, whereas Mary and Jesus' siblings remain present into the birth of the church. Bauckham suggests an alternative explanation. Perhaps his absence from the narratives reflects the fact that he did not become active in the post-resurrection Christian community as other members of the family did.[102]

Pauline Allen points out that when Augustine seeks to encourage the recipients of his letters with the example of biblical widows, he does not select Mary.[103] However, this is not sufficient evidence to demonstrate that he believed Joseph to have outlived Mary. It is likely that he chose to refer only to women explicitly described as widows in the Jewish Bible.

Jewish women in the first century generally married young (from 12 to 20 years of age) typically to men at least ten years older, and so generally experienced a time of widowhood.[104]

Given the incidence of infant and childhood mortality, it is likely that adults would be separated in age from surviving siblings by at least

---

102. Bauckham, *Jude and the Relatives of Jesus in the Early Church*, 6.
103. Allen, "A Case-Study of Augustine's Letters," 218.
104. Kraemer, "Typical and Atypical Jewish Family Dynamics," 141.

three years, on average.[105] It is likely, then, that Mary's childbearing phase of life spanned roughly eighteen years.

It must be admitted that few women at this time survived as many as seven births. Campbell argues that Joseph was probably married several times in order to have produced so many children.[106] However, the rarity of a woman producing seven children does not imply its impossibility.

It seems reasonable that Jesus, as the eldest son of a widow, may have waited until his younger siblings reached (official) adulthood before leaving the family home to embark on his itinerant ministry. This obligation would have been particularly pressing if he acted as their guardian in place of their father.[107] By this calculation, Jesus would have been about thirty by the time pressing family obligations would have allowed him to leave Nazareth.

The Gospels are silent concerning the extent to which family obligations determined the timing of Jesus' ministry. Emphasis is placed, instead, on the preparatory ministry of John the Baptist. Yet it is possible that family obligations could account for the difference in the timing of their ministries.[108]

Luke 1:39–45 indicates that John the Baptist and Jesus were roughly the same age, yet John commences his public ministry significantly earlier than Jesus. John was (presumably) the only child[109] of elderly parents. By the time he reached adulthood, or soon afterward, it is likely that his parents would have died, leaving him with no younger siblings. It is also likely that he had no wife, since the lifestyle described in Matthew 3:4 is not one that would support a family, and it is reasonable to assume that he would refrain from marriage since he knew he had been set apart from birth for a prophetic ministry. It is very likely, then, that by his early adulthood John was without family obligations and so was able to leave his home to commence his ministry much earlier than Jesus.

---

105. See Kraemer, "Typical and Atypical Jewish Family Dynamics," 146.

106. Campbell, *Kinship Relations*, 120.

107. See Kraemer, "Typical and Atypical Jewish Family Dynamics," 153–4.

108. Of course John's ministry, by its nature, could only be accomplished if it commenced before that of Jesus. Yet it is interesting to consider that family obligations, over which God is clearly seen to be in control in Luke 1, may have played a part in allowing John to start his ministry earlier.

109. Given that his parents are described as barren and old at the time of his conception, and that his conception is shown to be miraculous by the announcement of an angel, it is unlikely that Elizabeth and Zechariah produced other children.

It is therefore likely that Joseph had died at some time before Jesus entered public ministry and that Jesus' obligations to his family were those of an eldest son in the absence of a father. Certainty is not possible, but this seems the most likely explanation for Joseph's absence from the narratives.

Nazareth—Jesus' hometown

Nazareth[110] in Galilee was about six kilometers from Sepphoris, the capital city built by Herod Antipas, and near the fertile Bet Netofa Valley. Land in this area was extensively cultivated. About 80–90 percent of the population was involved in agriculture,[111] largely in the production of olives. Given that olive oil was a culinary staple throughout the Mediterranean, this region was in a position to support a large number of communities, including new towns that had been established during the reigns of Herod the Great and Antipas.[112]

Josephus speaks of 204 cities and villages in Galilee,[113] with three chief cities, Sepphoris, Tiberias, and Gabara.[114]

Lake Galilee, of course, was highly utilized commercially for fresh fish, salted fish, and fish sauces.[115] Galilee also boasted at least two important pottery production centers.[116] A barter system, which suited the needs of subsistence peasants,[117] had recently been replaced with the enforced use of minted currency,[118] increasing tax revenue and placing the necessities of life outside the reach of a few more peasants. It is likely that the richness of the land, "far from producing an improved situation

---

110. Moxnes believes that the fact that Matthew struggles to find scriptural significance for Nazareth in Matt 2:23 is good evidence that Matthew was convinced that Nazareth was the place where Jesus grew up. (Moxnes, *Putting Jesus in His Place*, 36.)

111. Oakman, *Palestine in the Time of Jesus*, 104–5.

112. S. Freyne, "Herodian Economics in Galilee," 29.

113. Josephus, "Josephi Vita," 235.

114. Josephus, "Josephi Vita," 123.

115. Freyne, "Herodian Economics in Galilee," 35.

116. Freyne, "Herodian Economics in Galilee," 36.

117. You can't eat a bronze coin—and you can't tax a loaf of bread.

118. Oakman, *Palestine in the Time of Jesus*, 123–5.

for all was highly exploitative in a way that led to social stratification and fragmentation."[119]

Hanson and Oakman explain that farmers and fishing families at this time rarely had the opportunity to exercise control over their own labor. Farmers were usually tenants on large estates owned by wealthy landlords, and tended to grow crops that suited the economic aspirations of the owners rather than the basic needs of their own families.[120] People who earned a living by fishing from the lake tended to be contracted to brokers associated with local rulers. Money from their work would pay debts to the brokers first, before providing for their families.[121] Of course, taxes were extracted at every point of transaction through highly unpopular and corruption-prone tax farming schemes.[122]

Josephus gives an indication of the level of exploitation and corruption under the Herods in *Antiquities* XVII.304–314. His charge against Herod the Great is summed up with the words, "there was no way of obtaining freedom from unjust violence, without giving either gold or silver for it."[123] Since this was the perspective of an estate owner, we must imagine the freedom and independence of the common artisans, tenant farmers, and day laborers, who had no gold with which to buy justice, were even more circumscribed.

For centuries, this region of the trans-Jordan had been fiercely contested, with a strong military presence reminding the Jewish population that they lived under foreign power. Freyne argues that this military presence, rather than instilling Greek and Roman culture in the local population, more likely increased their animosity towards their overlords.[124]

Freyne believes, quite reasonably, that one of the institutions that would have been put under great pressure by the economic changes of this time was the extended family.[125] "Family feuds must have occurred as a direct result of the social changes taking place and the invitation to join

---

119. Freyne, "Herodian Economics in Galilee," 43.

120. Oakman, *Palestine in the Time of Jesus*, 105–6.

121. Oakman, *Palestine in the Time of Jesus*, 106–110.

122. See Oakman, *Palestine in the Time of Jesus*, 113–6 for an analysis of the complex taxation systems of first-century Palestine.

123. Josephus, *Antiquities*, Book 17, 308.

124. Freyne, *Galilee*, 105–8.

125. Freyne, "Herodian Economics in Galilee," 43.

an alternative family would have resonated particularly with those who had become alienated or excluded in the prevailing social upheaval."[126]

How, then, might we imagine that the family of Jesus fared? What might have been their place within the social fabric of Nazareth? Here, again, we find that the Gospels give us little clear direction, noting only that the occupations of Jesus (Mark 6:3) and Joseph (Matt 13:55) could be described by the word τέκτων. Ken Campbell has argued convincingly that, "In the context of first-Century Israel, the τέκτων was a general craftsman who worked with stone, wood, and sometimes metal in large and small building projects."[127]

Campbell also argues, based on a linguistic analysis, that Jesus' teaching "has more affinity with what are now called 'middle-class values' than with any revolutionary agenda".[128] He finds that Jesus' vocabulary indicates "personal knowledge and experience of the world of business" and goes on to say that he "had clearly thought about these matters at length and developed a carefully nuanced philosophy of money management."[129]

While it may be possible that the family in which Jesus grew up was in some sense "middle-class",[130] this has not been settled by Campbell's linguistic argument. In any culture, those on lower rungs of the social hierarchy tend to be conversant with the business of those higher than themselves. This is particularly the case in honor–shame cultures where survival may depend on developing patron–client relationships. As builders, Joseph and his sons would have depended on good (possibly fiscal) relationships with those closer to the regional aristocracy in order to benefit from the many building projects that the new city of Sepphoris, in particular, would have required.

Luke, at least, seems to present a family that is closer to being poor than "middle-class." Their difficulty in finding accommodation in Bethlehem (Luke 2:7) and the small sacrifice given at Jesus' birth (Luke 2:24) point towards the young couple being far from wealthy. It may be, of course, that Joseph prospered as a builder after his marriage, aided in

126. Freyne, "Herodian Economics in Galilee," 45.
127. Campbell, "What Was Jesus' Occupation?" 512.
128. Campbell, "What Was Jesus' Occupation?" 517.
129. Campbell, "What Was Jesus' Occupation?" 517.
130. Note that Meier also concludes that Jesus would have been lower middle class. Meier, *A Marginal Jew*, 282.

time by his five sons. Yet it is hard to see that the needs of a growing family would not consume the increasing income of a growing business.

The designation of "middle-class" is also somewhat anachronistic here. The high levels of stratification in Palestine produced three social classes. The ruling class and their retainers would have comprised at most 10 percent[131] of the population. This included Herod and his family. The desperately poor and marginalized, πτωχος, would have comprised about 15 percent of the population. Those who had employment, land, or skills were not πτωχος but they may well have existed at a subsistence level,[132] as 75 percent of families in first-century Palestine did. Of this middle group, about 70 percent were peasant farmers and day laborers, while 5 percent were artisans.[133]

Guijarro identifies four different types of families that would have existed within these three strata. The very wealthiest were the "large families" who lived in mansions as extended family communities along with slaves and servants. The rest of the ruling class (tax collectors, wealthy soldiers, and people successful in business) existed in "multiple" type family groups where two or more conjugal families shared a courtyard house. Within both "large" and "multiple" families, support, solidarity, and sharing of resources in times of need would have been usual. These generally lived in the cities. Most members of the Galilean population would have lived in "nucleated" families, in single-room houses that could not accommodate more than a husband, a wife, and a small number of children. These would have maintained contact with, and given support to, other "nucleated" families in their kinship group, but would have been limited in this by long hours of labor and limited resources. "Scattered" families were the homeless, who would have been unable to offer any support to their kin.[134]

Given that there was so much work for builders in the region at the time it is probably not out of the question that Jesus' family lived in a courtyard house, but it is more likely that they lived in a single-room house.

---

131. These percentages reflect averages for agrarian societies, as this sort of data from the period is unavailable.

132. After taxes and rents had taken any surplus they did produce.

133. Guijarro, "The Family in First Century Galilee," 56.

134. Guijarro, "The Family in First Century Galilee," 57–61.

Conclusions

The brief portrait that I can now sketch of Jesus' family, based on the above evidence, is by no means one in which I can be completely confident of every detail. I rely at many points on likelihood and probability rather than certainty. Nevertheless, I have established in the above discussion that many of the likelihoods are quite high and so present the portrait with some confidence. Discussion of Jesus' kinship obligations in the remaining chapters will be, to a greater or lesser extent, based on this portrait.

Jesus was the eldest son of a family of five sons and at least two daughters. He learned the building trade from his father, Joseph, along with his brothers, in the town of Nazareth. Much of their work took them to the nearby city of Sepphoris where a great deal of building was taking place.

He grew up with a strong awareness of the sharp socioeconomic inequalities around him. His family just managed to support itself, with all able family members working very hard. He observed the wealth and luxury of the ruling class when in Sepphoris, and also observed the tragic consequences when people of his own class lost the means to support themselves.

He was recognized as an academically able child and was taught to read the Hebrew Scriptures and given the opportunity to study the Torah and the prophets.

Joseph died when Jesus, and one or two of his brothers, were fully productive adults but not yet married. Jesus assumed the responsibilities of head of the family. This meant continuing to work to support them financially and also, alongside his mother, Mary, training and disciplining the children and finding spouses for them at the appropriate time. As head of the family he was also able to choose not to marry, despite pressure to do so. Once his youngest sibling reached the age of twelve he considered that his family could now manage without him. He left the family home to commence his itinerant ministry. At times he placed his mother in the care of his brothers and at other times she travelled with him.

Much of this information would have been common knowledge among early Christians because of widespread curiosity in that culture about kinship relationships, because of the mobility of many Christians at the time, and because at least two of Jesus' close relatives, James and

Mary, were part of early churches in Jerusalem and (as is traditionally thought) in Ephesus.

It is already possible to begin to identify the tension Jesus faced between his obligations to his family and his call to teach, heal, and sacrifice his life. The next chapter will consider how that tension is described and understood in the Synoptic Gospels, and how his followers are called to manage that tension in their own life of discipleship and kinship.

3

Conflict between Discipleship and Kinship in the Synoptic Gospels and Other First-Century Sources

In Jesus the Word became flesh and dwelt among humanity. He grew to adulthood in a particular family with a particular place in a particular society. When he left his childhood home he did not fully divest himself of the influences and obligations that membership of this family entailed. He could not. They were as much a part of him as his hands and feet. Yet he unwaveringly pursued his mission in the face of his family's objections. This chapter will consider this tension between mission and family in Jesus' life and between discipleship and family in Jesus' teaching as it is described in the Synoptic Gospels. It will begin by defining some social-scientific terms and explaining their significance to the study of Jesus' family. It will then consider how two kinship groups, the biological family and the fictive kin of discipleship, are shown to be in conflict in the first three Gospels. This analysis will provide a basis for later comparison with the apparently very different treatment these two groups are given in the Fourth Gospel.

Key Questions to be addressed in this chapter:
- What is a fictive kinship group?
- Can Jesus' followers be described as a fictive kinship group?
- How is the tension between ministry and family evidenced in Jesus' life in the Synoptics?

- How is the tension between discipleship and family evidenced in Jesus' teaching in the Synoptics?

Definition of fictive kinship groups

Many cultures employ family language to describe relationships that are not based on blood ties. The anthropologist, Julian Pitt-Rivers, described these relationships as pseudo-kin.[1] He identifies three forms of pseudo-kin: figurative kin, fictive kin, and ritual kin. Figurative kinship language is often used when, for example, a young person calls an older woman "Auntie." There is no pretence of actual kinship here as the term simply recognizes that the woman is older and deserving of respect. An example of ritual kinship is blood brotherhood. Here a genuine change is made to the relationship through the ritual, but the new relationship involves quite different roles and obligations from biological brotherhood.[2] The form of pseudo-kinship of most interest to the study of the Gospels is fictive kinship.

Fictive kinship groups are, as the name suggests, groups that exhibit family-like structures and loyalties, but where relationship ties are not those of biological or adoptive kinship. In the ancient world, fictive kinship groups formed at times to provide support to individuals who had no kin[3] or who were estranged from their families, often because they had been forced to move from the country to the city in order to find employment. They also formed, at times, when the individual's kinship loyalties remained intact but were not sufficiently influential to support career advancement. This seems to be the case in many of the trade guilds that flourished at this time. Moxnes argues that the fictive kinship group into which Jesus' disciples were called was of the former kind: more of an alternative to biological family than an addition to it. "Those who leave the known and taken-for-granted household structure to follow Jesus," he says, "establish an alternative place as a fictive kinship household."[4] We will examine Moxnes' arguments in greater detail later in this chapter.

Hellerman's definition will serve our purposes here. A fictive kinship group is "a social group where members are related to one another

---

1. Pitt-Rivers, "Kinship," 408.
2. See Campbell, *Kinship Relations*, 4.
3. Dixon, *The Roman Family*, 115.
4. Moxnes, *Putting Jesus in His Place*, 48.

neither by birth nor by marriage but who nevertheless (a) employ kinship terminology to describe group relationships and (b) expect family-like behavior to characterize interactions among group members."[5]

Fictive kinship groups serve, to some extent, as surrogate families[6] and as such tend to mirror the family structure of the society in which they are formed. In such groups in the Ancient Roman world, the place of *pater familias* was generally taken by a patron. These patrons, rather than (or in addition to) preserving their honor through their descendants, would often endow shrines and institute annual birthday rites to preserve their memories.[7] A powerful patron could expect clients to demonstrate the kind of loyalty that would normally be demanded by the head of a household.

While ancient fictive kinship groups mirrored kinship structures, they also mirrored the political structures of their society.[8] An outworking of this is that, though fictive kinship groups tended to bring together people from a variety of social strata, they also tended to preserve the ranking system of their society. They were not the democratic havens we may romantically imagine them to have been.[9]

It is possible to argue, further, that some fictive kinship groups not only mirrored, but even had their own place within, the political structures of their day. Hanson and Oakman quote 1 Macc 14:40, "the Romans had called the Jews their friends and confederates and brethren," pointing out that the subjection of Judaea as a client state to Rome was expressed in (at least partially) kinship terms.[10]

It is possible that this provides one reason why emperors tended to view guilds and associations with suspicion. Such men were never eager to see their subjects' loyalties divided. Certainly, the "kinship" nature of the early Christian community was one of the factors that made it political. Those who call God alone "Father" no longer belong to the household of Caesar[11] even if they continue to obey the laws of Caesar (Matt 22:21).

---

5. Hellerman, *The Ancient Church as Family*, 4.

6. Duling, "The Matthean Brotherhood," 164.

7. Duling, "The Matthean Brotherhood and Marginal Scribal Leadership," 162.

8. Given that kinship structures and political structures tend to mirror one another, this is hardly surprising.

9. Duling, "The Matthean Brotherhood and Marginal Scribal Leadership," 162.

10. Oakman, *Palestine in the Time of Jesus*, 81.

11. Oakman, *Palestine in the Time of Jesus*, 127; See also Aristotle, "Politics" 1.1 [1252a7–17].

Duling believes that Matthew's extensive use of the term ἀδελφός to describe a fictive kinship relationship indicates that Matthew's community, even more than those of the other Gospel writers, understood itself in fictive kinship terms.[12] I will argue in chapter 9 that the author of the Fourth Gospel has a particular reason for reserving kinship language for the post-crucifixion scenes. Each of the Gospels employs kinship language and each does so to slightly different effect.

Genealogies

Genealogical research has become a popular interest in our time for a number of psychological and sociological reasons. I suspect that a feeling of dislocation and disconnection within our communities has driven people to look to their ancestors for insight into identity and direction.

Genealogies in the Roman Empire similarly served the purpose of defining an individual's identity, but they tended to do so in a much more deliberate and deductive manner. Published genealogies were ancestral *curricula vitae*, drawing attention to the highlights of the family tree and leaving out the less honorable details. Burridge points out that ancient biographies generally begin with an outline of the subject's ancestry that links the character to human or divine nobility.[13]

In his *Life of Brutus*, Plutarch describes two different possibilities for Brutus' ancestry, one ascribed by those who wished to honor him and another by those who wished the opposite. The former traced his ancestry to the Brutus who drove out the Tarquins; the latter to a plebeian steward.[14]

People in this world were inclined to believe, more than we generally do, the dictum "like father, like son." "'Son of' thus tells us not only *who* the genealogical subject is, but *what kind of person* we should expect him to be. In this way honour as precedence is connected with honor as virtue."[15] Genealogies delineate an individual's connection to a family group that "defines the present, is rooted in the past, and expresses future potentialities."[16] So, it was said of the sons of Oedipus, "For never can

---

12. Duling, "The Matthean Brotherhood and Marginal Scribal Leadership," 165.
13. Burridge, *What Are the Gospels?*, 141.
14. Plutarch, *The Life of Brutus*, 1.
15. Rohrbaugh, "Legitimating Sonship," 188. Italics in original.
16. Oakman, *Palestine in the Time of Jesus*, 51.

wrong be right, nor children of unnatural parentage come as a glory to the mother that bears them, but as a stain on the marriage of him who is father and brother at once."[17]

A key feature of a genealogy is the choice of apical ancestor—the one who appears at the head of the list. So, in the example of Brutus above, the apical ancestor is either Brutus who drove out the Tarquins or an obscure plebeian steward. The assumption is that the subject of the genealogy will show a family likeness to this key ancestor.

Another feature that may be unfamiliar to us is the lack of any attempt at comprehensiveness in ancient genealogies. These ancient lists of ancestors aim to tell a story, so only those characters whose lives carry forward the desired plotline are included.

Hanson and Oakman point out that while there were identifiable formats for genealogies, each particular example must be understood in terms of the intentions of the author and the literary context in which it is located.[18]

The genealogy with which Josephus begins his autobiography is clearly presented with the intention of claiming that someone from such an illustrious family must have a claim on the public ear. Notice how he begins:

Ἐμοὶ δὲ γένος ἐστὶν οὐκ ἄσημον, ἀλλ' ἐξ ἱερέων ἄνωθεν καταβεβηκός. ὥσπερ δ' ἡ παρ' ἑκάστοις ἄλλη τίς ἐστιν εὐγενείας ὑπόθεσις, οὕτως παρ' ἡμῖν ἡ τῆς ἱερωσύνης μετουσία τεκμήριόν ἐστιν γένους λαμπρότητος.[19]

Rohrbaugh claims that, "above all else, genealogies are honor claims. They seek to establish social status (ascribed honor) and thereby provide the all-important map for social interaction."[20] "To have a written pedigree, and especially a long one, was a mark of honor."[21] "Genealogies

---

17. Euripides, "The Pheonissae."

18. Oakman, *Palestine in the Time of Jesus*, 28.

19. Josephus, "Josephi Vita", 1. TR: "My family is not without distinction, but from the start has descended from priests; and just as for each one there is a different foundation for nobility, for us participation in the priesthood is a sure sign of a family's splendour."

20. Rohrbaugh, "Legitimating Sonship," 187; He draws here on Hanson, 75–84 and Hood, 4.

21. Rohrbaugh, "Legitimating Sonship," 188.

might be used to establish religious purity, rights to political leadership, inheritance rights, marriage eligibility, and ethnic connections."[22]

The function of genealogies in Luke and Matthew

Luke traces Jesus' descent from God through Adam, whereas Matthew chooses Abraham as the genealogical head and tells the story of Jesus' ancestry via David. Hanson and Oakman believe that Matthew, aware of ascriptions of kingship to Abraham in the LXX version of Gen 23:6 and in the *Testaments of the Twelve Patriarchs*, was here emphasizing Jesus' kingly descent, not just his Jewishness.[23] "The genealogy thus promotes Jesus' claim to Judean royal lineage, and the subsequent birth story promotes his claim to divine parentage by means of miraculous birth."[24]

Concerning Luke, on the other hand, Rohrbaugh believes it is significant that "the genealogy in Luke follows immediately on the baptism scene in which God acknowledges both paternity ("my beloved son"—*ascribed* honor; honor as precedence), and pleasure ("in whom I am well pleased"—*acquired* honor; honor as virtue) in regard to Jesus.[25]

We find in the genealogies of Jesus, both in Luke and in Matthew, a claim to honor that appears entirely out of keeping with the circumstances of his birth to a subsistence artisan father and a teenage peasant mother.[26] Such a claim to honor would naturally be tested, and in order to satisfy skeptical readers it must pass challenges mounted by suitably high-status adversaries.

Luke, therefore, moves Jesus out into the wilderness to be tested (πειραζόμενος) by Satan immediately after he has presented Jesus' genealogy. Note that the claim that Jesus is the Son of God has been made in the genealogy (Luke 3:38) and in the baptism scene (Luke 3:22). This claim is now tested by no less an adversary than the devil himself. Note how the devil begins, "*If* you are the son of God . . . " Jesus rises to that challenge. He answers as God's son by using the words of his Father, rather than his own words.[27] He refuses to alter the allegiance that he has

22. Oakman, *Palestine in the Time of Jesus*, 27.
23. Oakman, *Palestine in the Time of Jesus*, 53–54.
24. Oakman, *Palestine in the Time of Jesus*, 54.
25. Rohrbaugh, "Legitimating Sonship," 188. Italics in original.
26. Rohrbaugh, "Legitimating Sonship," 188.
27. Rohrbaugh, "Legitimating Sonship," 190.

already entirely devoted to God.[28] Finally, he counters the devil's claim to be entitled to speak in the name of the Father.[29] "In a classic Middle Eastern game of challenge–response he has bested an adversary that would frighten any mortal man."[30]

Bauckham dismisses this social-scientific approach to genealogies as reductionist.[31] Perhaps some advocates of social-scientific approaches to biblical exegesis are so enamored with their favorite approach that they forget to incorporate time-tested historical and literary methods into their work. Yet refusing to take account of social-scientific research because some of its advocates are reductionists is no more rational a position than focusing exclusively on social-scientific research. In any case, Bauckham's conclusions about Matthew's genealogy do not contradict those arrived at through social-scientific analysis.

Bauckham asserts that the genealogy in Matthew can be understood, like the genealogy at the start of 1 Chronicles, as a summary of "the story so far"[32] where a well-informed reader would be expected to recall the stories behind each of the names listed.[33] He argues that the role of the women mentioned by Matthew is to remind the reader of the ways God has incorporated Gentiles into the people of God in the past as a foretaste of the fulfillment of God's promise to bless all nations through Abraham's descendant—who Matthew announces as Jesus.[34]

Leaving home

Having briefly discussed the role of genealogies and fictive kinship groups in the Roman Empire, we are now able to bring those concepts together as we consider the ways in which the Synoptic Gospels present Jesus as one who calls disciples out of their families into a new type of kinship and gives them a new genealogy, with God as apical head.

28. Rohrbaugh, "Legitimating Sonship," 190–1.
29. Rohrbaugh, "Legitimating Sonship," 191–2.
30. Rohrbaugh, "Legitimating Sonship," 192.
31. Bauckham, *Gospel Women*, 27.
32. In the case of the genealogy in Matthew, we have "the story of the Messiah so far."
33. Bauckham, *Gospel Women*, 19.
34. Bauckham, *Gospel Women*, 22–23. Bauckham neatly sidesteps the problem of Mary then being the odd-woman-out by noticing that the role of the four women in the "story-so-far" is different from the role of the mother.

When Jesus speaks in Mark 10:29-30 of the sacrifices which may be expected from one who becomes his disciple, his primary image is that of leaving the family house (ἀφῆκεν οἰκίαν), and therefore being removed from mother, father, brothers, sisters, and children.[35]

Such a call does not sound greatly demanding to twenty-first-century Western ears. We see leaving the family and the family home as an indispensable part of growing up.[36] Yet in first-century Palestine this was only the case for young women, not young men. When a young woman married, she would leave her house, her parents, her brothers, and her sisters and enter her husband's home to live within the network of his family relationships:[37] with his father and mother, his brothers and sisters.[38] Men, on the other hand, stayed with their father in their father's home, pursuing the family trade and finding career advancement in kinship relationships and the family's social networks. The call to leave not only relatives but also house and fields reminds us that it was not just emotional security that Jesus called them to forsake, but economic security as well.[39]

Jesus called young men to abandon this security for the (humanly speaking) insecure and unstable life of a disciple. This chapter will outline just how central a theme this is in the Synoptic Gospels.

The house that Jesus calls disciples to leave in Mark 10:29-30 shelters three generations: mother and father; brothers and sisters; and children,[40] with the call to leave being addressed to the middle generation. Is this because these are the ones who are old (and young) enough to

---

35. It is worth noting that there is no mention of leaving husband or wife. Following this through would be outside the scope of this discussion, but it may well be that the value placed by Jesus on the marriage bond (e.g., Neyrey, "Loss of Wealth" Matt 19:3-9) precludes him from endorsing his disciples leaving their marriage partners for his sake. If that is the case, it is interesting to note that leaving children is not excluded in the same way, though we can reasonably assume that Jesus is speaking of adult children or children who will be cared for by those left behind. An (in my view unlikely) alternative put forward by Hellerman is that the marriage relationship is not mentioned because it is the least valued of kinship bonds. Hellerman, *The Ancient Church as Family*, 39.

36. See Moxnes, *Putting Jesus in His Place*, 46.

37. Hellerman, *The Ancient Church as Family*, 32-33.

38. Perhaps Jesus is deliberately phrasing his call to discipleship in terms of a marriage proposal?

39. See Moxnes, "What Is a Family?" 23.

40. See Moxnes, *Putting Jesus in His Place*, 30.

CONFLICT BETWEEN DISCIPLESHIP AND KINSHIP 61

live independently, while not being the household leader upon whom the others depend? Or is it simply that this was the group from which Jesus' disciples were generally drawn? I suspect it is the former but cannot be certain.

We hear echoes of Genesis 12:1 in Jesus' words about leaving home. Abraham was similarly called to leave house, kin, and land in order to form a new household; a household in which Abraham was to be father but YHWH was to be head.

Readers with knowledge of the Jewish Scriptures are also likely to think here of Ruth who, despite being told to stay with her own kin in her own land, insisted on giving her primary allegiance to Naomi and to Naomi's God, and making her home in Naomi's country.

Moxnes comments on the call of John and James in Mark 1:19–20: "when the brothers left that place, the effect was both that the livelihood of their household was threatened, and that their father[41] was dishonored and suffered a loss of authority."[42]

Yet Moxnes also notices that soon after Peter leaves everything to follow him we find Jesus (and Peter) at Peter's home. Peter, at least, seems not to have cut ties with his family completely.

Jesus called his disciples not only to leave their families, but even to hate them (Matt 10:37–9). Moxnes observes:

> to "hate" is more than an affective emotion, it carries with it an act of distancing, of separation. And the cross that one must take up is not a general suffering "for the sake of Jesus" (as in Mark), but implies the loss of community and alienation from family. Thus, it is the social location of the addressee, his or her primary place of identity, support, and loyalty, that is challenged by the demand to "hate" in order to be "worthy of Me."[43]

These words of Jesus find resonance with Philo's description of the stranger who makes his home among the people of Israel, τῷ μὲν ὅτι τοὺς συγγενεῖς, οὓς μόνους εἰκὸς ἔχειν συναγωνιστάς, ἐχθροὺς ἀσυμβάτους

---

41. Moxnes, commenting on Luke 9:59–60: "Life for the man who received the call from Jesus was rooted in obligations that derived their strength from the combined power of place and father, bound together in the location of the house and household." Moxnes, *Putting Jesus in His Place*, 55.

42. Moxnes, *Putting Jesus in His Place*, 56–7.

43. Moxnes, *Putting Jesus in His Place*, 58.

εἰργάσατο ἑαυτῷ μεταναστὰς εἰς ἀλήθειαν καὶ τὴν τοῦ ἑνὸς τιμίου τιμήν.[44]

Jesus rejected by his home town

Jesus' call to disciples to leave their homes is underlined by the account of the converse occurring in his own life. In Mark 6:4 and Mt 13:54–58 (cf., Lk 4:16–30 and John 4:44 where kin and house are not mentioned), household, kinship group, and village unite in their failure to honor the prophet among them.[45] Jesus' honor claims are tested in the "place where the most knowledgeable and critical audience possible is located."[46]

This audience seems on the verge of reacting positively to Jesus' teaching when some of them start to throw at Jesus the most extreme insult Mediterranean cultures have to offer—doubts about his lineage: "Is not this Joseph's son?"[47] When we culturally translate this question into something along the lines of "Who does he think he is?" we get some sense of the meaning, but miss the depth of the insult. We need to remember that "this is the way you get to someone in the Middle East. This is how you deflate overblown egos. This is how you cut down to size those who make claims all out of keeping with their proper place in the honor system. You remind them of where they were born."[48]

Rohrbaugh points out that Jesus' response as presented by Luke makes sense, then, as a response to an honor challenge. They have cast aspersions on his lineage; now he casts aspersions on theirs. Being children of Israel is not such a very great claim to status—God has often chosen

---

44. Philo, "Special Laws [Greek]", IV. 178; TR: "he has made his own kinsmen, whom alone it was natural for him to have as allies and champions, his irreconcilable enemies, by quitting their camp and taking up his abode with the truth, and with the honour of the one Being who is entitled to honour." Philo, "Special Laws [English]."

45. It may be that this uniting of village, kin, and house against Jesus gives us some insight into the journey of Jesus' mother towards discipleship in the Fourth Gospel. Her hometown refused to honor Jesus. Her sons refused to honor Jesus (John 7:1–5). Will she find the strength to leave behind her sons and her village in order to follow the son who is without apparent honour? And if she does, will she be left vulnerable as a woman on her own? It is certainly relevant that the next place his mother appears in John's Gospel is at the foot of the cross: the scene of Jesus greatest dishonor, and his greatest glory.

46. Rohrbaugh, "Legitimating Sonship," 193.

47. Rohrbaugh, "Legitimating Sonship," 194.

48. Rohrbaugh, "Legitimating Sonship," 193.

to overlook Israelites and show favor to those outside (Luke 4:25–7). The stakes have been raised and the game becomes deadly.[49]

The fact that the crowd then becomes violent is an indication to the Middle Eastern reader that the exchange has been won by Jesus. Rohrbaugh points out that violence is "an inadvertent admission that one has lost control of the challenge situation."[50] When wits fail, bullying takes over.

Moxnes points out that the "particular activity of this community in relation to the homecoming prophet is awarding or withholding honor."[51] "To be refused honor from that group was to be put outside of that location, to be marginalized and displaced."[52] In their view, the prophet "pretends to be something more than he is entitled to from his place in the village"[53] but Jesus refused to be bound by their paradigm.[54] Jesus dislocates himself from "the places that gave or withheld honor and identity, the household, and the village community. Thereby Jesus questioned the value of their activity as well as their power to grant or withhold honor."[55]

The narrative, which appears to be about Jesus being rejected by his hometown, turns out to be about Jesus rejecting his hometown. He rejects the basis on which they judge him; and he rejects their right to judge him.

While this narrative serves a number of functions within the four Gospels, one of its functions, in the Synoptics at least, is surely to reinforce Jesus' call on his disciples to leave family and hometown behind if they claim allegiance that belongs to Jesus alone. The teacher endured (indeed chose) dislocation from kin and village. Should the disciple expect anything less?

---

49. Rohrbaugh, "Legitimating Sonship," 195.
50. Rohrbaugh, "Legitimating Sonship," 195.
51. Moxnes, *Putting Jesus in His Place*, 52.
52. Moxnes, *Putting Jesus in His Place*, 67.
53. Moxnes, *Putting Jesus in His Place*, 52.
54. Moxnes, *Putting Jesus in His Place*, 53.
55. Moxnes, *Putting Jesus in His Place*, 68.

No turning back

Not only does Jesus call on his potential followers to leave family behind, but in Luke 14:25–33 (cf., Matt 10:34–39) he starkly warns them that considering the heavy cost of discipleship before committing themselves to his cause must include a resolve to hate father and mother.

The least we can draw from this warning is that, as Taylor has pointed out, "Early Christianity, like the broader ethnic-religious Judaism from which it emerged, attracted adherents who manifested varying degrees of commitment, and who were incorporated to varying degrees into the life of the Christian community."[56] Some must have given Jesus conditional loyalty that would not withstand pressure from their family to return to their previous way of life.

Luke certainly appears intent on shaming those who begin to follow Jesus but give up because it is too hard.[57] Yet there is more to Jesus' command here than merely "Make sure you know what you are getting yourself into." Neyrey comments:

> Both versions [Matthew and Luke] contain an exhortation to "take up one's cross" and become a member of Jesus' fictive kinship group. The "cross" must surely be a metaphor for negative experiences, possibly physical sufferings (begging, hunger) and/or social ones (loss of family/shame). These sufferings are not the result of taxation, drought, or some other "misfortune" but precisely the results of becoming Jesus' disciple. There would be, then, shame from the family and honour from Jesus.[58]

Moxnes goes further, to say that in these words, "The house as a structured place, as a microcosm of authority and order, of support and solidarity, is destroyed."[59]

Similar words of Jesus in Matt 8:22 and Luke 9:60 are hard indeed when set alongside Josephus' invective against zealots for seemingly doing just what Jesus commanded.

> οἱ δὲ εἰς τοσοῦτον ὠμότητος ἐξώκειλαν, ὡς μήτε τοῖς ἔνδον ἀναιρουμένοις μήτε τοῖς ἀνὰ τὰς ὁδοὺς μεταδοῦναι γῆς, ἀλλὰ καθάπερ συνθήκας πεποιημένοι τοῖς τῆς πατρίδος

---

56. Taylor, "The Social Nature of Conversion," 136.
57. Pilch and Malina, *Biblical Social Values and Their Meanings*, 101.
58. Neyrey, "Loss of Wealth," 150.
59. Moxnes, *Putting Jesus in His Place*, 58.

συγκαταλῦσαι καὶ τοὺς τῆς φύσεως νόμους ἄμα τε τοῖς εἰς
ἀνθρώπους ἀδικήμασιν συμμιᾶναι καὶ τὸ θεῖον, ὑφ᾽ ἡλίῳ
τοὺς νεκροὺς μυδῶντας ἀπέλειπον. τοῖς δὲ θάπτουσί τινα τῶν
προσηκόντων ὃ καὶ τοῖς αὐτομολοῦσιν ἐπιτίμιον θάνατος ἦν,
καὶ δεῖσθαι παραχρῆμα ταφῆς ἔδει τὸν ἑτέρῳ χαριζόμενον.[60]

Eisenman rejects the possibility that Jesus actually said such confronting words or made such unreasonable demands; claiming instead that these concepts, along with the sometimes negative portrayal of Jesus' family in the Gospels, are derived from an anti-Jewish bias in the early church. He claims that "this attitude of disparagement directed against what can only be called 'the Jewish apostles'—in effect comprising the nucleus of what is called 'the Jerusalem church'—is a retrospective one and part of the anti-family and anti-Jewish polemic of Pauline or "overseas" Christianity, not a historical one."[61]

It is not necessary here to address the question of how certain we can be that the Synoptic emphasis on forsaking family (to whatever extent) has its origin in the words of Jesus. My concern is to identify that emphasis and then to compare it with the picture painted by the Fourth Evangelist. Eisenman certainly finds an anti-family agenda in the Synoptic Gospels; so much so that he finds it too distasteful to attribute to Jesus. However, it is a commonplace of textual criticism to view distasteful elements as more—not less—likely to be original.

If this emphasis did originate with the Gospel writers, I must wonder where such an agenda might have come from in the first-century, and how it could be forceful enough to convince these followers of Jesus to put such unpleasant words into the mouth of their Messiah. Would Paul's anti-Jewish prejudices (if such existed) be sufficient for him to reject Jesus' brothers and then to reinforce such a rejection by inventing a rejection of family per se and planting this rejection in the mouth of Jesus? This hardly seems plausible. In chapter 7 it will be necessary to return to

---

60. Flavius Josephus, "De Bello Judaico Libri Vii," iv.381–3. TR: "But these zealots came at last to that degree of barbarity, as not to bestow a burial either on those slain in the city, or on those that lay along the roads; but as if they had made an agreement to cancel both the laws of their country and the laws of nature, and, at the same time that they defiled men with their wicked actions, they would pollute the Divinity itself also, they left the dead bodies to putrefy under the sun: and the same punishment was allotted to such as buried any, as to those that deserted, which was no other than death; while he that granted the favour of a grave to another, would presently stand in need of a grave himself." Josephus, *Antiquities, The Wars of the Jews* iv.381–3.

61. Eisenman, *James the Brother of Jesus*, 74.

this line of argument that drives a wedge between the family of Jesus in Jerusalem and the early Christians living elsewhere.

The *Gospel of Thomas* extends the words of Jesus in Matt 10 to say that the result of family conflict will be that one stands "solitary." This idea is completely absent from the Synoptic tradition, not just from this particular passage, but also from the whole thought world of these Gospels. The disciple who is rejected by family because of loyalty to Jesus does not stand solitary but is embraced by a hundred times more "houses, brothers and sisters, mothers and children, and fields," along with persecutions (Mark 10:30). Forsaken kin are not replaced by solitude but by fictive kin—and lots of them!

Cause or effect?

There is conflict among interpreters about whether Jesus' call to forsake family should be understood in the context of a kinship structure that, for political and economic reasons, was breaking down anyway.[62]

As the Athenian lawmaker, Solon, so aptly expressed it, political chaos has a way of breaking into the home:

> Οὕτω δημόσιον κακὸν ἔρχεται οἴκαδ' ἑκάστῳ,
> αὔλειοι δ' ἔτ' ἔχειν οὐκ ἐθέλουσι θύραι,
> ὑψηλὸν δ' ὑπὲρ ἕρκος ὑπέρθορεν, εὗρε δὲ πάντως,
> εἰ καί τις φεύγων ἐν μυχῷ ᾖ θαλάμου[63]

Moxnes believes that the move from the large clan tombs of earlier Israelite history to family ossuaries indicates the break-up of the extended family (beyond the household) as a unit of identity and support.[64] At this time, land was being consolidated into fewer hands, so small landowners and tenants found themselves under pressure.[65] Young males may have

---

62. See Moxnes, "What Is a Family?" 25.

63. Solon, "Lyrics," frag 4 West, 21.
TR: "Public ruin invades the house of each citizen,
and the courtyard doors no longer have strength to keep it away,
but it overleaps the lofty wall, and though a man runs in and tries to hide in chamber or closet,
it ferrets him out." Solon, "Greek Lyrics."

64. Moxnes, *Putting Jesus in His Place*, 42.

65. Moxnes, *Putting Jesus in His Place*, 42; Guijarro, "The Family in First-Century Galilee," 44.

needed to leave their households to find work in new cities being built by the Herods. This may have diminished the role and authority of the father as the leader of the household.[66]

Hanson and Oakman note that at this time in Palestine groups of bandits were becoming an increasing feature of the social and political landscape. These groups attracted disaffected young men who had lost their property and means of making a living. However, these tended to stay close to their villages and families, being sheltered by their communities and using the proceeds of their banditry to support their communities where possible.[67] Political dislocation, for at least some of these, then, did not involve dislocation from ties of kinship.

Jesus, though perhaps reaching a similar demographic, employs a very different strategy—one of total dependence on God as the ultimate patron, and of overriding loyalty to the fictive kinship group that renders all other loyalties relative and secondary.

The young men whom Jesus calls do not appear, on the whole, to be destitute or dislocated. They have occupations (as fishermen, tax collectors, etc.); and they have fathers, brothers, and cousins. As Moxnes points out, Jesus does not so much call destitute men to become his followers, as he calls ordinary young men to become destitute:

> The sayings of Jesus were primarily addressed to young men, calling them to leave their position in the household. Most of these young men did not seem to have been in a marginal position in society (e.g., poor or "sinners," sick, etc.,) but well integrated into their place in the house and village structure. Therefore, by leaving to follow Jesus they experienced the effects of separation: they became displaced; they were stripped of that which defined their position and status. They entered into a liminal stage, outside the known and accepted structure of their household and village society.[68]

The breakdown of household structures is not a cause behind Jesus calling young men away from family, nor is it seen as an unfortunate, unforeseen consequence of his call. Rather, it is something that Jesus

---

66. Moxnes, *Putting Jesus in His Place*, 42–3. See also Oakman, *Palestine in the Time of Jesus*, 78.

67. Oakman, *Palestine in the Time of Jesus*, 88–90.

68. Moxnes, *Putting Jesus in His Place*, 71.

intended.[69] Jesus appears to be quite deliberately challenging the power of family.

Here again, twenty-first-century Western Christians will miss the point if we come to these passages with only our own experience of family and community. Taylor reminds us that in the early church, "the degree of social dislocation involved in conversion, particularly to a religion with (in principle) absolute claims to exclusive devotion" was extreme.[70] Of course, many Christians today are in no danger of underestimating the dangers of conversion. Christians living in countries with dominant religions other than Christianity could teach us as much about dislocation as could those in first-century Palestine.

Neyrey believes that Jesus is here attacking "the basic solidarity and loyalty family members owe to one another. This passage implies that the division of the family occurs precisely because of Jesus ('I have come to . . .')"[71]

While the Synoptics depict Jesus shaming disciples who turn back from following him because of pressure from their families, they also show Jesus giving honor to those who choose, rather, to endure hardship. Hanson believes that the primary function of the Beatitudes is to attribute public honor, in most cases to those who are without honor.[72] Nayrey believes that the four best attested makarisms of Luke 6 and Matthew 5:

> describe the composite fate of a disciple who has been ostracized as a "rebellious son" by his family for loyalty to Jesus. This ostracism involves total loss of economic support from the family (food, clothing, shelter,) as well as total loss of honour and status in the eyes of the village (a good name, marriage prospects, etc.) Such persons would be "shameful" in the eyes of the family and village, but Jesus proclaims them "honourable" (*makarioi*).[73]
>
> In the case of the fourth makarism, public shame goes hand in hand with severe loss of wealth. The person described there is "driven out" (*dioxosin*) or "outlawed" (*aphorisosin*). This implies that he has lost his property: land (if he is a farmer) or market

---

69. Moxnes, *Putting Jesus in His Place*, 59.
70. Taylor, "The Social Nature of Conversion," 134.
71. Neyrey, "Loss of Wealth," 149.
72. Hanson, "How Honorable! How Shameful!"
73. Neyrey, "Loss of Wealth," 145.

stall (if he is an artisan). Total economic ruin, as well as corresponding collapse of social standing, quickly follow.⁷⁴

The word πτωχος does not mean one who is "just scraping by"; it indicates utter destitution. As Luz has succinctly put it, "The πενης has to work, the πτωχος has to beg."⁷⁵ When a man moves from being πενης to πτωχος he loses any capacity to maintain his social status or honor rating. He becomes worthless and invisible. This loss of honor had more serious consequences than the loss of wealth alone.⁷⁶

Neyrey also draws our attention to Matthew 6:25–35/Luke 12:22–32. He envisions a husband who is concerned about what to eat—the male preoccupation of the time being subsistence farming; and a wife being concerned about what to wear—the corresponding female preoccupation being the production of clothing.⁷⁷ He believes that since this couple is worried about these things they may have fallen below subsistence level. Neyrey suggests that this loss of wealth may be the result of drought, excessive taxation, or family conflict; but he believes that the way Jesus bestows honor (ποσω μαλλον ὑμεις διαφερετε) on disciples (μαθητας) implies that, like the makarisms, this saying of Jesus is also directed to people who have suffered the loss of honor and wealth precisely because they have been disinherited by their family because of their loyalty to Jesus.⁷⁸

In summary, Neyrey contends that Jesus' statements of comfort to those who are poor and suffering are addressed to "voluntary marginals"⁷⁹ who have suffered loss of honor and wealth in order to be disciples of Jesus.⁸⁰ Thomas Schmidt makes a similar comment in his discussion of whether hostility to wealth in the early Christian community is a function of the socioeconomic background of converts: "hostility to wealth exists independently of socioeconomic circumstances as a fundamental religious–ethical tenet consistently expressed in the Synoptic Gospels."⁸¹

---

74. Neyrey, "Loss of Wealth," 146.
75. Luz et al.,, *Matthew 1–7*, 231.
76. Neyrey, "Loss of Wealth," 154.
77. Neyrey, "Loss of Wealth," 151.
78. Neyrey, "Loss of Wealth," 152.
79. Neyrey here uses the language of Dennis C. Duling, "Matthew and Marginality."
80. Neyrey, "Loss of Wealth," 154.
81. Schmidt, *Hostility to Wealth in the Synoptic Gospel*, 164.

That is, the call to forsake wealth is not about making people feel better about their poverty. It is a genuine call to both rich and poor to reassess and realign their priorities. And it is a warning to those who wish to become followers of Jesus that poverty is a predictable result.

Evidence that opposition and dislocation from family did occur when people converted to Christianity is found outside the New Testament as well as within it. Tacitus wrote that converts to Judaism were told to "disown their country, to set at naught parents, children and brethren."[82] This overriding loyalty to their religion was bad enough in Jews, but when it turns up in the Christian sect it earns them the title of "haters of humanity."[83]

In relation to the well-known accusations of another second-century critic of Christianity, Stephen Barton says, "it is clear that Celsus perceives adherence to Christ as a strong threat to the network of ties and obligations which constitute a household. As Harnack points out,[84] Origen's reply does not deny that the new doctrine affects family ties: Origen claims instead that the children and women attracted to it are all the better for it."[85]

It is possible to see the household codes of Paul and Peter as apologetic responses to this kind of criticism.[86] If the new Christian movement was being accused of breaking down the solidarity of the family (and therefore of the empire) it would be wise for wives and slaves to fulfill society's expectations of them to any degree consistent with their Christian confession.

Walter Brueggemann comments in relation to the people of God in the Old Testament, "Perhaps the minority community of slaves is able to affirm the politics of justice and compassion because there is no other social vision in which to stand in protest against the oppression of the situation."[87]

One wonders, then, if the Synoptic writers are presenting Jesus calling disciples away from comfort and security in order to sharpen their

---

82. Tacitus, "History" V.5.

83. Tacitus, "The Annals" XV.44.

84. Harnack, *The Mission and Expansion of Christianity in the First Three Centuries*, 396.

85. Barton, *Life Together*, 4.

86. Barton, *Life Together*, 6; see also Balch, *Let Wives Be Submissive*, 109.

87. Brueggemann, *The Prophetic Imagination*, 29.

CONFLICT BETWEEN DISCIPLESHIP AND KINSHIP   71

vision, and implicitly that of the readers, and make concrete the transformation of priorities implicit in the confession of Jesus as Lord.

While other forms of social exclusion may also ensue, it is above all exclusion from family that leaves a person destitute in first-century Mediterranean society. "Issues of family loyalty and parental authority, not religious excommunication from the synagogue, emerge as an important locus of crisis in the lives of ordinary peasants."[88]

Moxnes argues that the families that reject Jesus' disciples "are trying to deal with disobedient sons and daughters, household members who have shown disregard for filial obligations and responsibilities toward the household. "Following Jesus" was hardly an excuse for this sort of behavior, which, when carried to the extreme, met with social ostracism."[89]

Who are my mother and my brothers?

We turn now to the key passage where the Synoptic Gospels depict the community of disciples as a fictive kinship group distinct from biological family ties; that is Mark 3:31–35 (Matt 12:46–50; Luke 8:19–21).

Mark chooses this event to introduce Jesus' family, and shows them behaving in a manner consistent with his later portrayal of them in 6:1–6. They are opposing Jesus' ministry and rejecting his claims.[90]

Jones comments that Mary's role in Matthew and Luke is to be the physical bearer of the Messiah. Her virtue is in her unquestioning obedience. In all three Synoptic Gospels, when she attempts to assert authority over Jesus she is seen as an impediment to his ministry.[91] She is not permitted to assume the prerogatives that her culture gave to motherhood.

Jesus here announces a substitution, not an addition. The disciples are not added into Jesus' biological family. Nor is his biological family added into his fictive kinship group. One is substituted for the other and the fictive kin become the only true kin.[92]

---

88. Neyrey, "Loss of Wealth," 155–6.
89. Moxnes, *Putting Jesus in His Place*, 63.
90. Moxnes, *Putting Jesus in His Place*, 60.
91. Jones, *The Women in the Gospel of John*, 6–7.
92. Moxnes, *Putting Jesus in His Place*, 60.

Pilch and Malina agree that the early Christian movement replaced family-centeredness with church-membership-centeredness and the church became the new family. [93]

Hellerman comments on the uniqueness of this call to changed allegiance:

> It is this resocialisation—at the kinship level—that marks early Christianity as distinct among the voluntary associations of Greco-Roman antiquity. The social solidarity characteristic of the family model, in turn, goes a long way to explain both the intimacy and sense of community so often cited as unique to early Christianity, and the attractiveness of the early Christian movement to displaced and alienated urbanites in the Greco-Roman world.[94]

Some implications

It may be worth briefly mentioning at this point some implications of this discussion. The Gospels draw a number of implications about life in Christian community from Jesus' use of family language. The most obvious is the expectation that sisters and brothers will share the family character and resemble their Father in heaven. I will mention just four others:

1. *Forbidding the use of honorary titles* (Matthew 23:8–12) on the basis that πάντες δὲ ὑμεῖς ἀδελφοί[95] ἐστε. In this kinship group there is no human who corresponds to the all-powerful *pater familias* because all authority resides with the Father in heaven.[96] Many denominations honor the letter of this law by ensuring that ordained clergy are not called "Father." But what of the spirit of the law? How often do we see autocratic church leaders, clergy or lay, who would never tolerate being called "Father," giving the clear message that belonging to their church means following their vision, following their program, and doing ministry the way they dictate? And for every autocratic leader there is a crowd of people who are more than

---

93. Pilch and Malina, *Biblical Social Values and Their Meanings*, 73.

94. Hellerman, *The Ancient Church as Family*, 25.

95. The NRSV's choice to obscure the family imagery here and elsewhere (e.g., 18:15) is extraordinary.

96. See Duling, "The Matthean Brotherhood," 165–6.

happy to be told what to do rather than exercising their own minds and their own responsibilities.

In post-Christian Australia, ministers carry very little honor or authority in the general community. This has been a painful transition for the church and we can respond to it by inflating the status of ministers within the church, or we can gratefully accept this reminder that we, the church, are all siblings, with God as our only Father.

2. *A high priority for forgiveness, repentance, and reconciliation.* Peter's question concerning the number of times he should forgive (Matt 18:21–22) is couched in the language of brotherhood. Similarly, Matthew 5:21–26 records Jesus forbidding the harboring of anger against a brother, and calling his followers to be reconciled with "your brother" as a matter of the highest priority.[97] Reconciliation in the church can be complex and has often been done very badly. Local churches need resources and training in managing reconciliation well, and it is necessary to reduce the stigma of requesting mediation and normalize the need for reconciliation.

3. *Providing for those in the family who are in need.* The sharing of resources is probably one of the most basic functions of any family.[98] In the first century, as in some parts of the world today, converts to Christianity could find themselves cut off from the resources of their biological families. The new family, formed around Jesus, would then be called upon to provide for those new members. It is no coincidence that the author of the Gospel of Luke, who so clearly warns that poverty is a possible consequence of following Jesus, presents readers of his sequel with a picture of a church where property is sold and given to the poor among them.[99]

In an age of international mass communication, Christians in the West can become overwhelmed and transfixed by the enormity of the needs of our international sisters and brothers. More thought needs to be put into the nature of our kinship obligations to one

---

97. See Duling, "The Matthean Brotherhood and Marginal Scribal Leadership," 169–170.

98. See, for example, Levi-Strauss, *The Elementary Structures of Kinship*, 29–41.

99. See Hellerman, *The Ancient Church as Family*, 21–22.

another and our capacity to act as faithful members of such a large family.

4. *Honoring faithfulness and perseverance among sisters and brothers.* Jesus honored disciples who were shamed by their families; and so disciples were able to follow his example: to despise the shame of discipleship for the sake of the glory and honor that was promised. Only a community that gives honor to the least honorable among them can stand in the place of the rejected/rejecting family for those who have lost all honor in the eyes of the world in order to follow Jesus.

Kinship and loyalty to God in other Jewish writings

It would be helpful to ascertain whether these words from the Synoptic Gospels are unique within the Jewish literary milieu of their time. A word about the treatment of conflict between kinship obligations and competing priorities in Jewish sources outside the New Testament is, therefore, necessary to complete this discussion before moving on to look closely at the Fourth Gospel.

Philo

When interpreting Deuteronomy 13:1-11, where family members are called on to execute false prophets among them, Philo indicates that allegiance to God renders secondary all other ties of kinship. His language is reminiscent of Mark 10:29f:

> ἔστω γὰρ ἡμῖν μία οἰκειότης καὶ φιλίας ἓν σύμβολον ἡ πρὸς θεὸν ἀρέσκεια καὶ τὸ πάντα λέγειν τε καὶ πράττειν ὑπὲρ εὐσεβείας· αἱ δ' ἐκ προγόνων ἀφ' αἵματος αὗται λεγόμεναι συγγένειαι καὶ αἱ κατ' ἐπιγαμίας ἢ τινας ἄλλας ὁμοιοτρόπους αἰτίας οἰκειότητες ἀπορριπτέσθωσαν εἰ μὴ πρὸς τὸ αὐτὸ τέλος ἐπείγονται, τὴν τοῦ θεοῦ τιμήν, ἢ πάσης ἑνωτικῆς εὐνοίας ἄλυτος δεσμός ἐστιν· ἀντιλήψονται γὰρ οἱ τοιοῦτοι σεμνοτέρας καὶ ἱεροπρεπεστέρας συγγενείας[100]

---

100. Philo, "Special Laws [Greek]" I.317; TR: "For we should acknowledge only one relationship, and one bond of friendship, namely, a mutual zeal for the service of God, and a desire to say and do everything that is consistent with piety. And these bonds which are called relationships of blood, being derived from one's ancestors,

Philo insists that ties of blood between worshippers of God are only valid if they support the bond of each to God. Kinship bonds can be renounced. The "one indissoluble bond" is the commitment of each to honor God. Those who renounce family bonds in this way find themselves worthy to be called "sons of God."

The obvious corollary of this, though not explicitly spelled out by Philo, is that those who are bonded to God in obedient sonship and renounce all contrary bonds because of that bond become a community of sons with one another. If those who place loyalty to God above loyalty to their family become sons of God, surely they then become brothers to all others who similarly place loyalty to God above all else.

Philo does make this connection explicit, though, in his discussion of *therapeutae*. There he comments that those who serve at their common meals, like legitimate sons, with affectionate rivalry minister to their fathers and mothers, thinking their common parents more closely connected with them than those who are related by blood, since in truth to men of right principles there is nothing more nearly akin than virtue.[101]

Barton comments:

> Here, then, we have a community of religious virtuosi in which the power of household ties and sexual identity is redirected—or better, reinterpreted—to form the basis of an alternative society where the pattern of relationships is determined by training in wisdom and piety rather than property-ownership and consanguinity, and sexual differences are transcended both in the ascetic quest for virtue and in ecstatic worship.[102]

For the *therapeutae*, privileging religious community over family meant renouncing family entirely and becoming celibate. Their example may be key to understanding the growing trend toward celibacy in the first to fourth centuries in the church, which Paul attempted to stall in 1 Corinthians 7. When breaking from a dearly held social construction, it is often easier to flip over to its opposite than to undertake the careful critique necessary to find a new (rather than opposite) way of being. Social

---

and those connections which are derived from intermarriages and from other similar causes, must all be renounced, if they do not all hasten to the same end, namely, the honour of God which is the one indissoluble bond of all united good will. For such men will lay claim to a more venerable and sacred kind of relationship." Philo, "Special Laws [English]."

101. Philo, *The Works of Philo*, "On The Contemplative Life," 72.
102. Barton, *Discipleship and Family Ties*, 29.

pendulums can take many centuries to find their equilibrium. Given the instances of sexual abuse in churches it is worth asking whether we have yet fully integrated healthy sexual expression into our understanding of the church as a family. This is a worthwhile area of investigation, but outside the scope of this book.

In Philo's descriptions of heroes of radical obedience, as well as his pictures of philosophic community, the renunciation of family ties is key. Abraham is Philo's exemplar for this choice of spiritual over physical comfort:

> μετ' ὀλίγων δὲ οὗτος ἢ καὶ μόνος ἅμα τῷ κελευσθῆναι μετανίστατο καὶ τῇ ψυχῇ πρὸ τοῦ σώματος τὴν ἀποικίαν ἐστέλλετο, τὸν ἐπὶ τοῖς θνητοῖς ἵμερον παρευημεροῦντος ἔρωτος οὐρανίου οὐδενὸς οὖν φροντίσας, οὐ φυλετῶν, οὐ δημοτῶν, οὐ συμφοιτητῶν, οὐχ ἑταίρων, οὐ τῶν ἀφ' αἵματος ὅσοι πρὸς πατρὸς ἢ μητρὸς ἦσαν, οὐ πατρίδος, οὐκ ἀρχαίων ἐθῶν, οὐ συντροφίας, οὐ συνδιαιτήσεως, ὧν ἕκαστον ἀγωγόν τε καὶ δυσαπόσπαστον ὁλκὸν ἔχον δύναμιν, ἐλευθέραις καὶ ἀφέτοις ὁρμαῖς ᾗ τάχιστα μετανίσταται[103]

Moses, similarly, is praised by Philo for both renouncing his inheritance from his adopted family in Egypt[104] and refusing to promote the interests of his own sons and nephews.[105]

In his discussion of Phineas, Philo goes beyond what is recorded in Numbers 25 to praise this man and his supporters for massacring without pity their own kin who had taken part in idolatrous rites.[106]

Barton comments that Philo's heroes, "by appearing to stand outside, above, or over against ties of natural kinship ... gain in holiness and

---

103. Philo, "On Abraham [Greek]," 66–7; TR: "But this man with a few companions, or perhaps I might say by himself, as soon as he was commanded to do so, left his home, and set out on an expedition to a foreign country in his soul even before he started with his body, his regard for mortal things being overpowered by his love for heavenly things. Therefore giving no consideration to anything whatever, neither to the men of his tribe, nor to those of his borough, nor to his fellow disciples, nor to his companions, nor those of his blood as sprung from the same father or the same mother, nor to his country, nor to his ancient habits, nor to the customs in which he had been brought up, nor to his mode of life and his mates, every one of which things has a seductive and almost irresistible attraction and power, he departed as speedily as possible, yielding to a free and unrestrained impulse." Philo, "On Abraham [English]".

104. Philo, *The Works of Philo*, On the Life of Moses I.149.

105. Philo, *The Works of Philo*, On the Life of Moses I.150; II.142.

106. Philo, *The Works of Philo*, On the Life of Moses I.303.

in proximity to God. Separation at one level makes possible identification at another."[107]

It is clear, then, that according to Philo all ties of loyalty must take second place to loyalty to God. He sees that it can be painful and costly to renounce family in the service of God, virtue, and the appropriate attribution of honor. Philo regards those who willingly pay that cost as heroes and as worthy to be called sons of God.

Josephus

Like Philo, Josephus expresses a high regard for those who leave family behind in order to focus on religious and philosophical ideals. He does not see the communal life of the Essenes as a disavowal of status and honor, but as a way of achieving status that is different from the societal norms. They are "a community of religious virtuosi where membership and status are a matter, not of what is ascribed according to marital and household ties, but rather of what is achieved by renunciation of marriage and family and by initiation into the Essene order itself."[108]

In contrast to Josephus' approbation of those who subordinate family ties to ideals that he approves, his scorn against rebels in the lead up to the Jewish Rebellion is expressed in the language of renunciation of family ties without any sense of approbation: καὶ πρῶτον μὲν ἐν οἰκίαις ἥπτετο τῶν ὁμονοούντων πάλαι τὸ φιλόνεικον, ἔπειτα ἀφηνιάζοντες ἀλλήλων οἱ φίλτατοι [λαοὶ] καὶ συνιὼν ἕκαστος πρὸς τοὺς τὰ αὐτὰ προαιρουμένους ἤδη κατὰ πλῆθος ἀντετάσσοντο.[109]

Breaking family solidarity in order to associate with people of common mind is clearly not a good in itself according to Josephus. He criticizes the Sicarii for doing exactly what would be praiseworthy if the cause were more glorious. ποία δὲ αὐτοὺς φιλία, ποία δὲ συγγένεια πρὸς τοὺς ἐφ᾽ ἑκάστης ἡμέρας φόνους οὐχὶ θρασυτέρους ἐποίησε; τὸ μὲν γὰρ τοὺς

---

107. Barton, *Discipleship and Family Ties*, 35.
108. Barton, *Discipleship and Family Ties*, 39.
109. Josephus, "De Bello Judaico Libri Vii", IV. 132; Translation "At the first this quarrelsome temper caught hold of private families, who could not agree among themselves; after which those people that were the dearest to one another, broke through all restraints with regard to each other, and everyone associated with those of his own opinion." Josephus, *Antiquities, The Wars of the Jews* IV.132.

ἀλλοτρίους κακῶς ποιεῖν ἀγεννοῦς ἔργον πονηρίας [εἶναι] ὑπελάμβανον, λαμπρὰν δὲ φέρειν ἐπίδειξιν ἡγοῦντο τὴν ἐν τοῖς οἰκειοτάτοις ὠμότητα.[110]

For Josephus, then, subordination of family ties can be a heroic act illustrating a higher commitment to a greater good; in which case it is worthy of honor. However, it can illustrate barbarity when the higher commitment is to a cause he does not approve. In either case, the subordination of family ties illustrates an extreme of social behavior, in either obedience towards God or barbarity towards people.

In line with Philo, Josephus sees Abraham as the primary exemplar of obedience to God, particularly in his willingness to sacrifice his son:

> Ἄβραμος δὲ τὴν ἰδίαν εὐδαιμονίαν ἐν μόνῳ τῷ τὸν υἱὸν ἀπαθῆ καταλιπὼν ἐξελθεῖν τοῦ ζῆν ἐτίθετο. τούτου μέντοι κατὰ τὴν τοῦ θεοῦ βούλησιν ἔτυχεν, ὃς διάπειραν αὐτοῦ βουλόμενος λαβεῖν τῆς περὶ αὐτὸν θρησκείας ἐμφανισθεὶς αὐτῷ καὶ πάντα ὅσα εἴη παρεσχημένος καταριθμησάμενος, ὡς πολεμίων τε κρείττονα ποιήσειε καὶ τὴν παροῦσαν εὐδαιμονίαν ἐκ τῆς αὐτοῦ σπουδῆς ἔχοι καὶ τὸν υἱὸν Ἴσακον, ᾔτει τοῦτον αὑτῷ θῦμα καὶ ἱερεῖον αὐτὸν παρασχεῖν ἐκέλευέ τε εἰς τὸ Μώριον ὄρος ἀναγαγόντα ὁλοκαυτῶσαι βωμὸν ἱδρυσάμενον· οὕτως γὰρ ἐμφανίσειν τὴν περὶ αὐτὸν θρησκείαν, εἰ καὶ τῆς τοῦ τέκνου σωτηρίας προτιμήσειε τὸ τῷ θεῷ κεχαρισμένον. Ἄβραμος δὲ ἐπὶ μηδενὶ κρίνων παρακούειν τοῦ θεοῦ δίκαιον ἅπαντά θ' ὑπουργεῖν ὡς ἐκ τῆς ἐκείνου προνοίας ἀπαντώντων οἷς ἂν εὐμενὴς ᾖ, ἐπικρυψάμενος πρὸς τὴν γυναῖκα τήν τε τοῦ θεοῦ πρόρρησιν καὶ ἣν εἶχεν αὐτὸς γνώμην περὶ τῆς τοῦ παιδὸς σφαγῆς, ἀλλὰ μηδὲ τῶν οἰκετῶν τινι δηλώσας, ἐκωλύετο γὰρ ἂν ὑπηρετῆσαι τῷ θεῷ, λαβὼν τὸν Ἴσακον μετὰ δύο οἰκετῶν καὶ τὰ πρὸς τὴν ἱερουργίαν ἐπισάξας ὄνῳ ἀπῄει πρὸς τὸ ὄρος.[111]

---

110. Josephus, "De Bello Judaico Libri Vii", 266. TR: "What friendship or kindred were there that did not make him more bold in his daily murders? For they looked upon the doing of mischief to strangers only as a work beneath their courage, but thought their barbarity towards their nearest relations would be a glorious demonstration thereof." Josephus, *Antiquities, The Wars of the Jews* VII.266.

111. Josephus, "Antiquitates Judaicae", I.223–5. TR: "Abraham also placed his own happiness in this prospect, that, when he should die, he should leave this his son in a safe and secure condition; which accordingly he obtained by the will of God; who, being desirous to make an experiment of Abraham's religious disposition towards himself, appeared to him, and enumerated all the blessings he had bestowed on him; how he had made him superior to his enemies; and that his son Isaac who was the principal part of his present happiness, was derived from him; and he said that he required this son of his as a sacrifice and holy oblation. Accordingly he commanded him to carry him to the mountain Moriah, and to build an altar, and offer him for

I have quoted this in full to illustrate the major points Josephus takes from the incident:

- Abraham's attachment to his son is such that his own happiness is bound up in Isaac's safety.
- All he has including his son comes from God. God's greatness and generosity therefore make Abraham's obedience both logical and necessary.
- Pleasing God was preferable to Abraham's greatest happiness.
- Abraham made wise choices about how to avoid interference as he carried out his plans to obey God.

Words placed by Josephus in the mouth of Moses carry a similar theme. After reminding the people that it is God who has delivered them from Egypt and given them the Torah, the same God who had created Adam, saved Noah, and chosen Abraham, in short the God who has provided them with everything they have and created in them everything they are, Moses reminds the people to keep the laws of this God:

> σεβάσμιοι δ' ὑμῖν γενέσθωσαν καὶ παίδων περιμαχητότεροι καὶ γυναικῶν· εὐδαίμονα γὰρ διάξετε βίον τούτοις ἑπόμενοι καὶ γῆς ἀπολαύοντες καρπίμου καὶ θαλάσσης ἀχειμάστου καὶ τέκνων γονῆς κατὰ φύσιν τικτομένων καὶ πολεμίοις ἔσεσθε φοβεροί· τῷ θεῷ γὰρ εἰς ὄψιν ἐλθὼν ἀκροατὴς ἀφθάρτου φωνῆς ἐγενόμην· οὕτως ἐκείνῳ τοῦ γένους ἡμῶν καὶ τῆς τούτου μέλει διαμονῆς.[112]

---

a burnt offering upon it; for that this would best manifest his religious disposition towards him, if he preferred what was pleasing to God, before the preservation of his own son. Now Abraham thought that it was not right to disobey God in anything, but that he was obliged to serve him in every circumstance of life, since all creatures that live enjoy their life by his providence, and the kindness he bestows on them. Accordingly he concealed this command of God, and his own intentions about the slaughter of his son, from his wife, as also from every one of his servants, otherwise he should have been hindered from his obedience to God; and he took Isaac, together with two of his servants, and laying what things were necessary for a sacrifice upon an ass, he went away to the mountain." Josephus, *Antiquities*, *The Antiquities of the Jews*, I.223-5.

112. Josephus, "Antiquitates Judaicae", III, 88. TR: "And let them be to you venerable, and contended for more earnestly by you than your own children and your own wives, for if you will follow them, you will lead a happy life; you will enjoy the land fruitful, the sea calm, and the fruit of the womb born complete, as nature requires; you will be also terrible to your enemies; for I have been admitted into the presence of God, and been made a hearer of his incorruptible voice; so great is his concern for your nation, and its duration." Josephus, *Antiquities*, *The Antiquities of the Jews*, III, 88.

Mattathias, who led the rebellion against Antiochus Epiphanes, is said by Josephus to have ἀπωδύρετο τοῖς τέκνοις τὴν κατάστασιν τῶν πραγμάτων καὶ τήν τε τῆς πόλεως διαρπαγὴν καὶ τοῦ ναοῦ τὴν σύλησιν καὶ τοῦ πλήθους τὰς συμφοράς, ἔλεγέν τε κρεῖττον αὐτοῖς εἶναι ὑπὲρ τῶν πατρίων νόμων ἀποθανεῖν ἢ ζῆν οὕτως ἀσεβῶς.[113]

He would soon lead his family into risk and privation by fleeing with them into the desert, leaving behind all their possessions. Josephus is clear that by acting counter to the worldly interests of his family, Mattathias believed he was acting for their good. Their interests were better served by obedience to God than by safety and prosperity.

It can easily be seen, therefore, that the call of Jesus in the Synoptics to leave family behind in order to honor and serve God is not unique among Jewish writing of its time. Not only can a similar call be found in Philo and Josephus but also in both men the theme follows from an exposition of Jewish Scripture. Both men see in the history of their people that God had always called faithful followers to lay aside all bonds and attractions that prevent them from honoring God above all.

What is new in the message of Jesus in the Synoptic Gospels is the call to "follow me." What is scandalous for the Jew in these words is not the call to give family bonds second place. They knew that family must take second place to loyalty to God. What is scandalous is that Jesus places himself in that place of ultimate loyalty. This would certainly appear blasphemous to his fellow Jews. Indeed it could only escape the charge of blasphemy if Jesus was himself utterly loyal to God and completely aligned with the will of God to the extent that following him was synonymous with following God. I might almost say that it would be blasphemous unless Jesus was himself God, but that may be claiming too much.

Conclusions

The Synoptic Gospels portray Jesus as calling his disciples away from family as their primary loyalty and into a fictive kinship group focused on the loyalty each disciple demonstrates toward Jesus. Family language

---

113. Josephus, "Antiquitates Judaicae", xii.267. TR: "lamented to his children the sad state of their affairs, and the ravage made in the city and the plundering of the temple, and the calamities the multitude were under; and he told them that it was better for them to die for the laws of their country than to live so ingloriously as they then did." Josephus, *Antiquities, The Antiquities of the Jews*, xii.267.

is used throughout the Synoptics, showing that the collection of followers around Jesus was not merely a band of displaced persons who happen to have found it easier to live together than apart; they saw each other as family, and made choices to break ties of biological kinship in order to follow Jesus. In this kinship group, all were called to honor one Father, and to acts as siblings with each other. This is not unique. Some other Jewish sects were so strict as to call for the breaking of family ties in order to live a life of complete devotion to God. What is unique is the way the Synoptics equate following Jesus with following God.

The call to place primarily loyalty in Jesus (and hence in God) is stark in these Gospels. Strong words like hate are used to describe the secondary priority to be given to family. Jesus speaks about his own biological family as if they were not his family at all unless they repented of their opposition to his ministry and sat with his disciples and heard from him the word of God.

How does this compare with the Fourth Gospel? Does the Jesus of John also insist upon such a change of loyalty? Certainly the idea that the Johannine Jesus calls for the overturning of many social and political institutions is uncontroversial. Barton, for instance, writes:

> the Gospel proclaims God's love for the world . . . Such a revelation transcends, displaces even, group boundaries of one kind—boundaries which the Pharisees, the Jews, Caiaphas and Pilate, amongst others, attempt to maintain. But in so doing, it proclaims as a reality a society of another kind. Members of this society are called "children of God" (*tekna tou theou*,) and include Jews, Samaritans and Greeks—for differences of race no longer symbolize differences of spiritual status . . . Gender differences no longer symbolize differences of spiritual status, either: hence the prominence in the Gospel of the mother of Jesus, the Samaritan woman, Martha and Mary with Lazarus, and Mary Magdalene.[114]

Our question in this book concerns the extent to which kinship is one of those institutions that Jesus overturns in John, and the extent to which the tension between biological kinship and the new fictive kinship created around Jesus is felt and described in the Fourth Gospel.

114. Barton, *The Spirituality of the Gospels*, 116.

Before beginning to answer that question, a better understanding of the nature of kinship relations in Jesus' culture is needed. Chapter 4 will, therefore, examine the nature and obligations of relationships between sons and mothers in New Testament culture.

4

Mother and Son

It is hard to imagine a culture where the relationship between a mother and her child is not typically intensely affectionate. Nine months of shared life, followed by a time in which most of her child's needs are supplied from her own body, cannot but produce deep emotional bonds. Yet there is variation to be found from culture to culture in the way this bond is expressed and in the way the gender of the child becomes a factor in the mother–child bond. This chapter will seek to clarify the values and expectations surrounding relationships between mothers and sons in first-century Palestine. Attention will first be given to current scholarship concerning gender relations and family bonds, and then the focus will move to ancient mother–son relationships in Greek, Roman, and Jewish literature to identify the extent to which the generalizations made by scholars are substantiated by those texts. Honor and shame will be the first topic discussed because any analysis of gendered relations in these cultures must be passed under this all-pervasive lens. I will move from there to a discussion of archaeological evidence for the roles of women and men within Galilean households and note any indications of the sort of contact that may have taken place between a mother and her adult sons. Ancient Greek, Roman, and Jewish literature will be explored for examples of mother–son bonds. I will then draw conclusions for the exploration of what the early readers of the Gospel of John may have expected of Jesus and his mother in their relations with one another.

Key Questions addressed in this chapter:
- What do modern socio-historical scholars say about this question?

- How well is this substantiated?
- What else can we find in Jewish literature?
- What else can we find in Galilean archaeology, especially about the division of household space along gender lines?
- What do we find in Greco-Roman literature and archaeology?
- To what extent can this be applied to Palestinian Jewish families?

There are commonalities that exist across most cultures and throughout history concerning the relationships between mothers and sons. G. P. Murdock's influential model of the nuclear family gives expression to some of these.[1] Campbell summarizes his findings concerning mother–son relationships in this way: "Dependency of son during infancy; imposition of early disciplines by the mother; moderate economic co-operation during childhood of son; early development of a lifelong incest taboo; material support by son during old age of mother."[2]

According to Hanson's[3] appropriation of Emmanual Todd's[4] model of family structure, three family types are of relevance to the study of the Fourth Gospel. Roman families tended to be the "exogamous community" type, which emphasized "paternal authority, equality between brothers determined by rules of inheritance, cohabitation of married sons with their parents, and no marriage between children of two brothers."[5]

Greek families tended to be the "egalitarian nuclear" type, which emphasized, "equality of brothers laid down by inheritance rules, no cohabitation of married sons with their parents, and no marriage between children of two brothers."[6]

Finally, Jewish families tended to be the "endogamous community" type, which emphasized, "equality of brothers established by inheritance rules, cohabitation of married sons with their parents, and frequent marriage between children of two brothers."[7]

Anthropologist, Raphael Patai, observed in the mid-twentieth century that traditional Middle Eastern families tended to be

---

1. Murdock, "The Nuclear Family."
2. Campbell, *Kinship Relations*, 90.
3. Hanson, "The Herodians and Mediterranean Kinship, 2 Pts."
4. Todd, *Explanation of Ideology*.
5. As summarized by Campbell, *Kinship Relations*, 92.
6. As summarized by Campbell, *Kinship Relations*, 92.
7. As summarized by Campbell, *Kinship Relations*, 93.

extended, patrilineal, patrilocal, patriarchal, endogamous, and occasionally polygamous.⁸

These models outline areas of commonality shared by most families and by certain types of family. Within this commonality variation can be observed between cultures, and when considering first-century culture the impact of honor and shame must be considered as a primary source of variation.

Honor and shame in the family

When we speak of honor in antiquity, we refer to the basic definition given by Pitt-Rivers that "honor is the value of a person in his⁹ own eyes, but also in the eyes of his society. It is his estimation of his own worth, his claim to pride, but it is also the acknowledgement of that claim, his excellence recognized by society, his right to pride."¹⁰

Rohrbaugh describes the pervasiveness of honor in this world, where it:

> determines dress, mannerisms, gestures, vocation, posture, who can eat with whom, who sits at what places at a meal, who can open a conversation, who has the right to speak and who is accorded an audience. It serves as the prime indicator of social place (precedence) and provides the essential map for persons to interact with superiors, inferiors and equals in socially prescribed or appropriate ways.¹¹

According to Neyrey, honor is also a family affair: "all members shared in the collective standing of the kinship group."¹² Therefore, "family loyalty—doing whatever is necessary to uphold the honor of the family in public—is the quintessential Mediterranean virtue."¹³ Where public humiliation is considered a fate worse than death¹⁴ it is not too great a stretch to imagine that the public humiliation of one's son could

---

8. Patai, *Golden River to Golden Road*, 84.
9. Gendered language in this case probably was intended by the author.
10. Pitt-Rivers, *The Fate of Shechem*, 1.
11. Rohrbaugh, "Legitimating Sonship," 184.
12. Neyrey, "Loss of Wealth," 142; see also Rohrbaugh, "Legitimating Sonship," 185.
13. Rohrbaugh, "Legitimating Sonship," 186.
14. Pilch and Malina, *Biblical Social Values*, 97.

be seen as a fate worse than bereavement. However, we shall note in our later discussion of 4 Maccabees that humiliation in the name of virtue may be accounted as honor.

Shame[15] is not generally considered to be simply the opposite of honor though in one sense it is a claim to worth that is publicly denied or repudiated. To be shamed is to be stripped of honor, which is always a negative experience. Kressel points out that three qualities of honor and shame prevent the words being directly antonymous:

1. Allocation of honor tends to be clearly scaled, while shame, if scaled at all, is less stratified.
2. Words connoting shame are more prevalent in daily speech than words associated with honor.
3. There is no clear midpoint or range of transition between honor and shame.[16]

According to Pilch and Malina, "having shame" is the virtue of being concerned about one's own honor and the honor of one's family.[17] Many social anthropologists agree that in a gender-based honor/shame society, honor tends to be a value embodied by men, while this positive aspect of shame is embodied by women.[18] It is also frequently argued that women did not enter into the contest for the accumulation of family honor. In fact, Philo goes so far as to say that it is more honorable for a man to be defeated in a contest for honor than to gain victory with the assistance of his wife.[19] Instead, women guard and maintain the family's (positive) shame by a veil of privacy and personal and sexual integrity.[20] A woman's sexual behavior and her fertility may contribute to or

15. Campbell, *Kinship Relations*, 88.
16. Kressel, "Shame and Gender."
17. See Pilch and Malina, *Biblical Social Values and Their Meanings*, 96.
18. Oakman, *Palestine in the Time of Jesus*, 26.
19. Philo, *The Works of Philo*, Book III,172–5. He is quite concerned that if a woman became involved in a battle with a man she might make use of that one way in which men are more physically vulnerable than women and, "proceed to such a degree of boldness as to seize hold of the genitals of one of the men quarrelling." This statement appears rather quaint to us until we read his conclusion: "And let the punishment be the cutting off of the hand which has touched what it ought not to have touched."
20. Pilch and Malina, *Biblical Social Values and Their Meanings*, 96. See also Oakman, *Palestine in the Time of Jesus*, 26.

detract from her husband's honor and her father's honor. Fathering many children, particularly male children, was a sign of virility for a man, and therefore increased his honor standing. A woman who produced illegitimate children brought great dishonor on her husband and his family.[21]

A daughter's chastity has been described as the weak link in a family's shame.[22] This is illustrated by the story of the rape of Dinah in Genesis 34, where her brothers decide that an act of violence and humiliation against her attacker's clan was the most appropriate way to redeem the lost honor of their family.[23] This vulnerability of a family to loss of honor through a daughter's (or sister's) sexuality may be one reason why women in such cultures tended to be married out of their fathers' (and brothers') households at what we would consider very young ages.

Kressel's study of Bedouin in Ramla, Israel and in the Negev Highlands introduces readers to a culture in today's world where a daughter's sexuality is perceived as such a threat to the family's honor that even very young girls are kept away from men outside the family, and are harshly disciplined for any infringement of propriety. Circumcision ensures that girls will never desire sexual intercourse for reasons other than child-bearing.[24]

This present-day example may help us in some way toward understanding gender in the ancient Mediterranean, but it would be a mistake to take the comparison too far. The projection of present-day ethnographic insights into the distant past is called "upstreaming" by anthropologists, and is considered an exercise that requires great care.[25]

Plutarch's words about women's virtues give us reason for caution about too complete a gender divide on the question of honor and shame:

> περὶ ἀρετῆς, ὦ Κλέα, γυναικῶν οὐ τὴν αὐτὴν τῷ Θουκυδίδῃ γνώμην ἔχομεν. ὁ μὲν γάρ, ἧς ἂν ἐλάχιστος ᾖ παρὰ τοῖς ἐκτὸς ψόγου πέρι ἢ ἐπαίνου λόγος, ἀρίστην ἀποφαίνεται, καθάπερ τὸ σῶμα καὶ τοὔνομα τῆς ἀγαθῆς γυναικὸς οἰόμενος δεῖν κατάκλειστον εἶναι καὶ ἀνέξοδον. ἡμῖν δὲ κομψότερος μὲν ὁ Γοργίας φαίνεται, κελεύων μὴ τὸ εἶδος ἀλλὰ τὴν δόξαν εἶναι πολλοῖς γνώριμον τῆς γυναικός· ἄριστα δ' ὁ Ῥωμαίων δοκεῖ νόμος ἔχειν, ὥσπερ ἀνδράσι καὶ γυναιξὶ δημοσίᾳ μετὰ τὴν

21. Pitt-Rivers, *The Fate of Shechem*, 78.
22. Oakman, *Palestine in the Time of Jesus*, 24, relying on Sir 7:24; 42:9–11.
23. See Brayford, "To Shame or Not to Shame," 166.
24. Kressel, "Shame and Gender."
25. Chance, "The Anthropology of Honor and Shame," 141–2.

> τελευτὴν τοὺς προσήκοντας ἀποδιδοὺς ἐπαίνους. διὸ καὶ Λεοντίδος τῆς ἀρίστης ἀποθανούσης, εὐθύς τε μετὰ σοῦ τότε πολὺν λόγον εἴχομεν οὐκ ἀμοιροῦντα παραμυθίας φιλοσόφου, καὶ νῦν, ὡς ἐβουλήθης, τὰ ὑπόλοιπα τῶν λεγομένων εἰς τὸ μίαν εἶναι καὶ τὴν αὐτὴν ἀνδρὸς καὶ γυναικὸς ἀρετὴν προσανέγραψά σοι[26]

Crook points out that Plutarch often praised women, not just for being chaste and submissive, but also for being witty, brave, aggressive, and loyal.[27] It is important to recognize that Plutarch's views in this respect were rather unorthodox, and to note that by today's standards he was no feminist. However, the fact that he wrote the above words demonstrates, at least, that the position of women with respect to honor in his time was not so fixed as to be beyond debate.

It is possible that honor and shame have become popular concepts that are called upon too readily and indiscriminately in interpretation of biblical texts. There have been calls for New Testament scholars of a social-scientific bent to demonstrate the relevance of concepts of honor and shame to the texts they study, rather than assuming that contests for honor are always in operation.[28] These calls must be attended to; but we must also remember that deeply held values are rarely made explicit in texts where author, characters, and presumed audience shared cultural assumptions.

Brayford points out that several Hebrew texts of the Pentateuch appear to view female sexuality, and indeed female honor, in a positive light. She notices that the LXX consistently translated these texts in such

---

26. Plutarch, *Bravery of Women* TR: Regarding the virtues of women, Clea, I do not hold the same opinion as Thucydides. For he declares that the best woman is she about whom there is the least talk among persons outside regarding either censure or commendation, feeling that the name of the good woman, like her person, ought to be shut up indoors and never go out.

But to my mind, Gorgias appears to display better taste in advising that not the form but the fame of a woman should be known to many. Best of all seems the Roman custom, which publicly renders to women, as to men, a fitting commemoration after the end of their life. So when Leontis, that most excellent woman, died, I forthwith had then a long conversation with you, which was not without some share of consolation drawn from philosophy, and now, as you desired, I have also written out for you the remainder of what I would have said on the topic that man's virtues and woman's virtues are one and the same.

27. Crook, "Honor, Shame, and Social Status Revisited," 605.

28. Downing, "'Honor' among Exegetes"; Lawrence, "They Have Received Their Reward," 688–9.

a way as to increase the honor of the men involved, while increasing the (positive) shame of the women.²⁹ Her apposite message is that we should not assume too complete a cultural continuity between the ancient Hebrew world and the world of the LXX and inter-testamental writings.

For the purpose of studying the New Testament, Bayford's research alerts us to the need to look to the LXX when the Old Testament is consulted as a resource for cultural background. Not only was the LXX the biblical text used by New Testament authors, it was also (for all its inaccuracies, and perhaps because of them) the version of the Old Testament that best reflects the cultural values and presuppositions of first-century Jews. Even so we also must keep in mind the fact that the LXX represents the values of Jews from Alexandria more than those from Judea.

Crook outlines epigraphic evidence of women being honored as patrons and benefactors by men. While the theory that women spent their lives inside the home, and outside of the world of honor accumulation, may hold as a general rule, it was clearly not an inviolable law.³⁰

Within the Gospels, Jesus' encounter with the Syrophoenician woman (Mark 7:24–30 cf. Matt 15:22–8) represents perhaps the only challenge–riposte encounter in which Jesus is defeated. The fact that Jesus appears delighted with this defeat may throw the actuality of his defeat into question, but it is nevertheless clear that a woman induced Jesus to give her what she asked for by performing well in a verbal interchange.

Crook sums up her argument with these words:

> There appears to have been an ideal world and a lived world, and in the lived world women *did* participate in public life, *did* compete for honor, *could* have greater honor than their husbands, did act as benefactors, and *were* given crowns, statues and seats of honor. The presence of women in areas *traditionally* demarcated as male, especially in the centuries on either side of the common era in Asia Minor, is too amply documented to be deemed counter cultural or exceptional.³¹

This may be an overstatement. I suspect that the attribution of significant honor to women at that time was somewhat exceptional. However, it was not unheard of.

---

29. Brayford, "To Shame or Not to Shame."

30. Crook, "Honor, Shame, and Social Status Revisited," 607–8.

31. Crook, "Honor, Shame, and Social Status Revisited," 609. Italics are from the original.

In addition to these concerns, Lawrence calls exegetes to remember that Pitt-Rivers described two different kinds of honor: honor precedence is public honor ascribed by members of one's group, while honor virtue is a person's private standing before their own conscience and/or an omniscient deity.[32] While Crook has argued that women were not entirely excluded from honor precedence, it is reasonably plausible that in such societies women are more able to accumulate honor virtue. If this were not the case then ethical instruction (in narrative or propositional form) would never be addressed to women.[33]

One might assume that a concern for the preservation of a family's honor, and particularly the safeguarding of the chastity of the women in the family, might be reflected in the architecture of such societies. A discussion of the architecture of first-century Galilee is, therefore, now in order.

Household space

In the last two decades archaeologists working in Galilee have identified three basic forms of household building. Eric Meyers gives a useful summary of their findings.[34] The *simple house* was a single-room structure, varying in size from 20 to 200 square meters. Some had a courtyard in front or behind. The majority of the population, especially in rural areas, probably lived in such structures.

The *complex house* involved various wings or housing units on three sides of a courtyard. This form of dwelling may have expressed prosperity or may have indicated that several branches of an extended family lived in their own units around a common courtyard.

Finally, the *courtyard house*, more common in urban areas, was built with an inner courtyard, with or without the classical innovation of columns. Such houses were clearly reserved for the wealthy, but archaeologists have not found sufficient evidence to be confident about the source of their wealth. The *peristyle house*, considerably less common than the others, is a form of courtyard house that shows a high degree of Roman influence. Banquet halls, mosaics, pools, and gardens set this

---

32. Lawrence, "They Have Received Their Reward."

33. Many ethicists, of course, did assume a completely male audience for their work.

34. Meyers, "The Problems of Gendered Space in Syro-Palestinian Architecture."

type of house apart as the home of only the wealthiest of Galileans. The presence of this type of house in Galilee indicates increasing levels of social stratification and consolidation of land in the late republic and early empire.[35]

Was household space gendered?

Philo wrote of "two kinds of states," cities and houses, with the former managed by men and the latter by women. He instructs adult women to keep themselves within their house and virgins to be kept safe in the very centre of the house.[36] Xenophon also spoke of men and women occupying different spheres.[37]

What use can be made of these instructions? They can only be genuinely useful to the extent that it is possible to discriminate between prescription, fantasy, and practice.[38] In other words, should Philo's instructions that women be concerned with the inside and men the outside of their homes be understood as reflecting reality at all, or was he seeking to encourage a form of gender segregation that was not in fact generally practiced?

The question of particular interest to this discussion is whether architecture gives any clues about how a mother may have been expected to act within the home, and particularly how she may be expected to have acted towards her adult sons.

It is relevant, then, to note Meyer's findings concerning a large residence in Meiron:

> The interior of the house does not represent private space as distinct from workspace. Rather, a variety of work was carried out there, consisting of food production, textile work, and carpentry. The public/private dichotomy simply cannot characterize this space where all manner of household, family activities were carried on. Though inscriptional supports are lacking for husbands and wives working together, the organisation of space

---

35. Guijarro, "The Family in First-Century Galilee," 55.
36. Philo, *The Works of Philo*, III, 169–170.
37. Xenophon, "Xenophon in Seven Volumes," 7:16–41. See also Plutarch, *Advice to Bride and Groom*, 9.
38. See Dixon, "Sex and the Married Woman in Ancient Rome," 114.

suggests such a possibility as well as the involvement of family members in a variety of household tasks.[39]

Further, he finds that even within a home that shows substantial evidence of priestly inhabitants, "It is virtually impossible to construct a scenario whereby men and women could have avoided each other either at home or outside the home."[40] In short, he concludes, "the material world of Roman-period Palestine clearly shows that women participated far more fully in crafts, daily household labors, and management, and hence had a much higher degree of recognition and responsibility than one might infer from literary sources alone."[41]

If it is not possible to identify gender segregation in the courtyard houses studied by Meyers, we must assume that men and women were even more likely to have shared space in the single-room houses of subsistence farmers and artisans, where segregation was even less practical. We are left to wonder whether this separation of genders remained for these families a desired but unattainable ideal, or an impractical and unpracticed rabbinic dream.

Patterson argues that even in classical Athens, where the practice of female domestic seclusion is assumed to have originated, there is evidence that it was not strictly observed.[42]

Given that ancient homes were places of production and industry,[43] the assumption that domestic space was gendered tends to lead to the conclusion that the labor of women was relegated to the domestic sphere (inside, away from the gaze of men) and the labor of men to the fields. However, in Galilee at least, it appears that men sometimes worked inside and that women sometimes worked in the courtyard.[44] It may even be

---

39. Meyers, "The Problems of Gendered Space in Syro-Palestinian Architecture," 59.

40. Meyers, "The Problems of Gendered Space in Syro-Palestinian Architecture," 67.

41. Meyers, "The Problems of Gendered Space in Syro-Palestinian Architecture," 86.

42. Patterson, *The Family in Greek History*, 126–9.

43. See also Meyers, "The Problems of Gendered Space in Syro-Palestinian Architecture," 58–59.

44. In large courtyard homes it may be that labor was carried out by slaves, who were without honor. The female slave had no shame to be hidden by keeping her inside, and the male slave had no honor to be demonstrated in the outside world.

that on occasion the harsh realities of subsistence agriculture could have taken women out into the fields.⁴⁵

The assumption of some social-scientific commentators that "men and women tend to move in two exclusive spheres which occasionally touch but rarely overlap"⁴⁶ is less apposite for Galilee than it might be for other areas in the Roman Empire; and is not a helpful assumption for exegesis of John 2 and 19.

Economic realities of home life

Moxnes points out that none of the relevant languages of this period have a word for family that means "nuclear family" in the modern sense.⁴⁷ These languages refer either to kinship more broadly or to "household," a more geographically focused term for a group of people who share a dwelling. The members of this group, apart from infants, shared in the economic activity of the household.⁴⁸

I have noted that in Galilee it is unlikely that domestic space was divided along gender lines,⁴⁹ but it is also important to understand that the labor that took place within these homes almost certainly was divided along gender lines.⁵⁰

In an exhaustive study by Treggiari, women in Rome were found in a far narrower range of occupations than were men (35 as opposed to 225). Women's work generally involved service industries and the production and (to a lesser extent) sales of market goods, particularly textiles.⁵¹ I believe that an assumption of a somewhat similar range of occupations of women in Galilee would be reasonable, but scarcity of data, and of academic studies based on that data, makes such an assumption tentative.

Treggiari also noted a large number of occupations, particularly in artisan classes, where husband and wife both participated.⁵² Though

---

45. R. Saller, "Women, Slaves, and the Economy of the Roman Household," 192; 198.
46. Ritva H. Williams, "The Mother of Jesus at Cana," 681.
47. Moxnes, *Putting Jesus in His Place*, 28.
48. Moxnes, *Putting Jesus in His Place*, 40–1.
49. Moxnes, *Putting Jesus in His Place*, 40–1.
50. Saller, "Women, Slaves, and the Economy of the Roman Household," 186.
51. Treggiari's study is referred to in Saller, "Women, Slaves, and the Economy of the Roman Household", 192.
52. Priscilla and Aquila seem to be an example of wife and husband working

Saller suspects that this participation of women was often little more than "minding the shop,"[53] it is an intriguing possibility that Mary and her daughters may have learned some basic building skills along with the men in their family.

There is also evidence that, in spite of Philo's disapproval, it was women who were primarily involved in the outside task of taking household produce to market and purchasing supplies from the market. DeSilva notes that Jewish women had greater access to this particular segment of the outside world than did their Roman and Greek counterparts.[54] As a mother in Nazareth, it is highly likely that Mary would have regularly walked to the market at the nearby city of Sepphoris.[55]

There is also substantial evidence that women and men dined together, at least on occasion. The Passover Seder required the presence of the whole family—men, women, and children. Men and women are also found at table together in Jewish inter-testamental literature.[56] We can even look to Luke 7:36–9 and notice that the Pharisee is shocked, not by the presence of a woman at a meal, nor even by the fact that she touched Jesus, but only by the fact that the woman touching Jesus was a sinner.

While considering the household as an economic unit, it is important to notice the economic importance of sons. Raising children was an expensive activity for families of limited economic means and it was generally done in the expectation that boys, in particular, would work to contribute to the family's income as soon as they were able.[57]

As we consider evidence of ancient household architecture we need to be mindful of the distinction between the household as an economic unit and the family as an affective unit of human relationship.[58] The two are interconnected, of course, but not interchangeable. A third interconnected concept is that of family as a political unit. After a century of universal adult suffrage in our society it is easy for us to overlook the significant role played by the head of the household in societies where he alone had the opportunity to participate in political processes.

---

together (Acts 18:1–3).

53. Saller, "Women, Slaves, and the Economy of the Roman Household," 194.
54. deSilva, *Honor, Patronage, Kinship & Purity*, 184.
55. Corley, *Women and the Historical Jesus*, 22–23.
56. Corley, *Women and the Historical Jesus*, 24–25.
57. Dixon, *The Roman Family*, 109.
58. See Moxnes, "What Is a Family?" 17.

Women at social occasions

In John 2 Jesus' mother is introduced in the context of a wedding celebration. This raises the necessity of considering where the place of women might have been and whether it was acceptable for her to approach Jesus in conversation.

While Greek tradition relegated respectable women to women's quarters,[59] there had been a move in Roman and Jewish circles to include wives at meals.[60] This, along with the likelihood that household space in Galilee was not divided along gender lines as in Greek homes,[61] leads to the conclusion that it was not inappropriate for Jesus' mother to be speaking to him at this wedding.

The courtyard seems to be the place where people of both genders gathered,[62] so we might imagine that the wedding guests, rather than mingling inside the house, were in the courtyard, or perhaps on the rooftop.[63]

Affective bonds

A Latin epitaph to a thirty-five-year-old Jewish man from ancient times in Rome is translated, "His mother did for her sweet son that which he should have done for her."[64] The affection and pathos of her words carry effortlessly across the centuries. Indeed, the untimely death of a young adult son is a greatly lamented tragedy in first-century life and literature.[65] Should we, then, assume that the affective bond between mother and son in ancient Rome was exactly the same as it is in our own culture? Or even that ancient Palestinian mother–son relationships were the same as those in ancient Rome? Further investigation is necessary to answer that question, and this will be the focus of the remainder of this chapter.

One of the main ways for a woman in this culture to gain honor for her family was through the bearing of sons, so it may be expected that a

---

59. Demosthenes, *In Neaer*, 24, The Wars of the Jews Isaeus *Pyr.* 13–14.
60. Love, "Hellenistic Symposia Meals in Luke," 200.
61. Moxnes, *Putting Jesus in His Place*, 40–41.
62. Moxnes, *Putting Jesus in His Place*, 41.
63. Moxnes, *Putting Jesus in His Place*, 41.
64. Leon, *The Jews of Ancient Rome*, 132.
65. Dixon, *The Roman Family*, 100; 112–3.

mother might take particular delight in her boys.⁶⁶ A young woman who entered her husband's home upon her marriage would find that her place in his family would not be consolidated or valued until she produced a son. That son who increased her status in the family would undoubtedly be highly valued. It seems reasonable then that a first-born son might be a particular focus of affection.

Malina contends, indeed, that in terms of affect the mother–son relationship was the closest of familial bonds. "While sibling relations may be close, the mother–son bond is perhaps the closest Mediterranean equivalent in intensity of what people in the US expect in the 'love' of a marriage relation."⁶⁷

This claim must be submitted to historical interrogation. Malina's habit of assuming that Mediterranean culture has not changed in significant respects in the past two thousand years is demonstrated by this statement: "If the evaluation and rearing of children in the Eastern Mediterranean are in fact traditional, there is little reason to expect first-century persons not to have shared the tendencies [of modern Mediterranean cultures]."⁶⁸

As it stands, this sounds like a breath-taking assumption. It must be admitted, though, that the study of comparable societies in today's world does help us conceptualize the ways in which ancient societies may have differed from our own.⁶⁹ It must also be noted that the traditional Mediterranean cultures of today will almost certainly be more similar to ancient Mediterranean cultures than any other culture existing today, and so provide the most potentially useful points of comparison. However, to imagine that any culture has remained unchanged for two thousand years is hardly credible, so any claim about ancient cultures based on today's cultures must be viewed with some skepticism and subjected to historical verification.

Malina's claim concerning the intensity of the mother–son bond must, therefore, be investigated in the light of whatever first-century evidence is available to us. We will concentrate here on literary evidence.

---

66. See Hellerman, *The Ancient Church as Family*, 33–34; Campbell, *Kinship Relations*, 102.

67. Malina, *The Social World of Jesus and the Gospels*, 110.

68. Malina, *The Social World of Jesus and the Gospels*, 112.

69. Guijarro, "The Family in First Century Galilee," 43.

Literary indications of the bonds between mothers and sons

The following analysis of literature relevant to first-century Mediterranean culture does not attempt to be exhaustive or quantitative. Rather, a number of key texts have been selected for close examination of what they reveal about relationships between mothers and sons.

Given recent developments in search technology it may be that qualitative textual analysis of a large range of sources is now possible, and may be fruitful in sharpening the light I am here able to throw on descriptions of relationships between mothers and sons in ancient literature. This would be a worthy doctoral book in itself and is beyond my constraints of space and time. As it is, I am indebted to the search tools at www.perseus.tufts.edu for directing me to the most relevant texts for my analysis.

Evidence from the New Testament

If we leave aside for the moment the particular relationship between Jesus and his mother, there is little discussion of mothers and sons in the New Testament. Moxnes believes that some mothers of Jesus' disciples appear to have become his followers along with their sons (Matt 20:20 and possibly 27:56) while this does not appear to be the case for their fathers.[70] There is insufficient evidence for any certainty on this and in any case it is not obvious what conclusions ought to be drawn from it. Possibly these women's husbands had died and they followed the sons on whom they depended as a matter of course.

Parents who brought children to Jesus for healing appear to be fathers slightly more often than they are mothers. This may simply reflect the difficulty of a woman approaching a man in this culture. Certainly the anxiety and desperation expressed by fathers appear just as intense as that expressed by mothers. For example, see Mark 5:22–3 (cf., 7:25–6). We can certainly say that the affective side of parenting does not appear in the Gospels to belong exclusively to mothers.

We might notice that the influence of Timothy's mother and grandmother was more significant for his faith development than his (presumably pagan) father (2 Tim 1:5).

---

70. Moxnes, "What Is a Family?" 35.

I suggest on this basis that there is too little evidence in the New Testament to make any clear assessment of the nature of mother–son relationships beyond the fact that emotional bonds existed between both parents and their children, and that the education of children could be influenced by mothers as well as by fathers.

Ancient Greek and Roman ethical literature

The work of Aristotle and Plato, while certainly not originating around the first century CE, was highly influential in this period and so is considered here as part of the intellectual milieu of the time. Aristotle taught that affection between parents and children is natural and universal: φύσει τ' ἐνυπάρχειν ἔοικε πρὸς τὸ γεγεννημένον τῷ γεννήσαντι καὶ πρὸς τὸ γεννῆσαν τῷ γεννηθέντι, οὐ' μόνον ἐν ἀνθρώποις ἀλλὰ καὶ ἐν ὄρνισι καὶ τοῖς πλείστοις τῶν ζῴων.[71]

Children, he believed, ought to demonstrate greater love toward their parents than they receive from their parents:

> ὅταν δὲ γονεῦσι μὲν τέκνα ἀπονέμῃ ἃ δεῖ τοῖς γεννήσασι, γονεῖς δὲ [υἱέσιν] ἃ δεῖ τοῖς τέκνοις, μόνιμος ἡ τῶν τοιούτων καὶ ἐπιεικὴς ἔσται φιλία. ἀνάλογον δ' ἐν πάσαις ταῖς καθ' ὑπεροχὴν οὔσαις φιλίαις καὶ τὴν φίλησιν δεῖ γίνεσθαι, οἷον τὸν ἀμείνω μᾶλλον φιλεῖσθαι ἢ φιλεῖν, καὶ τὸν ὠφελιμώτερον, καὶ τῶν ἄλλων ἕκαστον ὁμοίως· ὅταν γὰρ κατ' ἀξίαν ἡ φίλησις γίνηται, τότε γίνεταί πως ἰσότης, ὃ δὴ τῆς φιλίας εἶναι δοκεῖ.[72]

Parents not only bring their children into the world but also convey to them the established and time-tested wisdom that provides grounding and identity for family members within their culture.[73] Children, therefore, have a multitude of reasons to express gratitude and love toward

---

71. Aristotle, "Nicomachean Ethics" Book VIII, §3 TR: And the affection of parent for offspring and of offspring for parent seems to be a natural instinct, not only in [humans] but also in birds and in most animals.

72. Aristotle, "Nicomachean Ethics." Book VIII, §7.2. TR: when children render to parents what is due to the authors of their being, and parents to children what is due to them, then their friendships are permanent and good. In all friendships that involve the principle of inequality, the love also should be proportional; the better or the more useful party, or whoever may be the superior, should receive more love than he gives. For when love is proportioned to the merit, a sort of equality is established; and this equality seems to be a condition of friendship. See also §14.

73. Pilch and Malina, *Biblical Social Values and Their Meanings*, 71; Dixon, *The Roman Family*, 111.

their parents.⁷⁴ There was a deep-seated expectation in Greco-Roman culture that this gratitude would be displayed as children supporting their parents in old age and providing appropriate commemoration for them upon their death.⁷⁵

Even so, Aristotle notices that in fact parents love their children more than they are loved by them. The parent loves the child as part of themselves, whereas the child loves the parent as the source of his or her being. Aristotle concludes that this explains why mothers love their children more than fathers do.⁷⁶ That mothers do love children more than fathers appears to be self-evident to him. Mothers are held up as an example of love that does not insist upon a return of affection:

> δοκεῖ δ' ἐν τῷ φιλεῖν μᾶλλον ἢ ἐν τῷ φιλεῖσθαι εἶναι. σημεῖον δ' αἱ μητέρες τῷ φιλεῖν χαίρουσαι· ἔνιαι γὰρ διδόασι τὰ ἑαυτῶν τρέφεσθαι, καὶ φιλοῦσι μὲν εἰδυῖαι, ἀντιφιλεῖσθαι δ' οὐ ζητοῦσιν, ἐὰν ἀμφότερα μὴ ἐνδέχηται, ἀλλ' ἱκανὸν αὐταῖς ἔοικεν εἶναι ἐὰν ὁρῶσιν εὖ πράττοντας, καὶ αὐταὶ φιλοῦσιν αὐτοὺς κἂν ἐκεῖνοι μηδὲν ὧν μητρὶ προσήκει ἀπονέμωσι διὰ τὴν ἄγνοιαν.⁷⁷

Despite agreeing that children ought to be grateful to their parents, Plutarch is at pains to insist that parents ought not to bring children into the world in order to receive the rewards of their children's gratitude: ὡς τοῦ τεκεῖν καὶ θρέψαι τέλος οὐ χρείαν ἀλλὰ φιλίαν ἔχοντος.⁷⁸ Even very wealthy parents in the first century, who had no need for material support from their children, craved the companionship of their offspring in their old age.⁷⁹

---

74. See van der Watt, *Family of the King*, 284–5.
75. Dixon, *The Roman Family*, 108.
76. Aristotle, "Nicomachean Ethics," Book VIII, §xii.2.
77. Aristotle, "Nicomachean Ethics," Book VIII, §viii.3, TR: But in its essence friendship seems to consist more in giving than in receiving affection: witness the pleasure that mothers take in loving their children. Some mothers put their infants out to nurse, and though knowing and loving them, do not ask to be loved by them in return, if it be impossible to have this as well, but are content if they see them prospering; they retain their own love for them even though the children, not knowing them, cannot render to them any part of what is due to a mother.
78. Plutarch, "On Affection for Offspring," §i.3, 349 TR: the end and aim of bearing and carrying a child is not utility but affection.
79. Dixon, *The Roman Family*, 109.

Plato wrote of the great value of storytelling for the formation of the character of children, and assumed that mothers and nurses would be the primary storytellers.

> πρῶτον δὴ ἡμῖν, ὡς ἔοικεν, ἐπιστατητέον τοῖς μυθοποιοῖς, καὶ ὃν μὲν ἂν καλὸν μῦθον ποιήσωσιν, ἐγκριτέον, ὃν δ' ἂν μή, ἀποκριτέον. τοὺς δ' ἐγκριθέντας πείσομεν τὰς τροφούς τε καὶ μητέρας λέγειν τοῖς παισίν, καὶ πλάττειν τὰς ψυχὰς αὐτῶν τοῖς μύθοις πολὺ μᾶλλον ἢ τὰ σώματα ταῖς χερσίν: ὧν δὲ νῦν λέγουσι τοὺς πολλοὺς ἐκβλητέον.[80]

Plato was particularly keen to avoid little ears being scandalized by stories involving the mistreatment of mothers among the gods.[81]

The benefit of examining didactic ethical texts is that they identify the espoused values of a culture or a group within a culture. Their benefit for identifying actual practice is limited. It has been argued that the contradiction between espoused and practiced values is even greater in the Mediterranean cultures than elsewhere:

> Avowals of social egalitarianism coexist with marked socio-economic stratification; an ideology of male dominance often contrasts with a reality of matrifocality and a reliance on affines rather than agnates; the high value placed on family solidarity and the loyalty of siblings is counterbalanced by frequent intra-family hostilities; agonistic perceptions of one's neighbours co-exist with strong sociocentric sentiments; and women are said to be inactive economically despite their important contributions to the domestic economy.[82]

To this we must add two further cautions. Ethicists tended to express the views and values of their own class,[83] and only upper classes had sufficient leisure time for philosophical reflection. We cannot assume that they express as well the values of the artisan class.

In spite of these cautions, we can glean some basic generalizations about motherhood from the ethicists before moving into the realm of

---

80. Plato, "Republic" Book II, §337b,c. TR: Then the first thing will be to establish a censorship of the writers of fiction, and let the censors receive any tale of fiction which is good, and reject the bad; and we will desire mothers and nurses to tell their children the authorized ones only. Let them fashion the mind with such tales, even more fondly than they mould the body with their hands; but most of those which are now in use must be discarded. Plato, "The Republic,"

81. See Plato, "Republic" Book II §378d.

82. Chance, "The Anthropology of Honor and Shame," 146.

83. Guijarro, "The Family in First-Century Galilee," 47–48.

mythology. There appears to be an assumption that a mother's love is greater than a father's and demands less in return. There is also an assumption that mothers are more involved in the important role of passing on the values of culture and family through storytelling; and it is to those stories that I now turn.

Greek epic and mythology

Homer's epics, *The Iliad* and *The Odyssey*, present us with stories that are quintessentially Greek. They are not useful as sources of information about specific customs of the first century as they were written eight centuries earlier and reflect oral memory of a time even more distant. However, these stories were retained, remembered, and repeated because they encapsulated Greek values and re-presented those values to each new generation that heard them. These, above all others, are the stories that, in Plato's words, fashioned the minds of Greek children.

Our examination of them will concern the values that embody Homeric relationships between mothers and sons.

THE ILIAD

While this tale of Ilium gives the reader glimpses into many aspects of family life, including the depth of emotion between husbands and wives, it does seem that many of the scenes of greatest pathos are those between a mother and son.

When Hector comes in from battle to seek assistance from the gods, it is his "fond mother" Hecuba who greets him with expressions of concern. Hector asks her to make an offering to Minerva on behalf of the city. Immediately,

> αὐτὴ δ' ἐς θάλαμον κατεβήσετο κηώεντα, ἔνθ' ἔσάν οἱ πέπλοι παμποίκιλα ἔργα γυναικῶν Σιδονίων, τὰς αὐτὸς Ἀλέξανδρος θεοειδὴς ἤγαγε Σιδονίηθεν ἐπιπλὼς εὐρέα πόντον, τὴν ὁδὸν ἣν Ἑλένην περ ἀνήγαγεν εὐπατέρειαν: τῶν ἕν' ἀειραμένη Ἑκάβη φέρε δῶρον Ἀθήνῃ, ὃς κάλλιστος ἔην ποικίλμασιν ἠδὲ μέγιστος,ἀστὴρ δ' ὣς ἀπέλαμπεν: ἔκειτο δὲ νείατος ἄλλων. βῆ δ' ἴέναι, πολλαὶ δὲ μετεσσεύοντο γεραιαί.[84]

---

84. Homer, "Iliad," Book VI §263. TR: She went down into her fragrant storeroom, where her embroidered robes were kept, the work of Sidonian women, whom Alexandrus had brought over from Sidon when he sailed the seas upon that voyage

This episode shows a mother's deep concern for her son, and also gives an indication of the role of women in battles fought by men. Women may not fight, but mothers could make what was considered an essential contribution by sacrificing to the gods.

The love of a mother for her son, and particularly a mother's willingness to seek the assistance of the gods, had already come to the fore in Book I of *The Iliad*. When Achilles was distressed that Briseis had been taken from him, it was his goddess mother, Thetis, who immediately heard his cry,[85] shared his grief and anger, and promised to seek assistance in Olympus. The depth of her sympathy for her son was clear:

> τὸν δ' ἠμείβετ' ἔπειτα Θέτις κατὰ δάκρυ χέουσα· ὤ μοι τέκνον
> ἐμόν, τί νύ σ' ἔτρεφον αἰνὰ τεκοῦσα; αἴθ' ὄφελες παρὰ νηυσὶν
> ἀδάκρυτος καὶ ἀπήμων ἦσθαι, ἐπεί νύ τοι αἶσα μίνυνθά περ
> οὔ τι μάλα δήν· νῦν δ' ἄμα τ' ὠκύμορος καὶ ὀϊζυρὸς περὶ
> πάντων ἔπλεο· τώ σε κακῇ αἴσῃ τέκον ἐν μεγάροισι.[86]

Achilles is fortunate to have a mother who is uniquely able to give the assistance he needs by seeking the help of Jove. Later, Achilles attributes to his mother a dilemma that may be said to be at the heart of ancient motherhood:

> μήτηρ γάρ τέ μέ φησι θεὰ Θέτις ἀργυρόπεζα
> διχθαδίας κῆρας φερέμεν θανάτοιο τέλος δέ.
> εἰ μέν κ' αὖθι μένων Τρώων πόλιν ἀμφιμάχωμαι,
> ὤλετο μέν μοι νόστος, ἀτὰρ κλέος ἄφθιτον ἔσται·
> εἰ δέ κεν οἴκαδ' ἵκωμι φίλην ἐς πατρίδα γαῖαν,
> ὤλετό μοι κλέος ἐσθλόν, ἐπὶ δηρὸν δέ μοι
> ἔσσεται, οὐδέ κέ μ' ὦκα τέλος θανάτοιο κιχείη.[87]

---

during which he carried off Helen. Hecuba took out the largest robe, and the one that was most beautifully enriched with embroidery, as an offering to Minerva: it glittered like a star, and lay at the very bottom of the chest. With this she went on her way and many matrons with her.

85. See a repeat of this in Homer, "The Iliad," Book XVIII.

86. Homer, "Iliad" Book I, Line 413-18. TR: "Then Thetis answered him as she wept: 'Ah me, my child, why did I rear you, cursed in my child-bearing? Would that it had been your lot to remain by your ships without tears and without grief, [415] since your span of life is brief and endures no long time; but now you are doomed to a speedy death and are laden with sorrow above all men; therefore to an evil fate I bore you in our halls.'"

87. Homer, "Iliad" Book 9, Line 410-16. TR: "For my mother the goddess, silver-footed Thetis, telleth me that twofold fates are bearing me toward the doom of death:

What is a loving mother to wish for her son? A man who seeks honor in battle may well find death. A man who seeks long life in the safety of home will eventually die anyway but in that case his name, without honor, will die with him.

This desire of mothers for their sons to win glory in battle is also reflected in Hector's prayer for his son: ἐκ πολέμου ἀνιόντα· φέροι δ' ἔναρα βροτόεντα κτείνας δήϊον ἄνδρα, χαρείη δὲ φρένα μήτηρ.[88]

When the two much loved sons, Hector and Achilles, meet in battle they both have devoted mothers standing behind them. Hecuba, having previously been willing to support her son in battle, is now all too aware that she and her son are mortal, while his opponent is a demigod supported by a divine mother. Before this unequal contest she pleads with him in the most graphic terms to refrain from battle:

> μήτηρ δ' αὖθ' ἑτέρωθεν ὀδύρετο δάκρυ χέουσα
> κόλπον ἀνιεμένη, ἑτέρηφι δὲ μαζὸν ἀνέσχε·
> καί μιν δάκρυ χέουσ' ἔπεα πτερόεντα προσηύδα·
> Ἕκτορ τέκνον ἐμὸν τάδε τ' αἴδεο καί μ' ἐλέησον
> αὐτήν, εἴ ποτέ τοι λαθικηδέα μαζὸν ἐπέσχον·
> τῶν μνῆσαι φίλε τέκνον ἄμυνε δὲ δήϊον ἄνδρα
> τείχεος ἐντὸς ἐών, μὴ δὲ πρόμος ἵστασο τούτῳ
> σχέτλιος· εἴ περ γάρ σε κατακτάνῃ, οὔ σ' ἔτ' ἔγωγε
> κλαύσομαι ἐν λεχέεσσι φίλον θάλος, ὃν τέκον αὐτή,
> οὐδ' ἄλοχος πολύδωρος· ἄνευθε δέ σε μέγα νῶϊν
> Ἀργείων παρὰ νηυσὶ κύνες ταχέες κατέδονται.[89]

---

if I abide here and war about the city of the Trojans, then lost is my home-return, but my renown shall be imperishable; but if I return home to my dear native land, lost then is my glorious renown, yet shall my life long endure, neither shall the doom of death come soon upon me."

88. Homer, "Iliad" Book 6, Line 480f. TR: "may he bear the blood-stained spoils of the foeman he hath slain, and may his mother's heart wax glad."

89. Homer, "Iliad," Book 22, Line 79–89. TR: And over against him the mother in her turn wailed and shed tears, loosening the folds of her robe, while with the other hand she showed her breast, and amid shedding of tears she spake unto him winged words: "Hector, my child, have thou respect unto this and pity me, if ever I gave thee the breast to lull thy pain. Think thereon, dear child, and ward off yon foemen from within the wall, neither stand thou forth to face him. Cruel is he; for if so be he slay thee, never shall I lay thee on a bier and bewail thee, dear plant, born of mine own self, nay, nor shall thy bounteous wife; but far away from us by the ships of the Argives shall swift dogs devour thee."

Hecuba's concern here is not only for the preservation of her son's life, but also for his honor. A mother in this ancient world could seek honor for her son by sending him into battle with her blessing and her sacrifices to the gods on his behalf. Should he fall in battle, she could honor him in his burial as she wept over his body. If he should fall in battle and his body be kept and mistreated by the victors, then his grieving mother would have no means left to restore his honor or redeem his shame. In that case a father or brother could possibly raise an army and avenge the death, but the mother could do nothing. When Hector's dead body is at last returned to the city it is his wife and mother together who are first to rush to embrace him.[90]

The utter helplessness of Hecuba is contrasted with the resourcefulness of her counterpart. Thetis, to whom the divine blacksmith Vulcan is in debt, is able to promise her son a new suit of armor for the battle.[91]

Thetis is not only presented as a doting mother but also as a goddess whose motherly virtue is contrasted with the callousness of other deities. Indeed, her kindness toward the son of a less virtuous mother was the reason why she was in a position to make such a request of Vulcan. She had saved him when his mother had sought to get rid of him because he was lame.[92]

Vulcan, who here shows proper gratitude to the goddess who took him in when his mother rejected him, had earlier shown himself to be a virtuous son toward his own mother:

> μητρὶ φίλῃ ἐν χειρὶ τίθει καί μιν προσέειπε:
> 'τέτλαθι μῆτερ ἐμή, καὶ ἀνάσχεο κηδομένη περ,
> μή σε φίλην περ ἐοῦσαν ἐν ὀφθαλμοῖσιν ἴδωμαι
> θεινομένην, τότε δ' οὔ τι δυνήσομαι ἀχνύμενός περ
> χραισμεῖν: ἀργαλέος γὰρ Ὀλύμπιος ἀντιφέρεσθαι:
> ἤδη γάρ με καὶ ἄλλοτ' ἀλεξέμεναι μεμαῶτα
> ῥῖψε ποδὸς τεταγὼν ἀπὸ βηλοῦ θεσπεσίοιο,
> ...
> ὣς φάτο, μείδησεν δὲ θεὰ λευκώλενος Ἥρη,
> μειδήσασα δὲ παιδὸς ἐδέξατο χειρὶ κύπελλον: [93]

---

90. Homer, "Iliad," Book XXIV.
91. Homer, "Iliad," Book XVIII.
92. Homer, "Iliad," Book XVIII.
93. Homer, "Iliad," Book 1. Line 585–97. TR: "Be patient, my mother, and endure for all your grief, lest, dear as you are to me, my eyes see you stricken, and then I shall

In this vignette of family life we see a son siding with his mother to protect her from his father's violent temper. Because he is clever as well as loyal he manages to do this without dishonoring his father or running the risk of redirecting Jove's violence toward himself.

Another character, Phoenix, also speaks of taking sides with his mother against his father. He had left his family home because he was forced to:

> φεύγων νείκεα πατρὸς Ἀμύντορος Ὀρμενίδαο,
> ὅς μοι παλλακίδος περιχώσατο καλλικόμοιο,
> τὴν αὐτὸς φιλέεσκεν, ἀτιμάζεσκε δ' ἄκοιτιν
> μητέρ' ἐμήν: ἣ δ' αἰὲν ἐμὲ λισσέσκετο γούνων
> παλλακίδι προμιγῆναι, ἵν' ἐχθήρειε γέροντα.
> τῇ πιθόμην καὶ ἔρεξα: πατὴρ δ' ἐμὸς αὐτίκ' ὀϊσθεὶς
> πολλὰ κατηρᾶτο, στυγερὰς[94]

This discussion of *The Iliad* presents Greek mothers as being deeply conflicted in relation to their sons. Desire to keep their sons safe leads them to protect their sons with whatever means are at their disposal. Because the means of mortal women are limited, this protection often takes the form of imploring the intervention of the gods through prayers and sacrifices. Virtuous Greek mothers, however devoted they may be, send their sons into battle because they value their sons' honor above their sons' safety. The greatest fear of these mothers was, therefore, not their son's death in battle as such, but death in a battle where the victors shame the son by mutilating his body and feeding it to dogs. In death a mother may still honor her son by weeping over his body and performing the necessary funeral rites, but she can do this only if the body is returned.

A good Homeric son appears to return his mother's devotion by taking her side in disputes between his parents.

---

in no way be able to succour you for all my sorrow; for a hard foe is the Olympian to meet in strife. On a time before this, when I was striving to save you, he caught me by the foot and hurled me from the heavenly threshold; So he spoke, and the goddess, white-armed Hera, smiled, and smiling took in her hand the cup from her son.

94. Homer, "Iliad," Book 9, Line 448–55. TR: "fleeing from strife with my father Amyntor, son of Ormenus; for he waxed grievously wroth against me by reason of his fair-haired concubine, [450] whom himself he ever cherished, and scorned his wife, my mother. So she besought me by my knees continually, to have dalliance with that other first myself, that the old man might be hateful in her eyes. I hearkened to her and did the deed, but my father was ware thereof forthwith and cursed me mightily."

The intensity of the mother–son relationship here is certainly high, in agreement with Malina's assertion about mother–son relationships being the most emotionally intense in Mediterranean culture.

The Odyssey

While the adventures of Odysseus form most of the action in *The Odyssey*, his wife and son provide the backdrop of life in Ithaca in the absence of their husband and father. Penelope's faithfulness is tested by this extended absence during which she is inundated by suitors. Telemachus's patience is tested as he sees these suitors devouring his inheritance while his mother refuses to put an end to their visits by marrying one of them.

The relationship between Penelope and Telemachus lacks the affective intensity of Hecuba and Hector and of Thetis and Achilles, but *The Odyssey* does give us one extra piece of information about the behavior of a good son. Telemachus declares:

> οὔ τι διατρίβω μητρὸς γάμον, ἀλλὰ κελεύω
> γήμασθ᾽ ᾧ κ᾽ ἐθέλῃ, ποτὶ δ᾽ ἄσπετα δῶρα δίδωμι.
> αἰδέομαι δ᾽ ἀέκουσαν ἀπὸ μεγάροιο δίεσθαι
> μύθῳ ἀναγκαίῳ: μὴ τοῦτο θεὸς τελέσειεν. [95]

In the absence of Odysseus, Telemachus is de-facto head of his οἶκος, and that οἶκος is being eaten away by the hoard of suitors who are, no doubt, counting on his "numberless gifts." If Penelope had been his sister or daughter, it would have been his responsibility to choose a husband for her, and it would have been in his power to insist on her participating in the marriage. His comments imply that it was also in his power to insist on his mother marrying, but he forgoes the right to exercise that power because he "dare not" force his mother to leave the οἶκος against her wishes.

Penelope stands in a position with her son that is different from that of any other woman in his οἶκος. He has power over her but allows her to make her own decisions, even when her decisions are diminishing his wealth.

---

95. Homer, *The Odyssey*, Book 20, Line 341-4. TR (Murray): " in no wise do I delay my mother's marriage, but I bid her wed what man she will, and I offer besides gifts past counting. But I am ashamed to drive her forth from the hall against her will by a word of compulsion. May God never bring such a thing to pass."

The other mother–son relationship in *The Odyssey* of significance to this discussion is that between Odysseus and his mother. In this relationship we do find deep pathos. When Odysseus meets his mother's ghost he asks her why she died. This is her reply:

> οὔτ' ἐμέ γ' ἐν μεγάροισιν εὔσκοπος ἰοχέαιρα
> οἷς ἀγανοῖς βελέεσσιν ἐποιχομένη κατέπεφνεν,
> οὔτε τις οὖν μοι νοῦσος ἐπήλυθεν, ἥ τε μάλιστα
> τηκεδόνι στυγερῇ μελέων ἐξείλετο θυμόν·
> ἀλλά με σός τε πόθος σά τε μήδεα, φαίδιμ' Ὀδυσσεῦ,
> σή τ' ἀγανοφροσύνη μελιηδέα θυμὸν ἀπηύρα.[96]

Here again we see a mother cheated of the opportunity to see her son honored in victory or in death. The depth of her grief over that loss was sufficient to lead to her death.

The plays of Euripides

The plays of Euripides, written roughly four hundred years after Homer's epics were first written down, occupy the same world and are concerned with some of the same characters. These plays exemplify the advice given by Aristotle concerning the poetics of tragedy:

> ἂν μὲν οὖν ἐχθρὸς ἐχθρόν, οὐδὲν ἐλεεινὸν οὔτε ποιῶν οὔτε μέλλων, πλὴν κατ' αὐτὸ τὸ πάθος· οὐδ' ἂν μηδετέρως ἔχοντες· ὅταν δ' ἐν ταῖς φιλίαις ἐγγένηται τὰ πάθη, οἷον ἢ ἀδελφὸς ἀδελφὸν ἢ υἱὸς πατέρα ἢ μήτηρ υἱὸν ἢ υἱὸς μητέρα ἀποκτείνῃ ἢ μέλλῃ ἤ τι ἄλλο τοιοῦτον δρᾷ, ταῦτα ζητητέον.[97]

---

96. Homer, *The Odyssey*, Book XI, Lines 198–203; TR: Neither did the keen-sighted archer goddess assail me in my halls with her gentle shafts, and slay me, nor did any disease come upon me, such as oftenest with loathsome wasting sores takes the spirit from the limbs; no, it was longing for you and for your counsels, glorious Odysseus, and for your gentle-heartedness, that robbed me of honey-sweet life. Homer, "The Osyssey, Books 1–12."

97. Aristotle, *Aristotle's Ars Poetica* §1453b TR: (S.H. Butcher) If an enemy kills an enemy, there is nothing to excite pity either in the act or the intention—except so far as the suffering in itself is pitiful. So again with indifferent persons. But when the tragic incident occurs between those who are near or dear to one another—if, for example, a brother kills, or intends to kill, a brother, a son his father, a mother her son, a son his mother, or any other deed of the kind is done—these are the situations to be looked for by the poet.

These plays are of value in this study because they reveal ancient expectations about family relationships by contorting them with violence and tragedy.

Orestes is one of a series of plays about a family that tears itself apart in a chain of events as tragic as Aristotle could wish. King Agamemnon, before leaving to participate in the events depicted in *The Iliad*, kills his daughter as a sacrifice. His wife, Clytemnestra, in revenge for that murder, takes a lover while her husband is away and murders Agamemnon upon his return. Their son, Orestes, with encouragement from the god Apollo and from his sister, Electra, murders his mother for the death of his father.

The question driving this series of plays forward is this: can matricide ever be justified? The question will eventually be decided in court, but in *Orestes*, it is played out in the mind of the protagonist. After committing the act, Orestes is overcome by crushing cognitive dissonance. In Electra's words:

> ἐντεῦθεν ἀγρίᾳ συντακεὶς νόσῳ νοσεῖ
> τλήμων Ὀρέστης ὅδε πεσὼν ἐν δεμνίοις
> κεῖται, τὸ μητρὸς δ' αἷμά νιν τροχηλατεῖ
> μανίαισιν: ὀνομάζειν γὰρ αἰδοῦμαι θεὰς
> εὐμενίδας, αἳ τόνδ' ἐξαμιλλῶνται φόβῳ.
> ἕκτον δὲ δὴ τόδ' ἦμαρ ἐξ ὅτου σφαγαῖς
> θανοῦσα μήτηρ πυρὶ καθήγνισται δέμας,
> ὧν οὔτε σῖτα διὰ δέρης ἐδέξατο,
> οὐ λούτρ' ἔδωκε χρωτί: χλανιδίων δ' ἔσω
> κρυφθείς, ὅταν μὲν σῶμα κουφισθῇ νόσου,
> ἔμφρων δακρύει, ποτὲ δὲ δεμνίων ἄπο
> πηδᾷ δρομαῖος, πῶλος ὣς ὑπὸ ζυγοῦ.[98]

He is facing a likely sentence of death, but it is not fear that prostrates him but guilt and confusion. He has avenged his father's murder,

---

98. Euripides, "Orestes" Lines 34-44. TR: After this my poor Orestes, wasting away in a cruel disease, [35] lies fallen on his couch, and it is his mother's blood that drives him round and round in frenzied fits; I am ashamed to name the goddesses, whose terrors are chasing him—the Eumenides. It is now the sixth day [40] since the body of his murdered mother was committed to the cleansing fire; since then no food has gone down his throat, nor has he washed his skin; but wrapped in his cloak he weeps in his lucid moments, whenever the fever leaves him. Euripides, "Orestes."

and done so at the instigation of Apollo. Could that possibly be wrong? Yet he has taken his own mother's life. Could that possibly be right?

We see here a son caught between his mother and his father, with the extremity of this crisis leaving him no course of action that his own conscience can condone. We have seen in *The Iliad* that a good son takes his mother's side and protects her from his father, and a clever son does this without angering his father. Orestes takes his murdered father's side, and then collapses under the conflict in his polis and his psyche.

Conclusions from Greek epic and mythology

This sketch of the mother–son relationships found in ancient Greek literature has provided several insights into the significance placed on that relationship within Greek culture. The mother–son relationship is, indeed, portrayed as one heavy with affect and pathos. Mothers experience deep conflict between their desire for their son's safety and for his honor. A good mother will send her son into battle and weep over his dead body. Sons also experience deep conflict between their loyalty to father and their attachment to mother. A good son will side with and protect his mother, while striving where possible to keep himself clear of his father's anger.

Roman historical literature

First-century Rome was a time of legally enforced "family values," with laws given by Augustus requiring marriage and child-bearing, of the aristocratic classes at least. Cassius Dio puts these words in the mouth of Augustus as he seeks to convince a group of bachelor knights of the virtues of marriage and parenting:

> πῶς δ' οὐ μακαριστόν, ἀπαλλαττόμενον ἐκ τοῦ βίου, διάδοχον καὶ κληρονόμον οἰκεῖον ἐξ ἑαυτοῦ γεγονότα καὶ τοῦ γένους καὶ τῆς οὐσίας καταλιπεῖν, καὶ τῇ μὲν φύσει τῇ ἀνθρωπίνῃ διαλυθῆναι τῇ δὲ ἐκείνου διαδοχῇ ζῆσαι.[99]

---

99. Cassius Dio, "Roman History"; Cassius Dio Cocceianus, *Dio's Roman History*, Book LVI Chapter 3 §5. TR: "Is it not blessed, on departing from life, to leave behind as successor and heir to your blood and substance one that is your own, sprung from your own loins, and to have only the human part of you waste away, while you live in the child as your successor." Cassius Dio, "Roman History."

While there is reason to believe there was some reluctance among the upper classes to marry and raise children, children who were produced appear to have been held in affection by their parents.

In Plutarch's *Coriolanus*, Marcius is met by his mother, his wife, and his children while he is encamped against Rome with a Volscian army. The meeting is described in this way:

> γενόμενος δὲ τοῦ πάθους ἐλάττων καὶ συνταραχθεὶς πρὸς τὴν ὄψιν οὐκ ἔτλη καθεζομένῳ προσελθεῖν, ἀλλὰ καταβὰς θᾶττον ἢ βάδην καὶ ἀπαντήσας πρώτην μὲν ἠσπάσατο τὴν μητέρα καὶ πλεῖστον χρόνον, εἶτα δὲ τὴν γυναῖκα καὶ τὰ τέκνα, μήτε δακρύων ἔτι μήτε τοῦ φιλοφρονεῖσθαι φειδόμενος, ἀλλ᾽ ὥσπερ ὑπὸ ῥεύματος φέρεσθαι τοῦ πάθους ἑαυτὸν ἐνδεδωκώς.[100]

We notice here first that this general is carried away by a torrent of emotion at the sight of his mother, and second that it was his mother, rather than his wife or children, whom he embraced first. Next, we find that he is convinced by his mother's pleas to withdraw from Rome. He says to his mother, νενίκηκας,' εἶπεν, 'εὐτυχῆ μὲν τῇ πατρίδι νίκην, ἐμοὶ δ᾽ ὀλέθριον: ἄπειμι γὰρ ὑπὸ σοῦ μόνης ἡττώμενος.[101] His army, though not altogether happy with this outcome, praises his virtue in responding to his mother in this way. Commentators do not censure him for this outpouring of emotion. Though such emotional displays would usually be seen as inappropriate in a Roman general, it appears that emotional expression in relation to one's mother is acceptable.

One new element in the maternal bond that comes to the fore in Roman history is the exercise of power by women through their sons. Livia Drusilla, also known as Julia Augusta, as an archetypal powerful Roman woman, is said to have been "an imperious mother and an amiable wife . . . a match for the diplomacy of her husband and the dissimulation of her son."[102]

---

100. Plutarch, "The Life of Coriolanus," §34 TR: [from same source] "mastered by his feelings, and confounded at what he saw, he could not endure to remain seated while they approached him, but descended quickly from the tribunal and ran to meet them. He saluted his mother first, and held her a long time in his embrace, and then his wife and children, sparing now neither tears nor caresses, but suffering himself as it were to be borne away by a torrent of emotion."

101. Plutarch, "The Life of Coriolanus," §36 TR: [from same source] "Thou art victorious, and thy victory means good fortune to my country, but death to me; for I shall withdraw vanquished, though by thee alone."

102. Tacitus, "The Annals," Book V, AD 29–31. English translations have been used for Latin sources.

Such powerful mothers have a tenuous reputation in Roman history. Though more than one mother was the real power behind her less than competent emperor son, such mothers are often accused of committing monstrous crimes in order to hold onto their (sons') power. Some of these mothers were more guilty than others of the crimes attributed to them, but sorting fact from suspicion is not necessary for the present task of identifying the values that lie behind the historians' accounts of these mother–son relationships.

Agrippina and Nero are the most infamous example of such a powerful mother–son political team. Agrippina was in a unique position to demonstrate the use of power in, over, through, and for family relationships. She had been daughter, sister, wife, niece, and mother of a succession of emperors.[103] According to Tacitus, Agrippina maneuvered her son into power so that she could rule from behind the throne. Tacitus appears certain that she murdered her husband, even naming her co-conspirator, Locusta.[104] Once she attained her goal she found herself with a dilemma. Her son developed some of his own ideas about how to rule the empire, and even more of his own ideas about how to manage his life.

When Nero fell in love with a woman of whom Agrippina did not approve, Tacitus claims that the mother "raved with a woman's fury about having a freedwoman for a rival, a slave girl for a daughter-in-law."[105] The word "rival" is interesting. What was Nero's lover a rival for? Her son's affection or her own power? Tacitus does not attempt to answer that question, but seems to see the two as having been dangerously blurred as Agrippina became increasingly desperate.

After observing that reproaching her son only reduced her power over him, Tacitus indicates that she tried the opposite extreme and became overly indulgent and permissive: "The change did not escape Nero; his most intimate friends dreaded it, and begged him to beware of the arts of a woman, who was always daring and was now false."[106]

We see here that Agrippina had other rivals. Nero's "most intimate friends" were also keen to be the ones to pull his strings. Just how desperate she then became was a matter for debate. Tacitus claims that their

---

103. Tacitus, "The Annals," Book XII.
104. Tacitus, "The Annals," Book XII.
105. Tacitus, "The Annals," Book XIII.
106. Tacitus, "The Annals," Book XIII.

relationship became incestuous, though his sources disagree on whether it was Agrippina or Nero who initiated the seduction.[107]

Though a sexually permissive society, at least as far as the aristocratic classes were concerned, Rome had boundaries beyond which an honorable man could not go. Committing incest with his mother, or even appearing to be inclined to do so, was well beyond one of those boundaries.

Agrippina found herself in an intense and desperate spiral with the offspring who refused to play the part of dutiful son. Given the influence they each had to order assassinations at the drop of a hint, this spiral could not go on for long. According to Tacitus, Agrippina died the death of a scorned mother exclaiming, "Smite my womb," as the centurion raised his sword.[108]

The details of this low point in Roman mother–son affection cannot be known with certainty, but we can comment on the popular perception of the relationship at the time and shortly afterwards. Agrippina was one of many imperial wives who were suspected of murdering their husbands in order to establish their sons as emperors. What conceptions of family relationship make this a believable accusation?

Supposing, as Tacitus did suppose, that Agrippina acted out of a desire to increase her own political power and prestige, murdering her husband only makes sense if this end could be attained more fully as the emperor's mother than as the emperor's wife. In that case, there must have been a public conception that a woman might have more power over her son than over her husband.

What form might that power have taken? The increasingly desperate and manipulative actions attributed to Agrippina imply that her power over her son did not lie in any legal obligation that she could impose upon him. Rather, given that her actions towards him were thoroughly situated in the affective realm, it is reasonable to assume that the power at her disposal was primarily emotional. This accords with Malina's contention that the mother–son bond in this culture could have greater emotional intensity than any other.

This point can be demonstrated even more directly if Agrippina's supposed murder of Claudius can be attributed to affection for her son rather than hunger for her own power. In that case her emotional

---

107. Tacitus, "The Annals," Book XIV.
108. Tacitus, "The Annals," Book XIV.

attachment to her son must have been far greater than her attachment to her husband.

Conclusions from Roman historical literature

This brief examination of one particularly notorious mother–son relationship in first-century Rome parallels my observations of Greek culture. The relationship here is highly, indeed dangerously, intense. Here too the mother demonstrates an intense commitment to her son's honor. In this new context it is *honor as rank* that concerns her, rather than *honor as victory*, though these cannot be strictly separated. Attaining the rank of emperor could be seen as the ultimate victory.

Again we see deep conflict in the maternal psyche. Unlike the selfless Homeric mothers, Agrippina's conflict, if we are to believe Tacitus, was between her own need for power and her inability, as a woman of her time, to gain ultimate power other than through the men she sought to manipulate. She gained power for herself through giving it to her son; yet once her son received ultimate power she could not force him to give it back to her.

This example does not touch on the lives of ordinary women of the artisan class and so cannot be directly applied to the mother of Jesus. However, it does illustrate something of the intensity of the mother–son bond in the Roman world, and of the options available to a woman seeking power and influence in her world.

Ancient Jewish Literature

The obvious place to turn to investigate the mother–son bond in Jewish literature is 4 Maccabees. This tale of the triumph of a Jewish mother and seven sons over Antiochus Epiphanes illustrates the strength of the mother–son bond and brings us back to the conflicting maternal desires for her sons' honor and their safety.[109]

Four Maccabees must be handled as Jewish literature with some care because it would be inappropriate to assume that the Stoic philosophy it contains was widely held, particularly in Palestine. Even so, the Jewish setting, the high praise of Torah and the patriarchs, and the time of composition, along with its obvious relevance to the discussion of

---

109. See deSilva, "Love for Offspring."

mother–son relationships, are sufficient reasons for its inclusion as first-century Jewish literature here. Certainly, the mother–son bond is given a particularly Jewish flavor in this story.

In this account of the torture and martyrdom of seven sons, the author places great focus on the emotional torture endured by the mother who watched their suffering and death. Like Aristotle, and perhaps under his influence, this author believed that mothers feel "deeper sympathy" for their children than do fathers, and in this way stamp their own character on their children.

> ψυχῆς τε καὶ μορφῆς ὁμοιότητα εἰς μικρὸν παιδὸς χαρακτῆρα θαυμάσιον ἐναποσφραγίζομεν, μάλιστα διὰ τὸ τῶν παθῶν τοῖς γεννηθεῖσιν τὰς μητέρας τῶν πατέρων καθεστάναι συμπαθεστέρας. (4 Mac 15:4)[110]

Along with affective intensity, this story also illustrates the deep conflict that we have seen in Greek and Roman literature:

> μήτηρ δυεῖν προκειμένων, εὐσεβείας καὶ τῆς ἑπτὰ υἱῶν σωτηρίας προσκαίρου κατὰ τὴν τοῦ τυράννου ὑπόσχεσιν, τὴν εὐσέβειαν μᾶλλον ἠγάπησεν τὴν σῴζουσαν εἰς αἰωνίαν ζωὴν κατὰ θεόν. (4 Macc 15:2–3)[111]

> διὰ τὸν πρὸς τὸν θεὸν φόβον ὑπερεῖδεν τὴν τῶν τέκνων πρόσκαιρον σωτηρίαν. (4 Mac 15:8)[112]

This mother is torn between the desire to preserve her sons' lives and her desire for their honor. In this case, the honor sought is *honor as virtue*, which is rewarded by God. To this mother, the choice appears to have been clear, but the author is at pains to point out that a less courageous mother would be likely to take the other path of forsaking virtue for the sake of life (4 Mac 16:6–11).

The affection of the young men for their mother is not described as explicitly as her affection for them, but it is clear that her strength gave them courage to face their tortures and death: καθάπερ γὰρ σὺ στέγη ἐπὶ

---

110. TR: [NRSV] We impress upon the character of a small child a wondrous likeness both of mind and of form. Especially is this true of mothers, who because of their birth pangs have a deeper sympathy toward their offspring than do the fathers.

111. TR: [NRSV] Two courses were open to this mother, that of religion, and that of preserving her seven sons for a time, as the tyrant had promised. She loved religion more, the religion that preserves them for eternal life according to God's promise.

112. TR: [NRSV] because of the fear of God she disdained the temporary safety of her children.

τοὺς στύλους τῶν παίδων γενναίως ἰδρυμένη ἀκλινὴς ὑπήνεγκας τὸν διὰ τῶν βασάνων σεισμόν. (4 Mac 17:3)[113]

Towards the end of the account the author makes explicit the metaphor of the athletic contest that had been employed throughout the account:

> Ἀληθῶς γὰρ ἦν ἀγὼν θεῖος ὁ δι' αὐτῶν γεγενημένος. ἠθλοθέτει γὰρ τότε ἀρετὴ δι' ὑπομονῆς δοκιμάζουσα. τὸ νῖκος ἀφθαρσία ἐν ζωῇ πολυχρονίῳ. Ελεαζαρ δὲ προηγωνίζετο, ἡ δὲ μήτηρ τῶν ἑπτὰ παίδων ἐνήθλει, οἱ δὲ ἀδελφοὶ ἠγωνίζοντο, ὁ τύραννος ἀντηγωνίζετο, ὁ δὲ κόσμος καὶ ὁ τῶν ἀνθρώπων βίος ἐθεώρει, θεοσέβεια δὲ ἐνίκα τοὺς ἑαυτῆς ἀθλητὰς στεφανοῦσα. (4 Mac 17:11–15) [114]

This metaphor demonstrates the definition of honor given earlier by Pitt-Rivers:

> Honor is the value of a person in his own eyes, but also in the eyes of his society. It is his estimation of his own worth, his claim to pride, but it is also the acknowledgement of that claim, his excellence recognized by society, his right to pride.[115]

The sons were competing for honor against Antiochus and against their own pain thresholds. They are honored not only by God but also by those spectators, including the author and readers of 4 Maccabees, who claim that their humiliating deaths were, in fact, triumphs of virtue. Their victory, in part at least, was due to the presence of their mother cheering them on.

Here, then, we see a Jewish version of the conflict that appears to be at the heart of every first-century-CE Mediterranean mother in relation to her sons. She longs for their safety, health, and long life, and for them to marry and produce children. Yet she also longs for their honor and, if a good mother, longs most earnestly for them to be honored by God for their virtue and faithfulness. Where faithfulness compromises safety a

---

113. TR: [NRSV] Nobly set like a roof on the pillars of your sons, you held firm and unswerving against the earthquake of the tortures.

114. TR: [NRSV] 11 Truly the contest in which they were engaged was divine, 12 for on that day virtue gave the awards and tested them for their endurance. The prize was immortality in endless life. 13 Eleazar was the first contestant, the mother of the seven sons entered the competition, and the brothers contended. 14 The tyrant was the antagonist, and the world and the human race were the spectators. 15 Reverence for God was victor and gave the crown to its own athletes.

115. Pitt-Rivers, *The Fate of Shechem*, 1.

good mother will urge her sons toward faithfulness, though not without inner torment.

Tobit presents one more aspect of the mother–son bond in the sacred duty of an eldest son to provide for his mother after his father's death. The reason given for the son looking after his mother is not the care she has given him since his birth but rather the risks she took in her pregnancy as she brought him into the world. That is, his mother should be honored simply because she is his mother, and not because she is a good mother.

> καὶ καλέσας αὐτὸν εἶπεν Παιδίον, ἐὰν ἀποθάνω, θάψον με, καὶ μὴ ὑπερίδῃς τὴν μητέρα σου, τίμα αὐτὴν πάσας τὰς ἡμέρας τῆς ζωῆς σου καὶ ποίει τὸ ἀρεστὸν αὐτῇ καὶ μὴ λυπήσῃς αὐτήν. μνήσθητι, παιδίον, ὅτι πολλοὺς κινδύνους ἑόρακεν ἐπὶ σοὶ ἐν τῇ κοιλίᾳ, ὅταν ἀποθάνῃ, θάψον αὐτὴν παρ᾽ ἐμοὶ ἐν ἑνὶ τάφῳ. (Tobit 4:3f) [116]

Conclusions

This chapter has sought to identify some of the assumptions in current scholarship regarding relationships between mothers and sons in the Greek/Roman/Jewish region of Palestine and its neighbors.

The assumption that honor was a male value and shame a female value has been challenged and nuanced. Honor gained through victory in battle was almost exclusively male, but women could achieve honor through social and political rank, though in this they faced far more obstacles than men. Honor through virtue, particularly in Jewish culture the honor accorded by God, could almost be said to be equally accessible to women as to men.

Accordingly, honoring Mary, at least with the honor of virtue, is an option that was open to the Gospel writers.

The assumption that the world was divided into female (inside domestic) space and male (outside commerce and political) space is not substantiated by archaeological investigation into the architecture of

---

116. TR [NRSV] Then he called his son Tobias, and when he came to him he said, "My son, when I die, give me a proper burial. Honor your mother and do not abandon her all the days of her life. Do whatever pleases her, and do not grieve her in anything. Remember her, my son, because she faced many dangers for you while you were in her womb. And when she dies, bury her beside me in the same grave."

Palestine, though it was certainly asserted as an ideal by ethicists of the time.

It is reasonable to assume, then, that Jesus and his mother would have met and spoken frequently in the course of daily life while Jesus was living in the family home. A mother and son speaking together in the public space of a wedding party would not be at all culturally inappropriate.

The line taken by many modern socio-historical scholars that, generally speaking, the most intense affective kinship bond in this culture was that between mother and son has been shown to be highly feasible. More work would be required to prove this beyond doubt by comparing this bond with others, but that work is beyond the scope of this present investigation. It is sufficient to have noticed, by triangulating Roman, Greek, and Jewish literature, that this bond was perceived as highly intense in all those cultures that influenced life in first-century Palestine.

The nature of this bond has been consistently shown to be one in which the mother experiences deep conflict between her desire to send her son into the world to win honor (through war or politics or virtue) and her longing to keep him safe. Less selfless mothers also experienced a conflict between seeking honor for their sons and seeking it for themselves in a world where political power was only available to women through their husbands and sons.

Sons, in turn, had a sacred duty to provide for and protect their mothers after the death of their fathers. Sons also tended to act as their mother's defenders against harsh treatment from their fathers or others. An emotional plea from a mother appears to have had an enormous amount of weight with virtuous sons.

This description given by Williams is reasonably apt:

> For a woman, this maternal-filial attachment is a source of power which she can exploit to achieve her own ends. As her son grows and matures, he becomes her supporter and defender, first against his father, and later against his own wife. Even in adulthood an "honorable" son is expected to obey his mother.[117]

All aspects of this bond appear to be intensified when the son is the mother's first.

It is reasonable to assume that Mary felt intensely attached to her special eldest son, and that she also knew well the conflict between her responsibility to send him into the world to achieve the honor for which

---

117. Williams, "The Mother of Jesus at Cana," 682.

he was born, and her fears about how that harsh world may challenge his honor and mistreat him. Whether she, as the woman behind a powerful man, may have sought to exert power through her son is a question worth investigating.

Jesus, as the eldest son of a widow, would no doubt have felt to the full extent the pull of affection and obligation to meet his mother's needs and assent to her requests. How he dealt with this pull while steadfastly fulfilling the task given him by his heavenly Father is an important aspect of this book.

The following chapter will bring us, at last, into the presence of that mother and son as they celebrate a wedding in Cana. The exegetical difficulties posed by John 2:4 and the plethora of possible interpretations that have been urged by various commentators have led to the necessity of allocating two chapters to the subject. Chapter 5 will consider patristic interpretations of the passage and chapter 6 will examine more recent scholarship and will form conclusions.

5

Patristic Perspectives on the Cana Wedding, with a Comment on Symbolism

John 2:1–11 has created so much difficulty for exegetes throughout its history that two chapters will be necessary to analyze scholarship to date and present some conclusions.[1] This chapter will examine patristic commentators and preachers on this passage and will present some theologically surprising interpretations. The allegorical readings found in many of the Church Fathers create the necessity for discussing how Johannine symbolism is to be interpreted in this book. Establishing an approach to symbolic interpretation will be important for all chapters that focus on exegesis of passages in John.

Chapter 6 will then seek a path through the maze of more recent work on this passage and eventually ask what it means to accurately to exegete this enigma. Finally, conclusions will be drawn concerning what the author may be saying about Jesus' family relationships in John 2:1–11.

These two chapters will seek to answer the questions:

- When Jesus said Τί ἐμοὶ καὶ σοί; in 2:4, was he distancing himself from his mother and claiming that he had no obligation to act in response to her statement of need? This is the line taken by most commentators, but is that not inconsistent with the context?

- Given that it was highly unusual for a son to address his mother as γύναι, what do we to make of Jesus using this word here?

---

1. Indeed, the complexity of John 2:4 is such that it would be a worthy subject for a doctoral book on its own.

- By saying οὔπω ἥκει ἡ ὥρα μου, was Jesus saying "no" with his words and then "yes" with his actions?
- How did the Church Fathers interpret Τί ἐμοὶ καὶ σοί;?
- Did they observe distance, or even rudeness, in Jesus' words?
- How did they interpret the symbolism in this passage?
- What approach, based on scholarly and philosophical considerations, will be taken to Johannine symbolism in this book?

Because this book seeks to uncover cultural assumptions that may inform better exegesis, it seems appropriate to begin the task of exegesis with those commentators who are closest, chronologically and geographically, to the events in the narrative. Exegetes from the early church era can reasonably be assumed to be more conversant with first-century culture than we who examine these works from 1,500 years more distant. In particular, they are in the best position to consider whether there might be anything possibly offensive in Jesus' words to his mother.

English translations will be used for Latin and Hebrew sources.

Patristic puzzlement over John 2:1–11

"Did Jesus come to the wedding in order to dishonor his mother?"

This question from Augustine of Hippo takes us to the heart of the exegetical difficulties posed by John's account of the wedding at Cana. This giant of Christian thinking found a deep mystery lurking within this conversation between a son and his mother where the words Τί ἐμοὶ καὶ σοί, γύναι; οὔπω ἥκει ἡ ὥρα μου (John 2:4) were spoken. Was the sinless one being rude to his mother? Was Jesus intentionally setting an example of filial disrespect? These are the questions Augustine posed to his congregation.

Another great preacher of the early church, John Chrysostom began his sermon on John 2:4 by speaking of the hard labor involved in preaching, and indicating that it was no slight question that was proposed by this verse.[2]

Augustine and Chrysostom went on to give their congregations answers to those questions, of course, but not until the Christians at Hippo and Constantinople had been given ample time to ponder the mystery.

---

2. John Chrysostom, *Homilies*, XXII.

Following in their footsteps, I intend to leave verse 4 to the end of the discussion of patristic interpretations of Cana. I will begin with some generalities, move through early interpretations of some of the other elements of the sign at Cana, and then return to verse 4.

The usefulness of early interpretations

In the introduction to his work on early interpretations of the Fourth Gospel, Maurice Wiles wrote:

> There are some books of the Bible whose interpretation has been so completely revolutionized by modern critical methods that the exegesis of earlier centuries is unlikely to add much of value to our understanding of them. There is probably no book of which this is less true than the Fourth Gospel.[3]

In the half-century since Wiles wrote those words, the direction that biblical studies has taken has brought many of us to a greater appreciation of the early commentators. Narrative criticism and the use of social sciences have taught us to be a little more humble as we approach the work of our older brothers and sisters. The genres in which the New Testament was written were more familiar to those who were educated closer to its literary world. Early commentators are culturally closer to the presuppositions and values of the original authors and readers of the New Testament. Their perspective has a tendency to throw light on features of the text that we are most likely to overlook or to find confusing.

The miracle as sign

Many early commentators notice John's use of the word "sign" and infer that the author intended the miracles to point toward a deeper meaning[4] or a meaning beyond history.[5] At the very least, according to Augustine, the works of the man Jesus should direct our attention and praise to the God Jesus who created all things.[6] By doing the extraor-

---

3. Wiles, *The Spiritual Gospel*, 1.

4. e.g., Origen, *Commentary on the Gospel of John*, 13, 64.

5. Wiles notices that Origen never actually finds the significance in historical time, but always in the eschaton. (Wiles, *The Spiritual Gospel*, 42).

6. Augustine, "Tractate Viii"; Augustine, "Tractate Viii," §2.

dinary, God strikes people with wonder then with love and gratitude[7] so that, "He may rouse men as from sleep to worship him."[8] In the Old Testament, miracles were performed by God's spoken word, and in the Gospels by God's incarnate Word.[9]

For Irenaeus, this particular sign, along with the feeding of the 5,000, indicates that Christ is one with the creator.[10] Augustine says that it should be no surprise that the Lord turned water to wine since the same Lord turns water (in the form of rain) into wine (through the activity of grape vines) every day.[11] The identification of Jesus with the creator was important in the debate with Gnostics, including Manicheans, who held that creation was evil and the product of a lesser god.

For Origen, the main point of the sign is that Christ is the bringer of joy to his companions [12] and the location of this sign in Cana represents the calling of the Gentiles. For him, the water is the old wine of the law that has failed and is replaced by the good wine of the Gospel[13] and for Clement, the water of the law is turned into wine by the addition of Christ's blood.[14]

Chrysostom gives his congregation an interpretation that is at once more general and more readily applicable to their own lives. People who are "weak as water" can become strong when they come to the Lord. His description of watery men comes (perhaps dangerously) close to resembling the pompous yet transitory nature of the imperial court not far from the cathedral where he preached.[15] Similarly, Augustine tells his congregation that without Christ they were water, but now they have become wise in becoming wine.[16]

---

7. Augustine, "Tractate Viii," §3.

8. Augustine, "Tractate Viii," §1.

9. Augustine, "Tractate Viii," §1.

10. Irenaeus, "Against Heresies," Book III.xi.5; Wiles indicates that this line of thought is also found in Origen, Athanasius, and Chrysostom. See Wiles, *The Spiritual Gospel*, 42.

11. Augustine, "Tractate Viii," §1.

12. Origen, *Commentary on the Gospel of John*, Book XX.

13. Origen, "Fragments," §74.

14. Clement of Alexandria, "The Instructor," Book II.ii; Variations on this interpretation are found in most Alexandrian commentators. See Wiles, *The Spiritual Gospel*, 43.

15. Chrysostom, *Homilies*, XXII.

16. Augustine, "Tractate Viii," §3.

While several early commentators find Eucharistic imagery in the wine and the water, the sign as a whole does not tend to be interpreted sacramentally. Irenaeus has the greatest sacramental thrust, where he sees the imagery indicating that Mary wanted to partake of the cup ahead of time.[17] Jerome, in a discussion of baptism, finds it significant that Jesus' first miracle involved water.[18] Overall, though, Eucharistic imagery is a very minor theme in patristic interpretations of the Cana sign.

I now turn to analyze some of the details of patristic exegesis of this passage.

γάμος ἐγένετο

These words might easily pass without comment by modern exegetes. Not so those in the early church. Augustine tells his congregation not to be surprised that Jesus attended a wedding, as though there was some danger of them being scandalized by such an occurrence.

The presence of Jesus at a wedding seems to have forced Jerome reluctantly to concede that marriage may sometimes be an acceptable option for a Christian:

> For the Church does not condemn marriage, but only subordinates it. It does not reject it altogether, but regulates it, knowing . . . that 'in a great house there are not only vessels of gold and of silver, but also of wood and of earth; and some to honor and some to dishonor.[19]

Gregory Nazianzen also insisted that, though he attributed greater honor to virginity, he did not dishonor marriage, since Jesus had honored marriage through his presence at a wedding. [20]

Cyril of Alexandria sees that Jesus' presence at the wedding blesses and sanctifies the children to be born from that union, and removes the woman's sorrow in childbearing.[21]

Fourth- and fifth-century commentators tend unanimously to respond to Jesus' attendance at a wedding with embarrassed comments

17. Irenaeus, "Against Heresies," Book III.xvi.7; see also Wiles, *The Spiritual Gospel*, 44.
18. Jerome, "Letters of St Jerome," LXIX. To Oceanus.
19. Jerome, "Letters of St Jerome," XLVIII. To Pammachius, 71.
20. Gregory Nazianzen, "Select Orations," Oration XI. Xviii.
21. Cyril of Alexandria, "Commentary on the Gospel of John," ii.2,3.

along the lines of: "Of course we don't condemn marriage, after all Jesus went to a wedding . . . " The honor ascribed to virginity at that time was so widely and strongly felt that this wedding appears to have been a significant, and sometimes solitary, check against ascetic excesses.

Augustine allegorized Jesus' attendance at a wedding in a number of ways, including as the marriage between the Word and human flesh, in which Mary's womb became a bridal chamber.[22]

Later in his sermon Augustine takes this theme deeper. Referring to Ephesians 5:31–2, he asks in what way Jesus left his father and mother. His answer is that Jesus left his Father by the self-emptying described in Philippians 2:7; and he left his mother by "leaving the synagogue of the Jews, of which, after the flesh, he was born, and by cleaving to the church which he has gathered out of all nations."[23]

ἡ μήτηρ τοῦ Ἰησοῦ

Augustine implies that John uses the epithet, ἡ μήτηρ τοῦ Ἰησοῦ, rather than referring to Mary by name, in order to underscore the fact that Jesus was born as human to a human mother. Had John just called her Mary, the passage would have left room for Docetists to deny her role as the source of Jesus' humanity.[24]

ἦσαν δὲ ἐκεῖ λίθιναι ὑδρίαι ἕξ

For Augustine, the water represents prophecy in which Christ is not understood. Wine, he says, is latent within water. When the prophets are read through an understanding of the Gospel, they not only become delicious, they can even make you intoxicated![25] In this way, Jesus changed water into wine once again on the road to Emmaus as he taught the disciples to read the Scriptures in the light of his life, death, and resurrection.[26] Augustine argues that if Jesus had created the wine from nothing, rather than by turning water into wine, he would have appeared to reject the Old Testament Scriptures, but because he takes water and turns it into

---

22. Augustine, "Tractate Viii," §4.
23. Augustine, "Tractate Ix," §10.
24. Augustine, "Tractate Viii," §6.
25. Augustine, "Tractate Ix," §3.
26. Augustine, "Tractate Ix," §5.

wine he honors the water, the Old Testament,[27] and shows that it also is his, but is tasteless without him.[28]

Chrysostom, always less inclined to take an allegorical approach, believed that Jesus first had the pots filled with water in order to make the miracle more credible, so that the servants who filled them could be witnesses to the miracle, and to contradict those who believed him to be opposed to the creator God (i.e., Gnostics) by making use of created matter.[29] Irenaeus takes a similar line by insisting that the same God who created the earth and commanded it to produce fruit was at work here producing wine through his Son.[30]

κατὰ τὸν καθαρισμὸν τῶν Ἰουδαίων

Chrysostom believed that the detail given in John's description adds weight to the evidence for divine activity.[31] Because the pots were used for Jewish purification, we know that they could not have contained wine dregs that would have become weak wine when mixed with water.[32]

Origen similarly believed that the miracle was rendered more believable by the employment of servants, rather than disciples, to fill the pots.[33]

---

27. Augustine explained that the six water pots represent the six ages of humanity:
    1. Adam to Noah
    2. Noah to Abraham
    3. Abraham to David
    4. David to the Babylonian exile
    5. Exile to John the Baptist
    6. John the Baptist to the end of the world

Jesus turned all six pots of water into wine, that is, he made all prophecy from those periods tasty and inebriating when read with reference to himself. Augustine, "Tractate Ix," §5.

28. Augustine, "Tractate Ix", §5.

29. Chrysostom, *Homilies*, XXII. He fills out the latter point in words almost identical to Augustine's: "But now to show that is He who transmutes water in the vine plants, and who converts the rain by its passage through the root into wine, He affected that in a moment at the wedding which in the plant is long in doing."

30. Irenaeus, "Against Heresies," Book III, §xi.5.

31. See Wiles, *The Spiritual Gospel*, 26.

32. Chrysostom, *Homilies*, XXII.

33. Origen, "Fragments," §29.

φέρετε τῷ ἀρχιτρικλίνῳ·

Chrysostom insists that those entrusted with the management of a wedding remain sober and focused on their responsibility, regardless of how intoxicated the guests have become. He was then the one man who could be most relied upon to give sober judgment as to the quality of the wine.[34]

σὺ τετήρηκας τὸν καλὸν οἶνον ἕως ἄρτι.

According to a number of Church Fathers, including Augustine[35] and Cyril,[36] the new, better wine is the Gospel, the old wine the law. Chrysostom notes that the miracles of Jesus are better than the operations of nature.[37]

Clement, like many recent interpreters, is anxious to insist that Jesus' creation of wine here does not give permission for Christians to get drunk![38]

ἐφανέρωσεν τὴν δόξαν αὐτοῦ

Chrysostom wonders how Jesus' glory could have been manifest in a miracle that was so quiet and unobserved. He resolves this first by noticing that it did not stay in obscurity, but has become known to all Christians by its inclusion in John's Gospel; and second by asserting that it was appropriate for his disciples, who had already demonstrated some level of faith in him, to be the witnesses to this sign.[39]

Τί ἐμοὶ καὶ σοί, γύναι;

Jesus' apparent failure to acknowledge his mother is seen by Augustine as an "indubitable mystery," and so he asks, "Did he come to the marriage for the purpose of teaching men to treat their mothers with contempt?"[40]

---

34. Chrysostom, *Homilies*, XXII.
35. Augustine, "Tractate Ix," §2.
36. Cyril of Alexandria, "Commentary on the Gospel of John," ii.11.
37. Chrysostom, *Homilies*, XXII.
38. Clement of Alexandria, "The Instructor," Book II.2.
39. Chrysostom, *Homilies*, XXIII.
40. Augustine, "Tractate Viii," §5.

Augustine refers to some people (later identified as Manichaeans[41]) who infer from this phrase that Jesus was not born of the Virgin Mary. Of these he says that those who "appear to honour Christ in such wise as to deny that he had flesh, do nothing short of proclaiming him a liar."[42]

Augustine's words imply that, at least in a fifth-century context, these words sounded so dismissive that some could not believe Jesus could have said them to his mother.[43]

Augustine finds the answer to this mystery in the two natures of Christ. He amplifies Jesus' words to mean: "That in me which works a miracle was not born of you, you did not give birth to my divine nature; but because my weakness was born of you, I will recognize you at the time when that same weakness shall hang upon the cross."[44] Though he was both "the Lord of Mary and the son of Mary,"[45] at the time when he performed this miracle he was acting as Lord only, and so did not recognize her as his mother, but assured her that he would recognize her when his "hour" came.

Augustine did not have the benefit of the Council of Chalcedon's definition, which acknowledged that the two natures of Christ are unconfused, unchangeable, indivisible, and inseparable. He was not to know that his neat solution to this exegetical difficulty would sound like Nestorian heresy a couple of decades after his death. Yet Augustine was not alone in his interpretation.

Theodoret, who was deeply involved in the Nestorian controversy as one who wished to hold onto his orthodox credentials while refusing to be unfairly critical of Nestorius, wrote that just as Jesus could at one time call himself Son of Man and at another Son of God, so he could at one time honor his mother as her son and at another rebuke her as her Lord.[46]

More than a century after Chalcedon, Gregory the Great continued this line of interpretation. He begins with a paraphrase of Jesus' words:

41. Augustine, "Tractate Viii," §8.

42. Augustine, "Tractate Viii", §5.

43. It is worth noting, though, that in contrast to Augustine's struggle to understand, Cyril believed that Jesus' reply was entirely appropriate. It demonstrated that Jesus was not too hasty in performing miracles and also showed great honor to his mother because he did for her what he was not initially willing to do. (Cyril of Alexandria, "Commentary on the Gospel of John," ii.4).

44. Augustine, "Tractate Viii," §9 (language modernized).

45. Augustine, "Tractate Viii," §9.

46. Theodoret, "Dialogue Ii.—the Unconfounded," 194.

"That I can do a miracle comes to me of my Father, not of my Mother." For He who of the nature of His Father did miracles had it of His mother that He could die. So also, when He was on the cross, in dying He acknowledged His mother . . . He says, then, *Woman, what have I to do with you? My hour is not yet come.* That is, "In the miracle, which I have not of your nature, I do not acknowledge you. When the hour of death shall come, I shall acknowledge you as my mother, since I have it of you that I can die."[47]

It seems that it has always been the case that keeping the two natures of Christ unconfused and at the same time undivided is a challenge to the vocabulary as well as to the understanding.

Going back to the fourth century and into the heart of the Arian debate we find Athanasius saying of this verse: "He chid[48] His Mother, saying, 'My hour is not yet come,' and then at once He made the water wine. For He was Very God in the flesh, and He was true flesh in the Word."[49] Athanasius makes little attempt to be overly clear, but considers that the mystery of this verse is contained within the mystery of the incarnation.

Though modern scholars sometimes single out the use of the word γύναι as possibly being dismissive, it does not become a focus of concern for these Church Fathers. It is Jesus' question, not his form of address, that seems to trouble them.

οὔπω ἥκει ἡ ὥρα μου.

Chrysostom notices the other places in the Gospel where the hour is mentioned (7:30, 8:20, and 17:1) and infers that Jesus did all things at the right time in order to promote order and subdue chaos. In this instance, the time is not appropriate because Jesus had not yet been manifest to the majority of the people and had not finished gathering together his band of disciples.[50] He also suggests that Jesus would have preferred, rather than his mother, that those who wanted the wine had come to him to request the favor.[51]

---

47. Gregory the Great, "Selected Epistles," Epistle XXXIX (some modernization of language).

48. Archaic form of "chided."

49. Athanasius, "Discourses against the Arians," III.41 [Greek unavailable.]

50. Chrysostom, *Homilies*, XXII.

51. Chrysostom, *Homilies*, XXII.

Chrysostom then spells out the reasons why Jesus performed the miracle after an initial refusal:

1. To demonstrate that the creator of times and ages was not subject to fate.[52] The time was not right, but he was free to perform the miracle anyway. (Augustine similarly refutes the claim of astrologists that Christ was under fate[53] by quoting John 10:18.[54])

2. To show that he was not without power.

3. To honor his mother, because to refuse her request would have been to contradict and shame her.

4. Because we sometimes make ourselves worthy to receive through perseverance. On another occasion (Mat 15:21–8) Jesus granted the request of a Canaanite woman after an initial refusal. Jesus' mother also persevered because she took his refusal as a sign of humility.[55]

Augustine paraphrases Jesus' words in this way: "When I know that it is the fitting time for me to suffer, when my suffering will be profitable, then I will willingly suffer. That hour is not yet."[56] Origen[57] and Athanasius[58] also connect the hour with Jesus' suffering and death.

Augustine continues his argument by speaking again of the two natures of Christ:

> For he who hungered because he was man, fed so many thousands with five loaves because he was God; He who slept because he was man, commanded the winds and the waves because He was God. All these things had yet to be set forth, that the evangelist might have whereof to write, that there might be what should be preached to the church. But when he had done as much as he judged to be sufficient, then his hour came, not of necessity, but of will; not of condition, but of power.[59]

---

52. Chrysostom, *Homilies*, XXII.
53. Augustine, "Tractate Viii," §8.
54. Augustine, "Tractate Viii," §10.
55. Chrysostom, *Homilies*, XXII.
56. Augustine, "Tractate Viii," §12.
57. Origen, "Commentary on Matthew," 97.
58. Socrates, "Ecclesiastical History" Chapter VIII. — "Quotations from Athanasius," "Defense of his Flight."
59. Augustine, "Tractate Viii," §12.

Timely exegesis

Table 2 outlines the controversies of the early church that were drawn into the exegesis of John 2:1–11. The weight this table gives to fifth-century commentators does not indicate that the passage was employed any less in earlier centuries, merely that more documents have survived from the fifth century.

Initial conclusions concerning Patristic interpretations

Have the Church Fathers shed the anticipated light on John 2:1–11? I would initially concede that they have not been as insightful as I had hoped, but in three ways they have helped point the way forward.

Firstly, they have agreed that John 2:4 is an exegetical mystery. Jesus' address to his mother here sounds dismissive to twenty-first-century ears, and we might assume that we have missed an underlying tone of tenderness because of our cultural distance from the author. These teachers, who were much closer in time and culture, assure us that Jesus' words sounded just as dismissive to them as they do to us.

Secondly, we see the priority of pastoral care in the preaching of these men. These early interpreters have searched this text for anything that might feed their congregations and arm them against error. This one sign narrative has been enlisted in polemic against Docetists, Manicheans, Marcionists, Arians, astrologers, and (non-Christian) Jews. This one miracle declares the divinity and humanity of Jesus, the value of marriage, the dangers of wealth, and the superiority of the gospel over the law. These men are open to the accusation of eisegesis here, as are we all when we expect a passage such as this to answer our questions rather than allowing it to correct and interrogate us. Yet it was in the service of truth and for the good of their congregations that they overstepped the bounds of sound exegesis.

Finally, and centrally, though none of these men has conclusively demystified the passage, they have made it clear that the key to understanding it is to be found in the uniqueness of the relationship between Jesus and his mother. Mary's son was also her creator. Jesus' mother would find salvation only by kneeling before him as his disciple. That such a relationship might cause confusion in a social gathering is hardly surprising.

Theological Disputes Raised in Patristic Exegesis of John 2:1–11				
	2nd C	3rd C	4th C	5th C
Divinity of Jesus	Irenaeus			Augustine
Against Docetism (Jesus was fully human)				Augustine
Gospel superior to Jewish law; church superior to synagogue		Clement Origen		Cyril Augustine
Against astrology (Jesus not under fate)				Augustine Chrysostom
Against Gnosticism (Christ one with creator)	Irenaeus	Origen	Athanasius	Augustine Chrysostom
Virginity (marriage not to be forbidden)				Jerome Gregory Nazianzen John of Damascus
Two Natures of Christ			Athanasius	Augustine Theodoret [Gregory the Great]
Reliability of Scripture				Augustine
Against wealth and opulence				Chrysostom
Sacraments	Irenaeus			Jerome

Table 2

Allegorical and symbolic interpretation

One other point from these Fathers is worth noting. Their exegesis here provides an opportunity to comment on their use of allegorical interpretation. This continues to be of relevance to any exegete of the Fourth Gospel because the tension between literal and symbolic interpretation remains a source of dispute among commentators.

Dodd is among those who assert that because this miracle is described as a σημεῖον that revealed Jesus' δόξα it "is not to be taken at face value."[60] That is, the reader should not imagine a historical occurrence behind the text. Ridderbos makes a similar assertion, though from another direction. He claims that "to the degree that the 'theological' or 'symbolic' interpretation asserts itself, to that degree the form of the text (which presents itself as historical) must surrender more of its rights and must be interpreted ultimately as a distinct literary genre."[61]

However, he also insists that, "any suggestion that in the Fourth Gospel one can separate 'flesh' and 'glory,' history and revelation, violates the most specific aspect of that Gospel's character. Miracle is neither parabolic story nor symbolic action."[62]

Symbol need not override or undervalue history.[63] It is within history and flesh that symbol and glory are discerned. This is why most of John's signs include lengthy accounts of their meaning. They involve mystery and not everyone is able to "see" Jesus' glory in them.

In discussing John 10, van der Watt contends:

> The imagery functions with the presupposition that what applies to sheep farming can effectively express (by way of analogy) what is true of the spiritual world. This further presupposes a point of view that sees no tension between what happens on earth and the things on a spiritual level. That is why spiritual truths can be based on what is accepted to be true on an earthly level.[64]

---

60. Dodd, *Interpretation of the Fourth Gospel*, 297.
61. Ridderbos, *Gospel According to John*, 101.
62. Ridderbos, *Gospel According to John*, 100.
63. Hunter, *According to John*, 74.
64. van der Watt, *Family of the King*, 141.

Recent interpreters acknowledge that symbol and metaphor are not at all out of place in historical narrative.[65] Just as Jesus' glory was revealed in his flesh, spiritual meaning and theological insight can be discerned within the historical record of his life; in fact spiritual reality conveyed by means of earthly reality echoes the way the glory of God is conveyed in the flesh of Jesus of Nazareth.

At this point it is worth considering Watson's words in relation to allegorical interpretations of the Gospels. By *allegorical* Watson means a reading that looks only for the symbolic and places no importance on the literal meaning.

Allegorical interpretation subordinates the "letter" or "body" of a text to its "spirit," understanding the transition from one to the other as an *ascent* into spiritual realms that transcend bodiliness. In the case of allegorical interpretation of the Gospels, this scheme will have an obvious impact on Christology. The flesh of the incarnate Word—his concrete historical existence, its contingent unfolding in the context of other contingencies—is the subject matter only of the "letter" or "body" of the text, and is held to be significant not in itself but as an indirect disclosure of the higher reality of the Word itself in relation to the human spirit.[66]

Driving a wedge between the literal and the symbolic in the Gospels may implicitly be a denial of the incarnation. It is, in Watson's words, precisely in the "body" that the "spirit" is to be found.

Chapter 1 of this book observed that the Gospels were written in the genre of the ancient βίος. Given its affinity with portraiture, the employment of symbolism is particularly appropriate in this genre. The author of the Fourth Gospel has clearly employed symbolism carefully and deliberately in the way he has described the historical record of Jesus' life, making it clear that he had an extensive palate to draw from in painting this particular portrait (20:31; 21:25).

Differences of opinion about symbolism are not new. John Chrysostom and Augustine of Hippo have already been contrasted in this respect. Chrysostom confines his exegesis to the literal meaning of the text and only in his application does he become broad and encompassing of the needs and life situation of his congregation. Augustine presents his congregation with a more generous text; one with much more to offer than

---

65. Bruce, *Gospel of John*, 72; Borchert, *John 1–11*, 157; Morris, *The Gospel According to John*, 176; Tenney, "John," 43; Hunter, *According to John*, 74; Carson, *The Gospel According to John*, 166–67.

66. Watson, "Toward a Literal Reading of the Gospels," 214.

is found in its initial literal reading. Yet his sermons on John 2:1–11 draw a clear distinction between the authority of the literal, historical reading and that of his symbolic interpretation. In relation to the historical level of the text, he warned his congregation with these words:

> But if it be asked of you, why he made this answer to his mother, let him declare who understands; but he who does not as yet understand, let him most firmly believe that Jesus made this answer, and made it moreover to his mother. By this piety he will learn to understand also why Jesus answered thus, if by praying he knock at the door of truth, and do not approach it with wrangling.[67]

Piety demands that they first believe it and then try to understand it. Clearly, at this level, the text has authority that requires the submission and compliance of the intellect of the reader. In contrast, consider what he told them about the allegorical interpretations that he was presenting. "But there is also another meaning that must not be passed over, and which I will declare: let every man choose which he likes best. We keep not back what is suggested to us. For it is the Lord's table, and the minister ought not to defraud the guests."[68]

At the level of allegorical interpretation the intellect of the reader (and hearer) has authority over the symbol. The reader/hearer may exercise discrimination. Augustine likens preaching at this level to a banquet laden with dishes. Members of the congregation may fill their plates from whatever dish they choose.

Augustine's preaching certainly tended to be allegorical, but he did not downplay the historicity or authority of the literal reading or give undue authority to his symbolic interpretations.

In this Augustine gives helpful guidance to those attempting to exegete this Gospel today. Yet his guidance is not sufficient. Is symbolism really about picking and choosing as the reader sees fit? Surely, if the author included symbols in the text, as John certainly did, then he expected his readers to be able to interpret them as he intended.

Symbols never communicate with the same clarity as factual reports, but they are, nevertheless, a form of communication. What they communicate is often deeper, more elusively attractive, and more transformative than bare prose.

---

67. Augustine, "Tractate Viii," §7.
68. Augustine, "Tractate Ix," §9.

Symbols can be distracting, and Brown is helpful when he calls readers to focus on what the author focuses on:

> John does not put primary emphasis on the replacing of the water for Jewish purifications, nor on the action of changing water to wine (which is not described in detail) nor even on the resultant wine. John does not put primary emphasis on Mary or her intercession, nor on why she pursued her request, nor on the reaction of the headwaiter or of the groom. The primary focus is, as in all Johannine stories, on Jesus as the one sent by the Father to bring salvation to the world. What shines through is his glory, and the only reaction that is emphasized is the belief of the disciples.[69]

Yet, in any great portrait it is the light and shade of the "minor" details that draw the viewer's attention in the direction the artist intended. Misunderstanding those details may result in the viewer's attention being misdirected, especially when the portrait is literary rather than visual. Where symbol is used it is necessary to have some understanding of the symbolic conventions of author and assumed reader.

Convention forms a common ground of interpretation between author and reader that is generally assumed rather than made explicit in the text. This can be challenging because the present-day exegete does not naturally share that symbolic common ground with the author.[70] Particular symbols are sometimes "conventionalized" as internal symbols within a text where the reader is taught by repetition to relate a symbol to a particular meaning.[71] In John, the prologue orients the reader toward seeing symbolic undertones in references to light and darkness, birth, origin, and blood. Further on, repetition teaches the reader to see symbolism also in eating and drinking, water, time, seeing, and blindness. In addition to these internal symbols, the symbolic world of Judaism, particularly OT Scripture, was also regularly drawn upon in John's communication. Agricultural images (viticulture, shepherding) are also employed, and their symbolic import tends to be explained rather than assumed.[72] Whether pagan symbols were also employed is more controversial among commentators. This will become relevant in the discussion

---

69. Brown, *Gospel According to John (I-XII)*, 104.
70. van der Watt, *Family of the King*, 2.
71. van der Watt, *Family of the King*, 3.
72. van der Watt, *Family of the King*, 139.

of whether wine carried symbolic weight for Gentile as well as Jewish readers.

Meeks is quite incorrect, then, when he argues that John could not have been used in missionary endeavor because, "only a very rare outsider would get past the barrier of its closed metaphorical system."[73] The metaphorical system is sophisticated, certainly, but not closed. My suspicion is that Meeks sees the metaphorical system as closed because he reads meaning into the symbols that none of the early readers would have seen. Meeks decides what Johannine metaphors mean. He then points out that only those in the Johannine inner circle would have been able to see that meaning. He, therefore, concludes that the Gospel was written only for insiders. The question must be asked: if Johannine metaphor is completely opaque to all but the insiders in the Johannine community, how is it that a twentieth-century, social science, New Testament scholar like Meeks is able to penetrate it? Further, if it is such an insider document, why has this Gospel remained a text deeply beloved through two millennia by millions of people in a multiplicity of cultural and theological locations? If the Gospel was written in order to exclude outsiders, it has completely failed in its purpose.

A much more straightforward explanation might be that Meeks is incorrect in his reading of Johannine metaphor. If most first-century Christians would fail to see in this Gospel the things that Meeks sees, then perhaps Meeks is seeing things that are simply not there.

It is certainly true that language can be used to exclude outsiders. Speaking a foreign language or dialect tends to shut out those who cannot understand. Jargon often serves the same function. Campbell sees John as employing "Anti-Language," a halfway point between dialect and jargon that quite deliberately keeps outsiders in the dark.[74] While she correctly notices that the Fourth Gospel employs relexicalization (giving fresh meaning to familiar words) and overlexicalization (using a multiplicity of words to identify the same concept) which she claims are the major features of anti-language, she does not thereby prove her case that John's language is employed with the specific purpose of leaving outsiders in the dark. Relexicalization and overlexicalization are common to many poetic forms. Metaphorical language often has the potential of frustrating those who lack the energy, inclination, or tools to uncover its meaning, but this

---

73. Meeks, "The Son of Man in Johannine Sectarianism," 162–3.
74. Campbell, *Kinship Relations*, 163–80.

is very rarely its primary purpose. On the contrary, metaphor tends to be invitational, wooing the reader into closer engagement.[75]

Within the Fourth Gospel, symbols open meaning to new possibilities that bare prose may not communicate adequately. They are not closed but neither do they create infinitely open meaning. They remain a form of communication: a code that John's audience must have been in a position to interpret. Today we must take care to put aside the symbolic world of our own time and draw upon the symbolic world of the first century. "Sanctified restraint in interpretation is an important part of sanctified imagination."[76]

It is also important to keep in mind that within the narrative, seeing the reality behind the sign is not an intellectual exercise in deciphering metaphors. It is a matter of faith. Those who "see" are not merely understanding a form of communication; they are seeing Christ in the person of Jesus. Those who fail to acknowledge the deeper significance of the sign have not really "seen" the sign at all, regardless of how insightfully they have analyzed the metaphors.[77] Watt has rightly noted that, "faith is the literal theological description of what happens between a person and Jesus. To *see* falls under the metaphorical category. One sees the Agent of God, the Son of the Father, for who he is; overwhelmed by this reality, one submits to the Son and the Father. [Seeing] indicates 'full appreciation of true reality.'"[78;79]

Having examined the connection between the literal and metaphorical in this Gospel, a last word on the subject might be appropriately given to John Donne:

> My God, my God, thou art a direct God, may I not say a literal God, a God that wouldst be understood literally and according to the plain sense of all that thou sayest, but thou art also (Lord, I intend it to thy glory, and let no profane misinterpreter abuse it to thy diminution,) thou art a figurative, a metaphorical God too; a God in whose words there is such a height of figures, such voyages, such peregrinations to fetch remote and precious metaphors, such extensions, such spreadings, such curtains of allegories, such third heavens of hyperboles, so

---

75. See Barton, "Can We Identify the Gospel Audiences?" 192–3.
76. Borchert, *John 1-11*, 158.
77. Ridderbos, *The Gospel According to John*, 100.
78. Quoting Collins, *These Things Have Been Written*, 51.
79. van der Watt, *Family of the King*, 282.

harmonious elocutions, so retired and so reserved expressions, so commanding persuasions, so persuading commandments, such sinews even in thy milk, and such things in thy words, as all profane authors seem of the seed of the serpent that creeps, thou art the Dove that flies.[80]

Conclusions

Patristic scholarship has thrown some light on this complex and enigmatic passage. It has confirmed that we ought to wonder whether Jesus was being abrupt, if not rude, to his mother. It has also directed us toward the mystery of the incarnation as a way of understanding Jesus' words, or at least as a way of accepting that they cannot be fully understood.

I have demonstrated that many of the Church Fathers interpreted Τί ἐμοὶ καὶ σοί, γύναι; as a rebuke and read those words as the creator speaking to his creation rather than as a son speaking to his mother. They agree together that as words of a son to his mother they seem offensive. This is a significant discovery to take into the next chapter as it confirms that it is not simply our twenty-first-century cultural filter that makes modern readers wonder if Jesus was being impolite to his mother here.

Though modern scholars sometimes single out the use of the word γύναι as possibly being dismissive, it does not become a focus of concern for these Church Fathers. It is Jesus' question, not his form of address, that seems to trouble them.

Some of the Fathers, including Chrysostom, argued that one reason why Jesus went on to perform the miracle after an initial hesitation was to avoid shaming his mother with an outright refusal. Others speak of Jesus being fully in control of his own timetable rather than being subject to fate: though his hour for suffering had not yet come as there was so much to be done first, he was fully able to choose his hour to begin to manifest his glory through signs.

The Church Fathers of the first five centuries interpreted John 2:1–11 in light of the troubles and controversies of their own times. Their insights continue to be relevant because their own times were significantly closer to the writing of the Gospel than are ours.

Because their allegorical interpretations appear jarring to modern ears I have been encouraged to delve deeper into the nature and

---

80. Donne, *Devotions Upon Emergent Occasions*, XIX Expostulation.

interpretation of symbolism and to be cautious, though not pessimistic, in my reading of Johannine symbolism. Just as the first chapter of this book argued for the need to bring a better understanding of social context to our exegesis, so this chapter has argued that a thorough understanding of the symbolic world of the author and readers will enable us to fully and accurately appreciate the richness of this Gospel's metaphors.

Chapter 6 will explore more recent scholarship and present conclusions about what may reasonably be understood by the reader about Jesus' kinship relationships from this introduction of his mother into the narrative of the Gospel.

6

Οἶνον οὐκ ἔχουσιν. Exegesis of John 2:1–11

The wedding at Cana is a story that raises questions and poses conundrums which remain unanswered until later in the Gospel, leaving readers curious and seeking deeper meaning and significance in this simple story.[1] This deeper meaning remains just beyond our reach. I am concerned, therefore, to take care not to trample on the author's intention when approaching this sign narrative. If puzzlement is the author's aim for his readers here it is inappropriate to lay bare every veiled statement and sweep away every mystery, even if that were possible. However, it would be equally inappropriate to declare the passage a conundrum and take no steps toward solving its riddles.

Conundrums in John 2:4

The conundrums that will be considered in this chapter include:

- Is there anything culturally inappropriate about the way Jesus' mother speaks to him here? That is, did she do anything deserving of rebuke?
- When Jesus says Τί ἐμοὶ καὶ σοί; in 2:4, was he distancing himself from his mother and claiming that he had no obligation to act in response to her statement of need? This is the line taken by most commentators, but is that not inconsistent with the context?
- What does Τί ἐμοὶ καὶ σοί; mean in this context?

1. See Howard, "Minor Characters," 66.

- Given that it was highly unusual for a son to address his mother as γύναι, what do we make of Jesus using this word here?
- Is there anything at all that is culturally inappropriate about the way Jesus speaks to his mother here? Does he show her any disrespect?
- By saying οὔπω ἥκει ἡ ὥρα μου, was Jesus saying "no" with his words and then "yes" with his actions?
- What does "my hour" mean in this context? Is it used by the author to connect this passage with Jesus' crucifixion?
- Are there other pointers to the cross in this passage?

It could have been in reference to this passage in particular that Rensberger wrote,

> If this language serves to make the language all but opaque to the newcomer who does not know or admit its central secret, it also attracts and draws in by its very mysteriousness and its convoluted self-containment. The language of John is a kind of enchanting barrier, an irresistible obstacle that advertises a treasure within and yet seems designed to make the treasure all but inaccessible.[2]

This passage has, throughout its history, been both over-analyzed and under-analyzed. Every word has been plundered for multiple symbolic meanings, yet the key phrase, Τί ἐμοὶ καὶ σοί; has received surprisingly little academic attention. In particular, its use in the LXX has often been noted but, to my knowledge, has not previously been explored in the depth attempted here. This chapter will demonstrate that when this phrase's full Old Testament connotations are considered, the reader is in a much better position to understand the whole passage, and the message of the Fourth Gospel concerning Jesus' relationship with his mother.

Exegesis

This chapter will draw on findings presented in earlier chapters, particularly in chapter 4, concerning mothers and sons in first-century Palestine, and will conclude with observations about how the interaction between Jesus and his mother in John 2 contributes to our understanding of what the author sought to communicate about the relationship between

---

2. Rensberger, *Johannine Faith and Liberating Community*, 137.

kinship and discipleship. While the interaction between mother and son is the main concern of this chapter, all details of the passage will be examined. The following exegesis is very detailed and comprehensive, and necessarily so for a number of reasons.

- This passage has intrigued and puzzled many commentators, so there is a great deal of literature, and almost as many theories about the passage, needing to be addressed.
- The complexity of the passage necessitates careful, close, detailed examination.
- Although verse 4 is of particular interest, all details of the passage require attention so as to arrive at a reasonably accurate understanding of the whole. In fact, as will become apparent, close scrutiny shows verse 3 to be of almost equal significance.

τῇ ἡμέρᾳ τῇ τρίτῃ

Despite a great deal of speculation about the "days" in John 1 and 2, it is possible that the words are nothing more than a record of the historic sequence of the events being narrated.[3] The Mishnah (*Ket* 1:1) stipulates Wednesday, the third day of the week, as the day on which virgins should marry,[4] so it may be that the sequence simply points toward Jesus and his disciples arriving for the start of the wedding.

However, in a Gospel where time markers often carry symbolic weight, it is reasonable to ask whether greater depth of meaning may be intended. Some connection with the creation week is often suggested. Depending on how the days in John 1 are counted, the day arrived at may be the seventh day, symbolizing a new creation week,[5] or the eighth day, so that the first sign occurs immediately after a symbolic creation week. The latter could indicate a new phase in Jesus' ministry[6] or a (symbolic) Sunday, the day of resurrection.[7] If the author intended any one of these

---

3. Ridderbos, *Gospel According to John*, 103; Collins, *These Things Have Been Written*, 165; Hendrikson, *John*, 113; Tenney, "John," 42; Contra Waetjen, *Gospel of the Beloved Disciple*, 112.

4. Waetjen, *The Gospel of the Beloved Disciple*, 113; Morris, *The Gospel According to John*, 178.

5. Carson, *The Gospel According to John*, 168.

6. Neyrey believes this, but for different reasons (Neyrey, *The Gospel of John*, 63).

7. Malina and Rohrbaugh, *Social-Science Commentary on the Gospel of John*, 66.

symbolic undertones it is unlikely that he could have expected listeners to accurately identify it, particularly on their first hearing of the passage. This does not necessarily disqualify them, though, since there is much in this Gospel that is disclosed only on a second or subsequent reading. In any case, it is not necessary for the purposes of this chapter to come to a firm conclusion on this.

Waetjen argues that the appearance of τῇ ἡμέρᾳ τῇ τρίτῃ rather than the expected ἐπουριον, which had been repeated three times in chapter one, is a jolt that encourages the reader to look for deeper meaning.[8] He notes that deliverance often occurs in the OT on the third day (Gen 40:20–3, Exod 19:16, Hos 6:2).[9] Moloney connects τῇ ἡμέρᾳ τῇ τρίτῃ more particularly with the giving of the Law on Sinai (Exod 19:16),[10] and the mention of this event in 1:17 lends weight to such a connection.

The phrase τῇ ἡμέρᾳ τῇ τρίτῃ also occurs in the Synoptics (e.g., Matt 16:21) and in Paul (I Cor 15:4) as the day of resurrection so there is a reasonable possibility that the readers were familiar with it. A very similar phrase is found later in John 2 (v19) where it is also connected with Jesus' resurrection.

Dodd suggests that this places Jesus' entire incarnate ministry in the character of the third day of his glory.[11] That is, Jesus lives and works in the power and glory of the resurrection even before his death; he exists in the displaced timeframe of realized eschatology that all his followers are called to enter. I suspect that Dodd is incorrect in this. The Fourth Gospel, from the prologue forward, speaks of Jesus' origins, rather than his destiny, as the source of his power and glory.

It seems reasonable to conclude that τῇ ἡμέρᾳ τῇ τρίτῃ does not point the reader to one specific event, but raises the expectation of a great and decisive act of God, comparable to the giving of the law or the bringing of divine deliverance in the OT, or in the most decisive act of Jesus' resurrection.

---

8. Waetjen, *Gospel of the Beloved Disciple*, 112–4; contra Carson, *The Gospel According to John*, 167.

9. Waetjen, *The Gospel of the Beloved Disciple*, 113.

10. Moloney, *Belief in the Word*, 77; so Grassi, "The Wedding at Cana," 125.

11. Dodd, *Interpretation of the Fourth Gospel*, 300; so Borchert, *John 1–11*, 153; Koester, *Symbolism in the Fourth Gospel*, 82; contra Bruce, *The Gospel of John*, 68; Moloney, *Belief in the Word*, 77; Culpepper, *Gospel and Letters of John*, 130; Buby, *Mary of Galilee*, 118.

This will create dissonance as the reader continues. In what way can changing water into wine at a village wedding in a backwater province be compared with those other monumental turning points in history?

γάμος ἐγένετο

Wedding feasts were one of the high points of family and village life, lasting between three days and a week. Families would put on a public display of whatever wealth they had, such as clothing, eating utensils, music, food, and wine.[12] It was not uncommon for families to incur significant debts in the attempt to host the best wedding the village had yet seen.[13] It would be patronizing for me to mention this and fail to notice that weddings have a similar function in our own time, but one key difference is in the deeper shame attached to the failure of a wedding celebration. It could be socially crippling and could last for generations.

In contrast to patristic times, it is no longer commonplace for commentators to indicate that Jesus' presence at a wedding demonstrates his approval of marriage, but such a comment is still heard occasionally.[14] It is probably still worth noting that the Word whose glory was revealed in the flesh was not opposed to fleshly unions or to the gratification of the flesh through eating and drinking good celebratory fare.

It is almost beyond doubt that the mention of a wedding carries the symbolic OT overtones of messianic times (see Isa 25:6–8; 54:4–8; 62:4–5; Jer 2:2; Hos 2:19)[15] and of God's relationship with Israel (see Hosea).[16] Wedding imagery features in several of the Synoptic parables[17] and so must have been a symbol that could effectively catch the imagination of first-century Jews.

As such a key social and religious event, weddings must also have carried symbolic significance for pagans as well, but it is hard to find any clear reference to pagan wedding symbolism in this passage.

12. Neyrey, "Loss of Wealth," 142.

13. Malina and Rohrbaugh, *Social-Science Commentary*, 70.

14. Bruce, *Gospel of John*, 68; contra Borchert, *John 1–11*, 157; Carson, *Gospel According to John*, 168.

15. See Brown, *Gospel According to John (I–Xii)*, 104; so Dodd, *The Interpretation of the Fourth Gospel*, 297; Moloney, *Belief in the Word*, 80; Collins, *These Things Have Been Written*, 172; Culpepper, *Gospel and Letters of John*, 131.

16. Fehribach, *Women in the Life of the Bridegroom*, 29.

17. Dodd, *Interpretation of the Fourth Gospel*, 297.

By beginning his narrative with a wedding that takes place on the third day, (attended by the Word made flesh), the author is continuing to raise the reader's expectation that an event of great import—maybe even of eschatological import—is about to take place.

ἐν Κανὰ τῆς Γαλιλαίας,

It is easy for today's readers to miss the irony of this phrase. We have noticed that expectation has been built by the first two phrases of this sentence. Now the reader is told where this great event is to take place. In Cana. Of Galilee. A tiny village in a suspect region of Jewish territory. Great events just don't happen in Galilee, and certainly not in Cana. They happen in Jerusalem or, at least, in Bethlehem (7:42).

The author is here underscoring the unimpressiveness of the place where the δόξα of the λόγος would first be revealed.[18] In doing so he further underscores the scandal of the δόξα being revealed in the even more unimpressive location of human σάρξ (1:14).

The return to Cana for the second sign in 4:46–54 forms an inclusio around chapters two to four. More will be said later about the structure of these three chapters and the connection between these two sign narratives. At this point it is significant to note that the account of the second sign contrasts Cana with the more significant city of Capernaum. For those readers unfamiliar with the geography, it is clear that Capernaum is an important city because it is home to a βασιλικός. This is one of the rare occasions when Jesus refuses to visit a dying person but heals them from a distance. This type of healing certainly reveals Jesus' power and produces faith (4:53) but it also communicates the message that it was not necessary for him to leave Cana. Cana was not too humble a place from which Jesus might perform signs; just as human flesh was not too humble a place from which the λόγος might reveal the glory of the μονογενοῦς.

καὶ ἦν ἡ μήτηρ τοῦ Ἰησοῦ ἐκεῖ·

Because Jesus' mother is unnamed in the Fourth Gospel it is common for commentators to assume she has symbolic or representative significance in the Gospel. This need not necessarily follow. As Martin has argued,

---

18. See Ridderbos, *Gospel According to John*, 103; Waetjen, *Gospel of the Beloved Disciple*, 114, attributes this to Johannine irony.

it was common practice in Greek writing in the first two centuries CE to use the epithet, "Mother of X" rather than naming the mother.[19] The most usual situation in which this was done was when the mother's name was already well known to the assumed readers.[20] So, in spite of Lieu's rather implausible suggestion that the author did not know the name of Jesus' mother,[21] it is much more likely that the omission of her name implies that he and his readers were very familiar with her name, and probably with other aspects of her history.

Some other less than plausible suggestions about why she is not named include the avoidance of confusion with other women named Mary in Jesus' life[22] and that the author's practice was to refrain from naming himself or his close kin (Jesus' mother being assumed to be the sister of John's mother, Salome).[23] It is, however, plausible to notice a connection between Jesus' mother and the other significant unnamed character in the Gospel—the disciple whom Jesus loved. A discussion of that connection will be included in the exegesis of 19:25–7.

Neyrey's suggestion that, by refraining from naming her, John is casting doubt on her discipleship[24] is hardly credible when "the disciple whom Jesus loved" is also unnamed.

Among those commentators who envisage a symbolic role for Jesus' mother, some connect her with the church,[25] with "Mother Israel,"[26] and those "who faithfully await the messianic times,"[27] with the new Eve[28] and the mother in Revelation who gives birth to the messiah and all Christians.[29]

---

19. It is not comfortable for feminist readers to see women made invisible in this way. However, the author of the Fourth Gospel can hardly be judged by twentieth-century conventions or blamed for working with the literary conventions of his own day.

20. Martin, "Assessing the Johannine Epithet 'the Mother of Jesus'," 71.

21. Lieu, "The Mother of the Son in the Fourth Gospel", 63.

22. Bruce, *Gospel of John*, 68; Carson, *Gospel According to John*, 168.

23. Hendrikson, *John*, 114.

24. Neyrey, *Gospel of John*, 67.

25. Brown, *Gospel According to John (I–XII)*, 109; contra Bruce, *Gospel of John*, 68.

26. Waetjen, *Gospel of the Beloved Disciple*, 116.

27. Collins, *These Things Have Been Written*, 33.

28. Brown, *Gospel and Epistles of John*, 28–29; Dillon, "Wisdom Tradition and Sacramental Retrospect," 292.

29. Brown, *Gospel According to John (I–XII)*, 108.

Fehribach sees not so much symbolism as typology here. She characterizes Jesus' mother in the Fourth Gospel, along with the OT matriarchs and Hannah, as "mother of an important son."[30]

I will wait until the conclusion of the exegesis of this passage before making an assessment of the symbolic weight carried by Jesus' mother, but it should be noted that there is a verbal pointer in this verse to her significance in this narrative. Focal characters are usually introduced in this Gospel by using ἦν followed by the person's name or title (3:1; 4:46; 5:5; 11:1; 12:20)[31] as Jesus' mother is here.

ἐκλήθη δὲ καὶ ὁ Ἰησοῦς καὶ οἱ μαθηταὶ αὐτοῦ εἰς τὸν γάμον.

Priority is again given to Jesus' mother in that she is mentioned first, whereas Jesus and his disciples are merely "also invited":

> This order, in which Jesus' presence is subordinated to his Mother's, in a Gospel in which nothing is unintentional, signifies that the mother of Jesus and her presence at this wedding is of great importance. In other words, her symbolic importance is primary in this story of Jesus' first public miracle. Matthew and Luke focus their attention on Mary at the birth of Jesus. The wedding at Cana focuses on her role in the birth of his ministry.[32]

It is likely that Jesus' mother was closely involved with the catering arrangements for the wedding, as she seems to be one of the first to become aware of the shameful situation of the lack of wine. This probably implies that she was close to the family in which the wedding took place.[33]

It is also important to note Jesus' status as an invited guest. This underscores the fact that he acts later on his own initiative and not because of any responsibility which required him to act,[34] as would have been

---

30. Fehribach, *Women in the Life of the Bridegroom*, 25.

31. Lieu, "The Mother of the Son in the Fourth Gospel," 63.

32. Jones, *Women in the Gospel of John*, 7; so Lee, *Flesh and Glory*, 146; cf. Moloney, *Belief in the Word*, 80, who sees this as merely signifying her significance to this particular narrative.

33. Waetjen, *Gospel of the Beloved Disciple*, 116; Morris, *Gospel According to John*, 178; Carson, *Gospel According to John*, 169.

34. Bulembat, "Head-Waiter and Bridegroom," 65.

the case if, for example, the wedding had been for one of his younger brothers. Members of the groom's household would not have been invited; they would have been the hosts.

ὑστερήσαντος οἴνου

It has been suggested that the shortage of wine was in part due to the inability of Jesus and his disciples, in their poverty, to bring wine as a gift,[35] though most commentators agree that it was the responsibility of the host, not the guests, to provide the food and wine. In either case, this situation would have caused great embarrassment to the bridegroom, either because he could not supply enough wine,[36] or because he did not have enough friends with sufficient means to meet his need.[37]

λέγει ἡ μήτηρ τοῦ Ἰησοῦ πρὸς αὐτόν,

Two questions are raised by Jesus' mother's approach here. What did she believe Jesus to be capable of? And what did she think his intervention might achieve? The second question will be addressed first.

It is usual for commentators of a social-scientific bent to interpret this scene through the all-pervasive lens of honor and shame. According to this perspective she is usually seen to be acting as broker between the embarrassed host family and the head of her family in order to bring the two families into a patron–client arrangement that provides for the other family's need and increases the honor of her family.[38]

Malina and Rohrbaugh, mindful of the close relationship between mother and son in this culture,[39] believe that Jesus' mother is the most appropriate person to act as broker between the embarrassed host and Jesus, provided she does so discreetly.[40] It is therefore understandable that she might have been approached to take this role.

---

35. Derrett and Duncan, "Water into Wine"; Malina and Rohrbaugh, *Social-Science Commentary*, 66.

36. Bruce, *Gospel of John*, 69; Borchert, *John 1–11*, 154; Tenney, "John," 42.

37. Malina and Rohrbaugh, *Social-Science Commentary*, 66; so Williams, "The Mother of Jesus at Cana," 684.

38. Fehribach, *Women in the Life of the Bridegroom*, 28; so Williams, "The Mother of Jesus at Cana," 685.

39. See chapter 3 on Mother-Son relationships.

40. Malina and Rohrbaugh, *Social-Science Commentary on the Gospel of John*, 67.

Borchert sees this conversation as an encounter between the private (female) sphere and the public (male) sphere:

> Obviously the honor of the private realm was at stake, and Jesus' mother somehow was acting as the broker or mediator on behalf of the private realm. The question then was whether Jesus in a public setting should submit to the private authority of his mother, who by right of motherhood could use her son's resources to recoup her honor and [that] of her associates in the context of a failed situation that was soon to be evident in public at the feast.[41]

Williams is not afraid to tarnish Mary's saintly image, claiming that she may have been seeking to "remind her wayward son of his duty as head of the family."[42] That is, she was reminding him that he had a responsibility to increase the honor rating upon which she and her other children depended. Perhaps she had heard of his growing fame and wanted to ensure that his family and associates benefited from it.[43]

Two concerns arise from this interpretation. It is not clear that the host was aware of his embarrassment, and so may not have been in a position to seek assistance. In response to this, Williams suggests that it may have been a female member of the household who approached Jesus' mother and asked for her help,[44] and presumably sought to solve the dilemma without involving the groom or the headwaiter.

A more significant concern is that at this point in Jesus' ministry the host family would have had no reason to believe that Jesus could help them with their dilemma. He had achieved some public notoriety through John the Baptist (1:29–37) but this indicated neither wealth nor supernatural power. He was yet to perform his first sign, so they had no reason to think he could solve the problem in a miraculous way; and he appeared to have become an itinerant rabbi (1:37–51) so they had no reason to think he had the financial resources to resolve the situation. It is simply not credible that Mary would have been approached to act as broker between the host family and her eldest son; and, given the fact that John gives no indication of such an arrangement, it is reasonable to dismiss that line of thought.

---

41. Borchert, *John 1–11*, 155.
42. Williams, "The Mother of Jesus at Cana," 686.
43. Williams, "The Mother of Jesus at Cana," 686.
44. Williams, "The Mother of Jesus at Cana," 685.

However, the possibility that she saw in the situation an opportunity for Jesus to gain honor for himself and their family cannot be excluded. In her culture, that possibility could rarely be excluded from any social interaction, however mixed that motive might be with other, more altruistic concerns. As discussed in chapter 3, the driving concerns of mothers in this culture were the honor and the safety of their sons.

If Jesus' mother was not acting as broker for the host family, she must have approached Jesus on her own initiative,[45] having somehow discovered the host's difficulty. In addition to her concern for her son's honor, then, she was most likely acting from compassion for her friends. What, then, did she think Jesus might be able to do about the situation? Bruce suggests that she has learned from past experience that the best way to address a need is to bring it to the attention of her son.[46] As head of her family, Jesus would have been the person she would most readily turn to in a crisis; and it is reasonable to assume that the Jesus found in this Gospel would have been a particularly insightful and compassionate son. It may then be that she had no preconceived idea about what Jesus might do, but implicitly trusted him to find a solution.[47]

Is it possible, as Bultmann asserts,[48] that Jesus' mother is asking for a miracle? Does the author present the possibility that Jesus' mother knew her son to have such capabilities?

Some commentators answer this question by naively reading the nativity traditions of Luke and Matthew into the narrative here. Note, for example, Leon Morris:

> [Mary] knew that angels had spoken about Jesus before his birth. She knew that she had conceived him while still a virgin. She knew that his whole manner of life stamped him as different. She knew Jesus, in short, to be the Messiah, and it is likely that she now tried to make Him take such action as would show him to all as the Messiah she knew Him to be.[49]

---

45. The initiative Jesus' mother takes here will be contrasted later with her passive role at the foot of the cross. (See Lieu, "The Mother of the Son in the Fourth Gospel," 68.)

46. Bruce, *Gospel of John*, 69; so Carson, *Gospel According to John*, 170.

47. See also Jones, *Women in the Gospel of John*, 7.

48. Bultmann, *Gospel of John*, 116; contra Koester, *Symbolism in the Fourth Gospel*, 78.

49. Morris, *Gospel According to John*, 179.

Such commentators ignore authorial intention when they read John's Gospel through the lens of Synoptic tradition—unless they have good reason for believing that both the author and the assumed readers held that tradition as common knowledge. Morris does not express such a belief; in fact he writes energetically against the theory that the author of the Fourth Gospel depended in any way upon the first three,[50] though he does admit to a related oral tradition.[51]

Ridderbos is more circumspect, saying that "the evangelist evidently assumes that his readers knew enough of Mary and her unique involvement in Jesus' person and work to be able to understand such an initiative on her part."[52]

As was argued in chapter 1, there is good evidence, based on Johannine irony employed particularly in 7:40–44 and 6:41–42, that John and his readers were familiar with some elements of the Synoptic nativity tradition. There is good reason to believe, then, that an ideal reader of this Gospel, upon encountering the mother of Jesus for the first time in chapter 2, would assume her to be in on the secret of Jesus' identity to some extent. Would such a reader assume that Jesus' mother knew him to be capable of performing miracles? That is far less certain.[53] I contend that this remains an open question; one of the many puzzles that the author employs to draw his readers into deeper contemplation of this man who reveals God—and into more realistic analysis of themselves in relation to this man.

Campbell argues that Jesus is depicted in the Fourth Gospel as a holy man who is able to broker favor from God for petitioners. She considers it likely that his mother, and probably even the guests at the wedding, recognized him as such,[54] but this cannot be substantiated at this early point in the narrative.

Based on a comparison between this Gospel and Greek tragedy, Brant believes that Jesus' mother's speech is an index of her precognition of Jesus' status. What she believes he is capable of accomplishing

---

50. Morris, *Gospel According to John*, 35, 49–52.
51. Morris, *Gospel According to John*, 52.
52. Ridderbos, *Gospel According to John*, 104.
53. Carson, *Gospel According to John*, 169; Fehribach, *Women in the Life of the Bridegroom*, 28.
54. Campbell, *Kinship Relations*, 121–4.

is unclear, but her words to Jesus and the servants anticipate something extraordinary.[55]

Brant believes that Mary's words therefore carry significant weight in this narrative, so much so that they could be seen as the Johannine equivalent of the annunciation. That may be a little more than can be defended, but it is clear that the initiative taken by Jesus' mother leads into the miraculous action of this first sign account. When we consider the high note of expectation that began this narrative, it is clear that the appearance on the scene of the mother of God's son,[56] with a statement of need, must be designed to further increase the reader's sense that something big is about to happen.

Οἶνον οὐκ ἔχουσιν.

When Jesus' mother makes her request we find that it is not a request at all. It is a simple statement of fact, "They have no wine." Brown compares these words with those used by Jesus in the account of the feeding of the 4000 in Mark 8:2 and Matthew 15:32, "They have nothing to eat."[57] The words, "They have nothing to eat" on Jesus' lips were a challenge to the faith of the disciples. He presented his disciples with a need so that they would consider what resources they might be able to put toward meeting that need, and also so that they would later reflect on their failure to recognize that the man who presented the challenge also embodied all the resources they required.

A statement of need can be a challenge, just as an open request can be (cf. Matt 14:16); and the subsequent action in the narrative does imply that Jesus' mother's words were taken as a request.[58] However, they could hardly be seen as a demand, or an insistence upon maternal authority.[59]

Schnackenburg compares her words with those of Martha in 11:22, which are "imprecise, inspired by hope and confidence in Jesus, not excluding a miracle, and indeed, in the eyes of the evangelist, already

---

55. Brant, *Dialogue and Drama*, 89.
56. Or at least "God's chosen one" (1:34).
57. Brown, *Gospel According to John (I–XII)*, 99.
58. Brown, *Gospel According to John (I–Xii)*, 98; Hendrikson, *John*, 115; Buby, *Mary of Galilee*, 121; Morris, *Gospel According to John*, 179; Carson, *Gospel According to John*, 169.
59. Christian Paul Ceroke, "Jesus and Mary at Cana," 27.

hinting at it, while Jesus [taking] up her request, [turns] her mind from earthly hopes to the deeper significance of his action."[60]

However, I contend that the question of whether or not Jesus' mother or Martha was "hinting at" a miracle remains open in the narrative.

The statement "They have no wine," has clear symbolic referents for a community that knows its Old Testament. Wine is a symbol of God's blessing (Isa 25:6; Jer 31:12) and the reward of wisdom (Prov 3:10; 9:1–6) while a lack of wine indicates desolation (Jer 48:33,) particularly the desolation of divine judgment, as in Isaiah 24:5–11 (LXX):

> ἡ δὲ γῆ ἠνόμησεν διὰ τοὺς κατοικοῦντας αὐτήν,
> διότι παρέβησαν τὸν νόμον καὶ ἤλλαξαν τὰ προστάγματα,
> διαθήκην αἰώνιον.[61]
>
> πενθήσει οἶνος, πενθήσει ἄμπελος,
> στενάξουσιν πάντες οἱ εὐφραινόμενοι τὴν ψυχήν.
> πέπαυται εὐφροσύνη τυμπάνων, πέπαυται αὐθάδεια καὶ πλοῦτος ἀσεβῶν, πέπαυται φωνὴ κιθάρας.
> ᾐσχύνθησαν, οὐκ ἔπιον οἶνον, πικρὸν ἐγένετο τὸ σικερα τοῖς πίνουσιν.[62]
>
> ὀλολύζετε περὶ τοῦ οἴνου πανταχῇ, πέπαυται πᾶσα εὐφροσύνη τῆς γῆς.[63]

These words could describe a marriage celebration that is interrupted by catastrophic news. The silencing of the joy of wedding celebrations is a key symbol of judgment in Jeremiah (7:34; 16:9; 25:10; 33:11). "They have no wine": at a wedding feast this is a disaster in its own way, but the words hint at a greater disaster.[64] It is reasonable, then, for Dillon to say

---

60. Schnackenburg, *Gospel According to St John*, 327.

61. TR: The earth acted lawlessly because of its inhabitants; for they have transgressed law, altered the commands, the everlasting covenant.

62. TR: He will lament (strike? dry up?) the wine, he will lament (strike? wither?) the vine,
they will sigh deeply for all that makes the soul glad.
The merriment of the drum has been stilled.
Stubbornness and godless wealth have been annihilated
The voice of the lute has been silenced.
They have been dishonored, they do not drink wine;
strong drink has become bitter to those who drink it.

63. TR: There is an outcry concerning the wine everywhere; all merriment has been banished from the land.

64. See Waetjen, *Gospel of the Beloved Disciple*, 118; Brown, *Gospel and Epistles of*

"in the retrospect of the final age, Mary becomes the representative of the faithful of Israel, expressing the anguish of the captivity of sin which could not be removed under the old law."[65]

However, the fact that she expresses the anguish of judgment does not, in itself, make her a representative of Israel. An analysis of her representative role will need to wait until the end of this chapter.

It is possible that, by asking Jesus to address the problem of the lack of wine, his mother may be seen as asking him to assume the responsibility of the bridegroom.[66] Brant believes that, if that is the case, Jesus' response does not deny this responsibility but defers it to a later time, when his hour comes.[67] This possible line of interpretation will be discussed later.

Jesus' mother expresses a need that has deep symbolic undertones, though she may well have been unaware of the symbolic depth of the need her words express. Do her words indicate faith in her son? If so, does that faith look to him only for the immediate need, or also for the deeper need for release from sin and judgment?

Lieu believes that it is inappropriate to ask whether Jesus' mother at this stage has placed her faith in Jesus as Lord because, "For this narrative faith is the response to Jesus' act, not that which prompts the request."[68] In this she appears to oversimplify the subtle relationship in the Fourth Gospel between seeing and believing. Signs are a powerful impetus toward faith (2:11; 4:53 etc.) but on their own they are not an adequate basis for faith (2:23–5), and faith without seeing is more blessed (20:29). At Cana, the disciples come to faith because of the sign (2:11) but what about Jesus' mother? Did she come to faith at the same time? Did she already have faith beforehand? Or does she come to faith at a later time? These questions are not only appropriate, but appear to be deliberately raised by the author for the attentive reader to puzzle over.

The symbolic undertones of this statement do not obliterate the personal crisis in the event being narrated. A (presumably not very wealthy) family is at a point of social catastrophe. A new marriage is about to be burdened by crippling shame. The narrative tension increases through

---

John, 29; Ridderbos, *Gospel According to John*, 110.

65. Dillon, "Wisdom Tradition and Sacramental Retrospect," 291.
66. Fehribach, *Women in the Life of the Bridegroom*, 29.
67. Brant, *Dialogue and Drama*, 247.
68. Lieu, "The Mother of the Son in the Fourth Gospel," 64.

the intensification of the narrated situation and its symbolic undertones. The reader becomes impatient for the monumental event that the start of the narrative seemed to promise.

λέγει αὐτῇ ὁ Ἰησοῦς, Τί ἐμοὶ καὶ σοί,

At this point of narrative tension, Jesus says something that is almost incomprehensible to today's reader. This phrase is not only idiomatic, its meaning is also almost wholly dependent on context,[69] and the context here does not readily supply a clear meaning. It is hardly surprising, then, that this phrase has been notoriously difficult to translate and interpret. We noted earlier that patristic commentators found it troubling, so it is reasonable to assume that readers a few centuries earlier might also have struggled with it. If that is the case then presumably our author has chosen (again!) to be obscure and ambiguous rather than clear and precise.[70]

The phrase appears in the LXX, in the other Gospels, and also in the second-century philosopher, Epictetus. Each occurrence is analyzed in Appendix B. Before drawing on that analysis I will briefly survey the findings of recent scholarship concerning this verse.

Most commentators assert that the idiom is not necessarily offensive, but often has the sense of a sharp reprimand,[71] that it is "abrupt and draws a sharp line between Jesus and his mother."[72] Malina finds that Jesus is here "properly talking down to his mother."[73]

These words are sometimes compared with Jesus' refusal in 7:6 to act upon his brothers' instructions. "Here too the reader has the impression that Jesus acts differently from what his words in v. 8 would lead one to expect. But the evangelist sees no contradiction, since Jesus, following his appointed time, merely refuses to reveal himself publicly before the world (cf. v 4)."[74]

---

69. Williams, "The Mother of Jesus at Cana," 679; Ceroke, "Jesus and Mary at Cana," 19–20.

70. Lieu, "The Mother of the Son in the Fourth Gospel," 65.

71. Ridderbos, *Gospel According to John*, 105; Moloney, *Belief in the Word*, 81; Culpepper, *Gospel and Letters of John*, 130; Carson, *Gospel According to John*, 170; Schnackenburg, *Gospel According to St John*, 328.

72. Barrett, *Gospel According to St John*, 191; so Waetjen, *Gospel of the Beloved Disciple*, 117; Koester, *Symbolism in the Fourth Gospel*, 78.

73. Malina, *The Social World of Jesus and the Gospels*, 100.

74. Schnackenburg, *Gospel According to St John*, 329; So van der Watt, *Family of*

"His decisions are his own, and depend only on his Father's will";[75] so that "even his mother must yield place to his messianic call and work."[76]

There is near consensus among scholars that Jesus was placing himself beyond family relationships, just as he demanded of his disciples in Matthew 19:29.[77] Ridderbos compares this statement with Luke 2:49, showing that Jesus found it necessary to "observe sharply the boundaries of his authority" in relation to his mother.[78]

Bruce suggests that Jesus is bringing his mother up to date with the fact that things have changed since he left home. He has received power through the Holy Spirit to undertake the work of his Father. All other responsibilities must now be subordinated to this mission.[79] He therefore translates the phrase, "Why trouble me with that?"[80]

According to Bultmann, "the help for all man's perplexity is to be found in the miracle of the revelation; but the event of the revelation is independent of human desires and cannot forcibly be brought about by man's supplication; it comes to pass where and how God wills, and then it surpasses all human expectation."[81]

Malina and Rohrbaugh see here the first occurrence of a Johannine pattern of Jesus' dealing with in-group people who come to him with requests. They see this pattern (request—stalling reluctance—compliance—conflict with the Judeans) repeated in 4:46—5:1,18; 7:2–10 and 11:1–8.[82] Neyrey employs a similar scheme, but drops the fourth stage, so avoiding the implication of a closer link between the Cana wedding and the clearing of the temple than is justified by the text.[83]

---

the King, 261; Carson, *Gospel According to John*, 172.

75. Barrett, *Gospel According to St John*, 191; So Beasley-Murray, *John* 35; Borchert, *John 1–11*, 155; Bultmann, *Gospel of John*, 117; Carson, *Gospel According to John*, 171; Brown, *Gospel According to John (I-XII)*, 109; Culpepper, *Gospel and Letters of John*, 131.

76. Schnackenburg, *The Gospel According to St John*, 329.

77. Brown, *Gospel According to John (I-XII)*, 102; Fehribach, *Women in the Life of the Bridegroom*, 34.

78. Ridderbos, *Gospel According to John*, 105; So Carson, *Gospel According to John*, 171.

79. Bruce, *Gospel of John*, 69.

80. Bruce, *Gospel of John*, 69.

81. Bultmann, *Gospel of John*, 121.

82. Malina and Rohrbaugh, *Social-Science Commentary*, 67.

83. Neyrey, *Gospel of John*, 65.

Neyrey places this schema within the context of an honor challenge. A request from an insider (kin, client, or friend) puts the petitioned person on the spot because it may force him to do something he does not wish to do, or to admit to not having the resources to accede to the request. By first denying the request then choosing to take action himself, on his own terms, Jesus defends his honor and his independence from coercion, while at the same time meeting the need that has been brought to his attention.[84]

Campbell argues here that Jesus insists on acting humbly and so refuses his mother's request that he act to gain honor for himself and his family. His deep affection for his mother, however, ensures that he does act.[85]

Brant argues that Jesus risks shame by acting on the request of a woman[86] but this is incorrect. As I have argued in chapter 4, it was seen as honorable and virtuous in this culture for men to obey their mothers.[87]

Berenson Maclean wonders if Jesus is here engaging in deceptive speech, which is characteristic of the divine trickster motif that she sees Jesus embodying in the Gospel of John. Mary, as paradigmatic disciple, is not fooled, bewildered, or put off.[88]

Remembering that supplying wine was the bridegroom's responsibility, Fehribach contends that the ancient reader may have perceived Jesus' rejection of his mother's request as a refusal to heighten his own honor at the bridegroom's expense.[89] "Perhaps the author is emphasizing that Jesus, and Jesus alone, is the messianic bridegroom (3:27–30). He will supply the wine for the great banquet, and will do it at a time decided by his Father, not his mother."[90]

Some scholars detect a particular tension between the historical and symbolic senses of this verse. Dillon considered that at a conversational level it is a "highly artificial exchange" that owes more to eschatological redaction than to the original tradition.[91] He is certainly correct in point-

---

84. Neyrey, *Gospel of John*, 66–67.
85. Campbell, *Kinship Relations*, 131.
86. Brant, *Dialogue and Drama*, 214.
87. This is probably one example of modern Mediterranean practices being inappropriately read back into the first century.
88. Berenson Maclean, "The Divine Trickster," 70.
89. Fehribach, *Women in the Life of the Bridegroom*, 29.
90. Carson, *Gospel According to John*, 172–3.
91. Dillon, "Wisdom Tradition and Sacramental Retrospect," 290.

ing out that it is easier to understand the words as symbol than as a real conversation between a flesh-and-blood mother and son. It is reasonable to assume that the actual exchange may have been more comprehensive and less enigmatic than remembered here by John. This likelihood only sharpens the question of why the author chose these words to summarize the encounter.

Does Jesus' use of γύναι point toward a more symbolic and representational address to his mother? Does the idiom then reflect "the divergence in the thought-pattern between the implications of *mētēr* and the special sense the evangelist intends in *gynē*."[92]

Is Jesus indicating that his mother must be understood in a symbolic, rather than physical/biological, way: "Mary has approached Jesus in the only way she could approach Him—as His mother. Jesus chooses to view her in another light."[93] Lieu suggests that this other light remains ambiguous until at the cross Jesus says, "behold your son."[94]

Perhaps the author felt that his readers' confidence in Jesus' consistent sympathy in providing for human need would lead them to simply assume Jesus would perform the miracle, so he found it necessary to shock them into thinking more deeply about Jesus' motivations.[95] It seems, though, that this would be a more appropriate tactic later in the Gospel. At this point Jesus has not yet performed a miracle or provided for a human need.

Several problems emerge from this survey of current scholarship. Firstly, the near complete consensus that Jesus was distancing himself from his mother does not seem appropriate as a response to her humble communication of the need of the host family. Is it possible that the author could consider it appropriate for strangers to approach Jesus with their needs, but not appropriate for his mother to do so?[96] Does providing for a need she has identified imply that he is acting under her authority and not that of his Father? If so, are we to conclude that whenever he accepts a petition he is placing himself under the authority of the petitioner?

Most commentators agree that the last phrase in this verse, οὔπω ἥκει ἡ ὥρα μου, implies that Jesus is refusing his mother's implicit request.

---

92. Ceroke, "The Problem of Ambiguity in John 2:4," 339.
93. Ceroke, "The Problem of Ambiguity in John 2:4," 336.
94. Lieu, "The Mother of the Son in the Fourth Gospel," 69.
95. Ceroke, "The Problem of Ambiguity in John 2:4," 332.
96. Ceroke, "Jesus and Mary at Cana," 18.

It is possible to read this phrase as a question and therefore as an assent, but a detailed discussion of this possibility must be deferred until later. Reading this verse as assent removes the difficulty of explaining why, if Jesus said "no," his mother responded as if he said "yes." However, reading it as assent creates another problem. Τί ἐμοὶ καὶ σοί; must then be read, rather than distancing Jesus from his mother, as removing a hindrance to action:

> If one wishes to perceive assent in the use of the idiom in the reply of Jesus, the task is to establish an obstacle to the assent which Jesus is declaring removed or non-existent. If one wishes to perceive refusal in the idiom, one concedes the point from OT parallels and strives, then, to ascertain some religious aspect of Mary's petition that is not wholly satisfactory to Jesus or that diverges from his viewpoint as Messiah.[97]

It is possible to suggest an obstacle "which Jesus is declaring removed." Anxiety is one possibility, leading to a translation, "Why should we be worried about that?" but it is not possible to substantiate from the text that such was the author's intention.

At this point the phrase remains unfathomable. If Jesus is refusing his mother's request and distancing himself from her, then:

1. Why does the author fail to indicate what was objectionable about her approach?
2. Why does she respond as if Jesus had agreed to act?

If Jesus is agreeing to act, then

1. What does Τί ἐμοὶ καὶ σοί; refer to?
2. οὔπω ἥκει ἡ ὥρα μου must be translated in a way that is not its most obvious sense.

The other key problem raised in the above survey of scholarship is the tension between the literal account of a mother's conversation with her son and the symbolic meaning that the author intends his readers to find in that account. It is not at all unusual for there to be two levels of meaning in the Fourth Gospel, but they are generally smoothly and seamlessly overlaid. Sometimes one of the characters misses the significance of the metaphorical layer of meaning and initiates an opportunity

---

97. Ceroke, "The Problem of Ambiguity in John 2:4," 333.

for explanation (3:4). This passage is jarring in that neither level is at all clear and no explanation appears to have been given.

I contend that the author has deliberately placed a puzzle here to slow readers down and make them think. Calling it a puzzle should not cause readers to give up on finding a solution, rather it should energize them to look for the key.

At this point it becomes appropriate to consider the Old Testament (LXX) uses of the phrase, τί ἐμοὶ καὶ σοί;

Brown argued that there are two shades of meaning for this phrase when used in the Old Testament:

a. When one party is bothering the other, the injured party may use the phrase to mean, "What have I done to you that you should treat me this way?" (Judg 11:12; 2 Chron 35:21; 1 Kings 17:18; Mark 1:24; 5:7)

b. When someone is asked to get involved in something they believe to be none of their business they may use the phrase to mean, "This is your business, not mine." (2 Kings 3:13; Hos 14:8)

He acknowledges another possibility, based on 2 Sam 16:10, that the phrase might mean, "This is not *our* concern,"[98] but rejects this possibility because Jesus' reference to "my hour" implies that he is denying only his own involvement.[99]

I contend that Brown and other scholars have not looked closely enough at these OT texts. Brown has ascertained the possible meanings of the idiom, based on LXX usage, and has then sought to apply those meanings to John 2:4. He has not considered the possibility that John 2:4 may be an allusion to one or more of those texts. If it might be an allusion then it becomes necessary to take a much closer look at the contexts in which the idiom is used in the LXX.

Τί ἐμοὶ καὶ σοί; is a rare phrase in the LXX (appearing only seven times) and the New Testament (appearing five times outside John but always on the lips of a demon possessed man).[100] It is even more rare in literature outside the Bible, and so presumably (but not certainly) also rare in spoken communication. The author would, therefore, not have

---

98. So Tenney, "John," 42.

99. Brown, *Gospel According to John (I–XII)*, 99.

100. See Appendix A for a list of all occurrences of the phrase in the LXX and the NT.

been expecting too much of his readers if he hoped the Jews among them would connect the phrase with the passages they had heard in the Synagogue or read in their Scriptures[101] and would draw on that connection to discern what was meant by the phrase in this instance.

The phrase occurs only here in the Fourth Gospel, and not at all in any of the other NT books that may be attributed to the same author. It cannot be said to be a characteristic Johannine phrase, so it is reasonable to assume that the author had some particular reason for using it here, especially when some other phrase could have expressed his intentions more clearly.

The question of whether or not the Gospel recalls Jesus' exact words cannot be resolved. It is possible that he knew some Greek and might, perhaps, have used the Greek phrase here. It is also possible that he used the Hebrew phrase lying behind it. In either case, such a choice would have almost certainly been used with undertones of OT occurrences, since he would have been stepping outside his usual Aramaic. However, there is no clear evidence for this.

Appendix A examines all the uses of τί ἐμοὶ καὶ σοί; and related phrases in the LXX, the Gospels, and in Epictetus, and identifies four occurrences in the LXX that bear some affinity with the use in John 2. These are examined here.

Justice, mercy, and kingship in Israel

2 Samuel 16:10 and 19:23 place these words on the lips of King David. Links between David and Jesus are not so clear in John as in the Synoptics, since John neither gives him the title, "Son of David," nor situates him in a genealogy demonstrating his Davidic ancestry. However, Jesus is given the title, "King of Israel," twice in John. The first is spoken by Nathaniel in 1:49, only three verses before the Cana account. The second is in 12:13 as Jesus enters in triumph into Jerusalem. Not since David's son, Solomon, has a man been acclaimed "King of Israel" in Jerusalem! This title, along with the title, "Messiah" (1:41, 4:25, 7:26–41, 9:22, 11:27, 20:31) is sufficient to connect Jesus with David.

Throughout David's reign he was troubled by an ambivalent relationship with Joab and Abishai, the sons of Zuruiah. They were brilliant

---

101. Whether or not they had access to the Gospels is in doubt, so it is less likely that he expected his readers to take the NT occurrences into account.

and successful commanders of his army and were responsible for much of David's military success; but their strength was also their weakness. David laments in 2 Samuel 3:39, οὗτοι υἱοὶ Σαρουιας σκληρότεροί μού εἰσιν.[102] They execute the king's justice, but he cannot trust them because they never temper justice with mercy. Joab had been of use to David at the moral low point of his rule, when David sent Uriah the Hittite to him to be killed (2 Sam 11,) and this incident would have added to David's sense of ambivalence.

On the two occasions on which David uses the idiom he rebukes Abishai for being too ready to execute Shimei, who had been cursing David. David makes the startling objection that perhaps the Lord had directed Shimei to curse him.

Reference to these passages, therefore, recalls the conflict between justice administered through violence and justice tempered with mercy and submitted to the will of God. This does not appear simply to take the form of conflict between David and his commanders; the ambivalence seems to be more deeply lodged within David himself.

Reference to this frustration is entirely appropriate as a response to such a spiritually loaded comment as "They have no wine." It has already been noted that Jesus' mother's words would have brought to mind thoughts of God's judgment and God's mercy.

A man of God among sinners

In 1 Kings 17:18 these words are spoken to Elijah. There may be a link, though a tenuous one, between Jesus and Elijah in the Fourth Gospel. John the Baptist denies being the Messiah, Elijah, or the prophet in 1:20, raising the question: If he isn't, then who is? Jesus is called a prophet in John (4:19, 44, 9:17) and twice he is clearly called *the* prophet (6:14, 7:40). Elijah, however, is not mentioned again. Perhaps this raises, and leaves open, the question of whether or not Jesus is in some way presented as a new Elijah.

The context of these words, if not Elijah himself, is clearly relevant to a discussion of John 2:4. This is the only one of the four passages being alluded to that uses the exact words, Τί ἐμοὶ καὶ σοί. The words are spoken by the widow with whom Elijah is staying, when her son becomes

---

102. TR: "these sons of Zeruiah are too violent for me."

critically ill. In her distress, the widow begins to blame Elijah.[103] Is it his presence in her house that has brought this calamity upon them? As a man of God, has he brought her sins to God's remembrance and so brought God's judgment upon her?

What are the consequences for sinful humanity of the presence of a man of God among them? This is a central question in John's Gospel, where it is not merely a prophet, but the Word of God who has come to dwell among humanity (1:14). Is he there to bring God's judgment (3:17, 5:2–30, 8:16, 26, 9:39, 12:31,47)?

This is a complex question in John and there is no need to fully address it here. It is necessary only to point out the relevance of this question to both the literal and spiritual levels of the Cana wedding. What does it mean for the host family that the man of God, Jesus, is in their home? Is he there to bring blessing or curse? Will his presence result in calamity or abundance? This context may also throw light on Jesus' use of γύναι, where the word may be intended to recall this other conversation between a man of God and a woman in distress.

At a spiritual level, allusion to this passage raises the question of what it means for the Jews, who find themselves under God's judgment without the wine of God's blessing, that the Word of God has taken flesh and is living among them. Is he there to bless them or to curse them?

Assuming, as is usually considered most likely, that the canonical form of this Gospel took shape after 70 CE, is it perhaps possible that some were connecting the destruction of Jerusalem with Jesus' earlier presence there? If so (and I concede I am drawing a long bow here) the Cana passage, along with verses such as 3:17, would seem to be a denial of that. Jesus, and Elijah, came to bring blessing not curse, but people who reject God's servants bring curses upon themselves (3:18–20).

When will my bride be faithful?

In Hosea 14:9 God laments over the faithlessness of his bride, Israel. God's desire is to bless her but her faithlessness requires that he cut off his blessing in order to bring her back. The words here are τί αὐτῷ ἔτι καὶ εἰδώλοις;

---

103. This is an entirely ordinary thing for a grieving and frightened person to do in any culture.

What makes this occurrence of the idiom particularly relevant is the mention of wine in the immediately preceding verse, where God expresses the intention of blessing Israel again: ἐξανθήσει ὡς ἄμπελος τὸ μνημόσυνον αὐτοῦ, ὡς οἶνος Λιβάνου.[104]

Wine is one of the symbols of God's blessing in Hosea. It is one of the blessings God gives, then withholds and desires to give again. In this context, the comment, "They have no wine" places "them" in that middle time, the time of judgment and of withheld blessings. This implies faithlessness and the possibility of repentance on the part of those from whom blessing is withheld.

So we see again that this idiom is used in the context of tension between blessing and curse; between the need for justice and the desire to show mercy.

Conclusions regarding τί ἐμοὶ καὶ σοί;

Jesus' mother has approached him with the spiritually laden words, "They have no wine." The narrative gives us little evidence regarding whether or not she was aware of the deeper meaning of her words, but her response in 2:5 implies that her attention was fixed on the immediate need of the hosts to provide wine for their guests. Jesus, however, perceived their deeper meaning immediately; the Jews are experiencing God's judgment, not God's blessing. As with the Samaritan woman (4:10) and Nicodemus (3:3,) he seizes the opportunity to take the conversation onto a spiritual plane.

The OT allusions bring to mind the conflict in the heart of God (Hosea 14:8), of God's king (2 Sam 16:10; 19:23), and of God's prophet (1 Kings 17:28) regarding justice and mercy, blessing and curse. As God, as God's king, and as God's prophet, Jesus would have known such conflict all too well, as he knew that his mission was to bring justice and mercy together (Ps 85:10) in his own body, crucified. Mention of his "hour" is therefore entirely consistent.

Use of Τί ἐμοὶ καὶ σοί; as an OT allusion is therefore entirely appropriate, spiritually and theologically, in the Cana narrative, but is it appropriate as a conversational response from Jesus to his mother?

This question can begin to be answered by noticing that in these OT examples this idiom that apparently concerns the relationship between

---

104. TR: His memorial shall blossom like a vine, like the wine of Lebanon.

two people, always includes a third. David used the idiom because he believed that Abishai's course of action was not God's will. The widow used it because she believed Elijah's God was judging her. God used it because Israel was refusing to turn from idols. In all these examples, and most of the others examined in Appendix A, there is a sense of two parties opposed to a third, where either all three should be aligned or (as in Hos 14:8 and 2 Chron 35:21) the wrong two are aligned. The idiom does not create distance, as some commentators assume.[105] In these examples, it observes distance and wishes for a closer or different alliance.

Further, the idiom on its own does not dictate where the distance or conflict lies in the three-person relationship. This is best observed graphically.

FIGURE 1

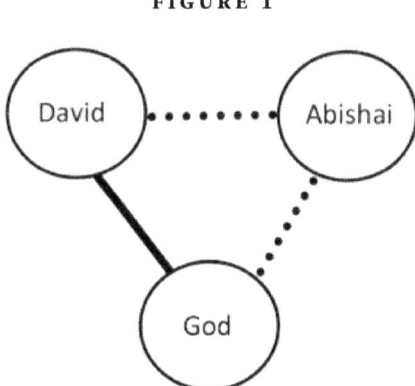

Figure 1 refers to 2 Samuel 16:10 and 19:23. There is distance between David and Abishai because there is already distance between Abishai and God—he is not in line with God's will.

Distance is therefore between the two people mentioned in the idiom and between the second person and God.

Figure 2 refers to 1 Kings 17:18. The idiom expresses distance between the widow and Elijah on the basis of distance between the widow and God (because of her sins).

---

105. Barrett, *Gospel According to St John*, 191; so Waetjen, *Gospel of the Beloved Disciple*, 117; Koester, *Symbolism in the Fourth Gospel*, 78.

FIGURE 2

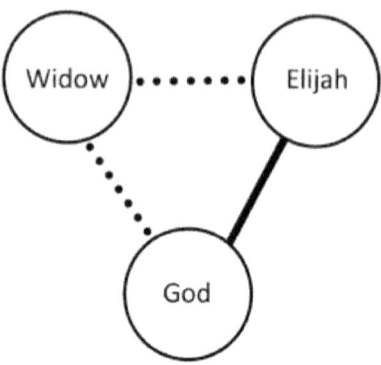

Distance is therefore between the two mentioned in the idiom and between the first person and the third (unnamed) party.

Figure 3 refers to Hosea 14:4. There is distance between God and Ephraim because there is alignment between Ephraim and idols.

FIGURE 3

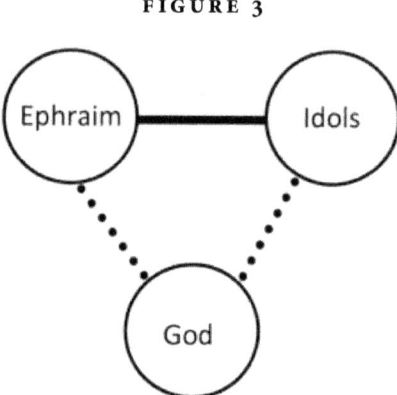

There is therefore alignment between the two mentioned in the idiom, and distance between each of them and the third (unnamed) party.

We find in three uses of the idiom three different configurations of distance and alignment. It is therefore not possible to be clear about the configuration based on the idiom alone. Clarity must be provided by the context.

Returning to John 2:4, it becomes necessary to discover the identity of the third party and the configuration of distance and alliance between the three. Before venturing further in that direction, however, the possibility that there was some ambiguity intended here should again be acknowledged. Perhaps John wished the readers to puzzle over where the problem may be in Jesus' relationship with his mother, and who the third party may be around whom there is distance. I consider this a real possibility, but I also believe there are clues that take us a little further.

Most scholars, as discussed earlier, believe that Jesus is distancing himself from his mother in order to emphasize his alignment with his Father.[106] They would, therefore, assume that the Father forms the third party in this triangle. The problem with this interpretation, as has been hinted at earlier, is that the context provides no evidence of distance or tension between Jesus and his Father or between Jesus' mother and God the Father. The phrase itself is the only evidence that something is amiss.

It is necessary, therefore, to consider all the other characters in the narrative. The disciples can be dismissed because, again, there is no indication of distance between them, Jesus, and Jesus' mother. The headwaiter and the servants perform specific functions in the narrative and the quality of their relationships with Jesus and his mother is not on view, except that the obedience of the servants implies that all is well there.

The remaining possibility is that the third party is the host family without wine. At a spiritual level they represent the Jews under God's judgment and denied God's blessing. In presenting their need to Jesus, his mother may be aligning herself with them and calling on Jesus to do the same. This may be what Ridderbos has observed when he wrote that "Mary herself represents the role of believing Israel, which impatiently awaits the breakthrough of the promised salvation but must await the moment when 'the time is fulfilled,' then the 'fullness of time' has come."[107]

Jesus' mother does not represent Israel, but she does align herself with Israel by presenting Israel's need to the Messiah. Jesus finds it necessary to challenge that alliance. Why? A couple of possibilities can be tentatively suggested.

Firstly, the Jews are estranged from God—they have no wine and therefore must be assumed to be under God's curse. The undertones of

---

106. Barrett, *Gospel According to St John*, 191; So Beasley-Murray, *John* 35; Borchert, *John 1–11*, 155; Bultmann, *The Gospel of John*, 117; Carson, *Gospel According to John*, 171; Brown, *Gospel According to John (I–XII)*, 109; Culpepper, *Gospel and Letters of John*, 131.

107. Ridderbos, *Gospel According to John*, 108.

conflict between mercy and justice that are found in the OT allusions are present here. Jesus' heart may be for mercy, but he is not about to compromise justice. Can he align himself with the Jews when their sin has estranged them from his Father?

Secondly, John 1:11 has already prefigured a rejection of Jesus by his own people, and a note of conflict between Jesus and "the Jews" has been hinted at in 1:19 and will resonate with increasing intensity throughout the Gospel until it leads to Jesus' death. The Jews have interrogated the one sent to bear witness to Jesus. Immediately after this pericope Jesus will travel to Jerusalem and create chaos in their temple. Mindful of this conflict and where it will lead, Jesus asks his mother to be careful about whose side she takes.

Of course, not all Jews will oppose Jesus. The disciples are Jews. Mary, Martha, and Lazarus of Bethany are Jews. Yet they will all be asked to reconsider what they have traditionally believed and practiced; they will find themselves marginalized by their own people and will learn to seek life in the person of Jesus rather than in the temple. There will be conflict for all who follow Jesus, especially for those who, like Jesus himself, continue to love the Jewish nation.

Τί ἐμοὶ καὶ σοί; in this context, can be translated, "Be careful of aligning yourself too closely with those who stand under God's judgment and among whom many will show themselves to be my enemies."

Would Jesus' mother have heard this meaning in his words? It is unlikely, unless they had previously discussed such things. In this Gospel it is not uncommon for Jesus to say things that his interlocutors could not be expected to understand. See, for example, 2:19; 3:5; 4:10; 6:51; 7:33; 8:28–29; 11:9–10; 12:23–26, 31–32. These enigmatic words from Jesus' lips seem to operate in a similar way to the parables of the Synoptics. They slow the reader down and call us to reflect on what could possibly be Jesus' meaning. They call the reader to gather, with the disciples, around Jesus and ask him, "What on earth are you talking about?" (Mark 4:10)

These enigmatic phrases also have a proleptic function in that the reader is more able to understand them after following the narrative to its conclusion. On several occasions Jesus tells the disciples that they will understand what he is saying later (13:7; 16:4–15, 25). Similarly, the readers of the Gospel gain deeper insight later, that is, after they have read to the end, perhaps several times, after they have reflected deeply on the narrative, and after they have received the Holy Spirit (e.g., 6:23).

Finally, these enigmatic words have an ironic function. The reflective reader, after examining the whole Gospel, is more able to understand Jesus' words than the characters in the narrative and so is "in on" secrets that are hidden from those characters.

γύναι

Γύναι is a polite form of address when spoken to a woman.[108] It is Jesus' usual form of address for women (Matt 15:28; Luke 13:12; John 4:21; 8:10; 20:13)[109] and it will be spoken by Jesus to his mother again when she stands at the foot of his cross (19:26). Josephus, in Ant 17:74, records it being used affectionately by a husband to his wife. There is no reason to think, then, that Jesus used the word to distance himself from his mother. However, this is the only place in the NT, or elsewhere in ancient literature, where a son uses this word to address his mother.[110] This is curious, so most commentators look for an explanation.

Some suggest that Jesus is stating that his mother may no longer seek his help on the basis of their mother–son relationship;[111] or that she must learn to look to him as Lord rather than son in order to limit her suffering at the time of his death.[112] "Jesus in His public ministry was not only or primarily the son of Mary, but 'the Son of man.'"[113]

The author is certainly not seeking to deny the mother–son relationship here, since the words ἡ μήτηρ τοῦ Ἰησοῦ are used four times in these twelve verses. It is unmistakably as ἡ μήτηρ τοῦ Ἰησοῦ that she appears in this narrative. Use of the word γύναι, alone, is insufficient reason to think that Jesus is here signaling a change to his relationship with his mother.

---

108. Bruce, *Gospel of John*, 69; Borchert, *John 1–11*, 154; Tenney, "John," 42.

109. See Brown, *Gospel According to John (I–Xii)*, 99.

110. Ridderbos, *Gospel According to John*, 105; Bultmann, *Gospel of John*, 116; Morris, *Gospel According to John*, 180; Carson, *Gospel According to John*, 170; Koester, *Symbolism in the Fourth Gospel*, 78; Lieu, "The Mother of the Son in the Fourth Gospel," 65; Williams, "The Mother of Jesus at Cana," 688.

111. Bruce, *Gospel of John*, 69; Waetjen, *Gospel of the Beloved Disciple*, 117.

112. Hendrikson, *John*, 115. Why she should suffer less at the death of her Lord than at the death of her son is not clear. Certainly, her maternal and protective feelings would be less engaged, but would those feelings really be more powerful than the feeling of utter devastation at seeing the master in whom she had placed all her hope humiliated and destroyed?

113. Morris, *Gospel According to John*, 181.

Commentators generally reach that conclusion only after deciding that the rest of the verse also signals distance.

Perhaps the use of her title rather gives her a symbolic and iconic role in the narrative,[114] but what she symbolizes is not clear. Could it be that the author is seeking to accentuate her femaleness,[115] so that she symbolizes women, perhaps as the new Eve? Perhaps she symbolizes Israel as the bride of YHWH?[116] None of these suggestions is very convincing.

Bulembat notices that every time this word is used by Jesus in the Gospels it is spoken to a woman in some distress, and seems to have been heard as a word of consolation.[117] If any explanation is needed for Jesus' use of this word, this seems the most reasonable. The words Τί ἐμοὶ καὶ σοί γυναι; seem to echo the words Τί ἐμοὶ καὶ σοί ἀνθρωπε; spoken to Elijah by another woman in distress (1 Kings 17:18). If this is the case, Jesus' words could well be heard as indicating that he will act to relieve the distress, as Elijah did.

οὔπω ἤκει ἡ ὥρα μου

The first dilemma that this phrase poses concerns whether it is a statement or a question. The translation of this phrase preferred by Gregory of Nyssa and Theodore of Mopsuestia—"Has my hour not now come?"[118]—is feasible and in some ways fits the context better than the usual translation. If Jesus' hour has come, meaning the hour for him to commence the sign phase of his ministry, then it is hardly surprising that he immediately performs his first sign.

Brown argues that this is unlikely here because:

1. No other use of οὔπω in John introduces a question expecting a positive answer,[119] though, a similarly constructed question is found in Mark 8:17.[120]

---

114. Jones, *Women in the Gospel of John*, 8; so Brown, *Gospel According to John (I–Xii)*, 99; Collins, *These Things Have Been Written*, 170.

115. See Brant, *Dialogue and Drama*, 213.

116. Ceroke, "The Problem of Ambiguity in John 2:4," 338.

117. Bulembat, "Head-Waiter and Bridegroom," 67.

118. A more recent argument for this reading is found in Collins, *These Things Have Been Written*, 169; and Williams, "The Mother of Jesus at Cana," 689.

119. Brown, *Gospel According to John (I–XII)*, 99.

120. Ceroke, "The Problem of Ambiguity in John 2:4," 326.

2. The first part of Jesus' reply is negative, so a negative construction of this phrase would be more fitting.[121] Of course, when the first part is not read as negative, this argument loses its force.

A better argument in favor of the phrase being a statement rather than a question is that in 7:30 and 8:30 virtually identical phrases indicate unambiguously that Jesus' hour has not come. I am persuaded by this connection with later use, but concede that a reader approaching the text (without punctuation) for the first time would be hard pressed to know how to read it.

It was in the author's power to be clear on this point, but he appears to have preferred ambiguity.[122] It is certainly true that every aspect of Jesus' response creates bafflement.[123] Ceroke argues that this tactic was taken in order to leave open to the reader the choice between interpreting ὥρα as the hour of signs or the hour of death, and also to leave open the question of whether or not Jesus was assenting to his mother's request.[124]

Carson sees the reference to ὥρα as an internal prolepsis, which indicates that the Gospel was intended to be read through more than once.[125] I heartily agree that this Gospel does not readily disclose its secrets on a single reading.

There is little doubt among commentators that throughout the Gospel ὥρα typically refers to Jesus' death,[126] or to Jesus death, resurrection, and ascension,[127] though for an opposing view see Ridderbos,[128] and for a nuanced view see Ceroke.[129]

---

121. Brown, *Gospel According to John (I–Xii)*, 99.
122. Ceroke, "The Problem of Ambiguity in John 2:4," 324.
123. Lieu, "The Mother of the Son in the Fourth Gospel," 66.
124. Ceroke, "The Problem of Ambiguity in John 2:4," 329.
125. Carson, *Gospel According to John*, 171.
126. Bultmann, *Gospel of John*, 121; Moloney, *Belief in the Word*, 82; Culpepper, *Gospel and Letters of John*, 131; Waetjen, *Gospel of the Beloved Disciple*, 118; Morris, *Gospel According to John*, 181–2; Koester, *Symbolism in the Fourth Gospel*, 81; Bulembat, "Head-Waiter and Bridegroom," 66; Lieu, "The Mother of the Son in the Fourth Gospel," 66.
127. Brown, *Gospel According to John (I–Xii)*, 100; Dillon, "Wisdom Tradition and Sacramental Retrospect," 284; Borchert, *John 1–11*, 156; Collins, *These Things Have Been Written*, 170; Tenney, "John," 42; Carson, *The Gospel According to John*, 171; Fehribach, *Women in the Life of the Bridegroom*, 30.
128. Ridderbos, *Gospel According to John*, 106.
129. Ceroke, "Jesus and Mary at Cana," 4–13.

The word ὥρα in John is rarely simply about telling the time.[130] Uses outside of 4:2 can be broken down as follows:

- Jesus' hour (death[131] and glorification): 7:30; 8:20; 12:23,27; 13:1; 17:1
- Sending of the Holy Spirit: 4:21,23
- Resurrection of humanity: 5:25,28
- Persecution of Jesus' followers: 16:2,4
- Woman in labor: 16:21
- When Jesus will speak plainly: 16:25
- When the disciples will be scattered: 16:32
- When the beloved disciple takes Jesus' mother into his home: 19:27
- Simple time reference: 1:39; 4:6; 4:53; 19:14

It is clear that, setting aside the few simple time references, those occurrences of ὥρα that do not refer directly to Jesus' death refer to events that are set in motion by Jesus' arrest, death, and resurrection. It is likely, then, that Jesus is pointing towards his death in 2:4 as well, though it must be noted that someone reading the Gospel for the first time will have no way of knowing this and may come to a very different conclusion. In particular, the context seems to point toward ὥρα referring to the hour of Jesus commencing his public ministry, though the reader will soon discover that Jesus' public ministry will lead to his death.

Fehribach observes that the implied reader, encountering the text for the first time, could well take Jesus' response to mean that it is not his time to get married: "What has this to do with me? It is not my wedding!"[132] It is the bridegroom's responsibility to provide wine, and Jesus is not the bridegroom. Such an interpretation is certainly open to the first-time reader, but a second-time reader will know to interpret ὥρα in light of its other uses in the Gospel.

Jennifer Berenson Maclean puts forward the intriguing idea that the hour is connected with Genesis 29:21 where Jacob announces that

---

130. Neyrey, *Gospel of John*, 62.

131. Notice also 7:6,8. It is interesting to note that the first occasion where Jesus makes a time reference that is clearly related to his passion he uses καιρὸς instead of ὥρα. See Ceroke, "Jesus and Mary at Cana," 7. Note also that in the raising of Lazarus, timing and glory are again significant, though the word ὥρα is not used.

132. Fehribach, *Women in the Life of the Bridegroom*, 31.

his "time is completed" and that Laban must give him Rachel in marriage.[133] Her point is that, unlike Jacob who seeks to control fate and seize his fortune, Jesus submits himself utterly to the will and timing of God. Berenson Maclean's comparison of John 2–4 with the Jacob narratives certainly has value. I would suggest, though, that this is more likely to be a subsidiary allusion than the author's main point.

According to Schnackenburg, ὥρα speaks primarily of the will of the Father that determines all Jesus' actions.[134] Though 7:30 and 8:20 refer unmistakably to Jesus' death, he believes that the concept is more distant in chapter 2. Jesus' death is certainly the primary event in which Jesus performs the Father's will and is glorified, but at this point it may be the Father's will, rather than the death itself that is highlighted.

Hence even when Jesus first speaks of it, this distant hour may be evoked, in the background; but first and foremost this "hour" here signifies the Father's sovereignty over Jesus, asserted precisely in view of Mary.[135]

Note again the wedge that commentators drive between Jesus and Mary and the Father. This is observable again in Waetjen:

> His "hour" . . . is that time when he will remedy the condition that the failure of wine symbolizes. That "hour" will be his response to his Father's will and not his mother's. But more immediately he will fulfil his mother's request, but only as a sign, a sign that pledges that by the fulfilment of his "hour" in death Israel will realize a messianic bounty of an intoxicating vintage that is far superior to anything that has been tasted and drunk in the past.[136]

Fehribach's conclusion that at this point in the narrative the implied author has eliminated any possibility of Jesus' earthly mother having any real influence over him[137] pushes the general consensus beyond credibility. Whatever has happened in verse 4, Jesus' mother is still his mother, travelling by his side, in verse 12.

---

133. Maclean, "The Divine Trickster," 63–4.

134. So Ridderbos, *Gospel According to John*, 106; Moloney, *Belief in the Word*, 82–83; Maclean, "The Divine Trickster," 64; Hendrikson, *John*, 115.

135. Schnackenburg, *Gospel According to St John*, 330.

136. Waetjen, *Gospel of the Beloved Disciple*, 119.

137. Fehribach, *Women in the Life of the Bridegroom*, 37.

Neyrey contends that Jesus' assertion about his hour sets Jesus apart from the others in the story, including his mother. He knows the time. Others do not.[138] This is certainly true, just as his special knowledge had set him apart in 1:47–51.

If Jesus' ὥρα indicates his death, how is οὔπω ἥκει ἡ ὥρα μου an answer to his mother's request? At the spiritual level it is a deferral until a later time: the hour has not yet come for me to bring in the day of eschatological abundance[139] when there will be wine for all God's people. At a literal level it says nothing about whether Jesus intends to address the problem of the shortage of wine at the wedding. It is neither assent nor refusal.

Campbell argues that Jesus' ὥρα begins with the raising of Lazarus. From that point, Jesus ceases to act in secret and allows himself to be publicly observed, publicly praised, and publicly mocked and executed. In his public shaming and death, Jesus is honored as king. His reference to his hour at Cana, therefore, implies that his hour for public scrutiny, action, and honor, that is, the hour for his identity to be revealed, has not yet come.[140] This is an interesting theory.

Notice that the announcement that the hour has come takes place immediately after some Greeks ask to see Jesus (12:20–3). This remains enigmatic in the text, but the informed reader in the early church, knowing that in their time the benefits of Jesus' death have been enjoyed by Gentiles, may have seen in these verses a hint that Jesus' ὥρα brings "wine" to Gentiles as well as Jews. Here is further reason for Jesus to challenge his mother's alignment with the Jews. Will she be able to watch her son die for Gentiles as well as her beloved Jews? Will she be willing to share his wine with all, especially when so many Jews will remain hostile and so unsatisfied?

It is unlikely that Jesus' mother understood all the implications of Jesus' words. Yet, unlike Nicodemus (3:4) and the Samaritan woman (4:11) she does not ask for clarification or express confusion. She simply hears his words, knows he will do what is right, and instructs the servants to do whatever he says. Even a first-time reader might be in a position to imagine that the mother of such a son will have experienced many

---

138. Neyrey, *Gospel of John*, 63–64.
139. Carson, *Gospel According to John*, 172.
140. Campbell, *Kinship Relations*, 132–4.

enigmatic conversations with him and will have either learned to interpret his riddles or else to smile and trust his wisdom.

λέγει ἡ μήτηρ αὐτοῦ τοῖς διακόνοις, Ὅ τι ἂν λέγῃ ὑμῖν ποιήσατε.

It comes as no surprise at this point that scholarship continues to be divided as to the import of these words. Perhaps she heard Jesus' words as a rebuke for approaching him as her son, and she now places her trust in him as her Lord to act as he sees fit?[141] Or, at the opposite extreme, could it be that she is ignoring her son's resistance and reasserting her parental authority over him?[142] A middle-ground interpretation would be that Mary's persistence won Jesus over to acting against his initial reluctance, as in Matt 15:25–7 and John 4:47–50.[143] According to Brown, Jesus' mother is the ideal disciple who "seems to have no doubt that Jesus will intervene and is uncertain only about the manner of intervention."[144]

For the reader, curiosity is aroused as to the capacity in which Jesus' mother gives orders to the servants, but this curiosity is not satisfied in the text. She is certainly presented as an insider with respect to the host family. She knew about the embarrassing situation when they were, presumably, trying to keep it quiet; and now she gives orders to their servants. It may be that the author is deliberately presenting her as a more effective headwaiter than the man who has that title and appears to be ignorant of the crisis.

The subjunctive, ὅ τι ἂν λέγῃ, makes no presupposition about what Jesus may tell the servants.[145] These words, therefore, perform three functions in the narrative. Firstly, they express trust and a transfer of authority to her son.[146] Secondly, they continue to heighten suspense about just what it is that Jesus might do now; and thirdly, they prepare the servants

---

141. Carson, *Gospel According to John*, 173.

142. Fehribach, *Women in the Life of the Bridegroom*, 31–32.

143. Brown, *Gospel According to John (I–XII)*, 102.

144. Brown, *Gospel According to John (I–XII)*, 100; so Bruce, *Gospel of John*, 70: "she knew he would do the right thing."

145. Schnackenburg, *Gospel According to St John*, 331; Fehribach, *Women in the Life of the Bridegroom*, 39; Ceroke, "Jesus and Mary at Cana," 15.

146. Borchert, *John 1–11*, 156; Bultmann, *Gospel of John*, 117; Moloney, *Belief in the Word*, 83–84, 86; Hendrikson, *John*, 116; Carson, *Gospel According to John*, 173.

to follow without astonishment[147] *whatever* Jesus tells them to do, however odd it may seem.[148] Their unquestioning obedience in the following verses indicates that they took her words seriously.

In these words there are echoes of two significant OT events. In Genesis 41:55 (LXX) very similar words are spoken by the Pharaoh to the people of Egypt,[149] ἐπείνασεν πᾶσα ἡ γῆ Αἰγύπτου, ἐκέκραξεν δὲ ὁ λαὸς πρὸς Φαραω περὶ ἄρτων, εἶπεν δὲ Φαραω πᾶσι τοῖς Αἰγυπτίοις Πορεύεσθε πρὸς Ιωσηφ, καὶ ὃ ἐὰν εἴπῃ ὑμῖν, ποιήσατε.[150]

Though the phrase is not verbally identical, it is extremely close, including the use of a subjunctive and with ποιησατε appearing at the end of the sentence in both cases. The sense of trust and transfer of authority also appears in both contexts. More importantly, the words appear in both cases in a time of need. The similarities are presented in the following table.

Genesis 41:55–7	John 2:3–5
The people of Egypt become hungry	The wine runs out
The people cry out to Pharaoh for bread	Mary tells Jesus they have no wine
Pharaoh says to the people "Whatever Joseph tells you, do."	Mary says to the servants, "Whatever Jesus tells you, do."
Joseph opens the storehouses	Jesus fills six enormous jars with water and changes it into wine.
More tentatively: Hungry people come from all over the world to purchase grain from Joseph.	In 12:20–3 Greeks come to Jesus and he recognizes that his hour has arrived.

---

147. Ceroke, "Jesus and Mary at Cana," 36.

148. Ceroke, "Jesus and Mary at Cana," 25.

149. See Dillon, "Wisdom Tradition and Sacramental Retrospect," 289; Ridderbos, *The Gospel According to John*, 106.

150. TR: The whole land of Egypt was starving and the people cried out to the Pharaoh for bread, and the Pharaoh said to all the Egyptians "Go to Joseph and whatever he says to you, do."

This comparison with Joseph presents Jesus as the man of true wisdom who has the resources to save his people in a time of need. Other points of contact might also be intended. Joseph was also wrongly arrested and punished as a criminal, while God used his unjust imprisonment to bring good to him and his family. Joseph also lived with the conflict between justice and mercy that we have observed earlier. His brothers had treated him dreadfully, but he sought their welfare for the sake of his father. Ultimately, Joseph, the brother who was rejected, became the savior of his people.

Whether all these themes were in the author's mind when he wrote those words is impossible to determine, but for the reader who is educated in the Old Testament one nod towards Joseph would bring to mind his entire story.

Moloney[151] believes these words also direct the reader's attention to the giving of the law (LXX Exod 19:8, cf. 24:3,7,) where the people at the foot of the mountain say, ἀπεκρίθη δὲ πᾶς ὁ λαὸς ὁμοθυμαδὸν καὶ εἶπαν Πάντα, ὅσα εἶπεν ὁ θεός, ποιήσομεν καὶ ἀκουσόμεθα.

The verbal similarity is not so close that conclusions about the author's intention here can be clearly discerned. It is significant that, here again, is the sense of trust and transfer of authority. Trust, here, is in all the words of the Lord; in John, believers are called to place their trust and allegiance in the Word of God. In this sense Moloney sees Mary as the prototypical disciple:

> The woman, the mother of Jesus, is the first person, in the experience of the reader, to manifest trust in the word of Jesus. Her relationship with Jesus transcends the limitations displayed by the disciples, who attempted to understand him within their own categories in 1:35–51. The mother of Jesus is deliberately shown by the author as the first who commands action based entirely on the word of Jesus, without offering any supporting cultural, religious, or historical motivation for such a command.[152]

ἦσαν δὲ ἐκεῖ λίθιναι ὑδρίαι ἕξ

Many commentators point out that stone jars were preferred for use in ritual cleansing because they could be cleaned if they became

---

151. Moloney, *Belief in the Word*, 83; so Grassi, "The Wedding at Cana," 126.
152. Moloney, *Belief in the Word*, 84.

ritually unclean, whereas earthenware jars would need to be broken (Lev 11:29–38).[153]

Stone vessels are among the most common finds on archaeology digs in Palestine[154] and some have been found embedded in the ground.[155]

In the number six, many commentators find symbolism of imperfection,[156] implying that Jewish purification rites do not give complete cleansing. Waetjen argues that the number represents the six *sederim* of the Mishnah, implying that the entire purity code is empty and must be replaced by a new moral order.[157] Almost certainly the use of purification vessels is symbolic of Jesus' intension to transform (not necessarily abolish) the purification rituals of his people.

κατὰ τὸν καθαρισμὸν τῶν Ἰουδαίων κείμεναι

Several variants omit κείμεναι or move it to an earlier point in the sentence. None of these alter the meaning of the sentence.

Dodd believes that these jars "stand for the entire system of Jewish ceremonial observance" and that this sign symbolizes that ὁ νόμος διὰ Μωϋσέως ἐδόθη, ἡ χάρις καὶ ἡ ἀλήθεια διὰ Ἰησοῦ Χριστοῦ ἐγένετο (1:17). This sign, in that case, "sets forth the truth that with His coming the old order in religion is superseded by a new order."[158]

Certainly these words are more than simply an explanation for Gentile readers,[159] particularly given the ominous tone the words οἱ Ἰουδαῖοι will take on as the Gospel proceeds. Just as the lack of wine symbolizes the Jewish people under God's judgment because of their sin, the jars

---

153. Schnackenburg, *Gospel According to St John*, 332; Borchert, *John 1–11*, 156; Carson, *Gospel According to John*, 173; Malina and Rohrbaugh, *Social-Science Commentary on the Gospel of John*, 69.

154. Moxnes, *Putting Jesus in His Place*, 42; Bruce, *Gospel of John*, 70.

155. Schnackenburg, *Gospel According to St John*, 332.

156. Moloney, *Belief in the Word*; Schnackenburg, *Gospel According to St John*, 332; Culpepper, *Gospel and Letters of John*, 131; contra Morris, *Gospel According to John*, 182.

157. Waetjen, *Gospel of the Beloved Disciple*, 119.

158. Dodd, *Interpretation of the Fourth Gospel*, 299; so Bruce, *Gospel of John*, 71; Moloney, *Belief in the Word*, 80; Berenson Maclean, "The Divine Trickster," 66; Carson, *Gospel According to John*, 173.

159. This is argued by Bruce, *Gospel of John*, 71; Bultmann, *The Gospel of John*, 117.

represent their unsuccessful attempts to cleanse themselves from that sin. Despite their purification rituals, they have no wine.

χωροῦσαι ἀνὰ μετρητὰς δύο ἢ τρεῖς.

Despite Augustine finding trinitarian imagery here,[160] it is much more likely that these words simply emphasize the enormous quantity (up to 720 liters) of water that is about to be transformed into wine. That abundance of wine will, in turn, point towards the arrival of messianic times (Gen 49:11; Hos 14:7; Amos 9:13–14; Isa 25:6; Jer 31:12)[161] and with it the end of God's judgment and the outpouring of God's blessing.

λέγει αὐτοῖς ὁ Ἰησοῦς, Γεμίσατε τὰς ὑδρίας ὕδατος. καὶ ἐγέμισαν αὐτὰς ἕως ἄνω.

The filling of such large jars to the brim (ἕως ἄνω) indicates, again, the lavishness of the miracle[162] and makes it clear that nothing extra could be added that might have affected the water.[163] The quantity of the miracle has been established and narration now turns to the quality.[164]

λέγει αὐτοῖς, Ἀντλήσατε νῦν

Note how νῦν here contrasts with the earlier οὔπω.[165] It was not his hour; but now he will act.

Westcott's well-known suggestion, on the basis that ἀντλήσατε usually refers to drawing water from a well, that the water that Jesus turns to wine is drawn from a well rather than the jars[166] is highly abrasive to the

---

160. See chapter 5.

161. Brown, *Gospel and Epistles of John*, 29; Brown, *Gospel According to John (I–XII)*, 105; so Ridderbos, *The Gospel According to John*, 108–9; Moloney, *Belief in the Word*, 79–80; Collins, *These Things Have Been Written*, 174; Carson, *Gospel According to John*, 174; Fehribach, *Women in the Life of the Bridegroom*, 29–30.

162. Schnackenburg, *Gospel According to St John*, 332.

163. Hendrikson, *John*, 115; Morris, *Gospel According to John*, 183.

164. Ridderbos, *Gospel According to John*, 107.

165. Ridderbos, *Gospel According to John*, 108.

166. This view is supported by Carson, *Gospel According to John*; Bruce, *Gospel of John*, 174.

context. There appears to be no reasonable explanation for the jars being filled if they are not then involved in the provision of wine.

Within the NT, ἀντλέω is used only here and in 4:7, 15, so no argument can be established upon NT usage. It is true that most LXX uses of the word refer unambiguously to drawing water from a well, but this is insufficient to exclude a slightly different meaning here. Consider the following definitions:

Strong's Lexicon 501: ἀντλέω antleō; from ἄντλος antlos (a ship's hold, bilge water in a ship's hold); to bail out, draw water:—draw(3,) drawn(1).[167]

47.1 ἀντλέω: to draw a liquid, normally water, from a container or well—'to draw water.' λέγει αὐτοῖς, Ἀντλήσατε νῦν 'he said to them, Draw it out now' Jn 2:8.[168]

Draw out (ἀντλήσατε). From ἄντλος, *the hold of a ship where the bilge-water settles*, and hence, *the bilge-water itself*. The verb, therefore, originally, means *to bale out bilge-water;* thence, generally, *to draw*, as from a well (4:15).[169]

The second definition, from Louw, may be open to the accusation of extracting the meaning from the text, so not too much encouragement can be drawn from its assurance that the word can be used in relation to a container. The other two definitions draw attention to the origin of the word. Word usage changes over time, and a word should not be considered too tightly bound to its roots, but it is interesting to notice that the word emerged from a context of shipping, not a context of extracting water from a well. To assert that by the first century this word has been first broadened and then narrowed to be exclusively associated with drawing water from a well seems unlikely.

It is more likely that this verb is used to accentuate the great size of the jars:[170] to indicate that drawing water out of them could be compared with drawing water out of a well. It is also entirely possible that the word was intended to prefigure its use in chapter 4 when Jesus converses with the Samaritan woman.

I tentatively suggest a third reason why the word is appropriate here. In the LXX we find it in Isaiah 12:3. Καὶ ἀντλήσετε ὕδωρ μετ'

---

167. Thomas, *New American Standard Hebrew-Aramaic and Greek Dictionaries*.
168. Louw and Nida, *Greek-English Lexicon of the New Testament*.
169. Vincent, *Word Studies in the New Testament*.
170. Morris, *Gospel According to John*, 183.

εὐφροσύνης ἐκ τῶν πηγῶν τοῦ σωτηρίου.[171] Note here that the water is drawn (ἀντλήσετε) not from a φρέαρ (well) but from a πηγαί (spring, or possibly well). This is therefore an example of a use of ἀντλέω which is not unambiguously related to a well. More importantly, the concept of joyfully drawing water from the spring of salvation is relevant to this context of Jesus addressing the tragedy of God's people living under God's judgment. It is possible that the use of ἀντλέω was intended as an allusion to this verse, though it is uncertain that many readers would be aware of it.

καὶ φέρετε τῷ ἀρχιτρικλίνῳ· οἱ δὲ ἤνεγκαν.

It seems that there is no reference to this role in Jewish literature, though there may be some connection with Sir 32:1 where a guest presides over the feast as a friend of the bridegroom. He appears to be both master of ceremonies and headwaiter, tasked with keeping the guests satisfied.[172]

It is quite possible that some contrast is intended between him and Jesus' mother, who seems to have assumed that role.

Use of the word "headwaiter" throughout this chapter concedes that it is not a perfect translation but that there does not seem to be a better translation available.

ὡς δὲ ἐγεύσατο ὁ ἀρχιτρίκλινος τὸ ὕδωρ οἶνον γεγενημένον

According to Bultmann, "It is in accordance with the style of ancient miracle stories that the miraculous process itself is not described; the divine action remains a mystery."[173] So here the reader is not told at what point, in time or space, the water became wine.

Barrett, following Bultmann,[174] points out that Dionysius was credited with both discovering and with transforming water into wine.[175] Most other commentators see insufficient evidence to make a clear

---

171. And you will draw water with joy from the spring of salvation.

172. Borchert, *John 1–11*, 156; Morris, *Gospel According to John*, 184; Tenney, "John," 42; Carson, *Gospel According to John*, 174.

173. Bultmann, *Gospel of John*, 118.

174. Bultmann, *Gospel of John*, 118–9.

175. Barrett, *Gospel According to St John*, 188.

connection with Dionysius.[176] It is interesting to note, though, that by the end of the fourth century the Cana reading had became part of the Epiphany liturgy[177] celebrated on January 6, the day of the feast of Dionysius in which fountains were said to run with wine.[178] Perhaps this was to demonstrate to pagans that Jesus was more powerful than Dionysius.[179] It is even possible that John narrated the sign in conscious opposition to pagan accounts of metamorphosis.[180]

Koester, making a connection between this passage and 12:20–3 via the use of ὥρα, believes that the Dionysian myths may have had a role, not as the origin of the Cana narrative, but as a way of communicating to Greeks as well as Jews that in Jesus God is present.[181] Ridderbos disagrees, arguing that this story is so decidedly set against a Jewish background that any search for links with paganism would be futile.[182] Yet, it is not inconceivable that the author may have intentionally included Greek imagery, alongside the Jewish, for the sake of communicating to a broader audience.

Dodd finds a clue to the Jewish background of changing water into wine in the writings of Philo concerning Melchizedek[183] where the phrase ἀντὶ ὕδατος οἶνος is used.[184] Other references to the wine of God in Philo include *De Somnis*[185] II 183, 190, 249, *Quod Deus Immutabilis* 158, Leg Alleg I. 84, De Fuga 166. Dodd summarizes Philo in this way:

> Thus the wine which the Priest-logos brings forth ἀντι ὕδατος stands for God's gifts of grace, joy, virtue, wisdom, and the like; in fact for all those things which for Philo characterize the higher or spiritual life. We may therefore recognize in it an apt

---

176. Beasley-Murray, *John*, 35; Schnackenburg, *Gospel According to St John*, 340; Ridderbos, *Gospel According to John*, 110–111; Buby, *Mary of Galilee*, 118; Carson, *Gospel According to John*, 167.

177. See Luther, *Sermons of the Gospel of St. John Chapters 1–4*, 214 for evidence of the continuation of that practice.

178. Brown, *Gospel According to John (I–XII)*, 101; Bultmann, *Gospel of John*, 119.

179. Brown, *Gospel According to John (I–XII)*, 101.

180. See Menoud, "Signification Du Miracle Selon Le Nouveau Testament," 182 for a contrast between the Cana sign and pagan accounts of metamorphosis.

181. Koester, *Symbolism in the Fourth Gospel*, 80–81.

182. Ridderbos, *Gospel According to John*, 111.

183. Philo, "Allegorical Interpretation" Book III, §79.

184. Dodd, *Interpretation of the Fourth Gospel*, 298–9.

185. Philo, "De Somniis."

symbol for all that the Fourth Evangelist conceives Christ to have brought into the world.[186]

καὶ οὐκ ᾔδει πόθεν ἐστίν, οἱ δὲ διάκονοι ᾔδεισαν οἱ ἠντληκότες τὸ ὕδωρ,

The headwaiter's ignorance about where the wine came from echoes and prefigures one of the major questions in this Gospel: where did Jesus come from?[187] At a more literal level it indicates his objectivity[188] and perhaps even his incompetence.[189] The fact that the servants appear to be willing to leave him in his ignorance does cause the reader to wonder whether they even recognized his authority over them.[190]

φωνεῖ τὸν νυμφίον ὁ ἀρχιτρίκλινος καὶ λέγει αὐτῷ, Πᾶς ἄνθρωπος πρῶτον τὸν καλὸν οἶνον τίθησιν καὶ ὅταν μεθυσθῶσιν τὸν ἐλάσσω·

Though there is no evidence in the literature that this was the common practice, it does seem a sensible expedient when keeping celebrations going for a week.[191] Schnackenburg suggests that it sounds like a joke,[192] while Bruce calls it a proverb.[193] Lack of extant attestation is insufficient reason to conclude that the tradition was an invention of the author.

Perhaps there is a suggestion of something morally wanting in the headwaiter speaking of drunkenness in such an off-hand manner.[194] Μεθυσόμαι appears only four times in the NT, always with negative connotations (Luke 12:45; Eph 5:18; 1 Thess 5:7; John 2:10).

186. Dodd, *Interpretation of the Fourth Gospel*, 299.

187. Schnackenburg, *Gospel According to St John*, 333; Bultmann, *Gospel of John*, 121; contra Ridderbos, *Gospel According to John*, 107–8; Moloney, *Belief in the Word*, 86.

188. Ridderbos, *Gospel According to John*, 108.

189. Bulembat, "Head-Waiter and Bridegroom," 62.

190. Bulembat, "Head-Waiter and Bridegroom," 63.

191. Brown, *Gospel According to John (I–Xii)*, 100; Borchert, *John 1–11*, 157.

192. Schnackenburg, *Gospel According to St John*, 323; so Koester, *Symbolism in the Fourth Gospel*, 78.

193. Bruce, *Gospel of John*, 71.

194. Bulembat, "Head-Waiter and Bridegroom," 61.

The most striking oddity about the headwaiter's speech is that he appears to have been completely unaware of the averted calamity concerning the supply of wine.[195] The reader is naturally puzzled about why Jesus' mother knew about this problem and the person whose responsibility it was did not. Could this point toward the Jewish leadership being unaware of the desperate spiritual state of the people, while those groaning under Roman oppression and the burden of Pharisaic legal tradition were all too aware that their people were not experiencing the wine of God's blessing?

σὺ τετήρηκας τὸν καλὸν οἶνον ἕως ἄρτι.

Schnackenburg sees the provision of the good wine at the end of the banquet as an indication of the eschatological nature of Jesus ministry.[196]

Neyrey sees here a challenge to the strongly held first-century Greek and Roman belief that older is better than newer, ancient better than modern. Jews also held this belief as they looked to Moses and were skeptical about the new gospel Jesus was declaring.[197] This sign points to the superiority of the new, against all expectations. Similarly, Berenson Maclean sees here a reference to Jacob, who embodied God's preference for the younger over the elder.[198]

According to Campbell, this speaks to the situation of Christian Jews who have been expelled from the Synagogue. She believes "The author presents Jesus as the one in whom persons who are no longer part of the synagogue community will not only find all that they have lost but much more. The replacement motif teaches people about Jesus while encouraging their deeper emotional anchorage in him and in the group."[199]

Undoubtedly, John intended these words in part as encouragement to people who had given up a great deal in order to follow Christ, or who were considering the implications of becoming a disciple. Many

---

195. Bulembat, "Head-Waiter and Bridegroom," 61.

196. Schnackenburg, *Gospel According to St John*, 338.

197. Neyrey, *Gospel of John*, 68.

198. Berenson Maclean, "The Divine Trickster," 66. She also points out that Justin Martyr (Dial. 134) interpreted Jacob's marriages allegorically in terms of the younger (Rachel = the Church) being superior to the elder (Leah = the Jews), and that Philo (Ebr. 47–51) makes similar use of the passage, asserting that the superior (Leah = philosophy) ought to come after the inferior (Rachel = elementary education).

199. Campbell, *Kinship Relations*, 183.

Christian Jews had experienced the pain of exclusion from fellowship with fellow Jews. However, this is unlikely to be the only sacrifice John had in mind. Pagan converts had similarly lost the fellowship around their local temple. By the end of the first century there were places in the Empire where Christians were losing their lives.

These words could also be seen as comfort to all Jews as they grieved the loss of their temple and their holy city. What had been lost has now been replaced by something much better.

Ταύτην ἐποίησεν ἀρχὴν τῶν σημείων ὁ Ἰησοῦς ἐν Κανὰ τῆς Γαλιλαίας

That this is the beginning of Jesus' signs implies a connection between this and the other signs in the Fourth Gospel.[200] This sign has been called the "foundation and pattern for everything that follows."[201] Just how much this is the case will be discussed below.

Only one other sign is numbered (4:54), so ἀρχὴν here may signal that the reader should read the two signs together or should understand that they operate as an inclusio around John 2–4.[202]

For Bultmann, ἀρχὴν τῶν σημείων is simply an indication that the σημεία source was numbered.[203] His reasoning appears to give the redactors far too little credit for their ability to combine sources smoothly and logically to suit their purposes.[204]

Σημείων may recall the Septuagint use of the word to describe the miracles that legitimized Moses as the one sent by God (Ex 8:4)[205] or perhaps the "sign acts" of the Hebrew prophets.[206]

Ridderbos does not see the word σημείων as referring primarily to deeper symbolic meaning behind Jesus' actions. He does, however, allow

---

200. Brown, *Gospel According to John (I-XII)*, 104; Grassi, *Mary, Mother and Disciple*, 84.

201. Ridderbos, *Gospel According to John*, 113; So Borchert, *John 1–11*, 153; Collins, *These Things Have Been Written*, 162; Waetjen, *Gospel of the Beloved Disciple*, 114; Buby, *Mary of Galilee*, 121; Hunter, *According to John*, 76.

202. Borchert, *John 1–11*, 152.

203. Bultmann, *Gospel of John*, 113.

204. See Moloney, *Belief in the Word*, 78.

205. Hunter, *According to John*, 70.

206. Hunter, *According to John*, 70. Bruce makes a similar point when he calls this story an enacted parable. Bruce, *Gospel of John*, 70.

for deeper (secondary) meanings to emerge and guide our reading.[207] For Bultmann, on the other hand: "The concepts of σημεῖα and ῥήματα (λόγοι) both qualify each other: σημεῖον is not a mere demonstration, but a spoken directive, a symbol; ῥῆμα is not teaching in the sense of communication of a set of ideas, but is the occurrence of the Word, the event of the address. 2:1–11 therefore can immediately be seen as a symbol."[208]

Signs in John (12:37), like the Gospel itself (20:30), are intended to draw people to believe that Jesus is the Messiah, the Son of God. Though there is great symbolic richness in each of them, their function as signs is to point to one thing: the divine origins of Jesus. Schnell expresses this well: "The miracle at Cana is . . . the beginning of the revelation of the δόξα of the Pre-existent One in space and time; it reveals the essence of the Son of God, whose whole activity John can designate as ποιεῖν σημεῖον (12:37; 20:30). As the "first sign," it anticipates further manifestations of the glory of Jesus Christ."[209]

The Cana sign presents a unique challenge within this Gospel in that there is no dialogue directing the reader's interpretation of the sign[210] other than the dialogue between Jesus and his mother. This places emphasis on that brief conversation as the reader seeks to identify just where this sign is pointing, and particularly as the reader seeks to interpret the other signs in the light of this one.

καὶ ἐφανέρωσεν τὴν δόξαν αὐτοῦ,

This phrase recalls 1:14, καὶ ὁ λόγος σὰρξ ἐγένετο καὶ ἐσκήνωσεν ἐν ἡμῖν, καὶ ἐθεασάμεθα τὴν δόξαν αὐτοῦ.[211] Jesus' glory is revealed in his σάρξ, but who are the ones who saw it, among whom the evangelist counts himself? Presumably not all he dwelt among. Presumably not those who αὐτὸν οὐκ ἔγνω (1:10,) or those who αὐτὸν οὐ παρέλαβον (1:11).

Jesus' glory was revealed at Cana, but who saw it? The servants saw what he did, but did they see his glory? We are not told. We are told that

---

207. Ridderbos, *Gospel According to John*, 113.
208. Bultmann, *Gospel of John*, 114.
209. Schnell, *Antidocetic Christology in the Gospel of John*, 75.
210. Ridderbos, *Gospel According to John*, 101.

211. Dodd, *Interpretation of the Fourth Gospel*, 297; Bruce, *Gospel of John*, 72; Borchert, *John 1–11*, 158; Moloney, *Belief in the Word*, 89.

the disciples believed, implying that they saw his glory in this miracle. What of Jesus' family, represented here by his mother and, presumably, his brothers, since they were with him immediately afterwards (v12)? He ἐσκήνωσεν ἐν them more literally than any other group of people. They were more familiar with his σαρξ than anyone else. Did they see his glory when it was revealed at Cana? This remains an open question, though his mother's initiative and trust seem to point towards her being a disciple.

Jesus' glory is seen, in John, in Jesus' σημεια (2:11; 11:40) and ultimately in his passion[212] (12:23; 17:24). Murray Rae believes that each sign in the Fourth Gospel is to be understood as "a foreshadowing of [Jesus'] glory and a participation ahead of time in the new life that is to come."[213] Schnell calls the miracles, "stages on the way to the cross."[214] They lead to the cross because they kindle both belief and unbelief. Belief will draw disciples to follow him. Unbelief will draw others into a conspiracy that will lead Jesus to his death.[215]

Schnackenburg, however, is wise to point out:

> It can hardly be right to reduce the present revelation of Jesus' glory to an anticipation of his future state. The eyes of faith see the doxa of Jesus even in his earthly work; it is precisely the doxa present in the incarnate Word which is spoken of in 1:14. It is not the primary or sole function of the "sign" to point to the future. It rather discloses—though only to believers—the saving power present in the person of Jesus.[216]

καὶ ἐπίστευσαν εἰς αὐτὸν οἱ μαθηταὶ αὐτοῦ.

Use of the aorist tense (ἐπίστευσαν) is interesting here. In John, the disciples appear to be in a process of intensification of faith, taking them from followers (1:35–42) to those who know that Jesus has the words of eternal life and so refuse to turn back (6:68,) to those who can say to Jesus, "My Lord and my God!" (20:28). However, here their belief seems to be focused at a particular point in time. ἐπιστεθσεν (again aorist) is used in 4:53 of the royal official whose son Jesus healed. The content of

---

212. Brown, *Gospel According to John (I-XII)*, 100.
213. Bauckham and Mosser, *Gospel of John and Christian Theology*, 303.
214. Schnell, *Antidocetic Christology in the Gospel of John*, 171.
215. Schnell, *Antidocetic Christology in the Gospel of John*, 171.
216. Schnackenburg, *Gospel According to St John*, 330.

his belief could not have been substantial after such a brief encounter with Jesus. It appears, then, that when πιστεύω is used in aorist tense here it refers to an appropriate response to Jesus on the basis of what they have just seen and heard. If a sign can be an act of communication, believing seems to be the appropriate answering act of response.

Hearing and responding appropriately, seeing and believing, are what sets disciples[217] apart from those who are merely observers.[218] These disciples are those who later become witnesses to Jesus' glory (1:14) and founders of the church (cf. 20:31).[219]

> John takes the incarnation so seriously that the veil of σάρξ is never removed, and the divine glory of Jesus is never displayed except to the eyes of faith . . . The φανεροθν is more than an external demonstration, such as the unbelieving brothers of Jesus ask for in 7:4; it is a manifestation (an "epiphany," when rightly understood) visible to the spiritually open eyes of the believer.[220]

It is interesting to note that though the verb πιστευω appears in its various forms more than a hundred times in the Fourth Gospel, the noun πιστις does not occur at all.[221] Perhaps the author is not interested in "faith" as an abstract notion, as a thing that a person may have or not have. Rather, the emphasis in this Gospel is on the act of believing, the act of responding appropriately (with trust, obedience, and humility) to Jesus. With respect to Jesus' mother, this Gospel does not encourage us to ask, "Does she have faith?" but rather, "Did she respond appropriately to Jesus? Did she express trust, obedience, and humility?" And the answer seems to be yes.

Dillon draws parallels between this sign and the call of Wisdom (Prov 9:5) to come to her banquet, eat her bread (cf. John 6), and drink her wine.[222] The disciples have been called in John 1;[223] now they drink the wine, indicating both that they have accepted the call and that Jesus

---

217. Schnackenburg, *Gospel According to St John*, 334; Thompson, *Humanity of Jesus in the Fourth Gospel*, 85.

218. Dillon, "Wisdom Tradition and Sacramental Retrospect." 283; Morris, *Gospel According to John*, 186.

219. Ridderbos, *Gospel According to John*, 99.

220. Schnackenburg, *Gospel According to St John*, 336–7.

221. Hunter, *According to John*, 72.

222. So Lee, *Flesh and Glory*, 139.

223. Brown, *Gospel According to John (I–XII)*, 105–7; so Schnackenburg, *Gospel According to St John*, 323.

acts in the role of Wisdom.[224] The disciples have followed (1:37); now they believe (2:11).[225] They have been promised greater signs (1:50f); now they have begun to see them.[226]

The prominence of Jesus' mother in this account, along with the mention of his brothers in the following verse,[227] raises the question for the reader: Are the members of Jesus' family numbered among those disciples who saw the sign, perceived Jesus' glory, and believed?[228] John 7:5 answers that question with respect to the brothers. At that later point in the narrative they did not believe. The readers might wonder if Jesus' brothers would have been at all happy with Jesus' performance at the wedding. Jesus' glory (honor) was revealed, but only privately to those who were already his followers. There was no public display that would build the eminence of his family.[229] Perhaps this disappointment is in view in 7:3.

Campbell suggests, on the other hand, that the brothers' presence on the journey to and sojourn in Capernaum may indicate that they sensed the potential benefit for their whole family to be derived from this extraordinary brother.[230] In this case a positive relationship with Jesus in John 2 somehow turns sour by John 7, perhaps because they sense that their elder brother's performances do not bring the honor to the family that they had hoped.

As far as Jesus' mother is concerned we must wait until John 19 for a clear answer,[231] but her trust in her son hints that she may be already a believer and a disciple. Some scholars call her the ideal disciple because she not only places unconditional trust in Jesus but she does so in a way that leads others to believe.[232]

---

224. Dillon, "Wisdom Tradition and Sacramental Retrospect."

225. Morris, *Gospel According to John*, 186.

226. Ridderbos, *Gospel According to John*, 99; Waetjen, *Gospel of the Beloved Disciple*, 120; Malina and Rohrbaugh, *Social-Science Commentary on the Gospel of John*, 69.

227. Moloney, *Belief in the Word*, 78.

228. Fehribach, *Women in the Life of the Bridegroom*, 41.

229. Williams, "The Mother of Jesus at Cana," 690.

230. Campbell, *Kinship Relations*, 136.

231. Neyrey, *Gospel of John*, 68.

232. Moloney, *Belief in the Word*, 92; Howard, "Minor Characters," 69; Ceroke, "Jesus and Mary at Cana," 36.

To what does this sign point?

All signs in the Fourth Gospel point to Jesus as the "Messiah, the Son of God" (20:31) yet they each do this in a unique way. Several suggestions have been put forward for the particular significance of the Cana portrayal of Jesus as Messiah and Son of God.

Dodd believes that John 1–4 can be summed up by Paul's words, τὰ ἀρχαῖα παρῆλθεν, ἰδοὺ γέγονεν καινά. (2 Cor 5:17).[233] Barrett sees the "supersession of Judaism in the glory of Jesus."[234] Brown argues that all the signs concern the replacement by Jesus of Jewish institutions and religious views.[235] Certainly in the Synoptic Gospels, new wine represents the shattering impact of Jesus' ministry upon Jewish institutions; and John 2–4 sees the overturning or transcending of much that was close to the heart of second temple Judaism. Purification rituals (2:1–11; 3:22–30), the temple (2:13–22), and the law (3:1–21), along with old rivalries and divisions (ch 4) are all challenged or symbolically replaced by Jesus. Even life itself is renewed (4:46–54). Why is it that so much needs to be challenged, transcended, and transformed? The answer is found in the words of Jesus' mother: Οἶνον οὐκ ἔχουσιν.

Wisdom motifs have also been observed in the invitation of the disciples to follow Jesus and come to the banquet, and also in the portrayal of Jesus as the new Joseph, the man of wisdom. Jesus is, therefore, both wisdom personified and the wise man—the Word of God become flesh. Wisdom, therefore, has also been made new in Jesus.[236] Now the wise person is the one who follows him, drinks his wine, and eats his bread (6:51).

Grassi points out that the only other place in the New Testament where the exact phrase, ἦν ἡ μήτηρ τοῦ Ἰησοῦ, is used is in Acts 1:14. There, Jesus' mother is gathered with the other disciples praying, as Grassi imagines, for the new wine of the Spirit. Her role in Acts 1–2, he argues, is the same as in John 2, that of asking Jesus for new wine.[237]

---

233. Dodd, *Interpretation of the Fourth Gospel*, 297; So Carson, *Gospel According to John*, 166.

234. Barrett, *Gospel According to St John*, 189; so Morris, *Gospel According to John*, 176.

235. Brown, *Gospel According to John (I-XII)*, 104.

236. 9:1–5 demonstrates the need for wisdom traditions to be renewed.

237. Grassi, "The Wedding at Cana," 125–6.

This puts a lot of weight on a verbal similarity that could easily be coincidental, but his argument is made more plausible by the fact that the geographical and sociological movement in John 2–4 matches the spread of the gospel in Acts 1–10.[238] This adds weight to the possibility that the authors of John and Acts were both reflecting on the birth of the church when they wrote their works. It is not necessary to posit dependence between John and Luke for such a link to be reasonable. The memory of Pentecost and its aftermath would have been alive throughout the first-century Christian community. It is not unreasonable to see John 2–4 as, in part, pointing towards the creation, by the messiah, of the new people of God.

There is a clear connection between the theme that "the new has come" and the birth of the church. The church, as Paul articulates, is the new temple (1 Cor 3:16), the new people of God. Both themes are also linked to the eschatological blessings of the advent of the messiah.

Fehribach believes that by providing wine for a wedding Jesus accepts the role of bridegroom, and therefore of messianic bridegroom,[239] the role of Yahweh, the bridegroom of Israel.[240] This resonates with the allusions to Hosea that have been noted.

Bulemont agrees that Jesus is presented as bridegroom and further argues that Jesus' mother takes the role of headwaiter.[241] I have already observed that Jesus' mother fulfills the role of headwaiter much more effectively than the man charged with the task, so Bulemont's argument is entirely plausible.

---

238. Culpepper, *Gospel and Letters of John*, 129.

239. So Bulembat, "Head-Waiter and Bridegroom," 55.

240. Fehribach, *Women in the Life of the Bridegroom*, 30; so Olsson, *Structure and Meaning in the Fourth Gospel*, who argues this point from Exodus 19–24.

241. She argues that the structure of the passage points to a parallel between vv3–5 and vv9–10 following the chiastic structure below:
A: vv1–2:   introduction
Ba: vv3–5:   action of the mother of Jesus—with Jesus
Bb: vv3–5:   action of the mother of Jesus—with servants
C: vv6–8   action of Jesus
B'b': vv9–10   action of the head waiter—with servants
B'a': vv9–10   action of the head waiter—with bridegroom
A': vv11–12:   conclusion
Bulembat, "Head-Waiter and Bridegroom," 57,60.

Malina and Rohrbaugh deny that Jesus takes the role of the bridegroom here.[242] They insist that he was acting as wedding associate and that, by providing so much wine, he showed himself to be a good friend to the bridegroom.[243] What makes their argument implausible is that the author has been quite clear about Jesus' status as an invited guest (2:2), whose invitation seems to be subsidiary to his mother's presence (2:1). This is not consistent with the role of wedding associate.

Lieu argues that the role exchanges are examples of narrative irony.[244] There is certainly irony involved when the bridegroom and headwaiter are unable to perform their functions while Jesus and his mother quietly do their jobs for them. However, it is a necessary next step to consider the function of the irony here. What does it mean that Jesus is acting like a bridegroom? What does it mean that his mother is acting like a headwaiter? What is the author seeking to communicate to the reader through such irony?

Israel, the bride of Yahweh, is experiencing the Lord's judgment rather than blessing. Οἶνον οὐκ ἔχουσιν. Jesus' mother brings this to the attention of her son. Whether she perceives the spiritual depth of her words or, more likely, is thinking only of the literal crisis of a wedding without wine is not clarified. What is clear is that Jesus perceived the full meaning of her words. In his reply, he warns his mother that aligning herself too closely with the Jews might bring her into conflict with him. In his ὥρα he intends to reconcile justice with mercy, but for now his mother's people are under God's judgment and must hear his charges against them, beginning symbolically in his first sign and verbally soon afterwards in 2:16. His mother's people are also his people, but they will reject him (1:10). The mother of the Word must take care where she places her allegiance.

Whether or not his mother heard all the undertones of his words is not clear, but she does not act as if she is confused. If anyone knows how to read the cryptic utterances of this man at this point in his life, surely it is the woman who has raised him and is in all likelihood the human who is closest to his heart.[245] It is not necessary to resolve the question of whether or not she understood. More important questions concern

---

242. This assertion is made by Fehribach, *Women in the Life of the Bridegroom*, 29.
243. Malina and Rohrbaugh, *Social-Science Commentary on the Gospel of John*, 69.
244. Lieu, "The Mother of the Son in the Fourth Gospel," 64.
245. See chapter 4 on mother–son relationships.

what is being communicated to the reader by John. What did the original readers/hearers understand on their first reading and on their tenth reading? What do we understand as modern readers on our first reading and what more do we understand when examining the Gospel at doctoral level?

Jesus' mother demonstrates her allegiance to her son by trustingly transferring her authority to him, telling the servants to do *whatever* he says. This recalls 1 Kings 17:18, where Elijah demonstrates his (challenged) allegiance to the widow by healing her son.

Jesus then miraculously meets the need in a way that points toward his messianic role without implying that Israel has escaped judgment. Use of the six purification jars is an implicit criticism of Jewish efforts to be ritually clean before God. Provision and criticism, mercy and judgment, therefore meet in this sign, while the sign points to the ὥρα when they will ultimately be reconciled.

The Cana sign is programmatic for the other signs in this respect. While Jesus acts in mercy he makes it clear that judgment has not been removed. While Jesus' glory is glimpsed in the signs, the signs point to the great ὥρα of Jesus' glory when he will take upon himself the judgment that has kept God and God's bride estranged.

What does this sign indicate about Jesus' mother, their family, and the nature of kinship among disciples?

Any conclusive observations about the message John is presenting about Jesus' family and about kinship relationships must wait until exegesis has been completed on all relevant passages, but some preliminary comments are appropriate now.

Contrary to the views of many scholars, and indeed to my own expectation at the start of this project, I have found that this passage does not express distance between Jesus and his mother.[246] Nor is it a statement of Jesus' choice to follow his Father rather than his mother.[247] The potential for distance between Jesus and his mother is present, if she were to align herself too closely with those Jews who are becoming his enemies, but this potential seems to be put aside as she demonstrates her

---

246. As argued by Barrett, *Gospel According to St John*, 191; Waetjen, *Gospel of the Beloved Disciple*, 117; Koester, *Symbolism in the Fourth Gospel*, 78, and many others.

247. As is argued by Howard, "Minor Characters," 67–9.

loyalty toward him. Ultimately, her loyalty will be clarified as she stands beside him as those Jews put him to death.

There has been no indication in this passage of the loyalties of Jesus' brothers. They are mentioned in 2:12 without comment. In 7:1–9 they are identified as unbelievers and are not found with Jesus in his death or resurrection.

It can tentatively be observed, then, that one of the roles of Jesus' family in John is to demonstrate that natural ties of kinship are not sufficient to align a person with Jesus. A clear choice, such as the one Jesus' mother seems to have made (and his brothers have not made) to place complete trust in Jesus and relativize all other loyalties, must be made, even by those closest to him, if they are to receive the blessings of his messianic ministry.

The presence of Jesus' mother at his first sign also demonstrates that he had a human, earthly origin as well as a divine, heavenly one (1:14).[248] Lieu points to the brief parable in 16:21 where a γυνὴ has her hour—the hour of giving birth. Her baby is given an unusual description. ἐγεννήθη ἄνθρωπος εἰς τὸν κόσμον[249] is an unmistakable reference to Jesus' incarnation within the Gospel of John (9:39; 16:28; 18:37).[250] Lieu concludes that the role of Mary is to pose the question of Jesus' divine and human origins but not to answer it.[251] This question probably does not have the prominence in the Cana account that many Church Fathers have given it,[252] but it cannot be denied that the mystery of the incarnation is partially embodied in Jesus' mother.

Finally, in addition to demonstrating the limitations of kinship bonds and presenting the mystery of the divine and human origins of the Word, Jesus' mother acts as an example to his followers by placing her trust in him and calling on others to obey him.[253]

Her role in this first sign is crucial, but she will not be seen again until she is found at the foot of Jesus' cross. Her younger sons do make another appearance before that climactic event, so the next two chapters

---

248. Schnell, *Antidocetic Christology in the Gospel of John*, 166–7.
249. A man has come into the world.
250. Lieu, "The Mother of the Son in the Fourth Gospel," 71–3.
251. Lieu, "The Mother of the Son in the Fourth Gospel," 77.
252. See previous chapter.
253. Moloney, *Belief in the Word*, 91; so Campbell, *Kinship Relations*, 182.

will examine fraternal relationships among first-century Jews and then analyze John 7:1–9 in detail.

Conclusions

Based on the discussion in chapter 5 of mother–son relationships this chapter has concluded that there is nothing culturally inappropriate about Jesus' mother approaching him at a wedding to discuss a problem that had arisen. Rather, it was very natural for her to approach her male guardian with such a problem. Jesus' words to her should not be read as a rebuke for shameful female behavior.

This chapter has shown that Jesus' words to his mother are more complex than a simple rebuke or assertion of emotional distance. He is not saying, "From now on I follow my Father's orders, not my mother's." Rather, he hears in his mother's words, Οἶνον οὐκ ἔχουσιν, a much deeper meaning than she intended. He hears a statement about the predicament of God's people living without the blessing of their God and without recourse for effectively calling God to act. These people who should have gloried in the honor of being God's chosen ones have been shamed by political, military, and financial subservience to nations who know nothing of the true God. A family wedding at which the wine runs out captures, in this culture that values hospitality so dearly, a glimpse of the shame of the people of God.

In response to his mother, Jesus says Τί ἐμοὶ καὶ σοί; God's people are living under God's judgment for a reason. They, as the bride of God, have been unfaithful. They are estranged. Is the Son of God to be called on to take sides here? And if so, how can he be expected to do other than side with God? And so the mother of the Son of God must take care. As she continues to be loyal to her son her relationship with her people may be desperately strained.

As the narrative continues toward Jesus' hour of shame and glory, the Jews (οἱ Ἰουδαῖοι) show themselves to be entrenched in their faithlessness by rejecting Jesus. They side against God's Son and therefore against God. Jesus' family, who are loyal and devout Jews, will be torn by this conflict. More will need to be said about how Jesus' brothers (chapter 8) and his mother (chapter 9) fare in this conflict.

Jesus was not impolite in addressing his mother as γύναι. Rather, by choosing this word John may be directing the reader towards a similar conversation between Elijah and the widow who showed him hospitality.

Jesus' words to his mother are unusual but do not indicate any breach in relationship or disrespect. If anything they show concern for the position of the mother of the Son of God when God sends the Son to judge as well as to save, and to be crucified as well as to be glorified.

Jesus' next words, οὔπω ἥκει ἡ ὥρα μου, need not be read as a refusal to act on the practical situation his mother has brought to his attention. His time to act decisively by bringing God's judgment and God's mercy to full expression has not yet come. He will deal with the plight of God's people living in shame under God's judgment, but not yet. However, the abundant eschatological wine of that day may spill over into the present predicament. The shame of one family can be turned to glory in the short term, while the whole of God's people await the ultimate reversal of their shame.

Close examination of mother–son relationships has thrown light on this first of Jesus' encounters with family members in the Gospel of John. The next chapter will turn to consider fraternal relationships to see if insights can be found there to illuminate Jesus' relationships with his brothers.

7

Brotherly Love

In preparation for examining Jesus' encounter with his brothers in John 7, this chapter will examine what can reasonably be known about expectations and obligations among brothers in their culture. As with chapter 4 on mothers and sons, I will first survey current social-science scholarship and then consider ancient literature from a selection of Greek, Roman, and Jewish sources for indications of how generalizations about brotherhood may (or may not) be evidenced in ethical, mythical, and historical writings.

Architecture need not be consulted in this analysis since it can reasonably be assumed that brothers tended to occupy the same space and pursue similar occupations.

Key Questions addressed in this chapter:

- What do modern socio-historical scholars say about first-century fraternal relationships?
- How well is this substantiated in ancient literature and archaeology dating to the first century or with influence continuing into the first century?
- What else can we find in Jewish literature?

Being a man

According to many current researchers into the sociology of the first-century Mediterranean, being a man was all about honor. Simply to be a man was an honor, but that honor was always in danger of being challenged[1] and so required constant, strenuous defense. Challenges could take the form of insults or neglect, but they could also take the more subtle form of gifts or compliments.[2] For the virtuous Jew in particular, honor challenges could also come in the form of temptation.[3] Humiliation ensues when a challenge is lost and also when it remains unanswered. Simply ignoring a challenge is not an option.[4] Sociologists have called these contests challenge/riposte encounters.

Honor tended to be associated with sexual and social dominance[5] and with a cluster of virtues such as strength, courage, daring, valor, self-control, generosity, and wisdom. Four virtues in particular formed the "cardinal virtues" recognized by the majority of Greco-Roman ethicists, including the Hellenistic Jew, Philo. These cardinal virtues were σοφία, σωφροσύνη, ἀνδρεία, and δικαιοσύνυ.[6] A lack of honor tended to be indicated by weakness, cowardice, and lack of generosity, and these tended to be the most despised of vices when found in men.[7]

Satlow argues that for Rabbinic Jews, self-restraint was the key virtue[8] associated with manhood, and this virtue was pursued through, and devoted to, the study of the Torah.[9] He argues that honor was, for some Jews, associated with the life of the mind[10] rather than the bodily life of sex and warfare. The Rabbinic period was, of course, later than the time under consideration here and clearly showed the scars of the Jewish War and the destruction of Jerusalem. Perhaps the life of the mind came into focus largely because of the devastating material losses that Jewish manhood had suffered. It seems likely, though, that the seeds of this focus on the mind had been planted long before in the Jewish wisdom tradition, just as similar seeds had been planted in many Greek cultures by their philosophical traditions. Wisdom of Solomon 3:14 indicates that a

---

1. Moxnes, *Putting Jesus in His Place*, 78.
2. Rohrbaugh, "Legitimating Sonship," 184.
3. Satlow, "Try to Be a Man," 27.
4. Pilch and Malina, *Biblical Social Values*, 100.
5. Moxnes, *Putting Jesus in His Place*, 78.
6. See Powell, "Did Paul Believe in Virtue?" 54.
7. Pilch and Malina, *Biblical Social Values*, 96.
8. Pilch and Malina, *Biblical Social Values*, 97; note that the details of what counts as weakness, cowardice, and folly are designated by the particular society.
9. Satlow, "Try to Be a Man," 20.
10. Satlow, "Try to Be a Man," 21.

man could be honored for his obedience to Torah even if he had lost his physical manhood.

However much wisdom and Torah were valued in the first century, it is clear from inscriptions in Palestine that many Jewish men at the time wanted to be remembered by the same traits valued by their non-Jewish contemporaries: wealth, piety, and public offices.[11]

Brothers in first-century societies: current anthropological research

Hellerman contends that sibling solidarity was at the heart of first-century family values.[12] The reciprocity of the kinship group meant that all property, including honor, was freely shared among brothers, and that wrongs between brothers were not avenged.[13]

According to Malina, competitions for honor occur between families, and not within families. Among brothers a man could rest, knowing that his own honor and his brothers' honor would not be questioned.[14]

As the family related to outsiders the preservation of honor tended to be a greater value than other virtues, such as truth telling. Deceptive behavior that protected the honor of a brother was generally considered appropriate.[15] This will be kept in mind in chapter 8 when considering whether Jesus deliberately deceived his brothers.

According to Hanson and Oakman, a brother who is the head of his kinship group would be responsible for arranging marriages for his siblings.[16] It is intriguing to consider whether Jesus, by leaving his home, failed to fulfill this responsibility; or whether this was one of the responsibilities that kept him at home so far into his adulthood. We might imagine that if he neglected this responsibility his siblings may have had cause to resent his ministry, but there is too little evidence to make such a case.

As this chapter moves from ideal to actuality, it will become clear that brotherly relationships were not always so blissful. Conflict between

---

11. Satlow, "Try to Be a Man," 39, relying on Naveh, *On Stone and Mosaic*, Roth-Gerson, *Greek Inscriptions*, van der Horst, *Ancient Jewish Epitaphs*.
12. Hellerman, *The Ancient Church as Family*, 35.
13. Hellerman, *The Ancient Church as Family*, 49.
14. Malina, *The New Testament World*, 33.
15. Hellerman, *The Ancient Church as Family*, 45–46.
16. Hanson & Oakman, *Palestine in the Time of Jesus*, 36.

brothers is a common theme in classic literature. Rather than seeing this as a contradiction to his hypothesis, Hellerman believes that the high value placed in this society on loyalty to this intense brotherly bond adds emotional tension to literature about rivalry between brothers.[17] I have previously observed that the pathos in conflict between mothers and sons in the literature is fuelled by the expectation that such relationships would normally be warm and affectionate. It seems to be equally the case that conflict or betrayal among brothers in ancient literature created tension and interest in the plot because of the expectation of loyalty between brothers. In our culture this plot tension is more often achieved by betrayal of a life-long friend.

It is also likely that the financial necessity of being on good terms with one's father in this patrilineal, patriarchal culture could create competition among brothers for their father's affection, and his property.[18] At the same time, the need to please their father would have often led brothers to at least portray a semblance of unity.

Ancient Greek, Roman, and Jewish ethicists will now be consulted to gain a more complete picture of what was expected of brothers, and afterwards historical and fictional works will be examined for the insight that they give into actual brotherly behavior. English translations will be cited for Latin works.

A view from the ethicist's study

A Greek view

Aristotle believed that common origin and upbringing ought to produce brotherly love and comradeship.

> ἀδελφοὶ δ' ἀλλήλους τῷ ἐκ τῶν αὐτῶν πεφυκέναι: ἡ γὰρ πρὸς ἐκεῖνα ταυτότης ἀλλήλοις ταὐτὸ ποιεῖ: ὅθεν φασὶ ταὐτὸν αἷμα καὶ ῥίζαν καὶ τὰ τοιαῦτα. εἰσὶ δὴ ταὐτό πως καὶ ἐν διῃρημένοις. μέγα δὲ πρὸς φιλίαν καὶ τὸ σύντροφον καὶ τὸ καθ' ἡλικίαν: ἧλιξ γὰρ ἥλικα, καὶ οἱ συνήθεις ἑταῖροι: διὸ καὶ ἡ ἀδελφικὴ τῇ ἑταιρικῇ ὁμοιοῦται.[19]

---

17. Hellerman, *The Ancient Church as Family*, 39–40.
18. Campbell, *Kinship Relations*, 108.
19. Aristotle, "Nicomachean Ethics" Book VIII, xii.3-4. TR: brothers love each other as being from the same source, since the identity of their relations to that source identifies them with one another, which is why we speak of "being of the same blood"

Because of the bond and obligations of brotherhood, it is more unjust to refuse aid to a brother than to a stranger.[20]

Epictetus' Stoic philosophy led him to a similar conclusion. Brothers ought to regulate their behavior toward each other according to the nature of the relationship, rather than other considerations: τὰ καθήκοντα ὡς ἐπίπαν ταῖς σχέσεσι παραμετρεῖται… ‛ὁ ἀδελφὸς ἀδικεῖ.' τήρει τοιγαροῦν τὴν τάξιν τὴν σεαυτοῦ πρὸς αὐτὸν μηδὲ σκόπει, τί ἐκεῖνος ποιεῖ, ἀλλὰ τί σοὶ ποιήσαντι κατὰ φύσιν ἡ σὴ ἕξει προαίρεσις… οὕτως οὖν ἀπὸ τοῦ γείτονος, ἀπὸ τοῦ πολίτου, ἀπὸ τοῦ στρατηγοῦ τὸ καθῆκον εὑρήσεις, ἐὰν τὰς σχέσεις ἐθίζῃ θεωρεῖν.[21]

Hesiod had earlier spoken of the appropriateness and importance of friendship between brothers by saying that a day when decency and respect disappear from the earth would be a day when οὐδὲ κασίγνητος φίλος ἔσσεται, ὡς τὸ πάρος περ.[22] Yet he was also realist enough to say: καί τε κασιγνήτῳ γελάσας ἐπὶ μάρτυρα θέσθαι.[23]

A Roman view

Plutarch's treatise, Περὶ Φιλαδελφίας;, is the most comprehensive ethical work on the subject of brotherly relationships surviving from the classical world.

Plutarch compares brothers with the members of a body, which work together for their mutual benefit. Difference and separateness or "of the same stock" or the like; brothers are therefore in a manner the same being, though embodied in separate persons. But friendship between brothers is also greatly fostered by their common upbringing and similarity of age; "two of an age agree" and "familiarity breeds fellowship," which is why the friendship between brothers resembles that between members of a comradeship.

20. Aristotle, "Nicomachean Ethics" Book VIII, ix.3.

21. Epictetus, *Epicteti Dissertationes Ab Arriano Digestae* §30 TR: Duties are universally measured by relations ... Is a brother unjust? Well, preserve your own just relation towards him. Consider not what he does, but what you are to do, to keep your own will in a state conformable to nature ... In this manner, therefore, if you accustom yourself to contemplate the relations of neighbor, citizen, commander, you can deduce from each the corresponding duties. Epictetus, *The Works of Epictetus: His Discourses, in Four Books, the Enchiridion, and Fragments.*

22. TR: "nor will brother be dear to brother as aforetime." Hesiod, "Works and Days."

23. TR: "even with your brother smile — and get a witness" Hesiod, "Works and Days," 371–2.

between them is intended by nature, not for opposition but, ὅπως χωρὶς ὄντες ἀλλήλοις μᾶλλον συνεργῶσιν.²⁴ When brothers do not cooperate, ποδῶν οὐθέν, οἶμαι, διοίσουσιν ἀλλήλους ὑποσκελιζόντων καὶ δακτύλων ἐμπλεκομένων καὶ διαστρεφομένων παρὰ φύσιν ὑπ᾽ ἀλλήλων.²⁵

He uses violent body imagery to condemn men who give preference to friends outside the family over a brother: ἀδελφὸς δὲ πολεμῶν ἀδελφῷ καὶ ὀθνεῖον ἐξ ἀγορᾶς ἢ παλαίστρας ἑταῖρον οὐθὲν ἔοικεν ἄλλο ποιεῖν ἢ σάρκινον καὶ συμφυὲς ἑκουσίως ἀποκόψας μέλος ἀλλότριον προστρίβεσθαι καὶ προσαρμόττειν.²⁶

Conflict with a brother becomes a disease that perverts natural appetites and engenders depraved cravings: ὡς γὰρ αἱ νόσοι τοῖς σώμασι μὴ προσιεμένοις τὸ οἰκεῖον πολλῶν ἐμποιοῦσιν ἀτόπων καὶ βλαβερῶν ὀρέξεις, οὕτως ἡ πρὸς τὸ συγγενὲς διαβολὴ καὶ ὑφόρασις ὁμιλίας ἐπάγεται φαύλας καὶ πονηρὰς εἰς τὸ ἐκλιπὲς ἔξωθεν ἐπιρρεούσας.²⁷

Friends are necessary, according to Plutarch, because humans are naturally communal, but friends outside the family are only shadows of the first friends we find in parents and brothers.²⁸ It is madness, he says, τοὔνομα σέβεσθαι καὶ τιμᾶν ἐν ἑτέροις αὐτὸν δὲ μισεῖν καὶ φεύγειν οὐχ ὑγιαίνοντός ἐστιν.²⁹

Cicero tempers this view somewhat by saying that a man ought not "to yield so much to his love for his brother as to think only of the welfare of his own relations, and to neglect the common safety of all."³⁰

Plutarch believed that one of a man's highest duties was to give pleasure to his parents. This duty ought to motivate men toward brotherly

---

24. Plutarch, "On Fraternal Affection" 250–1. TR: "that by being separate they might more readily co-operate with one another."

25. Plutarch, "On Fraternal Affection" 251. TR: "feet which trip up one another, and fingers which are unnaturally entwined and twisted by each other."

26. Plutarch, "On Fraternal Affection" 252–3. TR: "The man who quarrels with his brother, and takes as his comrade a stranger from the market-place or the wrestling-floor, appears to be doing nothing but cutting off voluntarily a limb of his own flesh and blood, and taking to himself and joining to his body an extraneous member."

27. Plutarch, "On Fraternal Affection," 252–3. TR: "For as diseases in bodies which cannot accept their proper diet engender cravings for many strange and harmful foods, so slander and suspicion entertained against kinsmen usher in evil and pernicious associations which flow in from outside to fill the vacant room."

28. Plutarch, "On Fraternal Affection," 254.

29. Plutarch, "On Fraternal Affection," 254–5. TR: "to reverence and honour the name 'brother' in others, but to hate and shun the person himself."

30. Cicero, "The Orations of Marcus Tullius Cicero," Sulla, 22.

goodwill. τίς οὖν ἐστι παρὰ παίδων γονεῦσιν ἢ πρᾶξις ἢ χάρις ἢ διάθεσις μᾶλλον εὐφραίνειν δυναμένη τῆς πρὸς ἀδελφὸν εὐνοίας βεβαίου; καὶ φιλίας;[31]

Plutarch was entirely aware that his ideals of brotherhood were not generally put into practice. He lamented, τὴν φιλαδελφίαν οὕτω σπάνιον οὖσαν, ὡς τὴν μισαδελφίαν ἐπὶ τῶν παλαιῶν.[32]

A Torah-informed view

The story of Cain and Abel, so early in the narrative, provides a violent setting for the discussion of brotherly bonds in the Old Testament. Here, it is jealousy over yhwh's preference that sparks fratricidal rage, so blame for Cain's behavior cannot be shifted to any overindulgent parent. God is assumed to be just, so Cain must take full responsibility for the murder. Later, when parental favoritism does become a factor in sibling rivalry, this story remains a signpost to brothers to keep their envy in check.

The conflict between Jacob and Esau is pivotal to the Jewish understanding of brotherhood, as is the later mistreatment of Joseph.[33] Once again, ideals are challenged by the actuality of human experience, and this challenge leads to further reflection on the nature of those ideals.

The book of Jubilees (35:22–27) includes a conversation between Rebecca and her sons on the night of her death. She first exhorts Esau that he and Jacob "will love each other and that neither will desire evil against the other, but mutual love only, and (so) ye will prosper, my sons, and be honored in the midst of the land, and no enemy will rejoice over you, and ye will be a blessing and a mercy in the eyes of all those that love you."

Esau first agrees that it is entirely appropriate for him to love his brother above all flesh, "for I have not a brother in all the earth but him only: and this is no great merit for me if I love him; for he is my brother, and we were sown together in thy body, and together came we forth from thy womb, and if I do not love my brother, whom shall I love?"

---

31. Plutarch, "On Fraternal Affection," 256–7. TR: "What deed or favour or disposition, which children may show toward their parents, can give more pleasure than steadfast goodwill and friendship toward a brother?"

32. Plutarch, "On Fraternal Affection," 249. TR: "brotherly love is as rare in our day as brotherly hatred was among the men of old."

33. See Assis, "Why Edom?"

Esau then wisely encourages his mother to give the same exhortation to his brother, and Jacob replies: "I shall do thy pleasure; believe me that no evil will proceed from me or from my sons against Esau, and I shall be first in naught save in love only."

The author of Jubilees had given a similar priority to brotherly love in 7:26–27 where Job begins to lose confidence in the future of the human race because of the behavior of his sons toward one another:

> ye do not walk in righteousness: for in the path of destruction ye have begun to walk, and ye are parting one from another, and are envious one of another, and (so it comes) that ye are not in harmony, my sons, each with his brother. For I see, and behold the demons have begun (their) seductions against you and against your children and now I fear on your behalf, that after my death ye will shed the blood of men upon the earth, and that ye, too, will be destroyed from the face of the earth.

These words reflect the belief that the first human blood to be shed on earth was motivated by fraternal envy (Gen 4:2–16)[34] and that, therefore, jealousy between brothers created a danger for the land.

Birth order is a fraught issue in Jewish thought, where the younger brother is so often chosen above the elder, or else usurps the place of the elder.[35] It is therefore debatable whether Herod the Great was expressing Jewish or Roman sentiments when, according to Josephus, he said of his sons, ὑμεῖς τηρήσατε μήτε ἀδίκους μήτε ἀνωμάλους τὰς τιμὰς διδόντες, ἑκάστῳ δὲ κατὰ τὸ πρεσβεῖον· οὐ γὰρ τοσοῦτον εὐφρανεῖ τις τὸν παρ' ἡλικίαν θεραπευόμενον, ὅσον ὀδυνήσει τὸν ἀτιμούμενον.[36]

Ben Sira 25:1 declares three things beautiful in the sight of the Lord and people: ὁμόνοια ἀδελφῶν, καὶ φιλία τῶν πλησίον, καὶ γυνὴ καὶ ἀνὴρ ἑαυτοῖς συμπεριφερόμενοι.[37] Perhaps the implication is that all three are as rare as they are beautiful, but at least one episode in Jewish inter-testamental literature portrays brothers behaving with honor and agreement.

---

34. See also Wisdom 10:3; Jubilees 4:1–6.

35. See Fox, "Stalking the Younger Brother."

36. Josephus, Book 1, Ch. 23, §5. TR: Do not you pay undue or equal respects to them, but to every one according to the prerogative of their births; for he that pays such respects unduly, will thereby not make him that is honored beyond what his age requires so joyful as he will make him that is dishonored sorrowful. F. Josephus, *The Works of Josephus*.

37. TR: unity of brothers, and affection of neighbours, and a wife and husband who suit each other.

The ideal Jewish mother of 4 Maccabees, whose encomium is examined in chapter 4, has seven sons who are equally lauded as ideal brothers in that they are in full agreement that torture and death are preferable to forsaking Torah.

> ὢ ἱερᾶς καὶ εὐαρμόστου περὶ τῆς εὐσεβείας τῶν ἑπτὰ ἀδελφῶν συμφωνίας. 4οὐδεὶς ἐκ τῶν ἑπτὰ μειρακίων ἐδειλίασεν οὐδὲ πρὸς τὸν θάνατον ὤκνησεν, 5ἀλλὰ πάντες ὥσπερ ἐπ' ἀθανασίας ὁδὸν τρέχοντες ἐπὶ τὸν διὰ τῶν βασάνων θάνατον ἔσπευδον. 6καθάπερ αἱ χεῖρες καὶ οἱ πόδες συμφώνως τοῖς τῆς ψυχῆς ἀφηγήμασιν κινοῦνται, οὕτως οἱ ἱεροὶ μείρακες ἐκεῖνοι ὡς ὑπὸ ψυχῆς ἀθανάτου τῆς εὐσεβείας πρὸς τὸν ὑπὲρ αὐτῆς συνεφώνησαν θάνατον. 7ὢ πανάγιε συμφώνων ἀδελφῶν ἑβδομάς. (4 Macc 14:3–7)[38]

Each brother is praised for his own courage and honor, but what appears to astonish the author most is the complete harmony with which the brothers go to their death together.

This brief survey of Jewish literature leads to the conclusion that harmony between brothers is seen as praiseworthy and rare, but at the same time natural. That such a natural state should be so rare as to be praiseworthy seems to indicate that humanity is out of step with its creator. Fraternal harmony, therefore, is somewhat of a religious duty. This is in line with concerns mentioned earlier about the danger of violence and chaos that brotherly chaos can pose.

Brothers in Greek mythology

Brotherhood, like all relationships, is painted in bold colors in Greek mythology. The Homerian tales present Hector as a hero who fights and dies in a war started by the impetuousness of his younger brother, Paris. Though he does not condone Paris' behavior, he also does not hesitate to go into battle to defend him.

Opposing Hector and Paris are the equally united brothers, Agamemnon and Menelaus. The elopement with Paris of the beautiful

---

38. TR: O holy and harmonious concord of the seven brothers concerning piety! Not one of the seven young men was afraid or even hesitated to face death, but all, as though running on the threshold of immortality, were hastening to death through torture. Just as the hands and feet harmoniously move the mind to action, so those holy young men, as though by a spirit of immortal piety, went in unison to death for it. O most holy seven, harmonious brothers!

Helen, Menelaus' wife, had precipitated the Trojan War. Agamemnon, King of Atreus, led the attack against his sister-in-law's lover. Agamemnon even sacrificed his own daughter[39] to ensure the favor of the gods for their endeavors. A brother's honor had been damaged, and it must be retrieved, along with the beautiful Helen.

Once the battle begins the younger brothers, Paris and Menelaus, remain relatively passive and submissive to their elder brothers. Their active role seems to end with the intervention of their brothers.

The Odyssey, however, casts some doubt on this picture of brotherly harmony between Agamemnon and Menelaus. At the end of the battle, the brothers quarrel over whether to depart immediately or take time first to placate Athena, whose son Achilles had been killed in the battle. In this account, Menelaus is not submissive to his elder brother, but takes half the ships and leaves immediately. This more complicated picture of fraternal relationship is further nuanced when Menelaus, after a long and difficult journey, finds his way home to live "happily ever after" with his beautiful Helen, while Agamemnon has an easier journey but is murdered upon his return by his wife and her lover. Menelaus is certainly not punished in the narrative for his disloyalty to his older brother.

A full analysis of what is communicated by these portrayals of brotherly relationship is beyond the scope of this chapter, but it would not be premature to note that *The Iliad* appears to present the ideal, or the conventional wisdom about brotherhood, while *The Odyssey* questions and nuances that ideal.

According to *The Iliad*, younger brothers must be ruled and protected by their elder brothers. Younger brothers ought to submit, and when they act on their own initiative they cause trouble for the whole family. In *The Odyssey*, Menelaus does get into trouble after splitting from his brother, but he is then able to redeem the situation without his elder brother's intervention. Not all younger brothers are as helpless as Paris. Agamemnon, who has acted honorably toward his brother and towards the gods, is not rewarded with a long life, but rather with a violent and dishonorable death. Life can be messy and the gods capricious.

Another example of an ideal brother is Polydeuces, who refused to accept immortality unless he could share it with his brother, Castor. Zeus

---

39. An action which would lead to his own death.

granted that the two brothers dwell, on alternate days, among the gods and among humans.[40]

Less ideal brothers also abound in Greek mythology. Acrisius and Proteus were twin sons of the king of Argos. Like Jacob and Esau, they quarreled even in the womb. Acrisius expelled Proteus from his inheritance, but Proteus gained support through marriage and compelled Acrisius to return half the kingdom to him. These brothers are then contrasted with their nephew Melampus who is promised a third of the kingdom in return for a favor, but refuses to proceed unless his brother, Bias, is given the same as himself.[41]

Polynices and Eteocles, sons of Oedipus, were supposed to rule Thebes in alternate years, but were unable to share the throne, and killed each other in battle. These brothers had done nothing to defend their father when he was shamed, blinded himself, and was driven from Thebes.[42] This mutual fratricide is lamented as a great crime and tragedy, adding greater pollution to a house already deeply troubled.[43]

Epictetus said of these brothers that, though they may have lived in harmony beforehand, once royal power became a matter of contention between them they turned on each other like two dogs fighting over a piece of meat.[44]

After the death of these brothers, Eteocles is given an honorable burial while Polynices' corpse is left to be devoured by birds. An edict promises death to anyone attempting to bury him. Their sister, Antigone, declares that nobody has the right to interfere with her sacred duty to honor her brother in death[45] and calls on her sister to help, telling her to demonstrate that she is an honorable woman.[46]

I noted in chapter 4 that funeral rituals were a way for women to give honor to their husbands, sons, and brothers in death. It is clear in this story that even for a sister an outrage against a brother, in his death, could not be tolerated. It would be reasonable to assume that a brother would be expected to join them in their anger and in any action they

---

40. Apollodorus, *Apollodorus, the Library*, 3.11.2.
41. Apollodorus, *Apollodorus, the Library*, 2.2.
42. Apollodorus, *Apollodorus, the Library*, 3.5.
43. Aeschylus, "Seven against Thebes," 734.
44. Epictetus, "The Discourses of Epictetus." 2.22.
45. Sophocles, "The Antigone of Sophocles." §1.39.
46. Sophocles, "The Antigone of Sophocles." §1.38.

should take in salvaging their brother's honor, but in the absence of a brother Antigone is willing to face danger in order to rescue her brother's body from disgrace.

Brothers in Roman mythology

Rome's foundation myths revolve around twin brothers, Romulus and Remus, so it could be expected that notions of brotherhood might be central to Roman identity. Romulus is said to have killed his brother for jumping over a sacred wall.[47] Plutarch states that his action arose ἐκ βουλῆς καὶ σκέψεως περὶ κοινῶν συμφερόντων.[48] This raises the possibility that conflict between duty to kin, duty to the gods, and civic duty might play out in the Roman psyche and history.

The historian's perspective

In general, Greek and Roman history bears out Epictetus' belief that all natural affections can easily be abandoned in the name of self-interest, especially where power and wealth are at stake.[49] Among the emperors, several sets of brothers can be found attempting to share power. While many of these grew suspicious of their brothers and some committed fratricide, a small number of highly confident and competent emperors succeeded in elevating their brothers to positions of power and then trusting them to fulfill the responsibilities of those positions.

The third-century emperor, Caracalla, placed himself at the low point in fraternal harmony among emperors, by having his co-regent brother, Geta, murdered in front of their mother while she was attempting to mediate between them.[50] While Caracalla's cruelty shocked observers at the time and from a historical distance, his dispatching of a brother as a competitor for power was not at all unprecedented. Nor was it a particularly Roman practice.

---

47. Plutarch, *Roman Questions*, 27.

48. TR: "from a deliberate investigation of the common welfare." Plutarch, "Comparison of Theseus and Romulus."

49. Epictetus, "The Discourses of Epictetus, with the Encheridion and Fragments." 2.22.

50. Smith, *Dictionary of Greek and Roman Antiquities*, 608.

Artaxerxes II, son of Darius II of Persia, exiled his brother, Cyrus, after being convinced by a false accusation that Cyrus was plotting against him. Upon his return, Cyrus assembled an army[51] in order to overthrow his brother and take the throne.[52] Cyrus was killed in the battle.

These brothers can be contrasted with Ariamenes and Xerxes son of Darius II. Ariamenes was on his way to contest Xerxes' right to the kingdom when Xerxes sent him gifts and offered him the highest position in his court. Xerxes kept his promise and the two worked peacefully together.[53]

Perseus of Macedon, son of Philip V, was envious of the popularity of his brother, Demetrius, with the Macedonians and the Romans, and so convinced his father to have Demetrius killed.[54] Livy implies that Perseus also planned to assassinate his father in order to seize the throne, and goes on to remonstrate, "He would find out in the ruin of his fortunes how hateful all this conduct was to the gods, for the gods bestowed their favour on natural affection and honourable dealing; it was by these that the Roman people gained their lofty position in the world."[55]

The Romans, of course, were by no means all paragons of natural affection and honorable dealing. Domitian grew up jealous and resentful in the shadow of his elder brother, Titus. Suetonius wrote that Domitian spread rumors after their father's death that Vespasian had intended for his sons to rule together, and that Domitian seriously considered bribing the army to make him emperor in his brother's place. When Titus died of an illness Domitian is remembered as neither mourning him nor honoring him sufficiently.[56]

Rome was not entirely devoid of heroic brothers. The historians are quick to praise men who do show affection and sacrifice for their brothers. Plutarch commends Lucullus for refusing honors and office until his younger brother, Marcus, was old enough to join him.[57] Livy praises

---

51. Xenophon, "Xenophon in Seven Volumes," Economics 4.
52. Xenophon, "Xenophon in Seven Volumes," Anabasis 1.1.
53. Plutarch, "Sayings of Kings and Commanders," 5.
54. Livy, "History of Rome," 40.5.
55. Livy, "History of Rome," 44.1.
56. Suetonius, "The Lives of the Twelve Caesars," Domitianus, 2.
57. Plutarch, "Lucullus," 1.6.

Marcus Valerius for sacrificing his life in battle in order to gain glory for his family and particularly for his brother Publicola.[58]

In my research I was surprised at not being able to uncover detailed studies of brotherhood in ancient history and literature. I believe this would be a very worthy subject for future research.

Based on my brief survey I can tentatively state that Roman historians held ideals about brotherhood that included a capacity to share rule and to take pleasure in seeing a brother honored, even at great sacrifice to oneself. Envy and rivalry are the opposite of the brotherly ideal and do not seem any less abhorrent to historians for being common.[59]

Conclusions

Throughout the first-century Mediterranean, ideals of brotherhood appear to have been similarly lofty, while actual brothers were similarly envious and self-seeking. Unity among brothers was highly valued, especially around ventures and values held in high esteem by their family. Among Jewish brothers, these values were often associated with knowledge of and obedience to Torah, while among Romans they were more likely to involve leadership and courage in battle. However, there was a common desire for brothers to act as one for the family's honor, rather than acting alone for their own honor.

Brothers were expected to show preferential treatment to one another compared with friends outside the family, and to share confidences that were kept from outsiders. Virtuous men made sacrifices for their brothers by sharing with them their honor and possessions and even, where necessary, by giving their lives. Men who envied their brothers and plotted against them were considered to be men of bad character.

The fact that brothers so rarely lived up to these ideals does not seem to have diminished the intensity with which the ideals were desired. Rivalry among brothers, like death and poverty, was not a reality that these cultures adjusted to. Rather it was a tragedy faced afresh by every generation of parents who hoped for better outcomes for and from their sons.

---

58. Livy, "Books I and 2 with an English Translation," 2.20.

59. Tacitus, "The Annals," 460.

Hellerman is correct in believing that sibling solidarity was at the heart of first-century family values.[60] Malina is less correct, and somewhat idealistic, when he contends that this value was so much in evidence that brothers could always find rest with each other when at home, away from the agonistic world of men outside their door.[61]

Fraternal conflict was a vice that added pathos to fictional plotlines and spice to historical recitation. The following chapter, by closely analyzing John 7:1–24, will consider what the conflict between Jesus and his brothers contributes to the narrative of the Fourth Gospel.

---

60. Hellerman, *The Ancient Church as Family*, 35.
61. Malina, *The New Testament World*, 33.

8

Glory and . . . Deception?

This chapter provides an opportunity to observe Jesus with his brothers. A close examination of John 7:1–24 will consider Jesus' apparent deception of his brothers concerning his intention of traveling to Jerusalem for the Feast of Tabernacles. After telling his brothers that he would not go up to Jerusalem for this festival, he travels there secretly and begins to teach in the temple courts. This raises intriguing ethical questions, which will be considered for what they may contribute to the focus of this chapter, that is the dynamics of Jesus' interaction with his brothers in which the brothers fail to understand the nature and source of Jesus' glory and Jesus chooses to leave his brothers outside his plans and his confidence.

This chapter will address the following questions:

- What were his brothers asking Jesus to do? Our distance from this culture can obscure the implications of their question.

- In verse 8, Jesus tells his brothers that he is not going to the festival and then in verse 10 he does go. Was he lying?

- Some scholars[1] have begun to identify hostility between the Gospel writers and Paul on the one hand, and Jesus' family, represented by James in his leadership of the Jerusalem church, on the other. What is their evidence for such hostility and is that evidence valid?

- What is being communicated in this passage about Jesus' brothers? Do they have any sort of representative function?

---

1. For example, see R. Eisenman, *James the Brother of Jesus*.

Unity

The Tabernacles Discourse binds together several chapters of the Gospel, from 7:1 to 10:21.[2] This entire unit, even more than the Gospel in general, is characterized by schism and conflict.[3] Within this large unit, several smaller units may be observed. Ellis points to the mention of Jesus being in hiding and of the Jews wanting to kill him forming an inclusio around 7:1–11 and 8:59.[4] He sees this section as one of the passages where John subtly refutes the charge of ditheism being leveled by Jews against his community.[5] Neyrey believes that John 7 is united by the motif of forensic proceedings, which provide the context for significant challenge–riposte encounters.[6]

While wanting to place Jesus' discussion with his brothers in the context of these large units of the Gospel I have also needed, for the sake of space, to restrict my examination here to a smaller section of text. I have chosen, then, to balance brevity against completeness by considering 7:1–24 in this chapter.

Undoubtedly, John 7:1–9 acts as an introduction to the Tabernacles Discourse. Unfortunately, it is difficult to find commentators who take it seriously as anything more than "setting the stage"[7] for the more important action at the feast in Jerusalem. I suspect that many commentators, embarrassed by an apparent lie on the lips of Jesus, are keen to rush past this section. Bultmann, however, does show that, even if this section is just an introduction, it is a "most suitable" one: "The introduction is obviously intended on the one hand to prepare the way for Jesus' appearance in Jerusalem, and on the other to make it clear that the motives for his appearance are not worldly ones, that his choice of the καιρὸς is not based on worldly considerations."[8]

It will be possible, later in this chapter, to analyze more clearly the way in which Jesus' interaction with his brothers introduces the whole of the Tabernacles Discourse.

2. Moloney, *Gospel of John*, 232–3.

3. Moloney, *Gospel of John*, 236.

4. Ellis, *Genius of John*, 138–9.

5. Ellis, *Genius of John*, 140. Other such passages include 1:1–18, 5:1–47, and 10:22–39.

6. Neyrey, *Gospel of John in Cultural and Rhetorical Perspective*, 196.

7. Köstenberger, *John*, 231.

8. Bultmann, *Gospel of John*, 288.

Καὶ μετὰ ταῦτα περιεπάτει ὁ Ἰησοῦς ἐν τῇ Γαλιλαίᾳ· οὐ γὰρ ἤθελεν ἐν τῇ Ἰουδαίᾳ περιπατεῖν, ὅτι ἐζήτουν αὐτὸν οἱ Ἰουδαῖοι ἀποκτεῖναι.

A small number of ancient authorities replace ἤθελεν with εἶχεν ἐξουσίαν. Schnachenburg believes the latter might possibly be the better reading.[9] This would be translated along the lines of, "he was not permitted to go about in Judea," implying that the choice to stay in Galilee was not in Jesus' hands. It is not difficult to imagine a scribe wishing to remove the implication that Jesus was motivated by fear. It is therefore more likely that ἤθελεν is original, particularly since it is included in the vast majority of early manuscripts.

This beginning to the section indicates heightened conflict. It will be apparent throughout this passage that, in Schnackenburg's words, "the forces of belief and unbelief are locked in struggle"[10] at this point in Jesus' ministry.

The phrase ἐζήτουν αὐτὸν οἱ Ἰουδαῖοι ἀποκτεῖναι recalls 5:18. This is the first of many links between chapter 7 and chapter 5, prompting a number of scholars to assert that the intervening material is a later insertion. I believe it is unnecessary to make such an assertion. At this point in the narrative Jesus is about to return to Jerusalem. The links between chapters 7 and 5 indicate that the author is at pains to ensure that the reader recalls the events of Jesus' last visit to that city.

Some ancient commentators are concerned to deny that fear kept Jesus from Judea, and are keen to provide other motivations. Cyril of Alexandria, for example, wrote that by spending his time with Gentiles he was warning the Judeans that if they continued to reject him he would give himself completely to outsiders.[11] He could instead have appealed to Aristotle's arguments against taking unnecessary risks, οὐκ ἔστι δὲ μικροκίνδυνος οὐδὲ φιλοκίνδυνος διὰ τὸ ὀλίγα τιμᾶν, μεγαλοκίνδυνος δέ, καὶ ὅταν κινδυνεύῃ, ἀφειδὴς τοῦ βίου ὡς οὐκ ἄξιον ὂν πάντως ζῆν.[12]

---

9. Schnackenburg, *Gospel According to St John*, 138.

10. Schnackenburg, *Gospel According to St John*, 136.

11. Cyril of Alexandria, "Commentary on the Gospel of John," 4.5.

12. Aristotle, "Nicomachean Ethics" Book IV, §iii, 23, 220–1. TR: (Rackham) "The great-souled man does not run into danger for trifling reasons, and is not a lover of danger, because there are few things he values; but he will face danger in a great cause, and when doing so will be ready to sacrifice his life, since he holds that life is not worth living at every price."

As his conversation with his brothers reveals, Jesus did not seem to consider that showing off his powers constituted μεγαλοκίνδυνο.

ἦν δὲ ἐγγὺς ἡ ἑορτὴ τῶν Ἰουδαίων ἡ σκηνοπηγία.

A brief description of the Festival of Tabernacles is in order here. Moloney suggests that the feast was both historicized and "eschatologised."[13] Historically, it commemorated the time the Israelites lived in tents in the wilderness after being delivered from Egypt (Lev 23:42–43). It was also the time when the annual harvest was celebrated (Deut 16:13–5) because harvests were made possible after they ceased to be nomadic and lived with some stability in the land of promise.[14] It may be this connection with harvest that gave this feast its eschatological focus as the people looked forward to the end-time harvest and the reign of the messiah. Moloney identifies a link between Zechariah 14 and each of the daily ceremonies of the feast,[15] indicating a probable eschatological significance being given to the festival in the first century after their return from Babylonian exile.

Extant Jewish documents giving details of the celebration of this feast date to the rabbinic period, so we cannot be certain of their applicability to early first-century practice. However, to the extent that they agree with Old Testament descriptions of the feast and with evidence from John's Gospel, rabbinic documents can reasonably be taken as reliable witnesses.[16] According to the Mishnah, the festival ran for seven days, with one extra day at the end, which was devoted to a call for rain.[17] Each of the seven days included the following features.

The Water Libation Ceremony

Priests, accompanied by Levites and a crowd of people, would process to the Pool of Siloam and gather water in a golden container. The water would then be carried back to the temple, through the Water Gate, which rabbinic literature links with the south gate of Ezekiel 47:1–5 through

---

13. Moloney, *Gospel of John*, 233; H.N. Ridderbos, *Gospel According to John*, 257.
14. Farley, *Gospel of John*, 128–9.
15. Moloney, "Narrative and Discourse at the Feast of Tabernacles," 157–9.
16. Moloney, "Narrative and Discourse at the Feast of Tabernacles," 156.
17. Moloney, "Narrative and Discourse at the Feast of Tabernacles," 157.

which waters of life would flow in the end times. Within the temple, they would process around the altar singing Psalms 113—18, and then the water, with wine, would be poured out into vessels on the altar.[18]

Messianic hope is linked with water and the Feast of Tabernacles in Zechariah 14. Messianic expectation also looked for a redeemer who, like Moses, would give water to the people.[19]

The Ceremony of Light

Four menorahs were lit in the court of women. Men would dance under these while the priests sang Psalms 120—34. These lights would illuminate the temple precincts, indeed the whole of Jerusalem,[20] for the seven nights of the festival. There would therefore be "no night" for the period of the feast.

Zechariah 14:6–8 links this illumination with the living waters that flow out of Jerusalem. The light probably also looked back to the pillar of fire that led the Israelites in the desert.[21]

The rite of facing the temple

When the rooster crowed on each of the seven mornings, the priests would proceed to the east gate and gaze toward the east. When the sun rose they would turn around and face the temple, saying, "Our fathers, when they were in this place, turned their backs toward the temple of the Lord and their faces toward the east, and they worshipped the sun toward the east; but as for us, our eyes are turned toward the Lord."[22] Moloney links this ceremony with Zechariah 14:9.[23]

Moloney asserts, therefore, that the Tabernacles Discourse should be read against the background of Israel's recognition of the one true God, to whom all praise and allegiance are due.[24]

---

18. Moloney, *Gospel of John*, 234.
19. Moloney, *Gospel of John*, 234; see *Ecclesiastes Rabbah* 1:8.
20. Moloney, "Narrative and Discourse at the Feast of Tabernacles," 158.
21. Moloney, *Gospel of John*, 235.
22. Moloney, *Gospel of John*, 236; see m. Suk. 5:4.
23. Moloney, "Narrative and Discourse at the Feast of Tabernacles," 159.
24. Moloney, "Narrative and Discourse at the Feast of Tabernacles," 159.

Initial comments on 7:1–10 as an introduction to the Tabernacles Discourse

Hoskins also argues convincingly that the Tabernacles Discourse points toward Jesus being the fulfillment not only of the promises of light and water but also of the temple itself.[25] This would align well with John 2:19–22.

The conflict in these chapters is related to Jesus' claims to be the fulfillment of what the festival signified (7:37; 8:12). The people of Jerusalem were being asked to accept that what they were celebrating was a "sign and a shadow"[26] of God's perfect gift in and through Jesus. They were being called to rethink their past through the present reality of the λόγος made σὰρξ among them. "History has not been abandoned but rendered Christological."[27] Yet for any people group the re-rendering of history is inevitably fraught with stress and conflict. Moreover, their hope for the future is also rendered christological. Jesus' καιρὸς may not yet have come (2:6) but he is already reconfiguring the Jewish calendar.

In this confusing period in which history is re-rendered and eschatology reimagined, it is reasonable to ask about the sense of timing embodied by those who should be closest to Jesus. How are his brothers telling the time? The introduction answers this question unequivocally. Jesus and his brothers do not share the same calendar. And if his brothers remain unconvinced, the people of Jerusalem are unlikely to accept this transformation without argument.

εἶπον οὖν πρὸς αὐτὸν οἱ ἀδελφοὶ αὐτοῦ, Μετάβηθι ἐντεῦθεν καὶ ὕπαγε εἰς τὴν Ἰουδαίαν

Though the brothers do not mention the festival, the use of οὖν implies a connection between the festival and their suggestion.[28] Jerusalem would have been bustling with people at the time, making it a very appropriate place for Jesus to publically manifest his great works, if that was his wish.

Of particular interest here is whether or not the brothers are aware of the Jews' plot to kill Jesus. Are they knowingly telling him to walk

---

25. Hoskins, *Jesus as the Fulfillment of the Temple*, 160–170.
26. Moloney, "Narrative and Discourse at the Feast of Tabernacles," 167.
27. Moloney, "Narrative and Discourse at the Feast of Tabernacles," 168.
28. Moloney, *Gospel of John*, 239.

into mortal danger? Köstenberger thinks not.[29] Yet in 7:25 we find that this news has filtered through to the people of Jerusalem. If it is known to Jesus in Galilee and to the people of Jerusalem, why should it not be known to Jesus' brothers?

Knowingly or not, they are asking Jesus to walk into danger. It may be that they had such confidence in their elder brother that they believed he would overcome any opposition. If he were to defeat such dangerous enemies then he would win even more honor, for himself and for his family, than he had earned by healing the sick and feeding the hungry.

However, their lack of concern for his safety is contrasted with the later attitude of the disciples who first warn Jesus to stay out of danger, and then align themselves with him to the extent that they resign themselves to die with him (John 11:7–16).[30] Here the disciples behave more like ideal brothers than do his biological kin.

Ridderbos suggests that Μετάβηθι ἐντεῦθεν implies more than a pilgrimage and may mean that the brothers want Jesus to move to Judea permanently.[31] This is certainly possible but cannot be verified with certainty.

It is notable that the brothers appear here without their mother.[32] Perhaps it is only the men in the family who are attending this festival, but Lee suggests that the author may be deliberately keeping her at a distance here. "Is there the suggestion of her dissociation (and that of the disciples) from those whose physical proximity to Jesus remains opaque and never moves beyond the material realm? Although encouraging Jesus' ministry (at one level) the *adelphoi* also express doubt and lack any understanding of the purpose of the "signs" (7:4b)."[33]

The only other time Jesus' mother will appear in this Gospel will be at the foot of the cross without her other sons but, importantly, with the beloved disciple.

---

29. Köstenberger, *John*, 230.

30. See Campbell, *Kinship Relations*, 137.

31. Ridderbos, *Gospel According to John*, 257; so Schnackenburg, *Gospel According to St John*, 139.

32. See Campbell, *Kinship Relations*, 27.

33. Lee, *Flesh and Glory*, 146.

ἵνα καὶ οἱ μαθηταί σου θεωρήσουσιν σοῦ τὰ ἔργα ἃ ποιεῖς·

This desire for Jesus' works to be seen in Judea must be understood in light of the recent defection of many disciples following Jesus' claim to be the bread of life (6:60–71). Brothers in this situation would almost certainly be sensitive to the dent in their family honor that would be caused by such a "setback." Urging their elder brother to take action that may win back some honor would be a natural next step for them.[34] The extent to which they expect to share Jesus' honor is not explicitly stated, but Neyrey believes this must have been their primary motivation in this exchange.[35] Indeed, in this culture it would be assumed that a brother's honor would reflect on his family. This does not necessarily imply that their motives were selfish. The honor of their family was at stake, not just the individual self-interest of the brothers.

Jesus has been an object of ridicule and threat from the great ones in Jerusalem. He has also lost the support of many who had been following him. A man who brought such dishonor upon his family could expect not only to be urged but even to be disciplined by his brothers in this culture, even if he was the eldest. For the brothers, sending Jesus to Jerusalem held the potential of solving the problem of family honor in one of two ways. Either he would perform great signs and gain honor for the family, as they openly suggest, or he might be put to death. Either way the crisis of family shame posed by Jesus would be averted.[36] It would be inappropriate to assume their thinking was quite so cynical, but the narrative certainly leaves that possibility open.

The brothers may be hoping that Jesus would recruit new disciples in Judea to help swell his recently diminished ranks,[37] but remembering that many Galileans would be in Jerusalem at this time[38] it could be that the brothers were thinking more in terms of winning back those disciples who had been lost[39] or gaining new disciples who would return with him to Galilee.

34. Kruse, *John*, 182; Waetjen, *Gospel of the Beloved Disciple*, 223.

35. Neyrey, *Gospel of John in Cultural and Rhetorical Perspective*, 222.

36. See Campbell, *Kinship Relations*, 139.

37. Ellis, *Genius of John*, 142.

38. Lenski, *Interpretation of St John's Gospel*, 530.

39. Moloney, *Gospel of John*, 239; Ridderbos, *Gospel According to John*, 257; Kruse, *John*, 181–2; also Köstenberger, *John*, 229.

Köstenberger, following Brown, suggests that the brothers might here be playing the role of Satan in the synoptic temptation narratives, urging Jesus to perform some great public act to compel belief.[40] Less diabolically, though along similar lines, they may be echoing the call of the crowds to make Jesus king in 6:15.[41] I suggest a more innocent connection to synoptic tradition. In light of the fact that when Jesus arrives at Jerusalem he does not perform ἔργα but rather engages in teaching and disputing, a likeness can be drawn between this passage and those, such as Mark 1:35–39, where Jesus asserts the priority of teaching over against the disciples' desire that he perform more miracles.

It is not uncommon for commentators to compare this passage with Jesus' mother's request in John 2.[42] However, it is more appropriate to see these passages in stark contrast. Jesus' mother brought a need to his attention and left him to decide how to meet that need. Here, the brothers urge him to act simply to bring glory to himself and his family. They are not at all suggesting that Jesus should go to Judea because there are many sick people there in need of healing. In similar contrast, there is no indication in John 2 that Jesus' mother was motivated by the worldly motives that concerned the brothers.

> οὐδεὶς γάρ τι ἐν κρυπτῷ ποιεῖ καὶ ζητεῖ αὐτὸς ἐν παρρησίᾳ εἶναι.

Schnackenburg points out the irony here: "it is of the essence of the revelation that Jesus proclaims it 'publicly' before the world (cf. 18:20); but it is only believers who grasp the meaning of this 'public' revelation, which in a deeper sense remains veiled."[43] Seeing, in this Gospel, is one path to belief (2:11), but not all who see believe (6:26), and not all who believe have need of sight (20:29).

When Jesus does reveal his glory fully it will be in a very public act in Judea. This act will not (at least initially) bring any honor to his family.

---

40. Köstenberger, *John*, 230; E. C. Hoskyns, *Fourth Gospel*, 311.
41. Lenski, *Interpretation of St John's Gospel*, 531; Hoskyns, *Fourth Gospel*, 311.
42. For example, Hoskyns, *Fourth Gospel*, 311.
43. Schnackenburg, *Gospel According to St John*, 139.

εἰ ταῦτα ποιεῖς, φανέρωσον σεαυτὸν τῷ κόσμῳ.

Moloney believes this conditional statement indicates doubt about whether Jesus was actually performing any significant works,[44] but it is much more likely that the brothers were well aware that Jesus was doing great works and were blind to the significance of those works. The εἰ should be read as "since." It might almost be appropriate (though uncharitable to the brothers) to paraphrase this as, "If you want to do party tricks you should go to the party!"

This entreaty of his brothers is in stark contrast to the way Jesus has been speaking of his ministry throughout this Gospel. Jesus insists that he has not come to show himself to the world but to make the Father known.[45] His brothers have failed to hear this message.

The word φανερόω has not been used since 2:11 and so provides another link with the Cana narrative.[46] At that point in my exegesis[47] I raised questions about whether Jesus' glory was revealed only to his disciples, or whether Jesus' family also saw it. The author says only that the disciples believed. Did the brothers see his glory and not believe, or did they not see it at all? These questions are left unaddressed in the Cana narrative. The possibility that the brothers may also have believed has waited until this point (7:5) to be addressed.

οὐδὲ γὰρ οἱ ἀδελφοὶ αὐτοῦ ἐπίστευον εἰς αὐτόν.

This statement from the narrator indicates to readers that the brother's comments are to be read as coming from a perspective that is not Jesus' own. This does not mean they should necessarily be read as hostile to Jesus[48] but they should certainly be seen as obstacles cast in the way of his mission.

---

44. Moloney, *Gospel of John*, 237; contra Ridderbos, *Gospel According to John*, 258; Köstenberger, *John*, 230; Schnackenburg, *Gospel According to St John*, 140; Lenski, *Interpretation of St John's Gospel*, 531; Hoskyns, *Fourth Gospel*, 311.

45. Moloney, *Gospel of John*, 237.

46. Lieu, "The Mother of the Son in the Fourth Gospel," 66.

47. Chapter 6.

48. Neyrey, *Gospel of John in Cultural and Rhetorical Perspective*, 222. Some scholars do argue that the brothers are hostile and that their hostility hints at later hostility between the Johannine community and the Jerusalem Church (Campbell, *Kinship Relations*, 61–62). This line of argument will be considered later in this chapter.

The prologue had already indicated that οἱ ἴδιοι αὐτὸν οὐ παρέλαβον (1:11). Here members of Jesus' family are explicitly numbered among his own people who do not receive him. In that sense the author makes Jesus' brothers representatives of unbelief and of the world,[49] examples of the darkness that will not make room for the light.

The imperfect tense of ἐπίστεθον implies on-going disbelief in the past. It is likely that readers are expected to know of the involvement of Jesus' brothers in the post-resurrection Christian community in Jerusalem.[50] This verse implies, in that case, that a person's stance toward Jesus need not be static.[51] Believers can become unbelievers, as evidenced by the defections in John 6. Unbelievers can also become believers. While some of the contrasts in this Gospel between belief and unbelief are very stark, such as darkness and light (3:19–21), it is clear that the gulf between the two can be traversed. The journey may be a long one, as it was for Jesus' brothers, but it is the ultimate destination that matters.

This possibility of transition implies that a charitable attitude toward outsiders is appropriate, but the author gives this implication without softening the boundaries between insiders and outsiders in the community of faith.

> λέγει οὖν αὐτοῖς ὁ Ἰησοῦς, Ὁ καιρὸς ὁ ἐμὸς οὔπω πάρεστιν, ὁ δὲ καιρὸς ὁ ὑμέτερος πάντοτέ ἐστιν ἕτοιμος.

The οὔπω of Jesus' καιρός in 7:6 looks back to the οὔπω of Jesus' ὥρα in 2:4.[52] This is certainly another link with the Cana narrative, but it is curious that the author should choose to use καιρός here instead of ὥρα. Schnackenburg believes that ὥρα refers to the Father's decree, whereas καιρός refers to the time of challenge in which Jesus must make a clear decision to follow that decree.[53] This is possible but is probably reading too much into the words.

Kruse proposes that καιρός is used here because theologically significant time is not in view here. Jesus is simply saying that if he were to turn up in Jerusalem at the start of the festival the people who wanted

---

49. Schnackenburg, *Gospel According to St John*, 139.
50. See chapter 1.
51. Waetjen, *Gospel of the Beloved Disciple*, 224.
52. Moloney, *Gospel of John*, 239.
53. Schnackenburg, *Gospel According to St John*, 140.

to kill him would be looking for him. He, therefore, had to choose his time carefully. His brothers did not have to worry about such things, as nobody was trying to kill them.[54] I find this unsatisfactory because the following verse places this contrast in the context of the world's attitude to Jesus, and so must be of more significance than Kruse implies. Apollinaris of Laodicea's argument that Jesus was indicating that it was not an appropriate time to feast, since the days are evil, is even less likely given Jesus' involvement in the Cana festivities.[55] Bultmann argues that καιρὸς is the world's time and that Jesus acts only in eschatological time.[56] This may be the most convincing argument but still appears to be reading into the text what the text does not suggest of itself.

It appears to me that καιρὸς is used because the word is applied to both Jesus and his brothers. Jesus has a ὥρα that he is moving towards and his brothers do not, but they all have a καιρὸς. They all have a calendar by which they live and a sense of past and future through which they understand their present.

The particular καιρὸς referred to here is the time when Jesus's work/s would be revealed to the world (7:4). Presumably, then, the καιρὸς of his brothers, which is ever-present, is also the time for their works to be manifest. This is the time for them to do the work of men in their culture, to pursue virtue in obedience to Torah, to acquire skill in their profession, and to earn and use wealth well for the benefit of their families. It is always time for this, but the time for Jesus to manifest his most important work is more specific. In 8:28 Jesus will tell the crowd in Jerusalem when they can expect his time to come. That time will arrive when Jesus is lifted up.[57] Jesus' time is not just a καιρὸς, it is a ὥρα.

καιρὸς here is, therefore, linked with the ὥρα of Jesus' death. In this context, καιρὸς is the more general term and ὥρα the more specific.

Most commentators, without much analysis, assume that καιρὸς is equivalent to ὥρα in this instance and believe that Jesus is saying, in effect, "I will reveal my glory to the world, but the right time has not yet come." Augustine argued that Jesus was thinking of a very different path to exaltation from the one his brothers suggested: a humble path that he will take soon, but not yet.[58] Ridderbos argues that this downward path

---

54. Kruse, *John*, 182.
55. Apollinaris of Laodicea, "Fragments on John," 32.
56. Bultmann, *Gospel of John*, 293.
57. Ellis, *Genius of John*, 138.
58. Augustine, "Tractate XXVIII" 5–7.

is necessary because of the nature of the people there. They represent not the ideal Israel but the hostile world:

> Awaiting Jesus in Jerusalem is not festively attired Israel prepared to meet the one sent by God, in the manner of the feast, to receive living water from the wells of salvation (Is 12:3), but "the world," those who, despite all their religiosity, are estranged from God, who do not recognize him for who he is because they do not recognize God (v28) and therefore do not believe in Jesus, but indeed hate him.[59]

Farley suggests that the brothers are asking Jesus here not simply to travel with them, but to lead the pilgrimage of Galileans to Jerusalem. This would have allowed him a triumphant entry into the city; such as he would lead later, but not now. That moment of publicity, which would soon be followed by his ultimate glorification on the cross, had not yet arrived.[60]

Schnackenburg sees in Jesus' words more than a statement of difference between Jesus and his brothers, but in fact a stern rebuke. Because Jews believed that all people and every moment stood under God's decree, he believes that Jesus is here "pronouncing on [his brothers] the annihilating verdict that their lives have become meaningless."[61] They experience appalling freedom from the constraints of God's will, because they are not people of God but people of the world.[62] I suspect he is correct, but only because of what Jesus goes on to say in v7. If Jesus had stopped at the end of v6 I do not believe we would have sufficient warrant for reading such harsh criticism into his words. Yet because Jesus does go on to accuse his brothers of being in league with the world, and therefore estranged from God, it is reasonable to read the whole speech as criticism.

οὐ δύναται ὁ κόσμος μισεῖν ὑμᾶς, ἐμὲ δὲ μισεῖ,

The brothers had called Jesus to reveal himself to the world, by which they meant that he should make his works more public. Jesus, however, sees that this misunderstanding of his mission indicates that the brothers

---

59. Ridderbos, *Gospel According to John*, 258–9.

60. Farley, *Gospel of John*, 129–30; so Lenski, *Interpretation of St John's Gospel*, 529.

61. Schnackenburg, *Gospel According to St John*, 141.

62. See also Campbell, *Kinship Relations*, 63–4.

had taken the side of the world. They have joined humanity in hostility to God, and brought themselves into conflict with their brother, who is God's son.[63] The meaning of κόσμος is transformed here by Jesus from publicity to hostility.[64]

The emphatic use of ὑμᾶς further broadens the gap between Jesus and his brothers.[65] Their status as brothers does not make them insiders with Jesus. Jesus' people, the Jews, are also set at a great distance from Jesus in their desire to kill him (7:1). They are presumably part of ὁ κόσμος, linked with the world in their hatred of Jesus. Again, the rejection of Jesus by his own kin is emphasized here. Those who should have received him have rejected him. This immediately raises the question of whether Jesus has any genuine ἴδιοι who do not reject him. If Jesus' own people are not those who are linked to him by kinship or race, who are they?

ὅτι ἐγὼ μαρτυρῶ περὶ αὐτοῦ ὅτι τὰ ἔργα αὐτοῦ πονηρά ἐστιν.

In v3 the brothers had urged Jesus to act in such a way that his disciples would see his ἔργα. Here ἔργα appears again, establishing a contrast between Jesus' works and the works of the world. Jesus' testimony that the works of the world are evil is partly verbal (as here) and partly through his action of refusing to do those works. His brothers are urging him towards worldly action, and he is refusing. The brothers, siding with the world, call Jesus to do the wrong sort of works; Jesus testifies that those works are evil.

Jesus is here doing what the world hates him for doing. Jesus here testifies to his brothers (representatives of the world) that their deeds (in calling him to manifest his glory at this time in Jerusalem) are evil (of the world and not of God). How will they respond to this accusation? Will they hate Jesus, as the world does, and join the world in calling for his death? Or will they accept his rebuke and change their works? Their reply is not recorded here, so this question remains open in John. Their absence from Jesus' execution does not augur well for them. However, readers of Acts (and presumably many members of the first-century church, including the first readers of this Gospel) know that they did eventually

---

63. Schnackenburg, *Gospel According to St John*, 141.
64. Lenski, *Interpretation of St John's Gospel*, 534–5.
65. Moloney, *Gospel of John*, 239.

repent. There was still hope for them, as there was still hope for others of the world, including the Jews.

> ὑμεῖς ἀνάβητε εἰς τὴν ἑορτήν· ἐγὼ οὐκ ἀναβαίνω εἰς τὴν ἑορτὴν ταύτην, ὅτι ὁ ἐμὸς καιρὸς οὔπω πεπλήρωται.

According to Moloney, the emphatic ταύτην indicates that Jesus intended to go to another festival, but not this one.[66] Chrysostom had earlier written that it was at the next Passover, not Tabernacles, when his time would come.[67]

Other commentators believe Jesus is simply making it clear that he will not go to the festival at the request of his brothers or for the reasons his brothers have given.[68] As with 2:4, some commentators emphasize that Jesus was following his Father's instructions, in his Father's time, rather than doing the will of his brothers.[69] Neyrey believes that Jesus is defending his honor by refusing to be manipulated.[70]

As will be seen later, many commentators are keen to insist that Jesus was not lying here, even if this strains the logic of the passage. Cyril of Alexandria argued that, "the Saviour says these things, not altogether saying that he will not go to Jerusalem . . . but minded that he will do this too and everything else at the proper time."[71]

Is it possible, with Epiphanius,[72] to read this phrase with a double meaning on the word ἀναβαίνω: "I will not ascend at this festival"? This may be the most promising line of enquiry, as it fits with John's theology and themes of glorification as well as with the brothers' coaxing of him to glorify himself. Hoskyns points out that cognates of ἀναβαίνω are used twice in this Gospel to refer to Jesus' ascent to the Father in heaven (3:13, 6:62).[73] Jesus will be lifted up (on the cross, in glorification, and in return to the Father) as he has said earlier (3:15) and will say again shortly (8:28), but this is not the festival at which his "lifting-up" will take place.

---

66. Moloney, *Gospel of John*, 238; so Schnackenburg, *Gospel According to St John*, 142.

67. Chrysostom, *Homilies*, 48.2.

68. Kruse, *John*, 182; also Köstenberger, *John*, 230–1.

69. Köstenberger, *John*, 231.

70. Neyrey, *Gospel of John in Cultural and Rhetorical Perspective*, 223.

71. Cyril of Alexandria, "Commentary on the Gospel of John," 4.5.

72. Epiphanius, *Pan. Haereses*, 51.25.

73. Hoskyns, *The Fourth Gospel*, 313.

Schnackenburg rejects this explanation on the basis that ἀναβαίνω εἰς τὴν ἑορτὴν must mean the same here as it means with reference to his brothers,[74] but this does not seem to be an adequate argument. It is not unreasonable that the author might use the same phrase in one place as a straightforward instruction and again soon afterward as a double (or triple?) entendre.

Ellis believes that John's original readers would easily have caught the implication from this verse that Jesus' hour for "going up" (on the cross) will not be at this feast.[75] He sees close parallels between 7:36 and 8:21–59 in the intention of the Jews to kill Jesus, the concept of secrecy, the accusation of demon possession, and the contrast between Jesus and the world.[76] This link may provide added evidence for use of ἀναβαίνω as a pun. 8:28 gives an answer to the questions raised in 7:6–8. His hour will have come when he is lifted up.[77]

Seeing a double entendre in this phrase adds depth to the discussion of honor and fame in this interaction. Jesus' plan for exalting himself is very different from his brothers' plan. Given the playfulness with words that characterizes this Gospel it is likely that such added depth was intended. However, this does not remove the difficulty of Jesus deceiving his brothers. A second level of meaning does not negate the surface meaning. Whatever else Jesus may have been communicating when he said, ἐγὼ οὐκ ἀναβαίνω εἰς τὴν ἑορτὴν ταύτην he was clearly saying that he would not go up to the festival.

> ταῦτα δὲ εἰπὼν αὐτὸς ἔμεινεν ἐν τῇ Γαλιλαίᾳ. Ὡς δὲ ἀνέβησαν οἱ ἀδελφοὶ αὐτοῦ εἰς τὴν ἑορτήν

In v9 some ancient manuscripts replace αὐτὸς with αὐτοῖς, some include both αὐτὸς and αὐτοῖς, and others omit both. None of these variations alters the meaning significantly.

It may possibly be that by going openly to Jerusalem the brothers are identifying themselves with οἱ Ἰουδαῖοι who are trying to kill Jesus.[78] What is clear is that Jesus' brothers do not share his danger. They can go

---

74. Schnackenburg, *Gospel According to St John*, 143; so Campbell, *Kinship Relations*, 63.

75. Ellis, *Genius of John*, 143.

76. Ellis, *Genius of John*, 138.

77. Ellis, *Genius of John*, 138.

78. Campbell, *Kinship Relations*, 60.

openly without fear, but Jesus would be in danger of being put to death if he were to go. If they had been closely identified with Jesus, or even if they were not estranged from him, surely they would attract some of the hostility that had been directed at Jesus. Surely, at the very least, they would be in danger of being targeted by those who might try to use those close to Jesus in order to trap him. Yet there appears to be no such danger. This adds to the sense in this passage that very little affinity exists at this point between Jesus and his brothers.

τότε καὶ αὐτὸς ἀνέβη

Edwards faces the question squarely: "Jesus says one thing and does another, with a subterfuge that is at once ineffectual and untypical of this Gospel."[79] Bultmann also admits that, "Jesus' actions contradict his own words."[80]

According to Moloney, Jesus' action here echoes that of 2:4–7 and 4:48–50 in that an initial unwillingness is reversed in order to indicate that Jesus is following orders, not from people but from God.[81] Certainly the author's intention in many places is to demonstrate that Jesus was beyond coercion[82] and was constantly doing the Father's will, yet this does not really help us here where Jesus says he will do one thing and then does another with no indication of a fresh word from the Father in the intervening time.

According to Waetjen, Jesus is being "inconspicuous, not surreptitious."[83] Köstenberger falls over himself grammatically in order to insist that Jesus was not being deceptive, "despite what might have seemed to be the implication from 7:1–9."[84]

The simple explanation that Jesus had not refused to go to the festival per se but had refused only in the context of the brothers calling on him to manifest himself there[85] may have some value. However, it does

---

79. Edwards, *John*, 82.
80. Bultmann, *Gospel of John*, 288.
81. Moloney, *Gospel of John*, 240; See the discussion of 2:4 in chapter 6.
82. Ellis, *Genius of John*, 143, so Schnackenburg, *Gospel According to St John*, 142.
83. Waetjen, *The Gospel of the Beloved Disciple*, 224.
84. Köstenberger, *John*, 231.
85. Schnackenburg, *Gospel According to St John*, 142–3; Lenski, *Interpretation of St John's Gospel*; Schnackenburg, *Gospel According to St John*; Schnackenburg, *Gospel According to St John*, 537.

not negate that plain meaning of his words. Jesus did not say, "I will not manifest my glory at this festival." He said, "I will not go up to this festival." Though in faith I assume that Jesus acted without sin[86] here, I must still ask why the author has chosen to give the impression that he lied to his brothers.

A distinction needs to be clearly drawn here between Jesus' words and John's reporting of those words. Since Jesus would have spoken in Aramaic, John was free to choose his Greek translation to suit the narrative. He used that freedom in a way that gives the impression that Jesus lied. Why would he do that when he has described Jesus as the very Word of God, πλήρης χάριτος καὶ ἀληθείας (1:14), and will describe him as ἡ ὁδὸς καὶ ἡ ἀλήθεια καὶ ἡ ζωή? Like every word in this profound Gospel, Jesus' words to his brothers here were deliberately chosen, and we should not overlook the message John is seeking to communicate in our rush to exonerate Jesus. I will seek, below, to unlock some windows toward clarifying this conundrum.

οὐ φανερῶς ἀλλὰ [ὡς] ἐν κρυπτῷ.

Though a majority of early manuscripts include ὡς it is easy to see how a scribe might have added it to soften any dishonor they considered may have been attached to Jesus acting in secret. It is likely, therefore, that it is not original.[87]

Surely this phrase is where the focus of the sentence is intended to lie. The question of whether Jesus went to the festival is less important to the author at this point than the way he went: not to show himself publicly as his brothers requested[88] but secretly, so as not to precipitate the καιρὸς that had not yet come. ἐν κρυπτῷ here echoes the ἐν κρυπτῷ of v4, showing that Jesus did not indeed want to be in public at this time.

Ridderbos points out that by following ἀνέβη, not with the expected εἰς τὴν ἑορτὴν, but with οὐ φανερῶς, the author is emphasizing the "wholly other" nature of Jesus' attendance at the feast.[89] Though Jesus did go to the festival, he did so in a completely different way than that envisaged by his brothers.

---

86. See below for a brief biblical ethic of deception.
87. Moloney, *Gospel of John*, 240.
88. Moloney, *Gospel of John*, 240.
89. Ridderbos, *Gospel According to John*, 260.

Edwards, following Hoskyns,[90] indicates that, to the rabbis, virtuous action performed in secret indicated humility.[91] It can at least be said that secrecy is seen in a positive light in Matt 6:4–6 and similar passages. The fact that Jesus acted in secret here need not trouble commentators who wish to exonerate Jesus. Wishing to avoid showing himself openly to those who were trying to kill him indicates discretion, not cowardice.

Augustine argued that Jesus was there in secret in the sense that those present did not perceive in him the ultimate reality behind the feast.[92] Bultmann takes this further by saying that Jesus' works are always ἐν κρυπτῷ to the world.[93] While this metaphorical reading may well be accurate it does not negate the surface level at which Jesus said he would not attend the festival and then did attend it in secret.

A fresh way forward will be introduced shortly, but firstly a number of conclusions based on the above considerations can be drawn about this ending to Jesus' conversation with his brothers.

Firstly, the fact that Jesus chooses to travel to Jerusalem separately from his extended biological family almost certainly indicates Jesus' increasing isolation from them.[94] Jewish pilgrimages were family and village affairs, but here the reader is not even told who Jesus traveled with. It is probably not too great a stretch to say that if we can identify those people with whom Jesus goes on pilgrimage we can identify whom he considers his kin. In this passage we are not told, but for his next pilgrimage, his last visit to Jerusalem, he will be accompanied by his disciples, not his brothers.

Secondly, it is clear that, though Jesus does travel to Jerusalem, he does not go there because his brothers invited him or with the intention of doing what they wanted him to do. They wanted him to manifest his glory. He insists that he will not do that at this festival. So, what does he intend to do there? We can assume that the answer to that question will also be important and for that reason, among others, analysis of verses 11–24 has been included later in this chapter.

Thirdly, in this culture open disclosure tends to be made only to insiders, to those who are trusted. Secrets are kept from outsiders and those who one believes cannot be trusted. By withholding from his brothers

---

90. Hoskyns, *Fourth Gospel*, 311.

91. Edwards, *John*, 82.

92. Augustine, "Tractate XXVIII" 9.

93. Bultmann, *Gospel of John*, 294.

94. Köstenberger, *John*, 231.

his intention to travel to Jerusalem Jesus is treating his brothers as outsiders, as Campbell explains: "If his relationship with his brothers was harmonious, Jesus would entrust himself to them and seek their support. Instead, he maintains strict boundaries by withholding the truth from them and by placing them squarely within the hostile world that he does not trust."[95]

Lastly, and more tentatively, I wonder if the author has introduced confusion over where Jesus is going as a prolepsis for the metaphorical discussion of Jesus' destination in 7:33–36.

A fresh way forward was suggested to me by Attridge's delightful essay "Genre Bending in the Fourth Gospel."[96] While Attridge does not touch on John 7, his demonstration of the tendency of the Fourth Gospel to take known narrative forms and distort them[97] raised the question for me of what known form or forms the author may be distorting in this case. The answer was immediately obvious: deceitful brother narratives in Genesis. Genesis, and indeed the Old Testament generally, is rich with brotherly conflict and deceit, as I have discussed in chapter 7. In the following pages Genesis will first provide a guide to developing an ethical framework for understanding Jesus misleading his brothers and will then supply a narrative template for understanding what is going on in this conversation between Jesus and his brothers.

Jewish ethics of deception

This fresh way forward may help readers to understand why John leaves open the possible interpretation that Jesus intentionally deceived his brothers. It appears to me that many commentators fail to delve deeply into this episode because of timidity about squarely facing this possibility. Once the apparent deception is explained away there is little left of interest in the episode. Commentators, therefore, generally move on very quickly to verse 11. I contend, rather, that there is a great deal of interest in this episode, and that much of it becomes accessible when we ask why John might have been so bold as to hint at Jesus deceiving his brothers.

---

95. Campbell, *Kinship Relations*, 141.

96. Attridge, "Genre Bending in the Fourth Gospel."

97. Martyn, *History and Theology in the Fourth Gospel*, 36 points to a similar reality when he writes of John taking the miracle story form and giving it a "dramatic expansion."

What Old Testament resonances might he have been alluding to in the concept of deception among brothers?

Williams identifies fifteen episodes of deception in the book of Genesis. These are:

1.	(Gen. 3:1–19)	The serpent's deception of Adam and Eve
2.	(Gen. 12:10–20)	Abram's deception of Pharaoh
3.	(Gen. 20:1–18)	Abraham's deception of Abimelech
4.	(Gen. 26:6–11)	Isaac's deception of Abimelech
5.	(Gen. 27:1–40)	Rebekah's and Jacob's deception of Isaac and Esau
6.	(Gen. 29:15–30)	Laban's deception of Jacob regarding his wife
7.	(Gen. 31:4–9, 38–42)	Laban's deception of Jacob regarding his wages
8.	(Gen. 31:17–18, 20–29)	Jacob's deception of Laban
9.	(Gen. 31:19, 30–35)	Rachel's deception of Laban
10.	(Gen. 34:1–31)	Jacob's sons' deception of the Shechemites
11.	(Gen. 37:29–35)	Joseph's brothers' deception of Jacob
12.	(Gen. 38:1–26)	Tamar's deception of Judah
13.	(Gen. 39:1–20)	Potiphar's wife's deception of Potiphar
14.	(Gen. 42:7–28)	Joseph's first deception of his brothers
15.	(Gen. 44:1–34)	Joseph's second deception of his brothers[98]

Williams contends that most of these incidents of deception are evaluated negatively in the narrative. However, he shows that the narrative depicts incidents 12, 14, and 15 in a positive light.[99] Anderson insists, in addition, that 8 and 9 are also viewed positively in the narrative, in that Jacob's deception is motivated by a dream given to him by God.[100] I

---

98. Williams, "Lies, Lies, I Tell You!" 11.

99. Williams, "Lies, Lies, I Tell You!" 2.

100. Anderson, "Jacob, Laban, and a Divine Trickster?"

suspect that incident 5 is at least ambiguous in that the deception obtains for Jacob the blessing that God had already declared to be his.[101]

Of the fifteen incidents of deception, there are only nine that are unambiguously presented by the narrative in a negative light. This alone ought to render questionable any notion that all forms of deception are entirely inconsistent with the character of God and God's people.

Williams argues that the principle tying together all positively viewed incidents (12, 14, and 15) is the use of deception to restore *shalom* after it has been disrupted.[102] He notes the following conditions for this principle to apply:

1. The deception must be limited to the person who caused the original wrong.
2. The deception must not disadvantage the deceived person.
3. The deception must not advantage the deceiver beyond his/her status prior to what it was before suffering the original wrong.[103]

It is obvious at this point why Williams chose only the three most unambiguous incidents of deception to include in his analysis. Only incidents 12, 14, and 15 comply in a straightforward manner with these three conditions. However, his conclusions are of significant value in discussing John 7 because they provide a maximal ethical framework by which to examine Jesus' deception of his brothers. There can be no doubt among readers familiar with Genesis that deception of this type is acceptable at least and may even be praiseworthy.

Anderson, by making a case for including incidents 8 and 9 among the positively presented examples of deception, is saying something broader and more ambitious than Williams. Anderson's perspective is also more theological than ethical.[104] What can be said about the God who not only fails to condemn certain acts of deception but even seems to initiate deception on occasion? For Anderson, the answer is clear:

---

101. It is unnecessary to make this case fully at this stage.

102. Williams, "Lies, Lies, I Tell You! " 14–15. I could argue that deceit which increases *shalom* is also morally acceptable, even if it is not a response to a previous disruption in *shalom*. A very simple example is the deceit involved in throwing a surprise birthday party. However, it is not necessary to make that case here.

103. Williams, "Lies, Lies, I Tell You! "15.

104. It should be noted that Williams also broadens his discussion to incidents where God endorses and initiates deception in the Old Testament. Williams, "Lies, Lies, I Tell You!" 19.

"God will stop at nothing to achieve His covenantal promise."[105] I would not be so bold as to agree with such a provocative statement. Rather I would say that God does not see certain minor forms of deception as impediments to the achievement of covenantal promises. To argue that God would stop at nothing implies that God is somehow above morality and so leaves the question of the morality of deception unaddressed. Noticing that God is unimpeded by the necessity of minor deception implies that those particular deceptions are morally acceptable to God.

In relation to the deception of Laban, Anderson argues that "the explicit deception is tempered by the covenantal overtones of the passage, which do not seek to exonerate God or Jacob from any type of deception but rather to convey that this deception should be understood as a means of carrying the covenantal promise and blessing to Abraham forward to its ultimate realization."[106]

Anderson and Williams can be brought together by noticing that fulfilling the covenantal promises is God's method of restoring the *shalom* disrupted by human sin. It can probably[107] be said that wherever God is implicated in deception in the Old Testament, God is fulfilling Williams' three criteria for acceptable deception motivated by the restoration of *shalom*.

Anderson's analysis is, therefore, a means of understanding God's actions, but it is not very helpful as an ethical principle for human interactions. Can I claim that any deceit on my part that advances God's covenantal purposes is morally acceptable? Are lies that make the Christian life appear more palatable than it really is acceptable because they bring people into the kingdom? Certainly not! The difference is that God's perspective is comprehensive and eternal and mine is not. I need a more tangible set of principles to guide my behavior. Williams is more helpful to me in that sense.

When I return to Jesus, though, I am struck again by the fact that I am discussing someone who is both God and human. It is reasonable, then, to apply both Williams' and Anderson's analyses to Jesus' possible deceit of his brothers?

---

105. Anderson, "Jacob, Laban, and a Divine Trickster?" 7.

106. Anderson, "Jacob, Laban, and a Divine Trickster?" 22.

107. More detailed work on a greater range of OT texts would be necessary to fully substantiate this claim.

Firstly, then, does this deception carry forward God's covenant purposes? If I am to affirm this I must argue that God's covenant purposes were furthered by both:

1. Jesus' attendance at the Festival of Tabernacles in Jerusalem, and
2. His brothers not knowing of his plans to attend.

The first point is straightforward. The Festival of Tabernacles becomes, in the Fourth Gospel, the occasion for Jesus' proclamations about being the water of life and the light of the world. The tension that builds during the Tabernacles discourses also moves Jesus towards his final confrontation on the cross and the ultimate fulfillment of God's covenant purposes. This case could be argued in greater detail, but it hardly seems necessary. God's covenant purposes were certainly forwarded by Jesus' attendance at the festival.

The second point requires a little more elaboration. Jesus' brothers wanted him to go to Jerusalem in a way that would bring fame and honor to himself and his family. They wanted the world to see bold displays of power. Had Jesus let them know that he was planning to travel to Jerusalem it is very likely that they would have sought to orchestrate opportunities for Jesus to perform such displays. Perhaps, as suggested earlier, they would have sought to make Jesus the leader of the Galilean procession into the city. It is likely that such actions would have precipitated events that, in God's planning for this climactic covenantal event, were not due to take place until the next festival. It was necessary, then, for the proper fulfillment of God's covenant purposes, that the brothers should be in ignorance of Jesus' plan to attend the festival.

So far Anderson's theological framework for deception has been followed by Jesus in this portrayal of his deception of his brothers. I turn now to Williams' three criteria for deception that restores *shalom*. These considerations take the discussion immediately out of the theological realm and focus on the interaction between a man and his brothers.

1. THE DECEPTION MUST BE LIMITED TO THE PERSON WHO CAUSED THE ORIGINAL WRONG

It is straightforward to argue that the deception was, indeed, limited to the brothers. It may have been repeated to others, but this is not revealed in the text. However, this criterion also requires that the brothers have wronged Jesus in a way that disturbed the *shalom* between them. Can this be substantiated?

There are certainly strong hints that the brothers' comments have disrupted their relationship with Jesus. The narrator makes it clear that their comments are to be heard as coming from unbelief in Jesus (7:5). Further, Jesus makes it clear that the brothers' suggestion demonstrates that they are siding with the world against him. If we return to the diagrams introduced in the discussion of Cana, the relationship as it stands in this pericope can be represented by Figure 4.

FIGURE 4

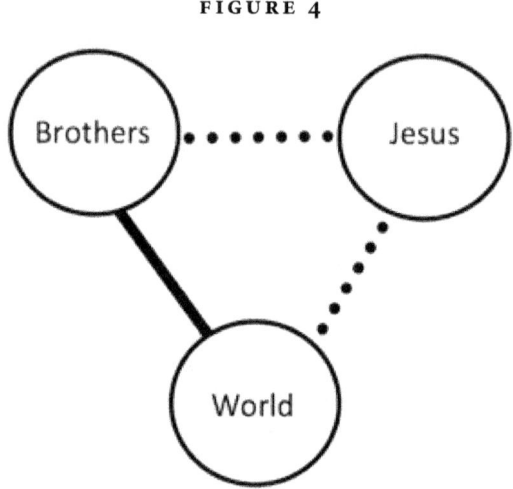

Rather than aligning themselves with Jesus, the brothers have aligned themselves with the world; the world that hates Jesus. This choice has placed Jesus at a distance from his brothers, and has certainly disrupted the *shalom* between them.

I have not included here the fact that the brothers urge Jesus to travel into territory where his life would be in danger. This almost certainly demonstrates a lack of love for their brother, but as it could also indicate confidence in his ability to overcome danger, I have not brought it into this discussion.

2. The deception must not disadvantage the deceived person

The deception denied the brothers the opportunity to make any advantage out of their brother's potential fame in the capital, but it did not take away anything that rightfully belonged to them.

Ultimately, as Jesus fulfils the Father's plans and goes, at the right time, to Jerusalem and to the cross, the brothers will benefit greatly, along with all humanity, when *shalom* is restored to Jesus' family and extends to us all.

3. The deception must not advantage the deceiver beyond his/her status prior to what it was before suffering the original wrong

Jesus here gains only the opportunity to go secretly to Jerusalem. This was presumably his plan before his brothers sought to make the journey public. By doing this, he gained the opportunity to teach and dispute in the capital, but again this is no more than he would have had if the brothers had not intervened.

Williams' three criteria for a morally acceptable deception are easily met by this encounter. We can be assured that we are not accusing Jesus of wrongdoing if we accept that Jesus deceived his brothers in this situation.

Yet most Christian people will not and cannot accept this explanation.[108] Jesus is not portrayed in this Gospel as just any person, bound by ordinary rules of morality. It is in his truth-telling in particular that he reveals his identity as λόγος and ἀλήθεια. I, therefore, propose another path toward ascertaining why John may have hinted at the possibility of Jesus deceiving his brothers.

Joseph and his brothers: a narrative template

The Old Testament contains many accounts of brothers deceiving each other, but only one in which the deceiver is held blameless in the narrative.

Joseph, son of the archetypal deceiver, Jacob, is throughout his life more the victim than the perpetrator of deception. Four of the fifteen

---

108. I have discussed this possibility with a number of Christian people and have noted that it is often found shocking and even heretical.

acts of deception in Genesis that are listed above concern Joseph. First, his brothers sell him into slavery and deceive their father with a story indicating that Joseph had died. Then, when he had become a trusted slave, his master's wife deceives his master with a story of Joseph attempting to rape her. Joseph, in spite of his family heritage, succeeds in reaching the highest echelons of power in Egypt without ever resorting to deception. At that point his brothers appear in Egypt and he has the opportunity to, in Williams' words, restore the family *shalom*.

The story of Joseph's interactions with his brothers is intricate, but can be roughly summarized as follows:

1. Joseph is elevated above his brothers by their father and apparently by God (as indicated by his dreams).
2. The envious brothers wrong Joseph.
3. Joseph rises to power.
4. The brothers come to Joseph with a request.
5. Joseph hides his identity from his brothers.
6. Joseph deceives them and is rude and rough.
7. They show themselves, in light of this treatment, to be repentant for their treatment of Joseph and so reconciliation is brought about.

Jesus' encounter with his brothers in John 7 is extremely brief and stylistic. It contains none of the color of the Joseph narrative, but it does contain many of the same basic elements.

1. Jesus is elevated above his brothers by God, his Father

Jesus' superiority to the other children of Mary is clear throughout the Gospel, but it is also apparent within 7:1–10. From the way the brothers appeal to Jesus' works it is clear that they are not similarly endowed with the power to perform such works.

2. Jesus' brothers wrong him

It is not explicitly stated that the brothers are envious of Jesus, though our knowledge of human nature may render a clear statement to that effect unnecessary! Whether or not they act from envy, they certainly do wrong him, as I have argued above.

3. Jesus' power is displayed in his ἔργα

Jesus is without political power but his brothers recognize that his works demonstrate a different sort of power.

4. Jesus' brothers come to Jesus with a request

In this case it is not gain but honor that the brothers seem to be asking from Jesus.

5. Jesus hides his plans by traveling in secret to Jerusalem

There are at least two layers of hiddenness in this brief account. Overt secrecy is portrayed in Jesus deceiving his brothers and traveling to Jerusalem incognito. Another level of secrecy can be observed in the fact that his brothers, though recognizing him on a superficial level, nevertheless fail to see his true identity, and so become deeply mistaken in the advice they give him.

6. Jesus deceives his brothers and is rude and rough

Before deceiving his brothers, Jesus accuses them of being in league with the world, and therefore out of step with God. These are not gentle words.

7. Repentance and reconciliation

It is at this point that the genre bending of the Fourth Gospel is encountered.[109] In this case it must be noted that one narrative does not a genre make, so I am calling it a template instead. I contend that this episode in the Fourth Gospel looks to the narrative of Joseph's deceit of his brothers as a template but deliberately omits the final element in the outline. Do the brothers repent? Do they become reconciled? Is the family *shalom*

---

109. Attridge, "Genre Bending."

restored? These questions are raised and not answered by the way the story is told but not "finished."

Readers today, and presumably many of the early readers as well, are aware that James and Jude, at least, did repent and were reconciled to their brother after the resurrection. Yet within the narrative of the Fourth Gospel this is left as an open question.

The function that this open question plays in the narrative of the Fourth Gospel will be discussed at greater length in the conclusion to this chapter. For now it is necessary only to notice that in Jerusalem Jesus will encounter many characters who find themselves in the same position as Jesus' brothers: upset by Jesus' pretentions; wronging Jesus with their words and actions; seeing Jesus' works but being unable to see what they mean; limited in their comprehension to what little Jesus has chosen to cryptically reveal about himself; accused by Jesus and ultimately left to decide between reconciliation and accelerated hostility.

A brief look at ethics of deception in Greek narrative

Homer's *Odyssey* provides an excellent study of deceit from a Greek narrative perspective, since its hero, Odysseus, is a master of trickery and is lauded as such. Even this trickster does not deceive indiscriminately but appears to be following some code of ethics. Two considerations seem to govern his deceit.

Firstly, Odysseus lies to preserve his own life in situations where such deceit brings honor to himself as a man of wit but not where lying would shame him as a man of cowardice. After boldly risking his life in the Trojan battles, he lies to the Cyclops about his name in order to save himself and his companions from being eaten.

Secondly, he seems very much more comfortable deceiving strangers and outsiders than his own kin. After deceiving his way through the mythical world, he chooses to return home in disguise so as to assess the strength of his position before again taking up his property and position. This disguise necessitates lying to his father and wife, and even this seasoned deceiver finds this extremely difficult.

A simple ethic of lying based on the Odyssey would therefore allow lying in situations where it preserves life and increases honor against opposition from outsiders, but only marginally accepts deceit among kin, and assumes that a person of honor will not find it easy, psychologically, to deceive close relations.

This is obviously an inadequate treatment of deceit in Greek narrative, let alone in Greco-Roman society, and little weight will be placed upon it. It is simply worth noticing that in *The Odyssey*, as well as in Genesis, there appear to be times when deceit is ethically acceptable. A simplistic view that all telling of untruth is wrong is not taken in these narratives and, I argue, is not expected of readers of the Fourth Gospel.

John 7:11–24

Now, having closely examined vv1–10 and considered some of the implications of Jesus telling his brothers a deliberate untruth, I will continue to examine the remaining verses in somewhat less detail in order to fill out the context of Jesus' discussion with his brothers.

οἱ οὖν Ἰουδαῖοι ἐζήτουν αὐτὸν ἐν τῇ ἑορτῇ καὶ ἔλεγον, Ποῦ ἐστιν ἐκεῖνος;

Here is another example of simple Johannine irony. The reader knows where Jesus is, but the Jews do not. This contributes another element to the theme in this passage of knowing and not knowing, understanding and not understanding.

Kruse believes that ἐκεῖνος reflects the antagonism of the Jews.[110] Schnackenburg also believes that the Jews in question here are hostile, not undecided, given that ἐζήτουν brings to mind v1 where the Jews are seeking to kill Jesus.[111] Certainly ἐζήτουν does not have a benevolent sense in this passage!

καὶ γογγυσμὸς περὶ αὐτοῦ ἦν πολὺς ἐν τοῖς ὄχλοις·

Farley suggests that γογγυσμὸς links this incident with the grumbling of the Israelites in the desert. They had seen God perform great signs, but refused to believe in God's ability to continue to provide for them. These

---

110. Kruse, *John*, 183.
111. Schnackenburg, *Gospel According to St John*, 143.

crowds had seen at least one great sign from Jesus and they, too, would not believe.[112]

Given the above discussion, it may be that another parallel can be drawn between the grumbling here: this time with the reaction of Joseph's brothers to his dreams and to his favored status with their father. In this case, Joseph's brothers set the direction for the people of Israel in their tendency to grumble at the obscurity of God's provision, which leads ultimately to their grumbling at the incomprehensibility of the Word becoming flesh. Thematic links are thereby formed between Jesus' brothers and Joseph's brothers and the Jews.

> οἱ μὲν ἔλεγον ὅτι Ἀγαθός ἐστιν, ἄλλοι [δὲ] ἔλεγον, Οὔ, ἀλλὰ πλανᾷ τὸν ὄχλον.

Neyrey sees the people as acting as witnesses for and against Jesus here.[113] John is putting on record the fact that the Jewish population was not united behind the leadership's rejection of Jesus.[114] Bultmann, on the other hand, argues that the disputes about Jesus here are not the true κρίσις that separates followers of Jesus from the world, but rather σχίσμα existing within the world because of the world's love for sensation.[115] They consider whether Jesus is good or is leading people astray, but they do not ask the most important question: Did God send him?

There is a great deal at stake in these discussions. The punishment for leading the people astray was death by stoning (Deut 13:6–11).[116] In later Jewish literature, Jesus will be called a deceiver.[117] Martyn, of course, suggests that members of John's community were also being accused of leading the people astray, and may even have suffered execution on that charge.[118]

---

112. Farley, *Gospel of John*, 131.

113. Neyrey, *Gospel of John in Cultural and Rhetorical Perspective*, 199.

114. Ellis, *Genius of John*, 143.

115. Bultmann, *Gospel of John*, 295.

116. See Schnackenburg, *Gospel According to St John*, 143.

117. b. Sanh. 43a; b. Sotah 47a. See discussion in Martyn, *History and Theology in the Fourth Gospel*, 78-83 and Köstenberger, *John*; Martyn, *History and Theology in the Fourth Gospel*, 232.

118. Martyn, *History and Theology in the Fourth Gospel*, 82–83. So Schnackenburg, *Gospel According to St John*, 144.

> οὐδεὶς μέντοι παρρησίᾳ ἐλάλει περὶ αὐτοῦ διὰ τὸν φόβον τῶν Ἰουδαίων.

There is a clear distinction being made here between οἱ Ἰουδαῖοι and ὁ ὄχλος, even though all the characters are presumably Jewish.[119] Whoever οἱ Ἰουδαῖοι are, they appear to be people who have already made up their minds about Jesus, while others puzzle over what his miracles and teachings might mean.[120]

The mention of τὸν φόβον τῶν Ἰουδαίων here underlines the sense of threat posed by the Jews that was introduced in v1 of this chapter.

> Ἤδη δὲ τῆς ἑορτῆς μεσούσης ἀνέβη Ἰησοῦς εἰς τὸ ἱερὸν καὶ ἐδίδασκεν.

On his first visit to Jerusalem in this Gospel Jesus had appeared like an Old Testament prophet, whip in hand and stern expression on face, condemning the misuse of the temple and purifying the building of all that had been preventing it from honoring God. On that occasion the Jews asked him for a sign to indicate his authority for taking such prophetic action (2:13–18). On his second visit to Jerusalem, Jesus appeared as a healer, telling a sick man to get up and carry his bed, so the Jews started persecuting him because he did this on a Sabbath (5:1–16). On his fourth visit he will enter Jerusalem as the eschatological king and the Jews will say, "Look, the world has gone after him!" (12:12–19). At that point the "world" will resolve into a few Greeks asking to see Jesus, and Jesus will acknowledge that his hour has come (12:20–23).

On Jesus' third visit to Jerusalem, he sits quietly in the temple courts and teaches his followers. He has revealed himself as prophet; he has revealed himself as healer; he will soon reveal himself as king; but here he reveals himself as rabbi, teacher.

We need not assume that his teaching at this point was loud and public,[121] though it will be on the last day of the festival (7:37). It seems more likely that he simply gathered his disciples around him in a quiet

---

119. Moloney, *Gospel of John*, 240–1.
120. Moloney, *Gospel of John*, 241–2.
121. Neyrey, *Gospel of John in Cultural and Rhetorical Perspective*, 194–5.

area of the temple courts and began to discuss with them the ways of his Father.[122]

Ridderbos notices that this Gospel makes few uses of the word διδάσκω in reference to Jesus (6:59; 8:20). It is significant here then, not only as a contrast with what Jesus' brothers had wanted him to do in Jerusalem, but also because Jesus here embodies the role of the messiah by making known to the people the words of God.[123] The people, therefore, immediately raise questions about his authority to be there and to do that.

> ἐθαύμαζον οὖν οἱ Ἰουδαῖοι λέγοντες, Πῶς οὗτος γράμματα οἶδεν μὴ μεμαθηκώς;

Jesus' teaching in the temple raises questions about his origins. He has not been taught in the traditions under a known rabbi, so how can he be teaching?[124] It is probably not his general education or knowledge of the Scriptures that surprised them. Many Jewish men were educated. What shocked them would have been the way he was interpreting the Scriptures, or indeed the fact that he took upon himself the task of interpreting Scripture at all, rather than repeating the words of greater scholars.[125] Indeed, what alarmed them may simply have been the fact that an unauthorized person like him had the audacity to set himself up as a rabbi.[126] They seem to be avoiding any response to the content of Jesus' teaching here; as Chrysostom said, "It is not his doctrine they admire, but another thing altogether."[127]

The main force of this verse is in its use of irony. The reader knows from 5:19–20 that Jesus has received the best possible education and the only genuinely significant authorization, from his Father.[128]

---

122. Lenski, *Interpretation of St John's Gospel*, 540.
123. Ridderbos, *Gospel According to John*, 261.
124. Moloney, *Gospel of John*, 242, Kruse, *John*, 184.
125. Köstenberger, *John*, 232–3.
126. Lenski, *Interpretation of St John's Gospel*, 540–1.
127. Chrysostom, *Homilies*, 49.1.
128. Ellis, *Genius of John*, 140.

Use of οὗτος here is clearly pejorative.[129] Indeed, Neyrey sees this questioning as tantamount to a charge of false teaching[130] and as an act of public shaming in a culture where young men were only as good as their teachers.[131] By teaching in the temple courts, albeit quietly, Jesus was laying claim to a form of honor that was highly esteemed among Jewish men,[132] that of understanding and being apt to teach the Scriptures. That claim is naturally challenged by the acknowledged teachers in Jerusalem. Jesus will then give his riposte.

ἀπεκρίθη οὖν αὐτοῖς [ὁ] Ἰησοῦς καὶ εἶπεν, Ἡ ἐμὴ διδαχὴ οὐκ ἔστιν ἐμὴ ἀλλὰ τοῦ πέμψαντός με·

If his teaching does not come from an authoritative rabbi, it would be natural to presume that it originated with himself; and to the Jews of his time that would look like arrogance,[133] if not heresy. However, Jesus insists that its origin is not with him but with the one who sent him.

Augustine notices the apparent contradiction here. How can the teaching be both ἐμὴ[134] and οὐκ ... ἐμὴ[135] at the same time? His solution is that, as Word of God, Jesus embodies the teaching of the Father. The teaching is his, in that it is himself. On the other hand, it is not his because it belongs to the Father, since Jesus belongs to the Father.[136]

Like so much in this pericope, Jesus' comments here refer back to 5:19–24.

ἐάν τις θέλῃ τὸ θέλημα αὐτοῦ ποιεῖν, γνώσεται περὶ τῆς διδαχῆς πότερον ἐκ τοῦ θεοῦ ἐστιν ἢ ἐγὼ ἀπ' ἐμαυτοῦ λαλῶ.

If a disciple accurately passed on what he had been taught, highly educated Jews would be able to identify which rabbi had taught him. Jesus

129. Moloney, *Gospel of John*, 245.
130. Neyrey, *Gospel of John in Cultural and Rhetorical Perspective*, 200.
131. Neyrey, *Gospel of John in Cultural and Rhetorical Perspective*, 220.
132. See chapter 7.
133. Kruse, *John*, 184; Köstenberger, *John*, 233.
134. Mine.
135. Not mine.
136. Augustine, "Tractate XXIX", 3–5.

claimed that this was so with him. He was accurately passing on the words of God, and anyone who knew God, anyone who genuinely wished to do God's will, would recognize the teacher in the disciple. The Jews show by their reaction that they do not recognize the God they claim to serve.

Jesus may be saying more than this. One who θέλῃ τὸ θέλημα αὐτοῦ ποιεῖν would also be a disciple of God, so their recognition of Jesus would not be the recognition of the disciple of another, but a fellow-disciple of the same master. Their failure to recognize him calls into question their devotion to God.

Jesus insists that in judging him negatively they are passing judgment on themselves, and declaring that they do not wish to do God's will. They had questioned the origin of his teaching, and now he questions the origin of theirs. Have they learned from God, or only from their rabbis?

Jesus refuses to play the role of defendant here. It is their own actions and motivations they should be judging, not his.[137] Jesus simply calls on their own words and actions as witnesses against them.[138] Behind all the forensic imagery of John 7 the question of who is really on trial here keeps being raised.[139]

ὁ ἀφ' ἑαυτοῦ λαλῶν τὴν δόξαν τὴν ἰδίαν ζητεῖ·

Mention of δόξα brings the reader's attention back to the questions of publicity raised by Jesus' brothers in vv4–5[140] and indicates that glory may be at the centre of their misunderstanding. Was Jesus seeking glory? If so, was he seeking his own or that of another?

This verse, then, provides another criticism of the brothers' challenge to Jesus. Not only has his hour not yet come, but his mission is to seek that glory of the one who sent him, not his own.[141]

In Cana, Jesus had revealed his glory and his disciples had believed in him (2:11); but was the revelation of his own glory really his goal? The author claims to be one of those disciples who saw Jesus' glory (1:14). What did he see? He says that he saw δόξαν ὡς μονογενοῦς παρὰ πατρός.

---

137. Waetjen, *Gospel of the Beloved Disciple*, 225.
138. Neyrey, *Gospel of John in Cultural and Rhetorical Perspective*, 192.
139. Neyrey, *Gospel of John in Cultural and Rhetorical Perspective*, 198.
140. Köstenberger, *John*, 233.
141. Attridge, "Thematic Development and Source Elaboration in John 7:1-36," 163.

This was not the sort of glory that could be shared with brothers. It was also not the sort of glory that could be sought through self-aggrandizement. This is the sort of glory that can only be seen as the Son reveals his ultimate family likeness; as the Son speaks the words of the Father, does the work of the Father, and wills the will of the Father.

Jesus seems to be appealing to their experience of true and false prophets in Jerusalem.[142] Their history books contained plenty of examples of both. He calls them to look at his behavior. Does he demonstrate a likeness to the false prophets (who were always telling people what they wanted to hear in order to gain glory for themselves) or the genuine prophets (who spoke an unpopular message and often endured great shame and persecution instead of glory)?

ὁ δὲ ζητῶν τὴν δόξαν τοῦ πέμψαντος αὐτὸν οὗτος ἀληθής ἐστιν

Jesus here claims to be a righteous agent—concerned only about the business of the one who sent him; not seeking anything for himself.[143] The correct response to his words, then, is not to question his credentials as a teacher, but to ascertain whether or not God had sent him. One way to test this would be to consider whose honor he was seeking.[144]

Those who were listening may have struggled to answer that question, but the readers, once they have read the whole story, can be in no doubt that a man who goes to his death in obedience to the one who sent him was seeking the sender's glory and not his own.

Once it is established that he is a genuine emissary from God there is no longer any need to ask questions about his education or upbringing. All such questions become irrelevant because he is not speaking or acting out of his upbringing or education. His speech and actions are determined by another, and they carry the authority of that other.[145]

---

142. Farley, *Gospel of John*, 133.
143. Kruse, *John*, 185.
144. Ridderbos, *Gospel According to John*, 263.
145 . See Aristotle, *Rhetoric* 1.9.17.

καὶ ἀδικία ἐν αὐτῷ οὐκ ἔστιν.

This seems to be about Jesus' teaching as such, rather than the purity of his behavior.[146] Because he seeks only the glory of the one who sent him, his teaching is not falsified by his desire to gain glory for himself. He is a righteous teacher.

Here is another reminder that, even if John does depict Jesus as deceiving his brothers, he does not see this as an unrighteous act or as proceeding from unrighteous motives.

οὐ Μωϋσῆς δέδωκεν ὑμῖν τὸν νόμον;

It is often argued that this mention of Moses, along with Jesus' remarks about the Jews' plot to kill him, belongs more with chapter 5 than here in the Tabernacles discourse.[147] However, once we note that Jesus is here defending his role as righteous teacher of the law, as against the recognized teachers who are neither righteous nor law-keepers, these words become entirely appropriate to their current context.

Moses, they all acknowledge, was acting as a genuine emissary from God when he delivered God's law to the people. They honor the law, not primarily because Moses gave it, but because it is God's law, delivered through a trustworthy agent.

καὶ οὐδεὶς ἐξ ὑμῶν ποιεῖ τὸν νόμον.

Though in the case of their law they are convinced that the emissary was genuinely delivering a message from God, Jesus claims that they do not place themselves wholly and utterly under that law.

τί με ζητεῖτε ἀποκτεῖναι;

That the Jews are seeking to kill Jesus is a clear indication that they are out of step with the law and out of step with Moses.[148] Murder is clearly outside the letter and intent of the law. So, who is in the best position

---

146. Moloney, *Gospel of John*, 245.

147. See for example Attridge, "Thematic Development and Source Elaboration in John 7:1-36," 165-7.

148. Moloney, *The Gospel of John*, 243-4; also Chrysostom, *Homilies*, 49.2.

to appeal to Moses? "Jesus, who healed a man on the Sabbath, or his adversaries, who for that reason wanted to kill him?"[149]

In this argument, Jesus has not simply proven that the Jewish leaders are sinners. He has shown that they are not legitimate teachers. They questioned his right to teach in the temple courts; he has shown that they are the ones who should be denied the right to teach.

The author here is almost certainly demonstrating pastoral concern by recalling this particular conversation of Jesus.

> ἀπεκρίθη ὁ ὄχλος, Δαιμόνιον ἔχεις· τίς σε ζητεῖ ἀποκτεῖναι;

Here is another instance of Johannine irony. They reply much as any crowd would respond, even today, to someone who appears to be so paranoid as to suspect that people are trying to kill them. "You are crazy!" Yet the reader knows that "the Jews" are trying to kill him (7:1).

The irony may have a deeper level, too, since the narrative gives some indication that the crowd did, in fact, know that the Jews were trying to kill Jesus. They were not speaking openly, for fear of the Jews (v13), and later some of them will ask if Jesus is the man they are trying to kill (v25). Neyrey suggests that the speakers are not at all in ignorance here, but are deliberately lying,[150] presumably in order to side with "the Jews" and put Jesus off his guard. It is difficult to be certain of this, and a number of scholars disagree with him,[151] yet in the context it is hard to read their words as entirely without guile.

"The Jews" give no answer here. It is only the crowd that speaks.[152]

> ἀπεκρίθη Ἰησοῦς καὶ εἶπεν αὐτοῖς,"Ἓν ἔργον ἐποίησα καὶ πάντες θαυμάζετε.

Jesus seems to be referring back to his last miracle in Jerusalem, the Sabbath healing at the Pool of Bethesda (5:1–18).[153]

---

149. Ridderbos, *The Gospel According to John*, 262.

150. Neyrey, *Gospel of John in Cultural and Rhetorical Perspective*, 201.

151. Ridderbos, *Gospel According to John*, 264; Moloney, "Narrative and Discourse at the Feast of Tabernacles," 163.

152. Lenski, *Interpretation of St John's Gospel*, 549.

153. Kruse, *John*, 186.

V22 clarifies that he is not implying that they were amazed by his healing powers, but rather by his decision to do this work on the Sabbath. By focusing in that direction they avoid asking themselves where Jesus' power came from. Jesus shows them where that false trail leads.

Augustine comments, amusingly, "They almost seem to imply that if any of them had recovered from a disease on the Sabbath, it was someone else who had made them well rather than he who had offended them by making one man whole on the Sabbath."[154]

διὰ τοῦτο Μωϋσῆς δέδωκεν ὑμῖν τὴν περιτομήν—οὐχ ὅτι ἐκ τοῦ Μωϋσέως ἐστὶν ἀλλ' ἐκ τῶν πατέρων—καὶ ἐν σαββάτῳ περιτέμνετε ἄνθρωπον.

Jesus appeals to the patriarchs as another group of reliable emissaries. The Jewish practice of circumcision came from God through Abraham, and was incorporated into the law through Moses.[155]

The Mishnah[156] (*Šabbat* 19.1–2) states that any work in relation to circumcision that cannot be done in advance on the eve of the Sabbath can legally be done on the Sabbath and so overrides the Sabbath law.

εἰ περιτομὴν λαμβάνει ἄνθρωπος ἐν σαββάτῳ ἵνα μὴ λυθῇ ὁ νόμος Μωϋσέως,

Jesus is saying something more profound here than simply that two laws sometimes come into conflict. He is saying that circumcising on the Sabbath fulfils the law. Indeed, as Ridderbos[157] argues, he may be saying that circumcision not only fulfils the circumcision laws, but also fulfils the Sabbath laws. Doing something that brings a fellow human being into the *shalom* of God is surely a Sabbath gift to them. According to this line of argument, Jesus is not claiming to have had a good excuse for breaking the Sabbath law. He is claiming that he fulfilled the Sabbath law by bringing rest to a man who had been laboring under a severe affliction. Indeed,

---

154. Augustine, "Tractate XXX," 3.
155. Ridderbos, *Gospel According to John*, 265.
156. *Mishnah*.
157. Ridderbos, *Gospel According to John*, 265.

Irenaeus argued quite reasonably that Jesus' entire ministry fulfilled the Sabbath law.[158]

This may reflect back on the earlier discussion of what the author was doing by implying that Jesus deceived his brothers. Readers are scandalized by that possibility, just as onlookers were scandalized when Jesus healed on the Sabbath. Was the author presenting readers with a similar puzzle to the one Jesus poses here? By meticulously and anxiously applying our own law are we, like the Jews who challenged Jesus, missing the point of the law and failing to see how Jesus fulfilled the law through his unorthodox actions? Is the author here, as he does so often, slowing readers down and tripping us up so that we will take the time to really see and meditate upon the Word made flesh?

ἐμοὶ χολᾶτε ὅτι ὅλον ἄνθρωπον ὑγιῆ ἐποίησα ἐν σαββάτῳ;

Maloney notes that Jesus here employs the Jewish legal technique of moving from the lesser to the greater: *qal wahomer*.[159] The connection between healing and circumcision seems to be via the Jewish understanding that circumcision was about bringing a person to wholeness.[160] *Yoma* 85b[161] states that if circumcision, which affects just one part of a man's body, overrides the Sabbath, a life-saving procedure must override the Sabbath even more.[162]

If the intent of the Sabbath law was to bring rest to God's people, Jesus is the greatest law-keeper in the narrative. Jesus brought healing in his life and release from the tyranny of sin in his death, whereas "the Jews" had turned a law about rest into a burden too heavy for the people to carry (cf. Matt 23:4).

μὴ κρίνετε κατ' ὄψιν, ἀλλὰ τὴν δικαίαν κρίσιν κρίνετε.

Here Jesus makes his most devastating accusation against his accusers. He has already exposed them for seeking to commit murder and for

---

158. Irenaeus, "Against Heresies," 4.8.2.
159. Moloney, *Gospel of John*, 246.
160. Waetjen, *Gospel of the Beloved Disciple*, 226.
161. *Mishnah*.
162. Quoted in Kruse, *John*, 186.

misunderstanding the law. Now he turns their accusation of him against them and exposes them as unjust judges.[163]

If the people set themselves up as judges they place on themselves the heavy obligation of judging righteously. Will they make a shallow judgment about Jesus, or will they look more closely and see that Jesus fulfilled the Sabbath law much more fully than they ever did or could?[164] All the challenges and accusations made to Jesus and about Jesus in this section are based on appearances. Jesus calls them to think more deeply.[165]

Is it possible that Jesus is calling on the crowd to make the right decision about who they will follow as their teachers? Will they follow "the Jews" who are trying to kill Jesus; or will they follow Jesus, the righteous (though not overly scrupulous) teacher of the Law?

This verse brings to a point of relative clarity the theme of secrecy that has run through this chapter. There is more to Jesus than what can be known κατ' ὄψιν. The complicating reality is that much of what is hidden about Jesus has been deliberately hidden by Jesus himself. Jesus travels to Jerusalem in secret. The people are told to look more closely, but Jesus has obscured their vision.

This is surely a parallel to Mark 4 where Jesus explains his use of parables to his disciples with the words,

βλέποντες βλέπωσιν καὶ μὴ ἴδωσιν,
 καὶ ἀκούοντες ἀκούωσιν καὶ μὴ συνιῶσιν,
  μήποτε ἐπιστρέψωσιν καὶ ἀφεθῇ αὐτοῖς. (Mark 4:11f)

It is only disciples who see and perceive. For everyone else, even his brothers, Jesus travels in secret. Yet, just as Mark (4:22) says, οὐ γάρ ἐστιν κρυπτὸν ἐὰν μὴ ἵνα φανερωθῇ, so in John 8:28 Jesus will say, Ὅταν ὑψώσητε τὸν υἱὸν τοῦ ἀνθρώπου, τότε γνώσεσθε ὅτι ἐγώ εἰμι, καὶ ἀπ' ἐμαυτοῦ ποιῶ οὐδέν, ἀλλὰ καθὼς ἐδίδαξέν με ὁ πατὴρ ταῦτα λαλῶ. καὶ ὁ πέμψας με μετ' ἐμοῦ ἐστιν· οὐκ ἀφῆκέν με μόνον, ὅτι ἐγὼ τὰ ἀρεστὰ αὐτῷ ποιῶ πάντοτε.

---

163. Neyrey, *Gospel of John in Cultural and Rhetorical Perspective*, 202.

164. Ridderbos, *Gospel According to John*, 266.

165. Attridge, "Thematic Development and Source Elaboration in John 7:1-36," 163.

Do the brothers have representative function?

Campbell, following Brown[166] and Martyn,[167] argues that the brothers represent a group of opponents to the Johannine community. She concludes that they represent refugees from the Jewish wars who have their roots in the ministry of James, Jesus' brother.[168] The view that the negative assessment of Jesus' brothers in this Gospel is a coded attack on such a group has followed the lead Brown set in the seventies with these words:

> In any case, the hostile portrait of the brothers of Jesus, without any hint of their conversion, is startling when we reflect that the Fourth Gospel was written after James, the brother of the Lord, had led the Jerusalem church for almost thirty years and had died a martyr's death. Since his name was revered as a teaching authority by Jewish Christians (James 1:1; Jude 1) are we having reflected in John a polemic against Jewish Christians, particularly in Palestine, who regarded themselves as the heirs of the Jerusalem church of James? Are their church leaders the hirelings of 10:12 who do not protect the sheep against the wolves, perhaps because they have not sufficiently distanced their flocks from "the Jews"?[169]

For a number of reasons, this line of argument can be dismissed. Firstly, as Barton[170] points out, we would expect James to be singled out for criticism in that case, rather than the brothers being treated as a whole. If the account in John 7 were intended as an attack on a rival community, surely sufficient verbal cues would be given for the reader to identify that community and understand the attack.

Secondly, such theories appear to have developed from imaginative exegesis rather than from historical evidence. There is no evidence that the Johannine community was at enmity with other Christian groups. The Johannine letters indicate concern over people who have left their community and abandoned the faith (1 John 2:19), but there is little

---

166. Brown, "Other Sheep Not of This Fold."
167. Martyn, *History and Theology in the Fourth Gospel.*
168. Campbell, *Kinship Relations*, 186–7.
169. Brown, "Other Sheep Not of This Fold," 13.
170. Barton, "Can We Identify the Gospel Audiences?" 184. Barton makes this comment in reference to similar claims that are made concerning Mark's Gospel. They are equally relevant to the Gospel of John.

reason to trace these to James, or to consider that these "antichrists" are a Christian community at all.

Thirdly, such theories must be considered with great caution because they appear to undermine the value of the Gospels and the validity of their message. As Johnson has challenged: "Reading everything in the Gospel narratives as immediately addressed to a contemporary crisis reduces them to the level of cryptograms, and the evangelists to the level of tractarians."[171]

If the Gospels were merely weapons in a slanging match between different Christian perspectives, how are we to trust what they reveal about the person and work of Jesus?

Similarly, what are we to think of the author of such a cryptogram? Is the great teacher of love to be unmasked as a sectarian who dismissed all fellow Christians who were not of his particular stamp? Certainly we should consider that possibility if clear evidence pointed in that direction. However, without such evidence it is more plausible to believe that the evangelist who spoke so much about love, and the community that was so often exhorted to love, did in fact live in love with their fellow believers.

Does it follow, then, that the brothers have no representative or symbolic function in the narrative. Not at all. The presence of brothers recalls the many instances of fraternal conflict in the Old Testament, and places the life of Jesus in the context of fraternal crisis. Will the less favored brothers be able to overcome their jealousy in order to participate in the blessings poured out by God on and through their more favored brother?

Like the brother of the prodigal, Jesus' brothers are left standing outside the party by the narrative at this point. Neither John 7 nor the parable intends final condemnation by this placement. The intention, rather, is invitation and suspense. Will they come in? Will the reader, who might identify with their skepticism, come in and embrace Jesus by faith?

The well-informed reader knows that some, at least, of the brothers will accept that invitation, and that knowledge brings hope to the suspense. Some of those who are currently outside will come in. The brothers, the Jews, and the world are not to be given up as lost.

The Jews, in the narrative and in the life of the early Christian community, struggled to respond to this man who is their own but did not belong to them. Seeing and not perceiving, they are blinded by Jesus until

---

171. Johnson, "On Finding the Lukan Community," 90; quoted in Barton, "Can We Identify the Gospel Audiences?" 186.

the moment of revelation has come, and are ultimately forced to confront their own wrongdoing and God's power in the cross and the empty tomb.

When Jesus is revealed to the world (cf. φανέρωσον σεαυτὸν τῷ κόσμῳ) he will also be revealed to his brothers. But his brothers will not be with him for that crucial moment of revelation. Only their mother will be there.

Conclusions

Schnackenburg believes that John uses the brothers as nothing more than "marginal figures" in the narrative, who can be brushed aside by Jesus.[172] Hopefully my discussion has demonstrated that they are much more than that.

The brothers show us that the community Jesus creates is not constituted by family ties. Jesus' brothers have no special access to him. They ask a favor of him: "Demonstrate your power in Jerusalem and bring honor to our family." This was a reasonable request in the terms set by their culture, but in terms set for Jesus by his Father it was out of the question. Jesus criticizes them sharply and leaves them out of his plans. (Whether or not his action constituted deceit is not ultimately decisive here.) Jesus treated his brothers as outsiders, while his disciples, who were related to him only by faith and following, are treated as insiders. This was shockingly counter-cultural.

The informed readers know that the brothers will eventually become insiders, when they accept the terms on which everyone else is welcomed into Jesus' community: faith and following. Like the Jews, they must find the humility to lay aside their right to special access to their brother and find salvation in him on the same basis as any other outsider.

At this point in the narrative, the brothers are not traveling with Jesus, but there is no mention of their mother. Is even she an unbeliever? The reader is kept in suspense for now but will meet her soon at the foot of the cross.

---

172. Schnackenburg, *Gospel According to St John*, 139.

9

Family Fractured and Reconfigured at the Cross

The final interaction in the Fourth Gospel between Jesus and a family member (19:26–27) will be examined in this chapter, along with some necessary discussion of its immediate context in the Johannine depiction of Jesus' passion. Themes of kinship are brought together in this passage, just as Jesus' mother and his beloved disciple are brought together at the cross.[1]

John 19:17–30, 38–39 will be closely examined in this chapter with the following questions in mind:

- Jesus appears to be acting as his mother's guardian here and handing over responsibility for her to another man as he faces his death. This would have been usual and appropriate in his culture. However, since Jesus had brothers, would this action not have been a significant affront to them? What is being communicated by this affront?

- Many commentators understand both Jesus' mother and the beloved disciple as representative characters in this scene. Is it reasonable to see them in this way, and what or who is it that they represent?

- What message is communicated by the way the presence of Jesus' mother forms an inclusio around the narrative of Jesus' public ministry?

---

1. A version of this chapter has been published as part of a collection of essays on grief. Margaret Wesley, "Family Fractured and Reconfigured."

- What other insights into the nature of kinship and discipleship might be obtained by close exegesis of John 19:17–30, 38–39?

A brief note on historicity

Points of contrast between this passion scene and those in the Synoptic Gospels have made it necessary for most commentators to discuss the historicity, or otherwise, of some details in John's depiction of Jesus' death. This discussion is clearly very important but does not need to be considered here because my approach is literary rather than historical.

Historicity becomes a consideration in literary analysis when an event is depicted which the reader knows to be impossible or highly improbable. This is a jolt to the reader, who will then either discount what the author has to say or stop to think about what symbolic, rather than literal, message might be conveyed by the depiction. For this reason I will comment—though only briefly—on historical plausibility in the following exegesis.

However, as I have stated in chapter 5, I do not believe it is John's practice to convey symbolic meaning through fictional events. In John the theological and symbolic are seen within the historical and physical, just as the divine Word is seen in the human person of Jesus of Nazareth. Indeed in 19:35 the author of the final version of this Gospel insists that this passion scene is eyewitness testimony. I see no reason to drive a wedge in this Gospel between the historical and the symbolic. What is historical here is pregnant with symbolic meaning; and what is symbolic here is discerned in the blood, flesh, dirt, and wood of events the author insists took place in history.

Introduction to Exegesis of John 19:17–30, 38–39

In order to place Jesus' words to his mother and beloved disciple in their immediate context, John 19:17–30 and 38–39 will be examined here. The intervening and surrounding verses are excluded purely for the sake of brevity.

There are many points of contact between John's account and parallel accounts in the Synoptic Gospels.[2] If we could be sure that he

---

2. Indeed, in many respects John's account is closer to the Synoptics in describing Jesus' death than in most of the rest of the Gospel. Smith, *John*, 354–5.

had read the other Gospels then we could assume that the points on which the fourth evangelist chose to diverge from the other accounts are particularly significant.[3] Those points include the writing of the sign above the cross in three languages, the seamlessness of Jesus' robe, and, most particularly for the current discussion, Jesus' words to his mother and beloved disciple. Thematically, a key difference between John's passion and the synoptic parallels is the emphasis on Jesus' kingship rather than his suffering and dereliction.

> Παρέλαβον οὖν τὸν Ἰησοῦν, καὶ βαστάζων ἑαυτῷ τὸν σταυρὸν ἐξῆλθεν εἰς τὸν λεγόμενον Κρανίου Τόπον, ὃ λέγεται Ἑβραϊστὶ Γολγοθα,

As an indication of the power of Rome, against which Jesus' sovereignty is asserted, the author moves immediately from Pilate's decision to the enacting of Jesus' sentence.[4] The Jews also, as will become clear soon, after handing Jesus over to the Romans, are now impotent. They are all in the hands of Rome. At least that is how it seems.

The comment here about Jesus carrying his own cross does not necessarily contradict the Synoptic report (Matt 27:32; Mark 15:21; Luke 23:26) that Simon of Cyrene was pressed into carrying the cross. In both accounts Jesus carried the cross at the start of the journey.[5] Desire to emphasize Jesus' resolute obedience to the Father,[6] and his regal self-sufficiency,[7] rather than his human weakness and suffering, led John to overlook Simon of Cyrene's contribution. Jesus acts here, as at all times in this Gospel, as king: the agent of his own destiny.[8] Leo the Great observed that when the crossbar was placed on Jesus' back sovereignty was laid on his shoulders (Isa 9:6).[9]

---

3. I argued in chapter 2 that it is very likely that he had access to the other Gospels, but of course that cannot be proved beyond doubt. See Carson, *Gospel According to John*, 608; Keener, *Gospel of John*, 1134.

4. Ridderbos, *The Gospel According to John*, 608.

5. Beasley-Murray, *John*, 550.

6. Carson, *Gospel According to John*, 609.

7. Stibbe, *John*, 197; Smith, *John*, 355; Bruce, *Gospel of John*, 366; Moloney, *Gospel of John*, 502.

8. Schnackenburg, *Gospel According to St John*, 270.

9. Leo the Great, "Sermons" 8.4.

Several early commentators,[10] including Tertullian,[11] compare Jesus here with Isaac, who also carried his own wood to a place of sacrifice. There may be fruitful reflection in that connection but it is unclear whether the author intended the allusion.

The place where Jesus is crucified is named twice, in Hebrew and in Greek. This may simply be a clarification for readers who may not be familiar with the geography of Jerusalem. There may be a symbolic undertone alluding to the apparent subjection of all things Jewish and Greek to Roman power. It is certainly likely that the repetition of the unsavory name is intended to underscore the horror of this place.

> ὅπου αὐτὸν ἐσταύρωσαν, καὶ μετ' αὐτοῦ ἄλλους δύο ἐντεῦθεν καὶ ἐντεῦθεν, μέσον δὲ τὸν Ἰησοῦν.

Jesus is crucified here simply with two *others*, and those others are not named as criminals as they are in the Synoptic Gospels. It may be that John wishes to emphasize Jesus' identification with humanity in his death, rather than focusing on his identification with sinful humanity. The placement of Jesus in the middle is also significant.[12] It may indicate his prominence among the three, as is appropriate for the "King of the Jews."[13] Indeed Augustine called his central position the judgment seat.[14] Perhaps it also indicates Jesus' centrality to the narrative[15] and indeed to human history. In the midst of human suffering Jesus suffers to bring relief to fellow-sufferers.

---

10. Elowsky, ed. *John 11–21*, 308; Note that Beasley-Murray, *John*, 550 also makes a good case for this allusion. Contra Schnackenburg, *Gospel According to St John*, 270.

11. Tertullian, "An Answer to the Jews," §13.

12. Bruce, *The Gospel of John*, 368; Moloney, *The Gospel of John*, 502.

13. Ridderbos, *The Gospel According to John*, 608; Beasley-Murray, *John*, 551; Schnackenburg, *The Gospel According to St John*, 270–1.

14. Augustine, "Tractate XXXI," §11.

15. Stibbe, *John*, 197.

> ἔγραψεν δὲ καὶ τίτλον ὁ Πιλᾶτος καὶ ἔθηκεν ἐπὶ τοῦ σταυροῦ· ἦν δὲ γεγραμμένον, Ἰησοῦς ὁ Ναζωραῖος ὁ βασιλεὺς τῶν Ἰουδαίων.

The theme of kingship hinted at throughout the Gospel is here given its fullest overt expression. The cross is where Jesus' kingship is established. In the middle of human suffering, Jesus is glorified.

Mention of Nazareth underscores Jesus' humble origins[16] and reminds the reader of Nathaniel's words in 1:46, Ἐκ Ναζαρὲτ δύναταί τι ἀγαθὸν εἶναι;

Johannine irony is beautifully at work here in that Pilate, determined to humiliate the Jews for manipulating him into acting against his better judgment (18:28—19:16), gives public assent to a truth he could not comprehend[17] and certainly did not believe. In so doing he has, against his own intention, become a prophet.[18] The author demonstrates the truth behind 19:11, "You would have no power over me unless it had been given you from above." It had appeared that all were impotent against the power of Rome, but in reality even Rome is impotent before the power of God.

> τοῦτον οὖν τὸν τίτλον πολλοὶ ἀνέγνωσαν τῶν Ἰουδαίων, ὅτι ἐγγὺς ἦν ὁ τόπος τῆς πόλεως ὅπου ἐσταυρώθη ὁ Ἰησοῦς· καὶ ἦν γεγραμμένον Ἑβραϊστί, Ῥωμαϊστί, Ἑλληνιστί.

These three languages represent the language of the local population, the administrative language of the empire, and the international language of commerce and cultural exchange. As all people are drawn to Jesus when he is lifted up (12:32), all people are able to read the charge/proclamation.[19] An implicit claim is made here regarding the universal kingship

---

16. Malina and Rohrbaugh, *Social-Science Commentary*, 268.

17. Bruce, *Gospel of John*, 368; Ridderbos, *Gospel According to John*, 609; Schnackenburg, *Gospel According to St John*, 271.

18. Bultmann, *Gospel of John*, 667.

19. See Malina and Rohrbaugh, *Social-Science Commentary*, 268-9; so Smith, *John*; Moloney, *Gospel of John*, 502.

of Jesus.[20] He is the King of the Jews for all humanity.[21] All may here look upon him and find eternal life (3:14–16).[22]

While it may seem implausible that soldiers would go to the effort of writing Jesus' charge in three languages, John tells the reader that the sign was written at Pilate's insistence. Since Pilate's intention was undoubtedly to humiliate the Jews it is quite plausible that he might maximize that humiliation by ensuring that all who saw the cross would know that Jesus was executed as the King of the Jews rather than as a bandit pretender to that title.

ἔλεγον οὖν τῷ Πιλάτῳ οἱ ἀρχιερεῖς τῶν Ἰουδαίων,

John's description of the Jews' concern is rather ironic here given their earlier statements about having no king but Caesar (19:15).[23]

Notice that the author has made it impossible for the reader, just as for the onlooker, to overlook the phrase Βασιλεύς . . . τῶν Ἰουδαίων. Within the paradox and irony of this narrative, Jesus is clearly portrayed as king.

ἀπεκρίθη ὁ Πιλᾶτος, Ὃ γέγραφα, γέγραφα.

It is at this point that the Jews discover that by inviting Rome into their dispute with Jesus they have lost control over the outcome. In seeking to rid themselves of Jesus they have found themselves impotent in the face of ridicule and humiliation.

Pilate refuses to allow himself to be further manipulated by the Jewish elite. Indeed he is determined to humiliate them. However, Johannine irony continues in that what Pilate has written continues to be "written" throughout history.[24] It is interesting to note that every other use of γράφω in this Gospel refers to Scripture[25] and Pilate's words have achieved similar longevity and authority. Indeed, his words are now part of Scripture, though of course the author could not have known that.

20. Stibbe, *John*, 197; Keener, *Gospel of John*, 1137.
21. Keener, *Gospel of John*, 1138.
22. Schnackenburg, *Gospel According to St John*, 270.
23. Smith, *John*, 357; Sloyan, *John*, 210.
24. See Malina and Rohrbaugh, *Social-Science Commentary*, 269.
25. Keener, *Gospel of John*, 1138.

There is certainly no reason to think, as Lindars seems to, that this was a "concealed confession of faith by Pilate."[26] Pilate's intention was to humiliate the Jews by declaring a bloodied, tortured, near-dead man to be their king. He showed no desire to honor Jesus. It is only with deep irony that we now read those words as tribute.

Οἱ οὖν στρατιῶται, ὅτε ἐσταύρωσαν τὸν Ἰησοῦν, ἔλαβον τὰ ἱμάτια αὐτοῦ καὶ ἐποίησαν τέσσαρα μέρη, ἑκάστῳ στρατιώτῃ μέρος, καὶ τὸν χιτῶνα. ἦν δὲ ὁ χιτὼν ἄραφος, ἐκ τῶν ἄνωθεν ὑφαντὸς δι' ὅλου. εἶπαν οὖν πρὸς ἀλλήλους, Μὴ σχίσωμεν αὐτόν, ἀλλὰ λάχωμεν περὶ αὐτοῦ τίνος ἔσται· ἵνα ἡ γραφὴ πληρωθῇ [ἡ λέγουσα],

Διεμερίσαντο τὰ ἱμάτιά μου ἑαυτοῖς
καὶ ἐπὶ τὸν ἱματισμόν μου ἔβαλον κλῆρον.

Appeal to Scripture at this point underscores John's contention that all of Jesus' life, and particularly his suffering and death, accords with the will of God.[27]

Note that while the Synoptic reference to Psalm 22:1 (Matt 27:46; Mark 15:23) is absent from John,[28] Psalm 22:18 is found here. The whole of this Psalm of anguished abandonment and distress was clearly central to early Christian understanding of Jesus' passion.

While the division of Jesus' clothes is highly plausible historically,[29] it was no doubt theological considerations that led the author to give it so much significance in his account. However, there is no agreement among commentators regarding the nature of those theological considerations.[30]

It may be that the seamlessness of the tunic and the fact that it is left intact represent the unity of Jesus' followers (17:11);[31] though some see a reference to high priestly garments[32] (Exod 39:27, 36:35). Chrysos-

---

26. Lindars, *Gospel of John*, 576.
27. See Carson, *Gospel According to John*, 612.
28. Bruce, *Gospel of John*, 370.
29. Keener, *Gospel of John*, 1139.
30. Sloyan's conjectures of a link with the rending of the temple curtain (Matt 27:51) is probably not worth mentioning. Sloyan, *John*, 211.
31. Moloney, *Gospel of John*, 503; Augustine, "Tractate CXVIII" §4.
32. Smith, *John*, 358.

tom, as always wishing to avoid allegorical interpretation, thought the style of garment here indicated Jesus' poverty and simplicity,[33] though commentators disagree on whether a tunic of this type was common or special.[34]

Cyprian contrasts the non-tearing of Jesus' garment with 1 Kings 11:29–32 where the prophet Ahijah tore Jeroboam's garment into twelve pieces to represent the division about to take place between the Northern and Southern tribes after Solomon's death.[35] Perhaps the author is indicating that after the death of the greatest King his kingdom will remain undivided; or perhaps even that his death will bring about the reunification of Israel, long hoped for in the Prophets.

This raises questions that must be addressed again later when discussing Jesus' words to his mother and beloved disciple. What is the kingdom over which this king reigns and how can it be identified after his death? Is the kingdom the church? Or is it the entire universe? And does this king, like Solomon, leave the kingdom to an heir who may or may not allow it to be divided? The answers to these questions may seem obvious but several recent scholars have been distracted by the kingship imagery into drawing unhelpful conclusions about the role of the church in the reign of Jesus.

The simplest implication of this scene is often overlooked because we involuntarily avert our gaze. The forced removal of Jesus' clothing, including his under-tunic, leaves him naked.[36] Outwardly, he is utterly degraded and stripped of all dignity as he hangs exposed. He is seen in this state by the women who come to mourn him. In this state he addresses his mother and his disciple. Here is the true king, not dressed in purple robes and sitting on a throne or driving a chariot, but naked, bloodied, and hanging on a cross.

---

33. John Chrysostom, *Homilies*, §85.2.
34. Keener, *Gospel of John*, 1140.
35. Cyprian, "On the Unity of the Church," 7.
36. Keener, *Gospel of John* , 1138; Perhaps the restraint of the soldiers in not tearing the tunic indicates God's honoring of Jesus' submission to humiliation. Schnackenburg, *Gospel According to St John*, 274.

> Οἱ μὲν οὖν στρατιῶται ταῦτα ἐποίησαν.

This sentence must be read alongside 16b. There the soldiers immediately carried out Pilate's command. Here they likewise immediately obey the will of God. Yet the nature of their obedience here is entirely different. Unlike Pilate's will, God's will here is not coercive. Those upon whom God's will acts on this occasion are not even conscious that they are carrying out God's orders.

This phrase is not a clumsy connecting clause as some have suggested.[37] It forms a part of the fabric of this scene, which is woven through with questions, negations, and assertions about human and divine power.

> εἱστήκεισαν δὲ παρὰ τῷ σταυρῷ τοῦ Ἰησοῦ ἡ μήτηρ αὐτοῦ καὶ ἡ ἀδελφὴ τῆς μητρὸς αὐτοῦ, Μαρία ἡ τοῦ Κλωπᾶ καὶ Μαρία ἡ Μαγδαληνή.

This is the second time that Jesus' mother appears in the narrative of this Gospel. This time, in contrast to the first, she is passive[38] and silent as befits the utter devastation any mother would feel in such a situation. Neyrey is therefore incorrect when he sees "radical character change" in Jesus' mother since the wedding in Cana.[39] The change is not in her character but in her situation. We first met her at a party, and now we find her at her son's execution.

Ambrose sees Jesus' mother comprehending that she could not at this time be of help to her son.[40] Unlike at Cana, when she could at least place the servants at Jesus' disposal, here she can only stand by in silence.

Some scholars doubt the possibility of the soldiers allowing mourners so near the cross (παρὰ τῷ σταυρῷ), especially when the Synoptic Gospels have them at a distance.[41] I would argue that four women and one man would hardly have been considered a threat to the security of the scene,[42] and at this point Jesus is so close to death that any attempt to rescue him would have been futile.

---

37. Schnackenburg, *Gospel According to St John*, 276.
38. See Fehribach, *Women in the Life of the Bridegroom*, 115.
39. Neyrey, *Gospel of John*, 314.
40. NPNF 2 10:472–3.
41. Schnackenburg, *Gospel According to St John*, 277.
42. Keener, *Gospel of John*, 1141.

The appearance of Jesus' mother at Jesus' execution is entirely plausible historically. Doubt is thrown on her presence only by her absence from the synoptic parallels,[43] though it should be noted that Luke does place her and her other sons in Jerusalem shortly afterward (Acts 1:13–14). The beloved disciple, who stands behind this Gospel (19:34; 21:24) and stands beside Jesus' mother here, might be expected to have access to unique historical details.

The presence of this mother at the execution of her son could not but recall the mother in 4 Maccabees who steadfastly watched her sons face death in preference to renouncing their faith.[44] This woman was, from the reference point of 4 Maccabees, the ideal mother: loving her sons and enduring inner torture at the sight of their suffering, yet balancing her love with courage and a desire for their glory. She is described as a woman of strong rationality because, in seeking her son's glory, she preferred the eternal glory of faithful obedience to the temporary glory of a strong body, a long life, and a multitude of grandchildren.

The silent presence of Jesus' mother could be read as steadfast support of her son's pursuit of the right sort of glory, at the expense of his life, in the face of murderous opposition.

Ambrose enters upon this theme when he notes Mary's piety and courage in remaining with Jesus when the disciples had fled. He contends that when she looked at the cross she, "did not look for the death of her offspring but the salvation of the world."[45] How much she actually understood of the significance of the cross to Jesus' mission can only be guessed, and does not seem to be the point the author is making. Rather, without fully understanding what her son is doing, she trusts him and stands by him, and so is seen here as a better disciple than the ten who fled. This implicit trust in her son, without understanding or explanation, is consistent with her behavior at Cana where she instructed the servants to do whatever he asked of them.

Chrysostom comments that the (weaker) women appear stronger than the male disciples because they endure with Jesus until the end,[46] and declares, "so entirely henceforth were all things transformed."[47]

---

43. Smith, *John*, 359–60.
44. See chapter 4.
45. Ambrose, "Epistle LXIII: To the Church at Vercellæ," §110.
46. Keener, *Gospel of John*, 1141.
47. Chrysostom, *Homilies*, 85.2.

Though the grammar of this verse allows for two, three, or four women it seems most likely that the list refers to four: Jesus' mother and her sister (unnamed), and two other Marys who are named.[48] It is possible that four women have been identified to balance and contrast the four soldiers just mentioned.[49]

Reading the list as four women seems logical as it removes the necessity of assuming two women in the same family bore the same name. However, we cannot be certain about this since Mary of Clopas may have been the sister-in-law of Jesus' mother. Eusebius recalled Hegesippus' belief that Clopas was Joseph's brother.[50] Two sisters-in-law may well share the very common Jewish name of Mary.

Fehribach points out that, unlike the synoptic parallels, none of the other women here are introduced using the formula, "mother of X." She sees this as setting Jesus' mother apart in her maternal role.[51] This is probably correct. Jesus' mother appears here not simply as a relative but specifically as a mother.

In comparing this list with the lists of women at the cross found in Matthew and Mark it is possible to correlate Mary of Clopas with Mary the mother of James[52] and Joses, and Salome with the sister of Jesus's mother (Mark 15:40).[53] If this Salome is the mother of the sons of Zebedee (Matt 27:56), and if the author of the Gospel of John and the beloved disciple and John the son of Zebedee are all the same person, then the beloved disciple may have been Jesus' cousin.[54]

If the beloved disciple was indeed Jesus' cousin it might seem natural for Jesus to place his mother into this cousin's care (v26). However, there are serious deficiencies in this argument. Firstly, the value of correlating the lists of women in each Gospel is undermined by Mark's mention of ἄλλαι πολλαί (Mark 15:41). If many other unnamed women were also present at the cross we cannot assume that each of the Gospel authors

---

48. Carson, *Gospel According to John*, 615–6; Bultmann, *Gospel of John*, 672; Keener, *Gospel of John*, 1142.

49. Stibbe, *John*, 194; Schnackenburg, *Gospel According to St John*, 273, 276–7; Keener, *Gospel of John*, 1141.

50. Eusebius, *History of the Church*, 3.11.2.

51. Fehribach, *Women in the Life of the Bridegroom*, 133.

52. So Jerome, *Perpetual Virginity of Mary*, 15.

53. Bruce, *Gospel of John*, 371.

54. See Carson, *Gospel According to John*, 616.

has chosen to highlight the same women.⁵⁵ This is demonstrated by the fact that John alone mentions Jesus' mother. Further, it is not beyond doubt that the beloved disciple is John the son of Zebedee, as he is never identified as such in the text.

More crucially, there is nothing in the text to indicate that John the son of Zebedee is Jesus' cousin. Historically it is possible, maybe even likely,⁵⁶ that they were related, but at a literary level there is no way for a reader to discern that relationship except by referring to both Mark and Matthew and then following the above logical sequence. It is highly improbable that the author expected his readers to perform such calculations.

It may be argued that if this Gospel was written for a closed community then the family ties between Jesus and the beloved disciple may have been common knowledge. Even then, however, some hint to jog the memory (such as is given in 11:2) would be expected if this were essential information needed for the reader to properly interpret vv26–27. It is therefore highly unlikely that the author intended the reader to take such a relationship into account when reading what follows.

It is certainly significant that John mentions the presence of Jesus' mother but says nothing about his brothers. The possibility that they may have been there, unmentioned by John, is negated by the fact that they also play no part in Jesus' burial. The burial of a brother was a sacred duty, as discussed in chapter 7, yet they are nowhere to be seen.

Carson makes the astonishing claim that their absence has no significance. Since their home was in Galilee, he argues, there is no reason why they should have been there.⁵⁷ While this is true, it must be taken into account that their mother is in Jerusalem with Jesus, and the brothers have been known in the past to travel with Jesus and his mother (2:12). They have also been seen quite recently to travel to Jerusalem and to encourage Jesus to go with them (7:3–4). Their absence at this most crucial moment in their brother's life cannot be without significance.

Campbell suggests that envy may have kept the brothers away.⁵⁸ She also wonders if they thought that Jesus had squandered his share

---

55. Schnackenburg, *Gospel According to St John*, 277.
56. Bauckham, *Jesus and the Eyewitnesses*, 47.
57. Carson, *Gospel According to John*, 617.
58. Campbell, *Kinship Relations*, 148.

(perhaps a double share as the eldest) of their father's property by becoming an itinerant preacher rather than building up the family business.[59]

In this culture the execution of a family member tended to result in one of two reactions from the family. If the family believed the executed one had behaved shamefully, bringing about his own death, the family would be likely to disown and cut themselves off from him. If, rather, the family believed the death to be unjust they would be likely to feel obliged to rage against this injustice and seek revenge, if possible, to re-establish the family's honor.[60] The presence of Jesus' mother at the foot of the cross and the absence of his brothers from his death and burial very probably indicate a family divided over whether Jesus' execution was just or unjust.

The absence of the brothers here, following their conflict with Jesus in John 7, makes it clear that Jesus and his brothers are estranged at this point. Campbell puts it rather starkly: "As no longer members of his family, the biological now superseded by the fictive, the brothers have no place at the scene."[61] Fehribach writes that the, "lack of faith of the brothers . . . combined with their absence at the foot of the cross, sets the stage for Jesus' giving his mother to a new son."[62]

Ἰησοῦς οὖν ἰδὼν τὴν μητέρα καὶ τὸν μαθητὴν παρεστῶτα ὃν ἠγάπα

While it is not possible to be certain about the identity of the beloved disciple, there is good reason to believe he was the author of the Gospel, or was at least closely connected with the author (19:35; 21:24). There is almost universal[63] agreement among early commentators that the author was one of Jesus' disciples. Ptolemaeus attributed the Gospel to "John, the disciple of the Lord."[64] Origen indicates that Heracleon believed the Gospel to have been written by a disciple.[65] The Anti-

---

59. Campbell, *Kinship Relations*, 148–9.
60. Campbell, *Kinship Relations*, 144–5.
61. Campbell, *Kinship Relations*, 151.
62. Fehribach, *Women in the Life of the Bridegroom*, 134.
63. The only contra voice may be that of the Alogoi, who Epiphanius believed to have taught that the Gospel was written by Cerenthus. Epiphanius, *Pan. Haereses*, 51, 2–3.
64. Quoted by Irenaeus, "Against Heresies," 1, 8, 5.
65. Origen, *Commentary on the Gospel of John*, 6, 3.

Marcionite prologue indicates that the Gospel was dictated by John to his disciple, Papias.[66] The Muratorian Canon describes a group of bishops and disciples encouraging the disciple John to make a written record of his recollections.[67]

Chrysostom believed that he gained the title "beloved" because of "some great and wonderful thing he had done."[68] Neyrey reads the title as an indication that he was the "consummate insider."[69] Wiles believes that, "The indirect method of referring to himself is regarded as a suitable means of emphasizing the unimpeachable nature of his authority without at the same time abandoning a proper humility."[70]

The most that can reasonably be said is that the beloved disciple is probably the disciple named John in the Synoptics, and is the author of this Gospel, or at least the eye witness whose testimony lies behind this Gospel.

λέγει τῇ μητρί, Γύναι, ἴδε ὁ υἱός σου. εἶτα λέγει τῷ μαθητῇ, Ἴδε ἡ μήτηρ σου.

There is a long tradition of seeing in these words that Jesus is giving an example of filial piety for others to follow. Augustine, for example, wrote, "The good teacher does what he thereby reminds us ought to be done, and by his own example he instructed his disciples that care for their parents ought to be a matter of concern to pious children."[71] Cyril of Alexandria points out that Jesus' example here is of honoring his mother in the most trying of times, and leaves us no excuse for disregarding

---

66. Anonymous, "Anti Marcionite Prologue to John."
67. Anonymous, "The Muratorian Canon."
68. Chrysostom, *Homilies*, 85.2–3.
69. Neyrey, *Gospel of John*, 314.
70. Wiles, *The Spiritual Gospel*, 9. Tom Thatcher proposes an intriguing theory, based on research among story-tellers in oral cultures, that "Beloved Disciple" was the name given to a legendary story-teller behind the Johannine tradition whose historical identity had been lost and whose role in the life of Jesus had been amplified by legend in the process of transmission (Tom Thatcher, "The Legend of the Beloved Disciple"). I consider this highly unlikely because the early church was intensely interested in the words and deeds of actual disciples, and so would not have allowed a fictional disciple to be invented so soon after the events portrayed in the Gospels.
71. Augustine, "Tractate CXIX," vv 24–30, §2.

our parents when life becomes difficult.[72] In this light it is interesting to note how quickly the church began to take responsibility for caring for widows (Acts 6:1–3), though it is impossible to be sure of any direct connection.[73]

Carson can hardly be blamed for taking a sentimental approach here: "If every mention of Mary during Jesus' years of ministry involves Jesus in a quiet self-distancing from the constraints of a merely human family . . . it is wonderful to remember that even as he hung dying on a Roman cross, suffering as the lamb of God, he took thought of and made provision for his mother."[74]

Clearly, Jesus is being a good son here, ensuring that his mother is protected and provided for after his death. However, it is just as clear that more is happening here than simple filial piety.

Jesus' use of the vocative, Γύναι, for his mother here cannot but draw the reader's attention back to his earlier use of that word (2:4). Similarly, on a second reading, the earlier use of the word cannot but draw the reader's eyes forward to the image of the son on the cross.

Ridderbos claims that by calling his mother Γύναι instead of Μητηρ Jesus is asking his mother to relinquish him as her son.[75] This would require that Jesus was similarly asking his mother to relinquish him in 2:4, and I have already argued that this is not so. Along similar lines, Carson suggests that this may be a Johannine equivalent of Matthew 19:29.[76] In losing one son, Jesus' mother has immediately gained another.

Perhaps this scene is a particular (and extreme) instance of 13:20 (cf. Matt 10:40).[77] One who receives Jesus' disciple receives Jesus, and so Jesus' mother has not really lost her son. Origen comments that no one can comprehend the Gospel of John who has not leaned on Jesus' breast or received Mary from Jesus.[78]

It may be that Tobit 7:12, σὺ δὲ ἀδελφὸς εἶ αὐτῆς, καὶ αὐτή σού ἐστιν, supplies a comparison as a legal formula declaring a change in

---

72. Cyril of Alexandria, "Commentary on the Gospel of John," 12.
73. Keener, *Gospel of John*, 1144.
74. Carson, *Gospel According to John*, 616-7.
75. Ridderbos, *Gospel According to John*, 612.
76. Carson, *Gospel According to John*, 618.
77. Ridderbos, *Gospel According to John*, 613.
78. Origen, *Commentary on the Gospel of John*, 1.23.

relationship between two parties, a marriage in the case of Tobit.[79] The verbal similarity is not sufficient to indicate a literary connection between the two texts, but it is certainly reasonable to see in Jesus' words a declaration of a new relationship.

One line of thought in current scholarship is that Jesus calls her Γύναι because she represents the disciples whom he is placing in the care of the new leader of the Christian community, the beloved disciple.[80] Indeed, for some recent commentators, this final act of love is reduced to an opportunity for sectarian point scoring in which the founder of the Johannine community, in preference to James, Peter, Paul, or any other contender, is made Jesus' successor.[81]

Ridderbos rightly takes exception to this view because it places ecclesiology, rather than Christology, at the centre of this scene, and of the Gospel:

> This symbolization is a radical *theological* shift in the point of the story. Mary and the Beloved Disciple symbolize—in the final act of the dying Jesus in his love for his own to the end—the ideal disciple and the community he founded. The Christological perspective is thus no longer primary and dominant but receives its content from ecclesiology, a reversal that may well be called crucial in the interpretation of the whole Gospel.[82]

Fehribach argues that Jesus' mother's role here is as an "exchange object," as can often be found in depictions of the death of a king in Greco-Roman literature. The exchange of women establishes kinship relationships in many cultures, and when it takes place at a king's death it gives an indication of the king's chosen successor.[83] This exchange also ensures that the women in the king's care will continue to be cared for.

The plethora of kingship references and imagery certainly argue in favor of Jesus' actions here being those of a king giving his last will and testament. However, two factors argue against Fehribach's conclusions. Firstly, the fact that Jesus' mother is given a role in relation to the beloved disciple implies that she is more than simply an "exchange object." Secondly, Fehribach assigns the beloved disciple two incompatible roles: that

---

79. Noted by Schnackenburg, *Gospel According to St John*, 278.
80. Campbell, *Kinship Relations*, 35.
81. Stibbe, *John*, 194; Campbell, *Kinship Relations*, 189.
82. Ridderbos, *Gospel According to John*, 615.
83. Fehribach, *Women in the Life of the Bridegroom*, 135–8.

of Jesus' successor and that of representative of Jesus' followers.[84] More will be said later about the possibility that the beloved disciple is here being made Jesus' successor.

What can be said without hesitation is that Jesus is here choosing to entrust his mother to the care of a disciple rather than a younger brother.[85] This was certainly unusual since "the ordinary procedure followed by the eldest son of a widow would have been to ask one of his other brothers to look after their mother at his death.[86] Jesus does not do that. He asks the beloved disciple to take care of Mary, which means that Mary is introduced into the fellowship of God's spiritual family."[87]

Campbell is quite right in seeing that in the thought world of this Gospel "Jesus cannot hand his believing mother over into the realm that hates him (John 7:7; 15:18), because by doing so he would be sending her from the realm of light and life into the realm of darkness and death."[88]

She is also correct to wonder if Jesus' mother's support of her eldest son had left her estranged from her other sons and therefore in need of this provision.[89] The fact that she appears at the cross without her other sons after the conflict between Jesus and his brothers in John 7 suggests this as a real possibility. Any estrangement already existing between Jesus' mother and his brothers would certainly have been exacerbated by Jesus placing her in the care of a man outside the immediate family.[90]

Fehribach sees this exchange as a devaluation of matrilineal descent because of the non-biological nature of the kinship bond established here.[91] Jesus' kin are from here described as children of a common father in heaven rather than of a common mother on earth. Certainly the earthly and heavenly origin of this spiritual parentage is important here, but it is far less clear that matrilineal descent, as such, is being undermined.

John 1:13 provides another contrast between the divine and human parentage of those who receive and believe Jesus. In this case it is the role

---

84. Campbell, *Kinship Relations*, 43.
85. Keener, *Gospel of John*, 1145.
86. See also Neyrey, *Gospel of John*, 310.
87. van der Watt, *Family of the King*, 261.
88. Campbell, *Kinship Relations*, 147.
89. Campbell, *Kinship Relations*, 146.
90. So Williams, "The Mother of Jesus at Cana," 691.
91. Fehribach, *Women in the Life of the Bridegroom*, 139.

of the human father that is downplayed. Assuming Fehribach is correct in seeing biological motherhood downplayed in the crucifixion scene, this must be placed alongside the downplaying of biological fatherhood in the prologue. Once these are viewed together we see it is not patrilineal descent that is being emphasized but heavenly, spiritual descent.

Here, then, a new relationship is formed that does not depend on bloodlines. This relationship is created by a speech-act.[92] Jesus' words do not simply describe an existing reality, nor do they command a new action, though new actions become necessary in light of the new relationship. Like the modern words, "I now pronounce you husband and wife," these words of Jesus from the cross, "behold your son," "behold your mother," are words of relationship-creation. The Word made flesh, who was from the beginning the agent of creation (1:3) is here, again, creating by a word.

More will be said later in this chapter about just what is created by this speech-act, but what must, at the very least, be noticed here is that we find "a new beginning at the moment when all is over."[93] At the point of Jesus' death a new relationship is born. At the end of Jesus' earthly ministry a new ministry is created. Despite my efforts to understand this fully, I recognize the need here to honor the mystery inherent in these few words.

καὶ ἀπ' ἐκείνης τῆς ὥρας ἔλαβεν
ὁ μαθητὴς αὐτὴν εἰς τὰ ἴδια.

The reference, at this climactic point, to Jesus' awaited ὥρα could not be coincidental.[94] Indeed Moloney argues that ἀπ', followed by the genitive here, may have a causative sense, "because of that hour . . ."[95] The author has prepared the reader to expect Jesus' ὥρα to be an hour of glory, but they find here an hour of pain, degradation, and death. They also find an hour of creation in the formation of a new relationship between a mother and a son.

---

92. The term "speech-act" is used here in the sense in which it is used by Wolterstorff, that is, speech that performs an illocutionary action. Nicholas Wolterstorff, *Divine Discourse*, 45, 75.

93. Lindars, *Gospel of John*, 573.

94. Stibbe, *John*, 195.

95. Moloney, *Gospel of John*, 503.

Here we also see a reversal of the indictment of humanity[96] found in the prologue, where the Word came εἰς τὰ ἴδια and was not received.[97] Not only that but, as Sloyan suggests, it is also a reversal of the scattering of the disciples predicted in 16:32, where each disciple would go εἰς τὰ ἴδια.[98]

Could it be, as Beth Sheppard argues, that the beloved disciple is a minor who was in Jesus' care, and is now made the foster-son of Jesus' mother?[99] There is insufficient evidence to claim that the beloved disciple was a minor, and good reason to assume that he was an adult. This verse makes it clear that this new relationship is one in which the new son cares for his new mother, more than the other way around.[100]

Campbell suggests that Jesus' mother is here made a witness to the superiority of the testimony of the beloved disciple.[101] This is an intriguing suggestion. The presence of Jesus' mother in the household of the beloved disciple would certainly add validity to his testimony, and the author is here at pains to demonstrate the validity of that testimony (19:35). It may well be that this verse has been included in this tightly disciplined passion narrative for that reason. However, Campbell's conclusion that this assertion of validity is made over against the testimony of other late first-century Christian groups is less convincing. It is much more likely that, as Campbell also suggests, Jesus' mother brings the beloved disciple into close and certain proximity with the greatest guarantee of Jesus' humanity—the woman who gave birth to him. It is therefore more likely that any claim to the superiority of the beloved disciple's witness is being made here over and against docetic objections, rather than against the witness of other Christian communities.

---

96. Or of the Jews in particular.

97. Moloney, *Gospel of John*, 503–4.

98. Sloyan, *John*, 211.

99. Sheppard, "Behold your Son," Unpublished paper cited in Campbell, *Kinship Relations*, 40–41.

100. Schnackenburg, *Gospel According to St John*, 280.

101. Campbell, *Kinship Relations*, 45.

Μετὰ τοῦτο εἰδὼς ὁ Ἰησοῦς ὅτι ἤδη πάντα τετέλεσται,
ἵνα τελειωθῇ ἡ γραφή, λέγει, Διψῶ

Here we find, at the very least, another witness to Jesus' humanity. The one who claimed to be able to supply living water (4:14; 7:39) is also subject to the common human condition of desperate thirst.[102] Indeed it seems that he must suffer thirst before he can pour out the living water of the Spirit.

This verse also underscores the significance of Jesus' words to his mother and disciple.[103] After this action of declaring a new relationship between his mother and disciple (μετὰ τοῦτο) all is accomplished.

Note the use of τελειωθῇ here instead of the customary πληρωθῇ. Scripture is here not simply fulfilled but brought to some form of completion.

Jesus had earlier in this Gospel said that his food was to do the will of his Father and to τελειώσω αὐτοῦ τὸ ἔργον (4:34); and in the garden where he was arrested he had insisted that he must drink the cup his Father had given him. Drinking the sour wine may signify that he has completed his Father's work: fully consumed all that had been required of him.[104]

Jesus' thirst could link to Psalm 22:15, given the earlier reference to that Psalm, but Psalm 69:21, "for my thirst they gave me vinegar to drink," is more likely, given the reference to sour wine immediately afterwards.[105] Certainly both Psalms stand in the background of this scene.

Ridderbos suggests that by indicating, but not quoting, Psalm 69 Jesus is referring to the fulfillment of the whole Psalm, rather than just to the particular verse about thirst.[106] It is certainly worth noting verse 8: "I have become a stranger to my kindred, an alien to my mother's children." Having become alienated from his brothers to the extent of giving his mother into another man's care, Jesus knows that all that remains for him to do is to admit to his own desperate thirst and to die.

Surely the reference to Scripture fulfillment is here, as Carson claims, an indication that "John wants to make his readers understand

---

102. Lindars, *Gospel of John*, 581.

103. Ridderbos, *Gospel According to John*, 616; Schnackenburg, *Gospel According to St John*, 287.

104. Schnackenburg, *Gospel According to St John*, 283.

105. Carson, *Gospel According to John*, 619, Bruce, *Gospel of John*, 372.

106. Ridderbos, *Gospel According to John*, 616.

that every part of Jesus' passion was not only in the Father's plan of redemption but a consequence of the son's direct obedience to it."[107] In this case, Scripture is knowingly and deliberately fulfilled, rather than being stumbled upon as the soldiers did when dividing Jesus' clothes.

Undoubtedly Jesus truly was desperately thirsty, but in this Gospel of the victorious Son there is always more going on than Jesus' need. Here he is determined to ensure that all that had been written about him would be accomplished[108] and that witnesses are in a position to accurately interpret these events.

Mention of thirst also recalls readers of this Gospel to 4:7 where Jesus asks a Samaritan woman for a drink. This demonstrates to the readers that the Word has entered into the experience of human thirst, not only at a physical level (though including that) but also at a spiritual level, and that by entering he has unstopped the fountain of living water for all come to him with their thirst. (4:13; 6:35; 7:37)

Ridderbos pulls these threads together:

> The regal power and authority—so prominent in John—with which Jesus accepts his suffering and goes out to meet his enemies in no way means that he is fundamentally immune to that suffering and passes through it unaffected. "I thirst" is not a proof of how strictly Jesus fulfilled Scripture but a lament wrung from him out of the depth of his suffering in which his solidarity with those who had lamented their suffering in Scripture consists above all in the fact that he and they took their suffering to God and laid it out before him.[109]

σκεῦος ἔκειτο ὄξους μεστόν· σπόγγον οὖν μεστὸν τοῦ ὄξους ὑσσώπῳ περιθέντες προσήνεγκαν αὐτοῦ τῷ στόματι.

The use of hyssop (ὑσσώπῳ/) is likely to be a link to Passover[110] narratives (Exod 12:22) and possibly to the timing of Jesus' death to coincide with

---

107. Carson, *Gospel According to John*, 619–20.
108. Smith, *John*, 361; Bruce, *Gospel of John*, 372.
109. Ridderbos, *Gospel According to John*, 616–7.
110. Bruce, *Gospel of John*, 373; Sloyan, *John*, 211; contra Schnackenburg, *Gospel According to St John*, 284.

the slaughter of Passover lambs.[111] Stibbe comments, "narrative chronology and narrative Christology are inseparable in John."[112]

However, the hyssop has aroused concern about plausibility because a hyssop branch would not be strong enough for the purpose. Our depiction of crosses as very tall structures probably adds to our incredulity here. In reality, Jesus' feet would have been just above the ground,[113] so the soldier would not have needed a long stick to reach his mouth.

Cyril of Jerusalem points to the faithlessness of Israel in this action. They were planted as a choice grape vine (Jer 2:21), but here in their gardener's time of need they provide vinegar, not wine.[114] However, most commentators agree that the drink would not have been vinegar as such, but a form of inferior wine that, though it tasted like watered-down vinegar, was a popular drink among the majority of the people.[115]

It is, however, very likely that the reader is expected to recall Jesus' earlier production in Cana of wine that was better than expected. Here he is given inferior wine but he is, through his death, creating the better wine that was prefigured at Cana. The inferior stuff, all that humanity can offer its king, is superseded by the superior wine that is given by the king to humanity, at the cost of his own life.

ὅτε οὖν ἔλαβεν τὸ ὄξος [ὁ] Ἰησοῦς εἶπεν, Τετέλεσται, καὶ κλίνας τὴν κεφαλὴν παρέδωκεν τὸ πνεῦμα.

The author is keen to demonstrate that Jesus remained in control, even to the point of choosing his own time to die (10:18).[116] Indeed, Malina and Rohrbaugh compare Jesus' lowering of his head with a sign of sanction from a king or god.[117]

Neyrey sees the handing over (παρέδωκεν) of the spirit here as a Pentecost event.[118] Malina and Rohrbaugh also believe Jesus is here giving his spirit to the community around the cross, referring back to 7:37–

---

111. Stibbe, *John*, 196.
112. Stibbe, *John*, 196.
113. Keener, *Gospel of John*, 1136.
114. Chrysostom, *Homilies*, §13.29; so Leo the Great, "Sermons" §55.4.
115. Schnackenburg, *Gospel According to St John*, 284.
116. See Carson, *Gospel According to John*, 621; so Smith, *John*, 361.
117. Malina and Rohrbaugh, *Social-Science Commentary*, 21.
118. Neyrey, *Gospel of John*, 311.

39 as a promise that the Spirit would be given when Jesus was glorified. They believe that this is what Jesus meant by bringing Scripture to its completion.[119]

It is very likely that a double meaning is intended here.[120] The literal meaning is certainly that he gives out his last breath in death.[121] The promised sending of the Holy Spirit to his followers is also probably in view here,[122] though it should be seen as proleptic in relation to 20:22 and Pentecost rather than as a giving of the Spirit ahead of time to a select group of disciples. Any assumption, based on this verse, that the Spirit is given exclusively to the beloved disciple and his community is overturned by 20:22, where Jesus breathed the Spirit on a more complete group of disciples.

For the sake of brevity, vv 31–37 are not analyzed here in detail. Vv 38–42 are, however, relevant to the current discussion so I move onto those verses now.

Μετὰ δὲ ταῦτα ἠρώτησεν τὸν Πιλᾶτον Ἰωσὴφ [ὁ] ἀπὸ Ἁριμαθαίας, ὢν μαθητὴς τοῦ Ἰησοῦ κεκρυμμένος δὲ διὰ τὸν φόβον τῶν Ἰουδαίων, ἵνα ἄρῃ τὸ σῶμα τοῦ Ἰησοῦ· καὶ ἐπέτρεψεν ὁ Πιλᾶτος. ἦλθεν οὖν καὶ ἦρεν τὸ σῶμα αὐτοῦ.

This secret disciple now acts publically.[123] Neyrey is mistaken in wondering whether, "[Joseph's] public act of burying Jesus finally cancels the stigma of his secret discipleship."[124] Other commentators who see him as advancing toward discipleship but perhaps not quite there are also incorrect.[125] They appear to miss the point that, by doing for Jesus what Jesus' brothers should have done, both Joseph and Nicodemus are shown to have progressed from secret disciples to open kin of Jesus.

119. Malina and Rohrbaugh, *Social-Science Commentary*, 271.

120. Smith, *John*, 362; Sloyan, *John*, 212.

121. Note that Moloney contends that this phrase cannot be a euphemism for death because he "hands over" and does not "give up" the spirit; and because it is *the* spirit, not *his* spirit that he hands over. Moloney, *Gospel of John*, 505.

122. Moloney, *Gospel of John*, 504–5.

123. Moloney, *Gospel of John*, 510; Ridderbos, *Gospel According to John*, 625; Lindars, *Gospel of John*, 592; Schnackenburg, *Gospel According to St John*, 295.

124. Neyrey, *Gospel of John*, 314.

125. Smith, *John*, 36.

We must note also that Joseph is spoken of with reverence by early Christian commentators,[126] who see no shame in his having until now been a secret disciple. Indeed, Chrysostom calls Joseph, "Not one of the Twelve, but perhaps one of the seventy."[127]

Carson claims that there is no significance in the absence of Jesus' brothers from the burial since they would have been refused an audience with Pilate if they had been the ones asking for his body.[128] This is true, but even if they could not personally take care of every detail they would be expected to be there. This is also true of Jesus' sisters, but since the sisters are not mentioned in this Gospel their absence here is not so conspicuous.

> ἦλθεν δὲ καὶ Νικόδημος, ὁ ἐλθὼν πρὸς αὐτὸν νυκτὸς τὸ πρῶτον, φέρων μίγμα σμύρνης καὶ ἀλόης ὡς λίτρας ἑκατόν

Neyrey again misunderstands what is happening here, claiming that Nicodemus "keeps the label of 'night-time' visitor, which negatively labels him as a 'fearful, secret disciple.'"[129] The point made in the text is that *at first*, τὸ πρῶτον, Nicodemus came to Jesus at night, but later he found the courage to speak up in the Sanhedrin (7:50–51) and now, even in the darkness and doubt of Jesus' death, he performs a public act to honor Jesus.[130] The amount of spice mentioned here could not have been carried secretly. In fact, several servants would have been required to transport it to the place where Jesus' body was prepared, in such a kingly fashion,[131] for burial.

Neyrey casts further doubt on Nicodemus' discipleship by saying that the spice indicated that Nicodemus had no faith that Jesus would be alive again soon.[132] However, these spices would not have been used for embalming, because the Jews did not practice embalming. The

---

126. Including Tertullian, "The Five Books against Marcion," 4.42–43.
127. Chrysostom, *Homilies*, 85.3.
128. Carson, *Gospel According to John*, 629.
129. Neyrey, *Gospel of John*, 314.
130. See Neyrey, *Gospel of John*, 315.
131. Bruce, *Gospel of John*, 379; Moloney, *Gospel of John*, 510; Stibbe, *John*, 197; Schnackenburg, *Gospel According to St John*, 295.
132. Neyrey, *Gospel of John*, 314–5.

spices would have been in powdered form, sprinkled on Jesus' body and between the linen cloths,[133] not to preserve Jesus' body, but to counteract the smell that after crucifixion would have been unpleasant even before decay began.

Also, the argument that Nicodemus' actions indicate a lack of faith in the resurrection could carry weight only if his actions were contrasted with other disciples who did demonstrate confidence in the resurrection at this time. However, it is the consistent witness of all four Gospels that none of the disciples expected Jesus' resurrection and all were surprised to see Jesus again on the Sunday. There is no justification for believing that any of Jesus' followers were expecting to see Jesus again in three days (20:9). Therefore, if no disciple demonstrated greater faith than Nicodemus, how could his incomplete faith preclude him from discipleship?

Just as Joseph of Arimathea came out of secrecy to honor Jesus in burial, so too Nicodemus[134] acts now in the daylight rather than the night. It is in Jesus' death that these two secret disciples found the courage to honor Jesus publically. As Jesus was lifted up they were drawn out of the shadows and into his light (12:32).[135] Mention of these two men is clearly intended to encourage other secret disciples to make their confession of Jesus public.[136]

Representative roles for Jesus' mother and his beloved disciple?

Bultmann famously made the claim that

> The mother of Jesus, who tarries at the cross, represents Jewish Christianity that overcomes the offense of the cross. The Beloved Disciple represents Gentile Christianity, which is charged to honor the former as its mother from whom it has come, even as Jewish Christianity is charged to recognize itself as "at home" within Gentile Christianity.[137]

---

133. Schnackenburg, *Gospel According to St John*, 297.

134. Martyn, *History and Theology in the Fourth Gospel*, 88; Ridderbos, *Gospel According to John*, 626.

135. Ridderbos, *Gospel According to John*, 626; Schnackenburg, *Gospel According to St John*, 297.

136. Moloney, *Gospel of John*, 512.

137. Bultmann, *Gospel of John*, 673.

Bultmann's interpretation has found no support in the academic community as there is nothing in the text to identify the beloved disciple with Gentile Christianity. However, many commentators have taken up the question of what, if any, representative roles Jesus' mother and disciple play in this account. I will discuss a number of these.

Does Jesus' mother, as Schnackenburg suggests, represent those who long for salvation? She had been honored with a foretaste of the messianic banquet at Cana, and now she receives its fulfillment.[138] This raises the question of what Jesus' mother actually received at the cross. A son? She already had sons. What is actually fulfilled in this new relationship established by Jesus from the cross?

Schnackenburg also suggests that the beloved disciple may represent the need to "take home" and make provision for all who seek salvation.[139] It may even be that it is primarily in the writing of this Gospel that this provision is made. Perhaps this is the task for which the Advocate would be sent, as promised in 14:25–26 at the meal where the beloved disciple is also mentioned as being present (13:23). Yet, can it really be said that Jesus' mother is a seeker any more than the beloved disciple? At Cana she was the one whose request provided the occasion for Jesus' first sign, she directed others to obey Jesus, and the outcome was a manifestation of Jesus' glory that led the disciples into deeper faith. Here at the cross she stands by Jesus when all but one of his male disciples have fled.

The beloved disciple has been called the "mediator and interpreter of Jesus' message"?[140] It could hardly be argued that he is not that, but what must be disputed is the claim that he is cast in that role within this Gospel in order to elevate the validity of one Christian sect above others who cannot claim such lofty authority for their founders. A full refutation of this line of argument is not possible within the scope of this book, and it has been touched upon already in chapters 5 and 8.[141]

---

138. Schnackenburg, *Gospel According to St John*, 278.

139. Schnackenburg, *Gospel According to St John*, 297; Does the disciple also represent the church, where seekers after salvation are always to be given hospitality? Scnhackenburg believes not, but argues that he is to "bring into being the church and lead it in the Spirit." Schnackenburg, *Gospel According to St John*, 280. Is this really the role of the beloved disciple?

140. Schnackenburg, *Gospel According to St John*, 279.

141. Richard Bauckham has ably refuted this argument in a number of works, especially in *The Gospels for All Christians*.

Much more potential is found in Lee's words: "Both figures ... symbolize different dimensions of the believing community, the mother of Jesus signifying its mothering capacity, inherited from Jesus himself, and the beloved disciple epitomizing its filiation, likewise having its origins in Jesus."[142]

The symbolic role of Jesus' mother ought, perhaps, not to be sought outside of the one thing we know about her with certainty in this Gospel—her motherhood. As a typical first-century mother her deepest longings would have been for her son's glory and her greatest dread for his suffering and death. As a literary portrayal of an ideal mother she desires the highest and most honorable form of glory for her son and is willing to watch him die in order to obtain it. These words from 4 Maccabees could have been written of her:

> Ὢ μῆτερ ἔθνους, ἔκδικε τοῦ νόμου, καὶ ὑπερασπίστεια τῆς εὐσεβείας, καὶ τοῦ διὰ σπλάγχνων ἀγῶνος ἀθλοφόρε. ὦ ἀρρένων πρὸς καρτερίαν γενναιοτέρα, καὶ ἀνδρῶν πρὸς ὑπομονὴν ἀνδρειοτέρα. καθάπερ γὰρ ἡ Νῶε κιβωτὸς ἐν τῷ κοσμοπληθεῖ κατακλυσμῷ κοσμοφοροῦσα καρτεροὺς ὑπήνεγκεν τοὺς κλύδωνας· οὕτως σύ, ἡ νομοφύλαξ, πανταχόθεν ἐν τῷ τῶν παθῶν περιαντλουμένη κατακλυσμῷ, καὶ καρτεροῖς ἀνέμοις ταῖς τῶν υἱῶν βασάνοις συνεχομένη, γενναίως ὑπέμεινας τοὺς τῆς εὐσεβείας χειμῶνας. (4 Macc 15:29–32)[143]

Within the church there must always be mothers. Just as the church continues to produce martyrs, the church must keep producing those who grieve and celebrate at the same time when Christians give their lives rather than abandoning the truth.

The beloved disciple, likewise, must be understood in terms of the role assigned to him. He is the son. The good son protects his mother and loves her with deep affection and loyalty. Ideally the most vulnerable members of the Christian community will always find such sons in the church.

---

142. D. Lee, *Flesh and Glory*, 156.

143. TR: 29 O mother of the nation, vindicator of the law and champion of religion, who carried away the prize of the contest in your heart! 30 O more noble than males in steadfastness, and more courageous than men in endurance! 31 Just as Noah's ark, carrying the world in the universal flood, stoutly endured the waves, 32 so you, O guardian of the law, overwhelmed from every side by the flood of your emotions and the violent winds, the torture of your sons, endured nobly and withstood the wintry storms that assail religion.

This disciple is not just a son, he is also a brother,[144] and his brotherhood is shared here by Joseph of Arimathea and Nicodemus who take on the fraternal responsibility of burying Jesus. The disciples will be called "brothers" by Jesus for the first time in 20:17. And so the church will always be made up of brothers. Christians, ideally, stand by each other in solidarity and equal regard, and less ideally, bicker and compete for our Father's attention. This is the church as pictured in this Gospel: a family with mothers, sons, and brothers.

Sisters are also represented by figures such as Mary Magdalene (20:11–18). It may be fruitful to investigate whether sisters are best included in this image by an enlargement of the role of brothers, or whether they have a separate role within the Gospel. This falls outside the scope of this book because the focus here is on Jesus' biological family in the Fourth Gospel and, although the Synoptic Gospels indicate that Jesus had sisters, they do not appear here. My assumption at present is that sisterhood is included within the concept of brotherhood in this Gospel, but closer analysis might demonstrate otherwise.

So, at the cross, a new family comes into being. Family of birth gives way to family of creation.[145] It is specifically at the cross[146] that this family is created and it is our relationship to Jesus that forms our filial, maternal, fraternal, and sisterly bonds. Lee's words are very helpful:

> Already at the foot of the cross the literal language of family begins to give way before the metaphorical: kinship imagery is now used of the community of faith. It is not that Jesus divests himself of kith and kin, but rather that the kinship bonds are transformed to become symbolic of a whole new understanding of "family" . . . the "brothers and sisters" of Jesus are no longer those who belong to his human family—unless they are themselves believers—but rather those who have entered the celestial family through birth in the Spirit, passing into the filial relationship of the Son to the Father.[147]

This new family is entirely christocentric. We are sisters and brothers of one another only because Jesus, at the cross, made himself our brother. By entering utterly into the reality of human experience, especially here

---

144. Howard, "Minor Characters," 68.
145. Park, "The Galilean Jesus," 429; Ridderbos, *Gospel According to John*, 614.
146. Moloney, *Gospel of John*, 504.
147. Lee, *Flesh and Glory*, 154.

the experience of suffering indicated by his fulfillment of Psalms 22 and 69, Jesus forged a fraternal bond with humanity that is stronger than the fraternal bonds of our biology.

Because Jesus has become our brother, God has become our Father (20:17). Note that in John, as in the Synoptic Gospels (Matt 23:9), there is no provision in the church for any Father other than God. The ultimate authority inherent in the first-century father can reside in no human in the church.

Conclusions

In this passage a dying king chooses as guardian for his mother a man who is not a family member in any literal sense. He chooses this guardian in spite of the fact that his mother has other sons who had every right and reason to expect that role to be theirs. As a last act of the Word made flesh, though, this is no mere insult against brothers who had rejected him. It is an act of family creation.

With these simple words, ἴδε ὁ υἱός σου . . . ’Ἴδε ἡ μήτηρ σου, Jesus creates a new reality. He is not bequeathing his kingdom or establishing a new authority structure, he is speaking a family into existence. Is it reasonable, then, to say that these words created the church? Probably, but not in the sense of the church as missional structure or the church as repository of doctrine; but it could be said the church as kinship group, as family, is brought into being here at the foot of the cross as the last act of the crucified king.

This is a specifically Johannine contribution to ecclesiology. The Synoptic Gospels use kinship language to refer to the disciples throughout Jesus' ministry, but in John it is not until after Jesus' death and resurrection that the disciples are called ἀδελφούς μου. By entering fully into human suffering, Jesus made humans his brothers, and made it possible for us to call God our Father.

The two appearances of Jesus' mother in this Gospel form an inclusio around Jesus' public ministry. She anticipates his first miracle and participates in his ultimate act of power and provision in humiliating death. She brings to Jesus' attention the lack of wine at the wedding, and at a deeper level the absence of the wine of God's blessing from the experience of God's people; and she is there when his blood is poured out to reverse God's judgment and bring the longed-for blessing to a new people of God. She is told that Jesus' hour was not yet; and she stands beside him when his hour comes. She pointed the disciples toward belief and obedience through her actions at Cana; and at the cross she joined the beloved disciple in witnessing Jesus' humiliation and glory.

She is introduced as the mother of Jesus, so the reader does not need to be explicitly told that she was there at the moment of incarnation and at the birth of the Messiah. This woman's presence at the beginning of Jesus' life, the beginning of his public ministry, and at his death, has encircled Jesus in a mother's love. The Word made flesh does not stride through life in regal independence. He has a mum. Like the rest of us, he has family responsibilities; he gives and receives family affection; he creates anxiety for his kin; he is part of—even the cause of—family conflicts. The Word has honored the human race, not only by taking on our physical form, but also by immersing himself in human social networks, and particularly that most crucial of social networks, the family.

The passion narrative in the Fourth Gospel is paradoxical. Throughout the horrific degradation of this scene, Jesus retains his majesty.[148] What looks on the surface like a status-degradation scene from Roman literature becomes a status-elevation scene: a triumph and a victory.[149] The overriding theme is one of kingship, and when all the references and allusions to kingship are taken together this passage can be seen as an act of regicide.[150] Indeed this Gospel depicts honorable, victorious regicide, not just because of the resurrection but also because of the way Jesus remains regally in control to his last breath.

The place of Jesus' mother and disciple at the foot of the cross is, therefore, a place of prestige.[151] This is not, as some have supposed, because one or the other of them is the heir of his kingdom. Jesus retains his kingdom, just as he retains his dignity. The dignity of Jesus' mother is in being the mother of the king and in retaining her motherhood in the new family created at the cross. The dignity of the beloved disciple is found in that his discipleship is transformed into sonship and brotherhood in that family. They need no greater role and no more significant symbolic function.

---

148. Schnackenburg, *Gospel According to St John*, 271.
149. Campbell, *Kinship Relations*, 143–6.
150. Stibbe, *John*, 197; Schnackenburg, *Gospel According to St John*, 268.
151. Campbell, *Kinship Relations*, 145.

This chapter brings to an end the cultural analysis and exegesis of this book. The remaining chapter will draw conclusions, consider implications, and make recommendations for further research.

10

Conclusions and Recommendations

No matter how often and how deeply one has read the Fourth Gospel there will always be times when something new catches our eye and we realize that we are still very far from exhausting the wisdom it has to offer. Eight years ago my eye was caught by the three interactions between Jesus and his close kin. Each one held mysteries and conundrums to be explored. Each one had been examined by devout scholars and wise Christian communities over many centuries, yet something still seemed to be missing in their analysis. This book has followed the trail of my curiosity in an effort to make a small contribution to the store of observations already accumulated about these verses and about this Gospel.

In the preceding pages I have sought to identify as accurately as possible what the implied readers of the Fourth Gospel would have discerned about kinship relationships (biological and fictive) from these three descriptions of interactions between Jesus and his family members (John 2:1–12; 7:1–10; 19:25–27). In particular, I have wondered whether they would have found in these three passages a theme of Jesus distancing himself from his biological kinship group as he established an alternative community of fictive kin. While these verses are verbally very distant from such synoptic passages as Matthew 12:46–50, Mark 3:31–35, and Luke 8:19–21, I have wondered whether a similar message might be discerned in them all. As I have followed this trail I have kept watch for other insights that might present themselves about the role of Jesus' family in this Gospel.

Summary of conclusions

A portrait of Jesus' family was sketched in the first chapter, based not on complete certainty but on solid probability. In this sketch Jesus was found to be the eldest son of a family of five sons and at least two daughters. All five boys would have learned the family trade of building from their father, Joseph. They lived in Nazareth, not far from the new Herodian city of Sepphoris where a great deal of work would have been available for builders.

With this rich city nearby, Jesus would have grown up with a strong awareness of the sharp socioeconomic inequalities around him. His family would have been just getting by, financially, with all able family members working hard. He would have had opportunity to observe the wealth and luxury of the ruling class when in Sepphoris, and around Nazareth he would have seen the plight of tenant farmers who paid a high percentage of their income on rent and various taxes. He would have observed the tragic consequences when people of his own class lost the means to support themselves and became destitute.

He would have been recognized as an academically able child and in this devout Jewish family this would have meant he was given the opportunity to learn to read the Hebrew Scriptures and to study the Torah and the Prophets under a local rabbi.

Joseph died when Jesus and perhaps one or two of his brothers were fully productive adults. Jesus assumed the responsibilities of head of the family. This meant continuing to work to support them financially and also, alongside his mother, Mary, training and disciplining the children and finding spouses for them at the appropriate time. As head of the family he was also free to choose not to marry, despite pressure to do so. Once his youngest sibling reached the age of twelve he left the family home to commence his itinerant ministry. At times he placed his mother in the care of his brothers and at other times she traveled with him.

Much of this information would have been common knowledge among early Christians because of widespread curiosity in that culture concerning issues of kinship. Any information that was available about Jesus' family would have traveled throughout the empire because of the mobility of many Christians at the time. At least two of Jesus' close relatives, James and Mary, were part of early churches in Jerusalem and (as is traditionally thought) in Ephesus. These two family members would have

CONCLUSIONS AND RECOMMENDATIONS 289

both embodied and supplied information to the early Christian community about Jesus' family.

It is, therefore, reasonable to assume that the author of the Fourth Gospel knew a great deal more about Jesus' family than is implied by the scant details that he included. It is very likely that the readers he originally envisioned also knew, or had access to, a great deal more information than they found in the Gospel, and this information formed the basis of background information and of some of the irony employed in this Gospel.

A number of early Christians were ostracized and disowned by Jewish or pagan family members who perceived their attachment to Christ as an act of disloyalty or even blasphemy. These people would have been sensitive to references in the Gospels to the tensions Jesus experienced between his obligations to his family and his call to teach, heal, and sacrifice his life.

The Synoptic Gospels portray Jesus as preparing his disciples for this dislocation from their kin. He calls them to actively choose to demote family from its place of primary loyalty and to give that loyalty to Jesus. Loyalty to Jesus in the Synoptics is equated to loyalty to God, as Jesus becomes the elder brother in the fictive family of faith in which God is the Father. In this kinship group, all were called to honor one Father, and to act as siblings with each other. This was not unique. Some other Jewish sects called for the breaking of family ties in order to live a life of complete devotion to God. There was recognition, even before and beyond the Christian community, that family could be a distraction from serving God. What is unique about the Christian call to demote family was the way the Synoptics equate following a person, Jesus, with following God.

The call to place primary loyalty in Jesus (and hence in God) is stark in the Synoptics. Strong words like "hate" are used to describe the secondary priority to be given to family. Jesus speaks about his own biological family as if they were not really his family at all unless they repented of their opposition to his ministry and sat with his disciples to hear from him the word of God.

The Fourth Gospel does not use this stark language. Nothing in John readily parallels Matthew 12:46–50, Mark 3:31–35, and Luke 8:19–21. If this theme of conflict between loyalty to family and loyalty to God exists in this Gospel it is not available on the surface to modern readers. A closer look at the way kinship was understood in this culture, along with detailed exegesis of the passages in which Jesus interacts with family members, has been necessary in order to excavate that theme for a culturally distant audience.

Very strong affective bonds held mothers and sons together in this culture. This is the conclusion of modern socio-historical scholars and it was also my conclusion after examining Roman, Greek, and Jewish literature that was influential in the first century.

Mothers of sons at this time were consistently seen in literature as experiencing deep conflict between their desire to send their sons into the world to win honor (through war or politics or virtue) and their longing to keep their sons safe. Less selfless mothers also experienced a conflict between seeking honor for their sons and seeking it for themselves in a world where political power was only available to women through their husbands and sons.

Sons, in turn, had a sacred duty to provide for and protect their mothers after the death of their fathers. Sons also tended to act as their mother's defenders against harsh treatment from their fathers and others. An emotional plea from a mother appears to have had an enormous amount of weight with virtuous sons.

All aspects of this bond appear to be intensified when the son is the mother's first, and it is reasonable to assume that Mary felt intensely attached to her special eldest son. She also knew well the conflict between her responsibility to send him into the world to achieve the honor for which he was born, and her fears about how that harsh world may challenge his honor and mistreat him. Jesus, as the eldest son of a widow, would no doubt have felt to the full extent the pull of affection and obligation to meet his mother's needs and assent to her requests.

The assumption that the world was divided into female (inside domestic) space and male (outside commerce and political) space is not substantiated by archaeological investigation into the architecture of Palestine, though it was certainly asserted as an ideal by ethicists of the time. It is reasonable to assume, then, that Jesus and his mother would have met and spoken frequently in the course of daily life while Jesus was living in the family home. In relation to the wedding at Cana, I found nothing to indicate that a mother and son speaking together in a public space would have been culturally inappropriate.

An investigation into Patristic interpretations of the Cana sign gave some insight into this complex and enigmatic passage. Noticing how Jesus' words were heard by people much closer, historically and culturally, to the original readers has confirmed that we ought to wonder whether Jesus was being abrupt with his mother. It is not only our twenty-first-century cultural filter that makes modern readers wonder if Jesus was being impolite to his mother here. For them it was not the address γύναι that seemed dismissive, but the question Τί ἐμοὶ καὶ σοί;

The Fathers have also directed us toward the mystery of the incarnation as a way of understanding Jesus' words, or perhaps as a way of accepting that they cannot be fully understood.

A deeper analysis of Jesus' words to his mother showed that they are more complex than a simple rebuke or assertion of emotional distance. He is not saying, "From now on I follow my Father's orders, not my mother's." Rather, he hears in his mother's words, Οἶνον οὐκ ἔχουσιν, a much deeper meaning than she intended. He hears a statement about the predicament of God's people living without the blessing of their God and without recourse for effectively calling God to act. These people who should have gloried in the honor of being God's chosen ones have been shamed by political, military, and financial subservience to nations who know nothing of the true God. A family wedding at which the wine runs out captures, in this culture that values hospitality so dearly, a glimpse of the shame of the people of God.

In response to his mother, Jesus says Τί ἐμοὶ καὶ σοί; God's people are living under God's judgment for a reason. They, as the bride of God, have been unfaithful. They are estranged. Is the Son of God to be called on to take sides here? And if so, how can he be expected to do other than side with God? And so the mother of the Son of God must take care. As she continues to be loyal to her son her relationship with her people may be desperately strained.

As the narrative continues toward Jesus' hour of shame and glory, the Jews (οἱ Ἰουδαῖοι) show themselves to be entrenched in their faithlessness by rejecting Jesus. They side against God's Son and therefore against God. Jesus' family, who are loyal and devout Jews, will be torn by this conflict. Will they stand with their son and brother and find themselves subjected to the same scorn and violence that Jesus experiences? Or will they side with "the Jews," and ultimately "the world" (7:7) against Jesus. Though the mention of Jesus' family in John is brief in each instance, they bring significant narrative tension to the Gospel.

Jesus' words to his mother are unusual but do not indicate any breach in relationship or disrespect. If anything they show concern for the position of the mother of the Son of God who has been sent by God to judge as well as to save, and to be crucified as well as to be glorified. Any sympathetic reader who is familiar with the whole story must pity this woman who, like every mother of a son in this culture, would have longed for his honor and his safety, and felt torn between the two.

Jesus' words, οὔπω ἥκει ἡ ὥρα μου, need not be read as a refusal to act on the practical situation his mother has brought to his attention. His time to act decisively by bringing God's judgment and God's mercy to full expression has not yet come. He will deal with the plight of God's people living in shame under God's judgment, but not yet. However, the abundant eschatological wine of that day may spill over into the present predicament. The shame of one family can be turned to glory in the short term, while the whole of God's people await the ultimate reversal of their shame.

Jesus' mother emerges at this point looking very much like a disciple. She has placed her confidence in Jesus, she has directed others to follow his instructions, and as a result his glory has been manifest and his disciples have been drawn into deeper faith. She then travels with him to Capernaum. On that journey her other sons were also present. Consideration of first-century fraternal bonds helps modern readers to form a picture of their relationship with their elder brother.

Throughout the first-century Mediterranean, ideals of brotherly love and unity appear to have been lofty. There was a common desire in Roman, Greek, and Jewish societies for brothers to act as one for the family's honor, rather than acting alone for their own honor. The sad reality for many families was that actual brothers were often envious, competitive, and self-seeking.

Virtuous men made sacrifices for their brothers by sharing with them their honor and possessions and even, where necessary, by giving their lives. Men who envied their brothers and plotted against them were considered to be men of bad character.

The fact that brothers so rarely lived up to these ideals does not seem to have diminished the intensity with which the ideals were desired. Rivalry among brothers, like death and poverty, was not a reality that these cultures adjusted to. Rather it was a tragedy faced afresh by every generation of parents who hoped for better outcomes for their sons.

Brothers were expected to show preferential treatment to one another compared with friends outside the family, and to share confidences that were kept from outsiders. The way Jesus chose non-family members as the disciples with whom he shared his life and his plans would undoubtedly have troubled his brothers and seemed unusual, even shameful, to most observers.

Fraternal conflict was a vice that added pathos to fictional plotlines and spice to historical recitation. The conflict between Jesus and his brothers would, no doubt, have caught the attention of early readers more than it does with those of us who have lower expectations of brotherhood.

The conflict between Jesus and his brothers described in John 7 shows us that family ties do not constitute the community Jesus is creating. Jesus' brothers have no special access to him. They ask a favor of him: "Demonstrate your power in Jerusalem and bring honor to our family." This was a reasonable request in the terms set by their culture, but in terms set for Jesus by his Father it was out of the question. Jesus criticizes them sharply and leaves them out of his plans. Jesus treated his brothers as outsiders, while his disciples, who were related to him only by faith and following, are treated as insiders.

Informed readers know that the brothers will eventually become insiders, when they accept the terms on which everyone else is welcomed into Jesus' community: faith and following. Like the Jews, they were the Word's own people who had rejected him (1:11) and they must find the humility to lay aside their right to special access and find salvation in their brother on the same basis as any other outsider.

The brothers were absent from the scene of Jesus' death where their mother stood by her eldest son and watched her darkest nightmares violently intrude on her reality. This was a failure of fraternal and filial affection and obligation on their part. Yet they were not the only ones who should have been there and were not. All but one of Jesus' disciples had also abandoned him, and on the other side of his resurrection disciples and brothers will need the forgiveness and reconciliation shown to Peter in 21:15–19. They would then become part of the new community created at the cross, even though so few of them were there.

As his last action on the cross Jesus spoke a few simple words, ἴδε ὁ υἱός σου . . . Ἴδε ἡ μήτηρ σου, and created a new reality. Though in the context of John's passion these words sound like the last will and testament of a king, Jesus is not here bequeathing his kingdom or establishing a new authority structure; he is speaking a new family into existence. The church as a kinship group is brought into being here at the foot of the cross as the last act of the crucified king. In John it is not until after Jesus' death and resurrection that the disciples are called ἀδελφούς μου.

By entering fully into human suffering, Jesus made humans his brothers, and made it possible for us to call God our Father.

The two appearances of Jesus' mother in this Gospel form an inclusio around Jesus' public ministry. She anticipates his first miracle and watches his humiliating yet glorifying death. She brings to Jesus' attention the lack of wine at the wedding and, at a deeper level (though probably unintentionally), the absence of the wine of God's blessing from the experience of God's people; and she is there when his blood is poured out to reverse God's judgment and bring the longed-for blessing to a new people of God. She was told that Jesus' hour was not yet; and then she stood beside him when his hour came. She pointed the disciples toward belief and obedience through her actions at Cana; and at the cross she joined the beloved disciple in witnessing Jesus' humiliation and glory.

The Word made flesh does not stride through life in regal independence. He has a mother. Like the rest of us, he has family responsibilities; he gives and receives family affection; he creates anxiety for his kin; he is part of—even the cause of—family conflicts. The Word has honored the human race, not only by taking on our physical form, but also by immersing himself in human social networks, and particularly that most crucial of social networks, the family.

The place of Jesus' mother and disciple at the foot of the cross is a place of prestige as well as horror. This is not, as some have supposed, because one or the other of them is the heir of his kingdom. Jesus retains his kingdom, just as he retains his dignity. The dignity of Jesus' mother is in being the mother of the king and in retaining her motherhood in the new family created at the cross. The dignity of the beloved disciple is found in that his discipleship is transformed into sonship and brotherhood in that family. They need no greater role and no more significant symbolic function.

The Fourth Gospel and the Synoptics

Tension between obligations to family and loyalty to God is described in the Synoptic Gospels by the dynamic of hating and leaving family members. The call to discipleship is an invitation to possible destitution that is only made endurable by hope in the coming kingdom and reliance on the abundant network of new fictive kin found in the community made up of all others who have heeded that call.

In John, this tension is not so stark or so explicit. It does not form a clear part of any of Jesus' teaching. Rather, it is in the way Jesus' family embodies and exemplifies this tension that readers learn about the need to count the cost of discipleship in the form of conflict and abandonment by kin.

Jesus' mother is consistently honored in the Fourth Gospel. Yet it is not her biological or nurturing function that is esteemed. It is her discipleship. She is shown to be a better disciple than most of the twelve. Without explicitly being told, the culturally astute reader can see how deeply this disciple's heart must be broken by her eldest son's suffering and also by the conflict between him and her other sons.

Christians who see their family broken over loyalty to Jesus can identify with this mother. They can join their voice to hers in calling Jesus to bring forward the day when all will enjoy the full messianic banquet. Then they can stand with her at the cross and know that Jesus' death has brought them into a new family in which all they have lost, including family, will be supplied just as surely as if he had said to them the words of Mark 10:28–30. Jesus' mother is a hero in this narrative, and as such calls readers to continue to stand beside her throughout life, even if their life should be as hard as hers.

Christians who experience misunderstanding and rejection from unbelieving kin can know that they are walking a path that Jesus has trodden. Even Jesus, who could simply say, "Come and see" (1:39) to potential disciples and have them follow him for life, had brothers who were skeptical about his ministry. It should be no surprise that Christian people have siblings, parents, spouses who misunderstand, accuse, and reject them because of their faith.

The informed reader knows that (some, at least, of) the brothers will come to faith, and will even become leaders in the young church. They give hope to Christians that unbelieving family members may at last come to faith, and they give heart to those who have once rejected Christ by showing them that there is a place for them in the church.

Is the message of the Fourth Gospel the same as the Synoptics regarding the conflict between kinship and discipleship? Not precisely the same. It is gentler, quieter. It draws the reader through narrative tension and characterization rather than sternly warning through the explicit words of Jesus. Yet all four Gospels present Jesus' fictive kin as the family group to which Jesus most truly belongs. The disciples are his "insiders," while brothers who are unbelievers are left outside his plans and fellowship. The family of faith and following consistently supersedes the family of biology. The faithful disciple chooses, like Jesus' mother, to stand at the cross and suffer rather than to stand at a distance with unbelieving kin. None of the Gospels pretends this is an easy thing to do, and all remind the Christian community to provide for and protect their fictive kin who have suffered for their loyalty to Christ.

Recommendations for future research

As I have carried out the research for this book I have become aware of a number of related questions that do not fall within the scope of my current work but that could be worthy subjects of future research. Among these questions are the following.

There is certainly more material about kinship in the Fourth Gospel than the three pericopes that have been examined here. For example, the fascinating narrative of the furor after Jesus healed the man born blind in John 9 illustrates many of the themes at the heart of this Gospel, including family tension as the man's parents refuse to be pulled in to the controversy.

Can the concept of brotherhood be used interchangeably with sisterhood in the Gospels? Because Jesus' sisters do not appear in the Fourth Gospel, this book has only examined brotherhood. My assumption is that the ecclesiological implications of the treatment of brotherhood in John apply to women in the same way as to men after the resurrection. This seems to be a reasonable assumption but one that might benefit from further research.

The connection between fourth-century Christian asceticism and belief in the perpetual virginity of Mary is a fascinating area of study. It would be particularly interesting to investigate the role of Jovinian, who was bold enough to question both.

In all four Gospels the tension between discipleship and kinship is expressed in terms of conflict between parents and children and between siblings. It never takes the form of conflict between a husband and wife, and certainly Jesus never calls a disciple to leave their spouse for the sake of the kingdom. Yet in the early church one of the most difficult positions for a believer was to be the wife of a pagan husband. This particular area of kinship conflict could be fruitful for research in all four Gospels.

When reading Philo, I noticed that for him celibacy seemed to be a natural corollary of privileging fictive kinship over biological kin. When ties of kinship were left behind for the sake of full devotion to God, family life can start to look like an unnecessary distraction. Given that the church did head in this direction in its first few centuries, I wonder if there is a necessary link here, or if a proper understanding of the church as fictive kin might have prevented what I consider a wrong turn in church history.

I am aware that my analysis of ancient literature in relation to mothers and brothers has been qualitative and selective. Research of a more substantial nature in these areas would be very welcome.

I am conscious that the call to leave family is often discussed in current psychology[1] and spirituality[2] literature as a (potentially) healthy movement towards autonomy and authenticity. At one time I thought I might integrate those insights into this book, but that task has proved too large. I simply mention this, then, and leave it to someone else, or to myself at a later time, to make the connections.

Final Conclusions

No matter how often and how deeply one has read this Gospel there will always be times when a previously unnoticed perspective opens up for us and we exclaim, "Ah! So that is what he means!" I have enjoyed many such moments in researching and writing this book, and cannot adequately sum up the joy of discovery that I have experienced over the last seven years.

I have had the pleasure of delving, diving, and even wallowing in that great ocean called biblical exegesis. There I have found infinite webs of connection between the Old Testament and the New, between ultimate realities and ordinary lives embedded in particular cultures, and between Christian people who, for centuries, have sought to understand and live by the truths to be found there.

As I finish I am aware that I stand in solidarity not only with thousands of Christian scholars who have completed doctorates in theology before me, but with millions of Christians who have struggled to make

---

1. To begin an exploration of this important issue in psychology, see Bowen, "On the Differentiation of Self."

2. See, for example, Rohr, *Falling Upward*.

loyalty to Christ their first priority in the face of pressure from their family to compromise. If I had given in to every call from my family to devote my energies to them I would not have completed this book. My family and I have made sacrifices, but not great sacrifices like those being made even now in communities where following Christ can result in violence and expulsion from family.

In my life of Christian scholarship I am deeply aware of my need for support from my fictive kin, the church universal. Much more am I aware of the need for support of my sisters and brothers who are suffering the agony of Jesus' mother at the cross in the very real experience of a sword slicing through their family (Matt 10:34–36).

I dedicate this book to them as I pray that the church will be the family it is called to be, and will enfold these sisters and brothers, giving them more sons and daughters and siblings than their arms can embrace, and protect them with the fierceness of a mother's heart.

Appendix: Τί ἐμοὶ καὶ σοί in the LXX, the NT, and Epictetus

Reference	Immediate Context	Situation Described	Implied Meaning
Judges 11:12	Καὶ ἀπέστειλεν Ιεφθαε ἀγγέλους πρὸς βασιλέα υἱῶν Αμμων λέγων Τί ἐμοὶ καὶ σοί, ὅτι ἥκεις πρός με σὺ πολεμῆσαί με ἐν τῇ γῇ μου;	The Ammonites have made war against Israel and Jephthah sends these words to their king. The king answers him "Because Israel took away my land…"	What is going on between us that you should do such a thing?
Significance	The king's reply makes it clear that he heard the words as a question about why he was behaving as he was toward Israel, in this case making war. Though the idiom is in first person singular, the question is not about Jephthah as an individual. It is about Israel (as the answer makes clear) and about Jephthah only as Israel's representative head. We will see shortly that the second party in this idiom can have a representative function; this example shows that the first party, too, can be representative. Given that the idiom is here used in response to hostility, and hostility cannot be discerned in Jesus' mother's words, it is unlikely that this passage is being specifically alluded to by John.		

Reference	Immediate Context	Situation Described	Implied Meaning
2 Samuel (Kingdoms) 16:10	καὶ εἶπεν ὁ βασιλεύς Τί ἐμοὶ καὶ ὑμῖν, υἱοὶ Σαρουιας; ἄφετε αὐτὸν καὶ οὕτως καταράσθω, ὅτι κύριος εἶπεν αὐτῷ καταρᾶσθαι τὸν Δαυιδ, καὶ τίς ἐρεῖ Ὡς τί ἐποίησας οὕτως;	David and his armies are in pursuit of his rebellious son, Absolom. Shimei, of the house of Saul, begins to curse King David. Abishai, son of Zeruiah, offers to take off Shimei's head. David tells him to leave Shimei alone because it may be that the Lord has directed him to curse David. This is not the first time Abishai and David have been in disagreement about the treatment of enemies. Abishai was with David when he found Saul asleep in a cave and chose to spare his life (1 Sam 26:6–9). Abishai would have taken a very different course of action. After Joab, Abishai's brother, had killed a man against David's orders in retaliation for the death of their brother, David lamented, "these men, the sons of Zeruiah, are too violent for me." (2 Sam 3:39) Later, he finds that men of violence can be useful. It is to Joab that he sends Uriah the Hittite when he wants him dead. (2 Sam 11)	You are not expressing my will or the will of God (. . . and I do not wish to be tempted to go your way when God is leading me in another direction.) cf. Mark 8:33

Reference	Immediate Context	Situation Described	Implied Meaning
Significance		This occurrence and the next are particularly relevant to a discussion of Jesus' words in John 2 because they come from Jesus' ancestor, David,[1] because they arise in the context of sin and forgiveness, and because they are addressed to an ally rather than an enemy. Use of the plural is interesting. David does not address Abishai as an individual but together with his brothers (Joab, the commander of the army, and Asahel, who had been killed) even though there is no indication that Joab was present, let alone that they were speaking as one. This appears to indicate that Abishai has a representative function here. From their history it is clear that his representative function is as a man of violence, or more precisely a man who seeks justice through violence and without mercy. David is, therefore, expressing a deep frustration here. As a king, he needs men of violence to lead his armies, but as a shepherd and man after God's heart he is inclined toward clemency. Τί ἐμοὶ καὶ ὑμῖν here not only expresses conflict between two people, it expresses conflict within David's soul, perhaps even within the very nature of kingship under YHWH. It expresses the sense of being caught between the will of YHWH and the voice of the accuser. "Get behind me, Satan" (Mark 8:33) is a reasonable parallel. Its repetition in 19:23 (below) gives this added emphasis.	
2 Samuel (Kingdoms) 19:23 (22)	καὶ εἶπεν Δαυιδ Τί ἐμοὶ καὶ ὑμῖν, υἱοὶ Σαρουιας, ὅτι γίνεσθέ μοι σήμερον εἰς ἐπίβουλον; σήμερον οὐ θανατωθήσεταί τις ἀνὴρ ἐξ Ισραηλ, ὅτι οὐκ οἶδα εἰ σήμερον βασιλεύω ἐγὼ ἐπὶ τὸν Ισραηλ.	Further to the previous occurrence. Absolom is now dead – killed against David's command by Joab. Shimei now begs forgiveness. Abishai again expresses a wish to put him to death. David makes a similar reply, saying that there should be no more death in Israel in that day.	You are not expressing my will or the will of God.

Reference	Immediate Context	Situation Described	Implied Meaning
Significance	Repetition here accentuates the frustration David is expressing. Does justice require violence, as the υἱοὶ Σαρουιας keep insisting? Does clemency express weakness? Is it shameful to weep over one's vanquished enemy? (2 Sam 19:5) Must justice and mercy always be opposed?		
1 Kings (3 Kingdoms) 17:18	καὶ εἶπεν πρὸς Ηλιου Τί ἐμοὶ καὶ σοί, ἄνθρωπε τοῦ θεοῦ; εἰσῆλθες πρός με τοῦ ἀναμνῆσαι τὰς ἀδικίας μου καὶ θανατῶσαι τὸν υἱόν μου.	The son of the widow with whom Elijah is staying becomes mortally ill. She accuses Elijah, as a man of God, of bringing her sins to God's remembrance, leading to her son's death.	What does it mean to me that you are here? (I thought you were a blessing; now I fear you have become a curse.)
Significance	Here again the idiom is used in connection with sin and judgment. The widow knows herself to be a sinner and so surmises that the presence of a man of God with her has brought her sins to God's remembrance. Elijah's reaction (becoming distressed and healing her son) shows that she is wrong. He is with her to bless her and not to curse her.		
2 Kings (4 Kingdoms) 3:13	καὶ εἶπεν Ελισαιε πρὸς βασιλέα Ισραηλ Τί ἐμοὶ καὶ σοί; δεῦρο πρὸς τοὺς προφήτας τοῦ πατρός σου. καὶ εἶπεν αὐτῷ ὁ βασιλεὺς Ισραηλ Μή, ὅτι κέκληκεν κύριος τοὺς τρεῖς βασιλεῖς τοῦ παραδοῦναι αὐτοὺς εἰς χεῖρας Μωαβ.	Moab has rebelled against Jehoram, son of Ahab, after his father's death. Jehoshaphat of Judah and the king of Edom have joined Jehoram to go into battle against Moab, following a route Jehoshaphat has advised. They find themselves without water and Jehoshaphat asks if there is a prophet of the Lord whose advice they could seek.	What makes you think you can come to me for help?

APPENDIX 303

Reference	Immediate Context	Situation Described	Implied Meaning
		When they approach Elisha he repels them with the words, Τί ἐμοὶ καὶ σοί; and tells Jehoram to go to his parents' prophets (of Baal). Jehoram tells him that he is wrong because the Lord had brought them there. (Presumably, he believed Jehoshaphat was following the will of YHWH.) Elisha agrees to seek a word from the Lord, but only out of respect for Jehoshaphat.	
Significance	Justice is again at the heart of this encounter. The son of Ahab wishes to seek the Lord through the successor of Elijah! Jehoram could hardly have found a man from whom he had less right to seek assistance. In an effort to overcome Elisha's resistance he blames the Lord for putting them in a position of need! The only solution to this standoff is a third party who Elisha can respect. It is very unlikely that this sense of the idiom applies in John 2. There is no history of animosity between Jesus and his mother and they certainly serve the same God. However, it is important to note that the idiom here expresses the great distance that already exists between the parties. Elisha is not creating distance here. He is drawing attention to distance that is unmistakably already there.		

Reference	Immediate Context	Situation Described	Implied Meaning
2 Chron 35:21	καὶ ἀπέστειλεν πρὸς αὐτὸν ἀγγέλους λέγων Τί ἐμοὶ καὶ σοί, βασιλεῦ Ιουδα; οὐκ ἐπὶ σὲ ἥκω σήμερον πόλεμον ποιῆσαι, καὶ ὁ θεὸς εἶπεν κατασπεῦσαί με, πρόσεχε ἀπὸ θεοῦ τοῦ μετ᾽ ἐμοῦ, μὴ καταφθείρῃ σε.	The words are spoken this time by Pharaoh Neco to Josiah, warning him not to come against him in war because Neco's quarrel is not with him but with Assyria. As a vassal king under Assyria, Josiah had clearly believed he was required to oppose Neco.	There is no need for you to oppose me. (You are not my enemy. Assyria is.)
Significance	It is interesting that what the two parties do not have in common in this instance is animosity. In other examples the idiom implies "we are not friends," here it implies "we are not enemies." While the atmosphere of hostility makes it unlikely that John is particularly directing his readers to this passage, it is instructive to notice the sense in which the idiom is used here.		
Hos 14:(9)8	τῷ Εφραμ, τί αὐτῷ ἔτι καὶ εἰδώλοις; ἐγὼ ἐταπείνωσα αὐτόν, καὶ ἐγὼ κατισχύσω αὐτόν, ἐγὼ ὡς ἄρκευθος πυκάζουσα, ἐξ ἐμοῦ ὁ καρπός σου εὕρηται.	God laments that Ephraim is still worshipping idols even though it is God who has protected them.	What is Ephraim still doing with idols?
Significance	Here the idiom is in second person and expresses the anguish of YHWH in the love triangle with Israel and foreign gods. Why are they in fellowship when one is my enemy and the other my beloved? A reference to wine in the verse immediately preceding this one gives weight to the possibility that this verse is one that the author was intending to bring to the minds of his readers in John 2:4. ἐπιστρέψουσιν καὶ καθιοῦνται ὑπὸ τὴν σκέπην αὐτοῦ, ζήσονται καὶ μεθυσθήσονται σίτῳ, καὶ ἐξανθήσει ὡς ἄμπελος τὸ μνημόσυνον αὐτοῦ, ὡς οἶνος Λιβάνου. (Hos 14:(8)7) Within Hosea, wine is one of the good things that God the husband has provided, but which Israel seeks outside of the covenant relationship. It becomes one of the good things which God ceases to provide because of Israel's faithlessness. As a response to the statement, "They have no wine", reference to Hos 14:8 is, therefore, entirely appropriate.		

APPENDIX 305

Reference	Immediate Context	Situation Described	Implied Meaning
Matt 8:29	καὶ ἰδοὺ ἔκραξαν λέγοντες, Τί ἡμῖν καὶ σοί, υἱὲ τοῦ θεοῦ; ἦλθες ὧδε πρὸ καιροῦ βασανίσαι ἡμᾶς;	Jesus gets out of his boat in Gentile territory and demons shout at him. ἦλθες implies that they are concerned that he has come into their locality specifically in order to destroy them.	What are your intentions toward us?
Significance	It is probably unfortunate for scholars of the Fourth Gospel that the only other uses of this idiom in the NT are on the lips of demons. This gives it a note of hostility that is not central to its semantic range. Notice that Jesus has not initiated the contact, yet the demons act as though he has. They act as though, simply because he is there, he must be there with the intention of destroying them. Judgment is again in view here. The demons know themselves to be under God's judgment, but they also appear to be aware that a time for judgment has been set and has not yet come. The time reference along with the idiom creates an interesting link with John 2:4. Notice in this and the following Gospel accounts that there are two places where demons say these words to Jesus: in Gentile territory and in the synagogue. Is it possible that the demons speak, not only on behalf of spiritual forces ranged against God, but also on behalf of the humans in their localities? Do they speak for Gentiles and for Jews and with one accord ask the Son of God why he has come to earth? More research on this question would be welcome. Has he come to destroy them? I am unable to demonstrate this here, but if that sense were present, this would be a connection with David's use of the idiom. It is for judgment or for mercy that the Son of God appears? Is it even possible that it could be for both?		

Reference	Immediate Context	Situation Described	Implied Meaning
Mark 1:24	λέγων, Τί ἡμῖν καὶ σοί, Ἰησοῦ Ναζαρηνέ; ἦλθες ἀπολέσαι ἡμᾶς; οἶδά σε τίς εἶ, ὁ ἅγιος τοῦ θεοῦ.	Jesus is teaching in the synagogue with astonishing authority. A demon cries out these words. ἦλθες again questions whether he has come there specifically for judgment.	What are your intentions toward us?
cf		In this case it is not clear who the ἡμᾶς are. Presumably demons, but could they be the Jews?	
Luke 4:34	Ἔα, τί ἡμῖν καὶ σοί, Ἰησοῦ Ναζαρηνέ; ἦλθες ἀπολέσαι ἡμᾶς; οἶδά σε τίς εἶ, ὁ ἅγιος τοῦ θεοῦ.		
Significance	The first person plural is interesting here, since the passage speaks of an individual man possessed by an individual demon. The plural suggests a representative function for the speaker. Is he speaking for the spiritual world or for the Jews? (See above.)		
Mark 5:7	καὶ κράξας φωνῇ μεγάλῃ λέγει, Τί ἐμοὶ καὶ σοί, Ἰησοῦ υἱὲ τοῦ θεοῦ τοῦ ὑψίστου; ὁρκίζω σε τὸν θεόν, μή με βασανίσῃς. 8ἔλεγεν γὰρ αὐτῷ, Ἔξελθε τὸ πνεῦμα τὸ ἀκάθαρτον ἐκ τοῦ ἀνθρώπου.	Jesus is in Gentile territory. On this occasion the demon cries out after Jesus has ordered it to come out of the man. The request that Jesus not torment him implies that his concern is not so much with why Jesus is there, but with what Jesus is going to do to him.	What are your intentions toward me?
Significance	This account resembles the Elisha narrative (2 Kings 3:13 above) in that an enemy of God begs a man of God to help him in God's name. Τί ἐμοὶ καὶ σοί would probably be more appropriate on Jesus' lips at this point.		

APPENDIX 307

Reference	Immediate Context	Situation Described	Implied Meaning
Luke 8:28	ἰδὼν δὲ τὸν Ἰησοῦν ἀνακράξας προσέπεσεν αὐτῷ καὶ φωνῇ μεγάλῃ εἶπεν, Τί ἐμοὶ καὶ σοί, Ἰησοῦ υἱὲ τοῦ θεοῦ τοῦ ὑψίστου; δέομαί σου, μή με βασανίσῃς. 29παρήγγειλεν γὰρ τῷ πνεύματι τῷ ἀκαθάρτῳ ἐξελθεῖν ἀπὸ τοῦ ἀνθρώπου.	Same situation as above, but with some differences in vocabulary.	What are your intentions toward me?
Significance	On the assumption that Mark was a source for Luke, it seems that Luke had removed the puzzling notion of the demon seeking mercy in God's name.		
Epictetus, Diss 1.1.16	τί ἄνεμος πνεῖ βοπεας τί ἡμῖν καὶ αθτῷ	You cannot control the wind so why should you let it worry you.	Why worry?
Significance	Given that Epictetus was a stoic philosopher, it is hardly surprising that in his use of the idiom the sense is almost always that of a lack of concern or anxiety.		
Epictetus, Diss 1.22.15	τί μοι καὶ αὐτῷ, εἰ οὐ δύναται, μοι βοηθῆς σαι... τί μοι καὶ αὐτῷ, εἰ θέλει μ᾽ ἐν τοιούτοις εἶναι ἐν οἷ εἰμι	Why should I care for Zeus if he cannot help me or if he wants me to be in this bad situation?	Why worry about Zeus?
Epictetus, Diss 1.27.14	λοιδόρω τον Δια καὶ τους θεους τους αλλους εἰ γὰρ μὴ ἐπιστρέφονται μου, τί ἐμοὶ καὶ α᾽θτοις	If a person does not believe in the gods he will insult them in a difficult situation because if they do not care for him why should they matter to him.	Why should they matter to me? Why should I take account of them?

Reference	Immediate Context	Situation Described	Implied Meaning
Epictetus, Diss 2.19.16	τί ἡμῖν καὶ σοί, ἄνθρωπε ἀπολλύμεθα καὶ σὺ ἐλθὼν παίζεις	What are your intentions toward us? We die and you come here to joke.	What are your intentions toward us?
Significance	Note the similarity between this and the use in the Synoptic Gospels.		
Epictetus, Diss 2.19.19	τί ἐμοὶ καὶ σοί, ἄνθρωπε ἀρκεῖ ἐμοὶ τὸ ἐμὰ κακά	I have enough problems of my own.	Why should I worry about you?
Epictetus, Diss 3.18.7	τί σοὶ καὶ τῷς ἀλλοτρίῳ κακῷ	A rare occurrence of the idiom being used in the second person. Also, the second party in the idiom is not a person but an abstract noun, κακῷ.	Why worry about another person's evil?

(Footnotes)

1 It should be noted, though, that the title, "Son of David" is not used of Jesus in the Fourth Gospel.

Bibliography

Aeschylus. *Seven against Thebes*. Translated and edited by Herbert Weir Smyth. Cambridge, MA: Harvard University Press, 1926.

Allen, Pauline. "The International Mariology Project: A Case-Study of Augustine's Letters." *Vigiliae Christianae* 60 no. 2 (2006) 209–30.

Allison, Dale C., Jr. "Divorce, Celibacy and Joseph (Matthew 1:18–25 and 19:1–12)." *Journal for the Study of the New Testament* 49 (1993) 3–10.

Ambrose. "Epistle LXIII: To the Church at Vercellæ." In *NPNF*. Translated and edited by Philip Schaff. Edinburgh: T&T Clark, 1888.

Anderson, John E. "Jacob, Laban, and a Divine Trickster? The Covenantal Framework of God's Deception in the Theology of the Jacob Cycle." *Perspectives in Religious Studies* 36 no. 1 (2009) 3–23.

Anonymous. "Anti Marcionite Prologue to John." *Revue Bénédictine*. Published by De Bruyne, no. 40 (1928).

———. "The Muratorian Canon." In *Das Muratorische Fragment Und Die Monarchianischen Prologue Zu Den Evangelien*, edited by Hans Lietzmann. Berlin: Kleine Texte, 1933.

Apollinaris of Laodicea. "Fragments on John." In *Johannes-Kommentare Aus Der Griechischen Kirche*, edited by J. Reuss. Berlin: Akademie-Verlag, 1966.

Apollodorus. *Apollodorus, the Library*. Translated and edited by Sir James George Frazer. Cambridge, MA: Harvard University Press, 1921.

Aristotle. *Aristotle's Ars Poetica*. Translated and edited by R. Kassel. Oxford: Clarendon, 1966.

———. "Nicomachean Ethics." Translated by J. E. C. Welldon. In *On Man in the Universe*, edited by L. R. Loomis. Princeton: Van Nostrand, 1943.

———. "Nicomachean Ethics." In *The Loeb Classical Library*, edited by Jeffrey Henderson. Cambridge, MA: Harvard University Press, 1975.

———. "Politics." Translated by H. Rackham. In *Aristotle in 23 Volumes*. Cambridge, MA: Harvard University Press, 1944.

Assis, Elie. "Why Edom? On the Hostility towards Jacob's Brother in Prophetic Sources." *Vetus Testamentum* 56 no. 1 (2006) 1–20.

Athanasius. "Discourses against the Arians." Translated by John Henry Newman and Archibald Robertson. In *Nicene and Post-Nicene Fathers, Second Series, Vol. 4*, edited by Philip Schaff and Henry Wace. Buffalo, NY: Christian Literature, 1892.

Attridge, Harold W.. "Genre Bending in the Fourth Gospel." *Journal of Biblical Literature* 121 no. 1 (2002) 3–21.

———. "Thematic Development and Source Elaboration in John 7:1-36." *Catholic Biblical Quarterly* 42 no. 2 (1980) 160-70.
Augustine. "Anti-Pelagian Writings." In *NPNF*, edited by Philip Schaff. Edinburgh: T&T Clark, 1888.
———. "Homilies on the Gospel of John Tractate CXIX." In *NPNF*, translated and edited by Philip Schaff. Edinburgh: T&T Clark, 1888.
———. "Homilies on the Gospel of John Tractate IX." In *NPNF*, translated and edited by Philip Schaff. Edinburgh: T&T Clark, 1888.
———. "Homilies on the Gospel of John Tractate VIII." In *NPNF*, translated and edited by Philip Schaff. Edinburgh: T&T Clark, 1888.
———. "Homilies on the Gospel of John Tractate XXIX." In *NPNF*, translated and edited by Philip Schaff. Edinburgh: T&T Clark, 1888.
———. "Homilies on the Gospel of John Tractate XXVIII." In *NPNF*, translated and edited by Philip Schaff. Edinburgh: T&T Clark, 1888.
———. "Homilies on the Gospel of John Tractate XXX." In *NPNF*, translated and edited by Philip Schaff. Edinburgh: T&T Clark, 1888.
———. "Homilies on the Gospel of John, Tractate CXVIII." In *NPNF*, translated and edited by Philip Schaff. Edinburgh: T&T Clark, 1888.
———. "Homilies on the Gospel of John, Tractate XXXI." In *NPNF*, translated and edited by Philip Schaff. Edinburgh: T&T Clark, 1888.
———. "The Writings against the Manichaeans and against the Donatists." In *NPNF*, translated and edited by Philip Schaff. Edinburgh: T&T Clark, 1888.
Balch, David L. *Let Wives Be Submissive: The Domestic Code in 1 Peter*. Chico, CA: Scholars, 1981.
Barrett, C. Kingsley. *The Gospel According to St John*. 2nd ed. London: SPCK, 1978.
Barton, Stephen C. "Can We Identify the Gospel Audiences?" In *The Gospels for All Christians*, edited by R. Bauckham. Grand Rapids: Eerdmans, 1989.
———. *Discipleship and Family Ties in Mark and Matthew*. Society for New Testament Studies Monograph. Cambridge[S.l.]: Cambridge University Press, 1994.
———. *Life Together: Family, Sexuality and Community in the New Testament and Today*. Edinburgh: T&T Clark, 2001.
———. *The Spirituality of the Gospels*. London: SPCK, 1992.
Bauckham, Richard, and Mosser, Carl. *The Gospel of John and Christian Theology*. Grand Rapids: Eerdmans, 2008.
Bauckham, Richard. "The Brothers and Sisters of Jesus: An Epiphanian Response to John P Meier." *Catholic Biblical Quarterly* 56 no. 4 (1994) 686-700.
———. "For Whom Were the Gospels Written?" In *The Gospels for All Christians*, edited by R. Bauckham. Grand Rapids: Eerdmans, 1998.
———. *Gospel Women: Studies of the Named Women in the Gospels*. Grand Rapids: Eerdmans, 2002.
———. *Jesus and the Eyewitnesses: The Gospels as Eyewitness Testimony*. Grand Rapids: Eerdmans, 2006.
——— "John for Readers of Mark." In *The Gospels for All Christians*, edited by R. Bauckham. Grand Rapids: Eerdmans, 1998.
———. *Jude and the Relatives of Jesus in the Early Church*. Edinburgh: T&T Clark, 1990.
Beasley-Murray, George R.. *John*. Word Biblical Commentary, Logos Edition 36. Dallas: Word, Incorporated, 2002.

———. *John*. Word Biblical Commentary 36, 2nd ed. Nashville: Thomas Nelson, 1999.
Berenson Maclean, Jennifer K.. "The Divine Trickster: A Tale of Two Weddings in John." In *A Feminist Companion to John*, edited by A. Levine. Cleveland: Pilgrim, 2003.
Borchert, Gerald L. *John 1–11*. The New American Commentary 25A, edited by E. R. Clendenen. Nashville: Broadman & Holman, 1996.
Bowen, Murray. "On the Differentiation of Self." In *Family Therapy in Clinical Practice*, edited by M. Bowen. New Jersey: Jason Aronson, 1985.
Brant, Jo-Ann A. *Dialogue and Drama: Elements of Greek Tragedy in the Fourth Gospel*. Peabody: Hendrickson, 2004.
Brayford, Susan A. "To Shame or Not to Shame: Sexuality in the Mediterranean Diaspora." *Semeia*, 87 (1999) 163–76.
Brown, Raymond Edward. *The Gospel According to John (I–XII)*. The Anchor Bible. Garden City: Doubleday, 1966.
———. *The Gospel and Epistles of John*. Collegeville: Liturgical, 1988.
———. *Mary in the New Testament*. Mahwah: Paulist, 1978.
———. "Other Sheep Not of This Fold: The Johannine Perspective on Christian Diversity in the Late First Century." *Journal of Biblical Literature* 97 no. 1 (1978) 5–22.
Bruce, F. F. *The Gospel of John*. Grand Rapids: Eerdmans, 1983.
Brueggemann, Walter. *The Prophetic Imagination*. Philadelphia: Fortress, 1987.
Buby, Bertrand. *Mary of Galilee*. New York: Alba House, 1994.
Bulembat, Jean-Bosco Matand. "Head-Waiter and Bridegroom of the Wedding at Cana: Structure and Meaning of John 2.1–12." *JSNT* 30 no. 1 (2007) 55–73.
Bultmann, Rudolf. *The Gospel of John: A Commentary*. Translated by G. R. Beasley-Murray. Oxford: Blackwell, 1971.
Burridge, Richard A. *What Are the Gospels? A Comparison with Graeco-Roman Biography*. Grand Rapids: Eerdmans, 2004.
Campbell, Joan Cecelia. *Kinship Relations in the Gospel of John*. Catholic Biblical Quarterly Monograph Series. Washington: The Catholic Biblical Association of America, 2007.
Campbell, Ken M. "What Was Jesus' Occupation?" *Journal of the Evangelical Theological Society* 48 no. 3 (2005) 501–19.
Carson, Donald A. *The Gospel According to John*. Grand Rapids: Eerdmans, 1991.
Cassius Dio Cocceianus. *Dio's Roman History*. Edited by Earnest Cary et al. Cambridge, MA: Harvard University Press, 1914.
Ceroke, Christian Paul. "Jesus and Mary at Cana: Separation or Appreciation?" *Theological Studies* 17 no. 1 (1956) 1–38.
———. "The Problem of Ambiguity in John 2:4." *Catholic Biblical Quarterly* 21 no. 3 (1959) 316–40.
Chance, John K. "The Anthropology of Honor and Shame: Culture, Values, and Practice." *Semeia* 68 (1994) 139–51.
Chrysostom, John. *The Homilies of S. John Chrysostom, Archbishop of Constantinople on the Gospel of St. John*. London: John Henry & Parker, 1852.
Cicero, M. Tullius. "The Orations of Marcus Tullius Cicero." London: Henry G. Bohn, 1856.
Clement of Alexandria. "The Instructor." In *ANF*, edited by Alexander Roberts and James Donaldson. Edinburgh: T&T Clark, 1885.

Cohick, Lynn H.. *Women in the World of the Earliest Christians: Illuminating Ancient Ways of Life*. Grand Rapids: Baker Academic, 2009.

Collins, Raymond F. *These Things Have Been Written: Studies on the Fourth Gospel*. Louvain Theological and Pastoral Monographs. Louvain: Peeters, 1990.

Corley, Kathleen E. *Women and the Historical Jesus: Feminist Myths of Christian Origins*. Santa Rosa: Polebridge, 2002.

Crook, Zeba. "Honor, Shame, and Social Status Revisited." *Journal of Biblical Literature* 128,no. 3 (Fall 2009) 591–611.

Culpepper, R. Alan. *The Gospel and Letters of John*. Interpreting Biblical Texts. Nashville: Abingdon, 1998.

Cyprian. "On the Unity of the Church." In *ANF*, edited by Alexander Roberts and James Donaldson. Edinburgh: T&T Clark, 1885.

Cyril of Alexandria. "Commentary on the Gospel of John." In *NPNF*, edited by Philip Schaff and Henry Wace. Edinburgh: T&T Clark, 1888.

Derrett, John., and Duncan, Martin. "Water into Wine." *Biblische Zeitschrift* 7 no. 1 (1963) 80–97.

deSilva, David A. *Honor, Patronage, Kinship & Purity*. Downers Grove: IVP, 2000.

———. "The Perfection of 'Love for Offspring': Greek Representations of Maternal Affection and the Achievement of the Heroine of 4 Maccabees." *New Testament Studies* 52 no. 2 (2006) 251–68.

Dillon, Richard J. "Wisdom Tradition and Sacramental Retrospect in the Cana Account (Jn 2:1–11)." *Catholic Biblical Quarterly* 24 no. 3 (1962) 268–96.

Dio, Cassius. "Roman History." In *Loeb Classical Library*. Cambridge, MA: Harvard University Press, 1924.

Dixon, Suzanne. *The Roman Family*. Baltimore: Johns Hopkins University Press, 1992.

———. "Sex and the Married Woman in Ancient Rome." In *Early Christian Families in Context*, edited by D. L. Balch and C. Osiek. Grand Rapids: Eerdmans, 2003.

Dodd, Charles Harold. *The Interpretation of the Fourth Gospel*. Cambridge: Cambridge University Press, 1970.

Donne, John. *Devotions Upon Emergent Occasions*. USA: Public domain, 1959.

Downing, F. Gerald. "'Honor' among Exegetes." *Catholic Biblical Quarterly* 61 no. 1 (1999) 53–73.

Duke, Paul D. *Irony in the Fourth Gospel*. Louisville: John Knox Press, 1985.

Duling, Dennis C. "The Matthean Brotherhood and Marginal Scribal Leadership." In *Modelling Early Christanity*, edited by P.F. Esler. London: Routledge, 1995.

———. "Matthew and Marginality." *Society of Biblical Literature Seminar Papers* 32 (1993) 642–71.

Edwards, Mark. *John*. Blackwell Bible Commentaries, edited by J. Sawyer, C. Rowland, and J. Lovacs. Oxford: Blackwell, 2004.

Eisenman, Robert. *James the Brother of Jesus*. London: Watkins, 2002.

Ellis, Peter F. *The Genius of John: A Compositional—Critical Commentary on the Fourth Gospel*. Collegeville: Liturgical, 1984.

Elowsky, Joel C., ed. *John 11–21*, edited by Thomas C. Oden, Ancient Christian Commentary on Scripture. Downers Grove: IVP, 2007.

Epictetus. "The Discourses of Epictetus, with the Encheridion and Fragments." London: George Bell and Sons, 1890.

———. *Epicteti Dissertationes Ab Arriano Digestae*, edited by Heinrich Schenkl. Leipzig: B. G. Teubner, 1916.

———. *The Works of Epictetus: His Discourses, in Four Books, the Enchiridion, and Fragments*. Translated and edited by Thomas Wentworth Higginson. New York: Thomas Nelson and Sons, 1890.

Epiphanius. *Pan. Haereses*. Edited by Jürgen Dummer, Vol. II. Berlin: Akademie Verlag, 1980.

Euripides. "Orestes." Translated by E.P. Coleridge. In *The Complete Greek Drama*, edited by Whitney J. Oates and Eugene O'Neill Jr.. New York: Random House, 1938.

———. "Orestes." In *Euripidis Fabulae*, edited by Gilbert Murray. Oxford: Clarendon, 1919.

———. "The Pheonissae." Translated by E.P. Coleridge. In *Euripidis Fabulae*, edited by Gilbert Murray. Oxford: Clarendon, 1919.

Eusebius. *History of the Church*. Translated by G. A. Williamson. Edited by Andrew Louth. London: Penguin, 1965.

Farley, Lawrence R. *The Gospel of John: Beholding the Glory*. The Orthodox Bible Study Companion Series. Ben Lomond, Ca: Conciliar, 2006.

Fee, Gordon D. *The First Epistle to the Corinthians*. The New International Commentary on the New Testament, edited by F.F. Bruce. Grand Rapids: Eerdmans, 1987.

Fehribach, Adeline. *The Women in the Life of the Bridegroom: A Feminist Historical-Literary Analysis of the Female Characters in the Fourth Gospel*. Collegeville, Minn: Liturgical, 1998.

Fox, Everett. "Stalking the Younger Brother: Some Models for Understanding a Biblical Motif." *Journal for the Study of the Old Testament* 60 (1993) 45–68.

Freyne, Sean. *Galilee: From Alexander the Great to Hadrian*. Edinburgh: T&T Clark, 1980.

———. "Herodian Economics in Galilee." In *Modelling Early Christianity*, edited by P. F. Esler. London: Routledge, 1995.

Fung, Ronald Y.K. *The Epistle to the Galatians*. The New International Commentary on the New Testament, edited by F.F. Bruce. Grand Rapids: Eerdmens, 1988.

Gaventa, Beverly R. *Mary: Glimpses of the Mother of Jesus*. Minneapolis: Fortress, 1999.

Grassi, Joseph A. *Mary, Mother and Disciple: From the Scriptures to the Council of Ephesus*. Wilmington, Del: Michael Glazier, 1988.

———. "The Role of Jesus' Mother in John's Gospel: A Reappraisal." *Catholic Biblical Quarterly* 48 no. 1 (1986) 67–80.

———. "The Wedding at Cana (John II 1–11): A Pentecostal Meditation?" In *The Composition of John's Gospel*, edited by D. E. Orton, 123–8. Boston: Brill, 1999.

Gregory Nazianzen. "Select Orations." In *NPNF*, edited by Philip Schaff. Edinburgh: T&T Clark, 1888.

Gregory the Great. "Selected Epistles." In *NPNF*, edited by Philip Schaff. Edinburgh: T&T Clark, 1888.

Guijarro, Santiago. "The Family in First Century Galilee." In *Constructing Early Christian Families*, edited by H. Moxnes. London: Routledge, 1997.

Hack, Roy Kenneth. "The Doctrine of Literary Forms." *Harvard Studies in Classical Philosophy* 27 (1916).

Hanson, Kenneth C. "The Herodians and Mediterranean Kinship, 2 Pts." *Biblical Theology Bulletin* 19 (1989) 75–84.

———. "How Honorable! How Shameful! A Cultural Analysis of Matthew's Makarisms and Reproaches." *Semeia* 68 (1994) 81–111.

Harnack, Adolf von. *The Mission and Expansion of Christianity in the First Three Centuries.* Vol. 1. London: Williams & Norgate, 1908.
Hellerman, Joseph H. *The Ancient Church as Family.* Minneapolis: Fortress, 2001.
Hendrikson, William. *John.* Edinburgh: Banner of Truth, 1954.
Hesiod. "Works and Days." Translated and edited by Hugh G. Evelyn-White. In *The Homeric Hymns and Homerica.* Cambridge, MA: Harvard University Press, 1914.
Hirsch, Eric Donald. *The Aims of Interpretation.* Chicago: University of Chicago Press, 1976.
———. *Validity in Interpretation.* New Haven: Yale University Press, 1967.
Homer. *The Iliad.* Translated by A.T. Murray. Cambridge, MA: Harvard University Press, 1924.
———. "Iliad." In *Homeri Opera in Five Volumes.* Oxford: Oxford University Press, 1920.
———. *The Odyssey.* Translated by A.T. Murray. Cambridge, MA: Harvard University Press, 1919.
———. "The Odyssey, Books 1–12." In *The Loeb Classical Library,* edited by G. P. Goold. Cambridge, MA: Harvard University Press, 1995.
Hoskins, Paul M. *Jesus as the Fulfillment of the Temple in the Gospel of John.* Paternoster Biblical Monographs, edited by I. H. Marshall et al. Milton Keynes: Paternoster, 2006.
Hoskyns, Edwyn C. *The Fourth Gospel.* London: Faber and Faber, 1947.
Howard, John M. "The Significance of Minor Characters in the Gospel of John." *Bibliotheca Sacra* 163 no. 649 (2006) 63–78.
Hunter, Alan M. *According to John.* London: SCM, 1968.
Hunter, David G. "Resistance to the Virginal Ideal in Late-Fourth-Century Rome: The Case of Jovinian." *Theological Studies* 48, no. 1 (1987) 45–64.
Ilan, Tal. "'Man Born of Woman . . .' (Job 14:1): The Phenomenon of Men Bearing Metronymes at the Time of Jesus." *Novum Testamentum* 34 no. 1 (1992) 23–45.
Irenaeus. "Against Heresies." In *ANF,* edited by Alexander Roberts and James Donaldson. Edinburgh: T&T Clark, 1885.
Jerome. "Against Jovinianus." In *NPNF,* translated and edited by Philip Schaff. Edinburgh: T&T Clark, 1888.
———. "Letters of St Jerome." In *NPNF,* translated and edited by Philip Schaff. Edinburgh: T&T Clark, 1888.
———. *The Perpetual Virginity of Mary.* In *NPNF,* translated and edited by Philip Schaff. Edinburgh: T&T Clark, 1888.
Johnson, Luke Timothy. "On Finding the Lukan Community: A Cautious Cautionary Essay." In *Society for Biblical Literature Seminar Papers.* Missoula: Scholars, 1979.
Jones, Judith Kaye. *The Women in the Gospel of John.* St. Louis: Chalice, 2008.
Josephus, Flavius. "Antiquitates Judaicae." In *Flavii Josephi Opera,* edited by B. Niese. Berlin: Weidmann, 1895.
———. "De Bello Judaico Libri Vii." In *Flavii Josephi Opera,* edited by B. Niese. Berlin: Weidmann, 1895.
———. "Josephi Vita." In *Flavii Josephi Opera,* edited by B. Niese. Berlin: Weidmann, 1890.
———. *The Works of Josephus.* Translated by W. Whiston. Edited by W. Whiston. Peabody: Hendrickson, 1987.

Keener, Craig S. *The Gospel of John: A Commentary*. Vol. II. Peabody: Hendrickson, 2003.
Koester, Craig R. *Symbolism in the Fourth Gospel: Meaning, Mystery, Community*. Minneapolis: Fortress, 1995.
Köstenberger, Andreas J. *John*. Baker Exegetical Commentary on the New Testament, edited by R. Yarbrough and R. H. Stein. Grand Rapids: Baker Academic, 2004.
Kraemer, Ross S. "Typical and Atypical Jewish Family Dynamics." In *Early Christian Families in Context*, edited by David L Balch and Caroline Osiek. Grand Rapids: Eerdmans, 2003.
Kressel, Gideon M. "Shame and Gender." *Anthropological Quarterly* 65 no. 1 (Jan 1992) 13.
Kruse, Colin G. *John*. Tyndale New Testament Commentaries, edited by L. Morris. Nottingham: IVP, 2003.
Lawrence, Louise Joy. "'For Truly, I Tell You, They Have Received Their Reward' (Matt 6:2): Investigating Honor Precedence and Honor Virtue." *Catholic Biblical Quarterly* 64 no. 4 (2002) 687–702.
Lee, Dorothy. *Flesh and Glory*. New York: Herder & Herder, 2002.
Lenski, Richard C. H. *The Interpretation of St John's Gospel*. Minneapolis: Augsburg, 1943.
Leo the Great. "Sermons." In *NPNF*, edited by Philip Schaff. Edinburgh: T&T Clark, 1888.
Leon, H. J. *The Jews of Ancient Rome*. Peabody: Hendrickson, 1995.
Levi-Strauss, Claude. *The Elementary Structures of Kinship*. Translated by J. H. Bell et al. Boston: Beacon, 1969.
Levin, Yigal. "Jesus, 'Son of God' and 'Son of David': The 'Adoption' of Jesus into the Davidic Line." *Journal for the Study of the New Testament* 28 no. 4 (2006) 415–42.
Lieu, Judith. "The Mother of the Son in the Fourth Gospel." *Journal of Biblical Literature* 117 no. 1 (Spr 1998) 61–77.
Lightfoot, Joseph Barber. "The Brethren of the Lord." In *Dissertations of the Apostolic Age*, edited by J.B. Lightfoot. London: Macmillan, 1892.
Lindars, Barnabas. *The Gospel of John*. New Century Bible. London: Oliphants, 1972.
Livy. "Books 1 and 2 with an English Translation." In *History of Rome*. Cambridge, MA: Harvard University Press, 1919.
———. "History of Rome." New York: E. P. Dutton and Co, 1912.
Louw, Johannes P., and Eugene Albert. Nida. *Greek-English Lexicon of the New Testament: Based on Semantic Domains*, 2nd ed. New York: United Bible Societies, 1996.
Love, Stuart L. "Hellenistic Symposia Meals in Luke." In *Modelling Early Christianity*, edited by P. F. Esler, 198–210. London: Routledge, 1995.
Luther, Martin. *Sermons of the Gospel of St. John Chapters 1–4*. Luther's Works, Edited by J. Pelikan. Vol. 22. Saint Louis: Concordia, 1957.
Luz, Ulrich, et al. *Matthew 1–7: A Commentary*. Hermeneia. Minneapolis: Augsburg Fortress, 2007.
Malina, Bruce J., and Richard L. Rohrbaugh. *Social—Science Commentary on the Gospel of John*. Minneapolis: Fortress, 1998.
Malina, Bruce J. *The New Testament World: Insights from Cultural Anthropology*. Louisville, Kentucky: Westminster/John Knox, 2001.

———. *The Social World of Jesus and the Gospels*. London & New York: Routledge, 1996.
Martin, Troy W. "Assessing the Johannine Epithet 'the Mother of Jesus.'" *Catholic Biblical Quarterly* 60 no. 1 (1998) 63–73.
Martyn, J. Louis. *History and Theology in the Fourth Gospel*. The New Testament Library, 3rd ed. Louisville: Westminster John Knox, 2003.
Mayor, Joseph B. "Brethren of the Lord." In *A Dictionary of the Bible*, edited by James Hastings. Edinburgh: T&T Clark, 1898.
McHugh, John. *The Mother of Jesus in the New Testament*. London: Darton, Longman & Todd, 1975.
Meeks, Wayne A. "The Son of Man in Johannine Sectarianism." In *The Interpretation of John*, edited by J. Ashton. Philadelphia: Fortress, 1986.
Meier, John P. "The Brothers and Sisters of Jesus in Ecumenical Perspective." *Catholic Biblical Quarterly* 54,no. 1 (1992) 1–28.
———. *A Marginal Jew*. New York: Doubleday, 1991.
Menoud, Philippe H. "Signification Du Miracle Selon Le Nouveau Testament." *Revue d'histoire et de philosophie religieuses* 28 no. 3 (1949) 173–203.
Metzger, Bruce M. *A Textual Commentary on the Greek New Testament*. London: United Bible Societies, 1971.
Meyers, Eric M. "The Problems of Gendered Space in Syro-Palestinian Architecture: The Case of Roman-Period Galilee." In *Early Christian Families in Context*, edited by David L. Balch and Caroline Osiek. Grand Rapids: Eerdmans, 2003.
Moloney, Francis J. *Belief in the Word: Reading the Fourth Gospel, John 1-4*. Minneapolis: Augsburg Fortress, 1993.
———. *The Gospel of John*. Sacrina Pagina, edited by Daniel J. Harrington. Collegeville: Liturgical, 1998.
———. "Narrative and Discourse at the Feast of Tabernacles." In *Word, Theology, and Community in John*, edited by John Painter et al. St Louis: Chalice, 2002.
Morris, Leon. *The Gospel According to John*. The New International Commentary on the New Testament, edited by F.F. Bruce. Grand Rapids: Eeddmans, 1971.
Moxnes, Halvor. *Putting Jesus in His Place*. Louisville: Westminster John Knox, 2003.
———. *Theology in Conflict: Studies in Paul's Understanding of God in Romans*. Leiden, Netherlands: E.J. Brill, 1980.
———. "What Is a Family?" In *Constructing Early Christian Families: Family as Social Reality and Metaphor*, edited by Halvor Moxnes. London: Routledge, 1997.
Murdock, George Peter. "The Nuclear Family." In *Readings in Kinship and Social Structure*. New York: Harper and Row, 1971.
Naveh, Joseph. *On Stone and Mosaic: The Aramaic and Hebrew Inscriptions from Ancient Synagogues*. Tel-Aviv: Maariv, 1977.
Neyrey, Jerome H. "Despising the Shame of the Cross: Honor and Shame in the Johannine Passion Narrative." *Semeia* 68 (1994) 113–37.
———. *The Gospel of John*. The New Cambridge Bible Commentary. New York: Cambridge University Press, 2007.
———. *The Gospel of John in Cultural and Rhetorical Perspective*. Grand Rapids: Eerdmans, 2009.
———. "Loss of Wealth, Loss of Family and Loss of Honour." In *Modelling Early Christianity: Social-Scientific Studies of the New Testament in Its Context*, edited by P.F. Esler. London: Routledge, 1995.

———. "The Sociology of Secrecy and the Fourth Gospel." In *What is John? II, Literary and social readings of the Fourth Gospel*, edited by Fernando F. Segovia. Atlanta: Scholars,1998

Oakman, Douglas E. and Hanson Kenneth C. *Palestine in the Time of Jesus*. Minneapolis: Fortress, 1998.

Oberlinner, Lorenz. *Historische Überlieferung Und Christologische Aussage*. Stuttgart: Verlag Katholisches Bibelwerk, 1975.

Olsson, Birger. *Structure and Meaning in the Fourth Gospel: A Text—Linguistic Analysis of John 2:1–11 and 4:1–42*. Coniectanea Biblica, New Testament Series 6. Lund: Gleerup, 1974.

Origen. "Commentary on Matthew." Translated by John Patrick. In *ANF*, edited by Philip Schaff. Edinburgh: T&T Clark, 1885.

———. *Commentary on the Gospel of John*. Edited by A. E. Brooke. Eugene: Wipf & Stock, 2009.

———. "Fragments." In *ANF*. Edinburgh: T&T Clark, 1885.

Osborne, Grant R. "Historical Narrative and Truth in the Bible." *Journal of the Evangelical Theological Society* 48 no. 4 (2005) 673–88.

Park, Sophia. "The Galilean Jesus: Creating a Borderland at the Foot of the Cross (Jn 19:23–30)." *Theological Studies* 70 no. 2 (2009) 419–36.

Patai, Raphael. *Golden River to Golden Road: Society, Culture, and Change in the Middle East*. 3rd ed. Philadelphia: University of Pennsylvania Press, 1969.

———. *Sex and Family in the Bible and the Middle East*. Garden City, NY: Doubleday, 1959.

Patterson, Cynthia B. *The Family in Greek History*. Cambridge, MA: Harvard University Press, 1998.

Perry, Timothy. *Mary for Evangelicals*. Downers Grove: IVP Academic, 2006.

Philo. "Allegorical Interpretation." In *The Works of Philo: Greek Text with Morphology*, edited by Peder Borgen et al. Bellingham, WA: Logos Bible Software, 2005.

———. "De Somniis." In *The Works of Philo: Greek Text with Morphology*, edited by Peder Borgen et al. Bellingham, WA: Logos Bible Software, 2005.

———. "On Abraham [English]." In *The Works of Philo: Complete and Unabridged*, edited by Charles Duke Yonge. Peabody, MA: Hendrickson, 1995.

———. "On Abraham [Greek]" In *The Works of Philo: Greek Text with Morphology*, edited by Peder Borgen et al. Bellingham, WA: Logos Bible Software, 2005.

———. "Special Laws [English]." In *The Works of Philo: Complete and Unabridged*, edited by Charles Duke Yonge. Peabody, MA: Hendrickson, 1995.

———. "Special Laws [Greek]." In *The Works of Philo: Greek Text With Morphology*, edited by Peder Borgen et al. Bellingham, WA: Logos Bible Software, 2005.

———. *The Works of Philo: Complete and Unabridged*. Translated and edited by C. D. Yonge. Peabody: Hendrickson, 1993.

Pilch, John J., and Bruce J. Malina. *Biblical Social Values and Their Meanings: A Handbook*. Peabody: Hendrickson, 1993.

Pitt-Rivers, Julian. *The Fate of Shechem, or the Politics of Sex*. Cambridge: Cambridge University Press, 1977.

———. "Kinship: Pseudo-Kinship." In *International Encyclopedia of the Social Sciences*, edited by David L. Sills. USA: Macmillan and the Free Press, 1968.

Plato. "Republic." In *Platonis Opera*, edited by John Burnet. Oxford: Oxford University Press, 1903.

Plutarch. *Advice to Bride and Groom*. Cambridge, MA: Harvard University Press, 1928.
———. "Bravery of Women." Translated by W.C. Helmbold. In *Moralia* Vol. III., Loeb Classical Library, edited by J. Henderson. Cambridge, MA: Harvard University Press, 1987.
———. "Comparison of Theseus and Romulus." In *Plutarch's Lives*. Cambridge, MA: Harvard University Press, 1914.
———. "The Life of Brutus." In *The Parallel Lives*. Cambridge, MA: Harvard University Press, 1918.
———. "The Life of Coriolanus." In *The Parallel Lives*. Cambridge, MA: Harvard University Press, 1916.
———. "Lucullus." In *Plutarch's Lives*. Cambridge, MA: Harvard University Press, 1914.
———. "On Affection for Offspring." In *Moralia*, edited by W.C. Helmbold. Loeb Classical Library. Cambridge, MA: Harvard University Press, 1939.
———. "On Fraternal Affection." In *Moralia*, edited by W.C.Helmbold. Loeb Classical Library. Cambridge, MA: Harvard University Press, 1939.
———. "Roman Questions." Translated by Frank Cole Babbitt. In *Moralia*. Vol. IV, Cambridge, MA: Harvard University Press, 1936.
———. "Sayings of Kings and Commanders." In *Moralia*. Cambridge, MA: Harvard University Press, 1931.
Powell, Brian W. "Did Paul Believe in Virtue?" PhD diss., Macquarie University, Sydney, 1995.
Provan, Iain, et al. *A Biblical History of Israel*. Louisville: Westminster John Knox, 2003.
Quintilian. *Institutio*. Translated by Harold Edgeworth Butler. Edited by Harold Edgeworth Butler. Cambridge, MA: Harvard University Press, 1920.
Rensberger, David. *Johannine Faith and Liberating Community*. Philadelphia: Westminster, 1988.
Resnick, Irven M. "Marriage in Medieval Culture: Consent Theory and the Case of Joseph and Mary." *Church History* 69 no. 2 (2000) 350–71.
Ridderbos, Herman N. *The Epistle of Paul to the Churches of Galatia*. The New International Commentary on the New Testament, edited by F.F. Bruce. Grand Rapids: Eerdmans, 1953.
———. *The Gospel According to John*. Translated by J. Vriend. Grand Rapids: Eerdmans, 1997.
Rohr, Richard. *Falling Upward: A Spirituality for the Two Halves of Life*. San Francisco: Jossey-Bass, 2011.
Rohrbaugh, Richard L. "Legitimating Sonship — a Test of Honour." In *Modelling Early Christianity*, edited by P. F. Esler. London: Routledge, 1995.
Roth-Gerson, L. *The Greek Inscriptions from Synagogues in Eretz—Israel*. Jerusalem: yad Ben-Zvi, 1987.
Saller, Richard P. *Patriarchy, Property and Death in the Roman Family*. Cambridge: Cambridge University Press, 1994.
———. "Women, Slaves, and the Economy of the Roman Household." In *Early Christian Families in Context*, edited by D.L. Balch and C. Osiek. Grand Rapids: Eerdmans, 2003.
Satlow, Michael L. "'Try to Be a Man': The Rabbinic Construction of Masculinity." *HTR* 89 (1996) 19–40.
Schmidt, Thomas E. *Hostility to Wealth in the Synoptic Gospel*. Journal for the Study of the New Testament Supplement. Sheffield: JSOT, 1987.

Schnackenburg, Rudolf. *The Gospel According to St John*. Translated by K. Smyth. Vol. 1. London: Burns & Oats, 1968.

———. *The Gospel According to St John*. Translated by C. Hastings, et al. Vol. 3. London: Burns & Oats, 1980.

———. *The Gospel According to St John*. Translated by C. Hastings, et al. Vol. 2. London: Burns & Oats, 1980.

Schnell, Udo. *Antidocetic Christology in the Gospel of John*. Translated by L. M. Maloney. Minneapolis: Fortress, 1992.

Seneca, Lucius Annaeus. "De Beneficiis." In *Moral Essays*, edited by John W. Basore. London and New York: Heinemann, 1935.

Shanks, Hershel, and Ben Witherington. *The Brother of Jesus: The Dramatic Story and Significance of the First Archaeological Link to Jesus and His Family*. New York: HarperCollins, 2003.

Sloyan, Gerard. *John*. Interpretation, edited by James Luther Mays. Atlanta: John Knox, 1988.

Smith, D. Moody. *John*. Abingdon New Testament Commentaries, edited by Victor Paul Furnish. Nashville: Abingdon, 1999.

Smith, William. *Dictionary of Greek and Roman Antiquities*. Boston: Little, Brown, 1870.

Socrates. "Ecclesiastical History." In *NPNF*, edited by Philip Schaff. Edinburgh: T&T Clark, 1888.

Solon. "Greek Lyrics." Translated by R. Lattimore. Chicago: University of Chicago Press, 1960.

Sophocles. *The Antigone of Sophocles*. Translated and edited by Sir Richard Jebb. Cambridge: Cambridge University Press, 1891.

Stibbe, Mark W. G. *John*. Sheffield: JSOT, 1993.

Suetonius. "The Lives of the Twelve Caesars: An English Translation, Augmented with the Biographies of Contemporary Statesmen, Orators, Poets, and Other Associates." Edited by J. Eugene Reed. Philadelphia: Gebbie & Co., 1889.

Swift, Jonathan. *A Modest Proposal*. USA: Public Domain—Gutenberg ebook #1080, 1997.

Tacitus. "The Annals." Translated and edited by Alfred John Church et al. In *Complete Works of Tacitus*. New York: Random House, 1942.

———, "History." Translated and edited by Alfred John Church et al. In *Complete Works of Tacitus*. New York: Random House, 1942.

Taylor, Nicholas H. "The Social Nature of Conversion in the Early Christian World." In *Modelling Early Christianity*, edited by P. F. Esler. London: Routledge, 1995.

Tenney, Merrill C. "John." In *John—Acts*, edited by F. E. Gaebelein. The Expositor's Bible Commentary. Grand Rapids: Regency, Zondervan, 1981.

Tertullian. "An Answer to the Jews." In *ANF*, edited by Allan Menzies. Edinburgh: T&T Clark, 1885.

———, "The Five Books against Marcion." In *ANF*, edited by Allan Menzies. Edinburgh: T&T Clark, 1885.

Thatcher, Tom. "The Legend of the Beloved Disciple." In *Jesus in Johannine Tradition*, edited by Robert Fortner and Tom Thatcher. Louisville: Westminster John Knox, 2001.

Theodoret. "Dialogue II—the Unconfounded." In *NPNF*, edited by Philip Schaff. Edinburgh: T&T Clark, 1888.

Thomas, Robert L. *New American Standard Hebrew—Aramaic and Greek Dictionaries: Updated Edition*. Anaheim: Foundation Publications, 1998.

Thompson, Michael B. "The Holy Internet: Communication between Churches in the First Christian Generation." In *The Gospels for All Christians*, edited by R. Bauckham. Grand Rapids: Eerdmans, 1998.

Thompson, Marianne Meye. *The Humanity of Jesus in the Fourth Gospel*. Philadelphia: Fortress, 1988.

Todd, Emmanuel. *Explanation of Ideology: Family Structure & Social System*. Oxford: Blackwell, 1989.

van der Horst, Pieter W. *Ancient Jewish Epitaphs: An Introductory Survey of a Millennium of Jewish Funerary Epigraphy, 300 BCE–700 CE*. Contributions to Biblical Exegesis and Theology. Kampen, Netherlands: Kok Pharos, 1991.

van der Watt, Jan G. *Family of the King: Dynamics of Metaphor in the Gospel According to John*. Biblical Interpretation Series 47, edited by R. A. Culpepper and R. Rendtorff. Leiden: E. J. Brill, 2000.

Vanhoozer, Kevin J. *Is There a Meaning in This Text? The Bible, the Reader, and the Morality of Literary Knowledge*. Grand Rapids: Zondervan, 1998.

Various. *The Greek New Testament, Fourth Revised Edition (with Morphology)*. Edited by Kurt Aland et al. Deutsche: Bibelgesellschaft, 2006.

———. *The Mishnah: A New Translation*. Translated and edited by Jacob Neusner. New Haven, CT: Yale University Press, 1988.

———. *Pseudepigrapha of the Old Testament*. Edited by Robert Henry Charles. Bellingham, WA: Logos Bible Software, 2004.

———. *Septuaginta: With Morphology*. electronic edition. Stuttgart: Deutsche Bibelgesellschaft, 1979.

Vincent, Marvin Richardson. *Word Studies in the New Testament*. Bellingham, WA: Logos Research Systems, Inc., 2002.

Waetjen, Herman C. *The Gospel of the Beloved Disciple*. New York: T&T Clark, 2005.

Watson, Francis. "Toward a Literal Reading of the Gospels." In *The Gospels for All Christians*, edited by R. Bauckham. Grand Rapids: Eerdmans, 1998.

Wesley, Margaret. "Family Fractured and Reconfigured." In *Loss and Discovery*, edited by Margaret Wesley. Preston, Vic.: Mosaic, 2013.

Wiles, Maurice F. *The Spiritual Gospel: The Interpretation of the Fourth Gospel in the Early Church*. London: Cambridge University Press, 1960.

Williams, Michael James. "Lies, Lies, I Tell You! The Deceptions of Genesis." *Calvin Theological Journal* 43 no. 1 (2008) 9–20.

Williams, Ritva H. "The Mother of Jesus at Cana: A Social-Science Interpretation of John 2:1–12." *Catholic Biblical Quarterly* 59 no. 4 (1997) 679–92.

Witherington, Ben. *Conflict and Community in Corinth*. Grand Rapids: Eerdmans, 1995.

Wolterstorff, Nicholas. *Divine Discourse*. Cambridge: Cambridge University Press, 1995.

Wright, N. T. *The New Testament and the People of God*. Christian Origins and the Question of God Series. Minneapolis: Augsburg Fortress, 1989.

Xenophon. "Xenophon in Seven Volumes." Edited by Carleton L. Brownson. Cambridge, MA: Harvard University Press, 1922.

www.ingramcontent.com/pod-product-compliance
Lightning Source LLC
Chambersburg PA
CBHW050617300426
44112CB00012B/1543